SHAKESPEARE, EINSTEIN, AND THE BOTTOM LINE

DAVID L. KIRP

SHAKESPEARE, EINSTEIN, AND THE BOTTOM LINE

The Marketing of Higher Education

Harvard University Press
Cambridge, Massachusetts, and London, England

To Brian

Gracias a la vida

First Harvard University Press paperback edition, 2004

Library of Congress Cataloging-in-Publication Data

Kirp, David L.
    Shakespeare, Einstein, and the bottom line : the marketing of higher
education / David L. Kirp.
      p.   cm.
    Includes bibliographical references and index.
    ISBN 0-674-01146-5 (alk. paper)
    ISBN 0-674-01634-3 (pbk.)
    1. Universities and colleges—United States—Marketing.
  2. Education, Higher—Public relations—United States. I. Title.

LB2342.8.K57 2003
378.73—dc21   2003049914

Contents

Hugh Fennyman: Uh, one moment, sir.

Ned Alleyn: Who are you?

Hugh Fennyman: I'm, uh . . . I'm the money.

Ned Alleyn: Then you may remain so long as you remain silent.

—*Shakespeare in Love* (1998)

Introduction: The New U

The university is a community of scholars and students engaged in the task of seeking truth.

—Karl Jaspers, *The Idea of the University* (1946)

Knowledge is a form of venture capital.

—Michael Crow, quoted in
Chronicle of Higher Education (2000)

The two campuses are a half hour's drive and a psychological light year removed from each other. Between them, they mark the outer boundaries of the new higher learning in America.

One is a modern rendering of the ivied college, a place of learning set apart from the humdrum world. The verdant landscape, camouflaged from neighboring office parks, is a real park dotted with ponds and meandering trails, a setting that invites conversation among students and teachers. The buildings are unobtrusively contemporary, and the classrooms, many of them seminar-sized, are wired for the electronic age. This is a highly selective school, which draws its students and its faculty from around the globe. Students report that they are pleased with their education as well as with the opportunity to make the kinds of contacts that make careers.

The other campus is a faux-Gothic refuge from a dicey urban neighborhood, Oxbridge amid the ghetto. But until recently the telltale signs of neglect were everywhere evident, from the physics labs, state of the art circa 1950, to the swimming pool used to train competitors for the Olympics—the 1908 Olympics, that is. Throughout its history, the institution has regularly been in financial trouble. Twice in earlier years it came close to moving away; and its annual deficit, projected to run $10 million, was eating away at its relatively modest endowment. While its alumni have always been fiercely loyal, many were saying that the place was so brutal they wouldn't send their own children there. Attracting new students had become harder and harder. More than 60 percent of those who applied were

1

admitted to the class of 2000, and fewer than a third of those who were accepted actually enrolled.

The second of these schools is the University of Chicago. The first is Hamburger University, McDonald's corporate training headquarters.[1]

To speak of McDonald's and the University of Chicago in the same breath is blasphemy, at least in Hyde Park. But the rise to prominence of schools like Hamburger U—not your father's higher education, certainly, but an accredited institution nonetheless—as well as the hard choices that confront a quintessential academy of higher learning like Chicago illustrate a much larger phenomenon. For better or worse—for better *and* worse, really—American higher education is being transformed by both the power and the ethic of the marketplace. It is this story that is recounted in succeeding chapters: the strategies devised to navigate this complex market terrain, as well as the values of university life that those strategies place at risk.

The notion that higher education is a "market" needs to be unpacked, because the system doesn't look like the market portrayed in any Economics 101 textbook. In the realms of commerce, when demand exceeds supply, firms are supposed to expand or else jack up their prices, a practice that encourages new entrants. But this isn't at all how higher education operates.

While enrollment in postsecondary institutions has increased by more than half since 1970, much of that growth has been absorbed by community colleges, which enroll over 30 percent of all undergraduates, and regional public universities. The very idea of expansion is anathema to the elite—imagine Yale setting up shop in the Bay Area. Instead, these schools set ever-higher standards for admission. The most selective reject seven out of eight applicants, almost all of whom are qualified.

Nor do universities raise their prices to discourage would-be students. Even though tuition continues to rise, as universities engage in what economists term "positional warfare" to protect their place in the hierarchy, revenue from tuition doesn't pay the bills. It is hard to identify a nonprofit university that doesn't subsidize its students; and the higher up in the pecking order, the greater the subsidy. Schools at the top of the heap attract desirable graduate students with lavish stipends that used to go only to star quarterbacks.[2]

Sensing the possibility of making money in this increasingly competitive environment, new institutions have entered the field. But these for-profit schools do not embody the rugged individualism of the classic market. They receive massive subsidies in the form of federal and state loan programs, an act of public generosity beyond the wildest dreams of a new trucking firm or microchip manufacturer. Because most students at for-profit schools need the loans to pay their college bills, these institutions would have to retrench if they didn't receive infant industry treatment.

To further complicate the story, the "sellers" in this peculiar market, the universities, seek out the most attractive "buyers"—that is, students. BMW doesn't care much who buys its cars, but "the university's consumers are one of the most important inputs in its production process, and this is not the case for producers of typical private goods and services. . . . [Elite institutions] need top students every bit as much as top students need them." If the higher education marketplace is best understood as a metaphor rather than a precise economic model, the metaphor packs a wallop.[3]

Despite all their obvious faults, American universities have long aspired to be communities of scholars, places for free thought. The century-long campaign for academic freedom represents an effort, against long odds, to secure a degree of intellectual distance from quotidian pressures, to allow breathing room for scholars to critique the conventional wisdom of the day.[4]

It is important not to romanticize academe, not to slip into nostalgia for a time that really never was. Dollars have always greased the wheels of American higher education; were it otherwise, the term "legacy" would not have a meaning specific to universities. There is no returning to Cardinal Newman's nineteenth-century *Idea of a University*, where "useful knowledge" is a "deal of trash"—no returning, either, to the world envisioned more than eighty years ago by Thorstein Veblen in *The Higher Learning in America*, where pure research is the only proper activity of the university, and developing usable applications (as well as educating undergraduates) is the business of lesser places.[5] Ever since Harvard College and the College of William and Mary opened their doors over three centuries ago, money has been a pressing concern, and the need for a useful and usable education has been a theme in American public policy at least since the launching of the land grant universities with the Morrill Act of 1862.

What *is* new, and troubling, is the raw power that money directly exerts over so many aspects of higher education. Even as public attention has been riveted on matters of principle such as affirmative action and diversions like the theater-of-the-absurd canon wars, the American university has been busily reinventing itself in response to intensified competitive pressures.[6] Entrepreneurial ambition, which used to be regarded in academe as a necessary evil, has become a virtue. "We are a business," the provost of the University of Connecticut flatly states; "our shareholders are students, faculty, and the state of Connecticut," even as the president of the University of California proclaims that "the University of California means business."[7]

Priorities in higher education are determined less by the institution itself than by multiple "constituencies"—students, donors, corporations, politicians—each promoting its vision of the "responsive" (really the obeisant) institution. Strong leadership used to be regarded as crucial in the making of great universities, but nowadays presidents are consumed with the never-ending task of raising money. The new vocabulary of customers and stakeholders, niche marketing and branding and winner-take-all, embodies this shift in the higher education "industry." This is more than a matter of semantics and symbols, for the business vocabulary reinforces business-like ways of thinking. Each department is a "revenue center," each student a customer, each professor an entrepreneur, each party a "stakeholder," and each institution a seeker after profit, whether in money capital or intellectual capital.[8]

Opting out of the fray by fleeing the market is not a realistic possibility. Any school that adopted the Thoreau-like position that, in education as in the design of a mousetrap, quality is all that matters, would be courting self-destruction. Even—perhaps especially—the elite schools are ever vigilant, lest a rival steal an edge (or a professor or a major donor). Prestige is the coin of the realm among the leading research universities and liberal arts colleges; and since prestige is a scarce commodity, the losers will far outnumber the winners.

Prestige means more than bragging rights for trustees and alumni. It brings tangible benefits, and small differences in reputation have large consequences. The more highly regarded the institution, the more top students and prized professors it attracts, and the more readily it can secure the biggest gifts (for it is a truism among fund-raisers that money follows money, not need), the largest research grants from government and foundations, and often the most lucrative industry contracts. Those successes reinforce a school's place in the pecking order. "To those who have," as the Book of Matthew decrees, "more shall be given"—in other words, the more, the more. "To an extent rivaled perhaps only by the market for trendy nightclubs," writes economist Robert Frank, describing what he calls a "winner-take-all" market, "higher education is an industry in which success breeds success and failure breeds failure."[9]

Whether the rivalry is over undergraduates, faculty, contributions, or commercial deals, the fighting has grown much fiercer in recent years. Top students are more knowledgeable about their options, as publications such as *U.S. News & World Report*'s annual survey of "America's Best Colleges" wield outsized influence; more mobile; and more demanding about everything from plush accommodations and tuition "discounts" to inflated grades.[10] The most sought-after faculty regard their primary attachment as not to their school nor to their discipline but to themselves. For those favored few, every spring becomes a season of greed, as competing offers are weighed, not just in terms of salary but also in terms of research support, reduced teaching obligations, and the like.[11]

With the advent of Big Science, research has turned into an ever more high-stakes proposition. Recruiting a renowned social scientist might set the institution back a quarter-million dollars, but it costs upwards of $20 million to attract a star biochemist, complete with retinue and laboratory. Snagging such a figure is regarded as an investment as well as a coup, since the findings from those labs potentially have immense commercial potential—nine-figure income streams for the most successful universities, the equivalent of the income generated by a multibillion-dollar endowment. It's no wonder, then, that raising research money, negotiating patent rights, and establishing a presence on the Internet are contact sports.

Even as higher education has become more stratified at the top, it has also become more widely available. The proportion of high school graduates going to college keeps increasing, and more working adults are returning to the campus. On the lower rungs of the academic ladder, what matters are money and enrollment figures, not prestige. Less selective and non-selective schools—four out of five American college students attend such institutions—vie to fill classroom seats, resorting in the extreme to Priceline.com-type discounting and hiring firms that make cold calls on prospects.[12]

Since the 1970s, there has been a massive shift in student interest away from the liberal arts and toward what has been dubbed the "practical arts," and most universities have had to adjust their offerings accordingly.[13] The new generation of for-profit schools targets this segment of the market. The best of those institutions bear no resemblance to the old "matchbook" trade schools; and while they enroll barely 2 percent of all students, they have been able to cherry-pick the most lucrative fields. No one is warring over prospective philosophy majors. It's the University of Phoenix versus University of Texas–El Paso for business students, DeVry

University versus University of Northern Illinois for software engineers. Moreover, the for-profits have learned how to clone themselves without sacrificing quality, something that neither public nor nonprofit schools know how or want to do, and they have been quick to take advantage of the market potential of the Internet.[14]

As if this challenge to traditional institutions weren't powerful enough, more than a million students, many of whom would otherwise be enrolled in four-year schools, have opted instead for the "parallel postsecondary universe" of information technology courses that prepare them for careers as, for instance, Cisco- or Microsoft-certified engineers.[15] It isn't just the for-profits and community colleges that are chasing after these students; selective universities, through their extension arms, are in the game as well. Here, as in distance education, familiar distinctions among elite, mass, and universal institutions are becoming blurred, and neither renown nor quality guarantees success in this arena.

In a sense, this is history repeating itself. A century or so ago, the University of Chicago stripped Clark University of its best professors by offering them outsized salaries; the University of Southern California opened a real estate school; Columbia University ran a factory-like correspondence school; and at MIT, General Electric started a corporate-sponsored laboratory on the campus.

What is decisively different is the magnitude of these forces. A "revolution" is how David Riesman and Christopher Jencks, writing in 1968, characterized the shift from Mr. Chips's tranquil pre–World War II world of the academic village to Clark Kerr's teeming "multiversity"; and "revolution" is at least as good a description of the present, what Kerr himself has called "*the* greatest critical age" for higher education.[16] New educational technologies; a generation of students with different desires and faculty with different demands; a new breed of rivals that live or die by the market; the incessant demand for more funds and new revenue sources to replace the ever-shrinking proportion of public support; a genuinely global market in minds: taken together, these forces are remaking the university into what has variously been called the site of "academic capitalism," the "entrepreneurial university," and the "enterprise university."[17]

This is how the world seems naturally to work when, as now, the zeitgeist is the market. If health care, museums, even churches have been caught up in, and reshaped by, intense competitive pressures, why should higher education be any different?[18] In all these instances, the best answer is the same. "There is a place for the market," as economist Arthur Okun wrote some years ago, "but the market must be kept in its place."[19] So, too, in higher education. As the narratives that follow make plain, market forces lead some schools to forget that they are not simply businesses while turning others into stronger, better places. Still, embedded in the very idea of the university—not the storybook idea, but the university at its truest and best—are values that the market does not honor: the belief in a community of scholars and not a confederacy of self-seekers; in the idea of openness and not ownership; in the professor as a pursuer of truth and not an entrepreneur; in the student as an acolyte whose preferences are to be formed, not a consumer whose preferences are to be satisfied.[20]

In the balance of the book I look at how the pull and tug of competition plays out across the landscape of American higher education. Multimillion-dollar deals with semiconductor firms and the privatization of a public university's business school; strategies to create "buzz" in liberal arts education and legal education; efforts to corner the "high-end market" and initiatives to give away courses on the Internet; battles for the soul of a boastfully traditional university and a for-profit college; collaboration among classics departments and competition for information technology certification courses; the scavenging for students and the hunt for faculty superstars: the book relies on case studies, tales that signify beyond their particulars, to make sense of this new world.

  Do these narratives show the benign workings of the invisible hand, the decline of the West, or—like it or not—the shape of things to come? Some describe schools that have learned how to combine the best of both worldviews, the academic commons and the marketplace, becoming successful and principled competitors in the higher education bazaar. Others look at institutions that have struck bargains only Faust could love. Which model will come to dominate the higher education landscape is anyone's bet. One thing is clear, however: the answer, as it emerges, will map the future direction of higher education.

PART I

THE HIGHER EDUCATION BAZAAR

This Little Student Went to Market

"No matter what it is called, who does it, or where in the institution it is being done, universities are engaging in marketing." That message startled university administrators when a marketing professor named Richard Krachenberg first delivered it in a 1972 *Journal of Higher Education* article.[1] What schools referred to as recruiting was really a euphemism for advertising, Krachenberg pointed out, financial aid was pricing, and the bloodletting ritual of revamping the curriculum was nothing more than product development.

Nowadays the marketing is right out front. Universities on the make hire image creators to give themselves an academic face-lift, what the trade calls a new "brand." Schools at the very top of the ladder battle to maintain their elite position. Harvard created a Technology and Entrepreneurship Center in 2000 to compete with Stanford for budding high-tech entrepreneurs. In the spring of 2002, several staff members at Princeton's admissions office went so far as to hack into Yale's admissions website, peeking at the files of eleven students who had been accepted by both schools, among them Lauren Bush, fashion model and niece of President George W. Bush. "The pressures on admissions folks and on schools to get the best candidates is enormous," Alvin P. Sanoff, a higher education consultant and former managing editor of *U.S. News & World Report*'s annual college guide, told a reporter from the *Chronicle of Higher Education*. "The elite schools are like warring software companies, each trying to best the other, and so one very strong possibility was that this was an effort to see who Yale was admitting to help Princeton in landing the students it wanted."[2]

Top college applicants are treated like pampered consumers whose demands must be satisfied. The notion that these are adolescents who are supposed to be *formed* by a college education is dismissed as quaint.

11

"The objective of the enrollment process," says William Elliott, Carnegie Mellon's vice president for enrollment management (good-bye admissions director, hello corporate-speak), "is to improve your market position."[3]

With elite schools rejecting as many as seven out of eight applicants, students are also busy distinguishing themselves in the ever-growing crowd of aspirants. They and their parents believe that, because of its scarcity value, a degree from a top-ranked school will pay off handsomely in future earnings and status.[4] Sixties-style idealism has long since given way to pragmatism. These aspirants are Jay Gatsbys in training, who regard an elite pedigree as their ticket to the new aristocracy. What matters most in picking a college, students report, is not the quality of its education but rather its prestige.[5] In a 2001 national survey, the most commonly mentioned reasons to go to college included getting career training, getting a better job, and making more money.[6] Parents spend upwards of $25,000 on coaches to help their scions package themselves—signaling, as economists would say, that they deserve to be selected, branding themselves so that they are especially appealing to the school of their choice.

In this new regime, the savvy customers and management consultants are royalty. Colleges improve their market fortunes with a variety of contrivances, including changing their names, and an otherwise little-noticed news magazine, *U.S. News & World Report,* produces a statistically dubious ranking system that has become higher education's *Michelin Guide.*[7]

All this behavior is consistent with what the model of rational economic behavior predicts. More information is becoming available; buyers and sellers are doing the best job they can to promote themselves; and money talks.[8] But "the danger," as Robert Reich writes, "is that the increasing competition—to be selected and to be selective—will exacerbate the widening inequalities that are raising the stakes in the first place."[9]

▪ Identity Theft

Until recently, Beaver College, just outside Philadelphia, was losing badly in the competition for students. The school used to be a women's liberal arts college a cut below the Seven Sisters, but as that niche vanished in the 1970s, it suffered what one longtime faculty member describes as an "ongoing identity crisis." With enrollment dropping and an endowment of just $400,000, the school was forced to use deposits sent in by the following year's incoming class to pay off its creditors. In 1972 it started admitting men, lowering its admissions standards to do so, and over the next fifteen years it tacked on vocational programs for physicians' assistants, physical therapists, and genetic counselors, as well as an associate's degree program open to anyone who could pay.

At the advice of the consulting firm KPMG, the school revamped its administrative structure. In 1992 it hired Dennis Nostrand for the new position of vice president of enrollment management, with responsibility to recruit more and better students. What made Nostrand an appealing choice, says dean of admissions Mark Lapreziosa (whose own title morphed into "director of enrollment management"), was the fact that "he knew the technology and the marketing techniques."

"Customer orientation" is Dennis Nostrand's watchword. He introduced a database system that could personalize student mailings, getting rid of those generic "Dear Student" letters. He began awarding merit scholarships to tempt better applicants. And he created a "total quality management" team (an idea lifted from the corporate management textbooks) that, among its other activities, sought to make the campus visit a more memorably pleasant experience.

Still, there remained the ticklish problem of the school's name. Beaver College had been named after the western Pennsylvania county where it was founded in 1853, but pop culture had long since turned an innocent animal into a double entendre. ("Nice beaver," says Leslie Nielsen to the ladder-climbing Priscilla Presley in *The Naked Gun*. "Thanks," she replies, bringing a taxidermied animal into view. "I just had it stuffed.") Nostrand began lobbying for a name change the minute he arrived. The name scared off prospective applicants, he argued, and the Internet content filters on many high school computers even blocked them from accessing the college's website.

Companies give themselves new names all the time, so why not a school? But once news of the pending name change was leaked, TV talk show hosts like Jay Leno and David Letterman had a field day. Unwelcome "suggestions" poured into the office of Bette Landman, Beaver's longtime college president. "How about Gynecollege?" one wag suggested, or "University of the Southern Region?" Landman hired a firm of marketing consultants to come up with a name that would, as she puts it, "reflect the brand." That meant something short and punchy, its first letter coming at the beginning of the alphabet to ensure early mention in college guidebook listings; something pleasing-sounding, easy to say and read—something, Landman said, that could "become a strong trademark."

"Arcadia University" emerged as the winner among the focus groups to which the school, at the behest of Nostrand and the marketing consultants, turned for inspiration. The name evoked pastoral images ("artistic, in a pretty setting," observed one focus group member) and "sounds like a fun place to be." Similarly, the "college" became a "university" because the focus groups liked "university" better. Nostalgic alums plumped for University of Grey Towers, after the campus's historic first building, but the focus groups thought that name made the school sound like a prison. Still, tradition had to be part of the brand; the name change had to reflect the new while not discarding the virtues of the old. New T-shirts reflected the marketers' solution: "Arcadia University: Since 1853."

But what does this altered identity really signify? To set itself apart, the school currently promotes the fact that it sends many of its freshmen on a heavily subsidized weeklong trip to London over spring break. This "London Preview" is just the kind of gimmick that a consultant might concoct—"Arcadia = Fun." But at a school chronically strapped for funds, what is the message about academic priorities?

Arcadia University was able to laugh off the criticisms and witticisms when, after changing its name, it found that the number of applications jumped by a third. In the fall of 2002, there were more than five hundred freshmen, the biggest class in the school's history. "Inadvertently, the fact that our own name was the butt of many jokes meant that people across the country and outside the country heard the fact that we were changing our name," says President Landman. "That was unexpected advertising."

▪ Doing It Maguire's Way

Not only was Richard Krachenberg's 1972 missive intended to alert college administrators to the fact that, like it or not, they were marketing their wares—it was also a wake-up call to do the job better. Even as higher education had started "wisely borrowing some management and operating techniques from other institutions, especially business and government," Krachenberg wrote, marketing was "poorly done and with a keen lack of appreciation for all the tools" of the trade.[10]

In its initiatives, Beaver College was late off the mark, for the changes that Dennis Nostrand introduced have elsewhere been de rigueur since the 1980s. The task of matching students and colleges, long regarded as a counseling and hand-holding job, has become management science.

This new model was first tested in the mid-1970s in the admissions office of Boston College, a Catholic school that was having a hard time fill-ing its classrooms. Jack Maguire, an assistant professor of physics and a loyal son of the college, became the admissions director.[11] As an outsider to the field, he didn't like how the job was typically done. Maguire began what he describes as "a process that brings together often disparate func-tions having to do with recruiting, funding, tracking, retaining and replac-ing students as they move toward, within and away from the University . . . to reduce fragmentation by systematizing and integrating these fields into one grand design."[12] Everything pitched to the "customer base," he de-cided, should be the responsibility of a single administrator, with the new title of "enrollment manager."

In 1985, Maguire opened his own consulting firm. His approach rap-idly became common practice. There is now a handbook for the college admissions "profession" that describes enrollment management as "a comprehensive process designed to achieve and maintain the optimum re-cruitment, retention and graduation rates of students."[13] "Comprehen-sive" is the key term. Enrollment managers are supposed to get involved in almost everything that happens on campus, from setting financial aid pol-icy to deciding what should be built on the campus, from encouraging a student-friendly curriculum to improving the cafeteria food, even, as in Beaver's case, to deciding on the school's name. "Any factor that influ-ences a student's decision to attend or to continue enrolling" is regarded as the business of the enrollment manager.[14] And while admissions officers had always ranked low on the institutional totem pole, a vice president for enrollment management like Nostrand at Arcadia now reports directly to the president. Detecting a market niche, the University of Miami has started a master's program in this new field.[15]

Financial desperation powered this revolution in the care and feeding of prospective students. In the 1950s, higher education enrollments swelled because of the GI Bill, and the baby boom generation kept college enroll-ments high; but in the late 1970s, the number of high school graduates began to decline. At the same time, state legislatures began underwriting a smaller fraction of public universities' budgets, a trend that has continued ever since; and, in a shift in policy, federal financial aid was funneled di-rectly to students, not to institutions. The resulting fiscal squeeze forced universities to rethink how they pitched their appeals to prospective stu-dents.

In actuality, there was a 31 percent increase in college enrollment be-tween 1979 and 1999. That's not because the demographic projections were wrong—the annual number of high school graduates, which peaked at nearly 3.2 million in 1979, decreased by 300,000 students—but because a much higher percentage of high school graduates has been going to college: more than 65 percent in 1999, compared with 50 percent a generation earlier.[16] One reason is the assiduous use of the techniques of enrollment management.

When Philip Kotler, whose marketing texts are widely used in undergraduate business courses, published his book *Strategic Marketing for Educational Institutions* in 1985, the point was plain: enrollment management is just an application of general marketing principles to the specialized problem of attracting college students. The task is not very different from boosting tourism or increasing membership in church congregations, two other topics on which Kotler has written.[17] Explicitly and unapologetically, enrollment managers regard students as customers and see a college education as the product students consume. In marketing terms, their assignment is to advertise and recruit customers, to set a price for their product, and to make sure that product matches the demand.

▪ Trolling for Students: The Bait

Gordon Gee had a problem. The president of Brown University moved to Nashville in 2001 to take the top job at Vanderbilt. His new school was just as good as his old one, Gee believed, but because it didn't carry the cachet of higher education's most valuable brand—the Ivy League—it couldn't attract the best students.[18]

Gee went about solving his problem in a most unusual way; he opened a Hillel House and revived a Jewish studies program. The intention, he says, was to recruit Jewish students, who "by culture and by ability . . . make a university a much more habitable place in terms of intellectual life." What's even more remarkable, religiously affiliated schools like Southern Methodist University and Texas Christian University are doing the same thing.[19]

A Rip Van Winkle admissions officer who fell asleep in the 1970s and awoke today wouldn't recognize his own profession. Even as students have changed—they are more willing to consider going to school away from home and apply to more schools—the easygoing world of registrars who counted things and counselors who played matchmaker has vanished. While "the general admission objectives and some of the admission folkways persist," writes Donald Stewart, the former president of the College

Board, "much that is done now on the admissions landscape would be foreign territory to many of them."[20]

The University of Chicago is a prime example of how things currently work.[21] When Michael Behnke became vice president and associate dean of college enrollment in 1997, he walked into a daunting job. A university that prided itself on being "a dirty, intense place"[22] was scaring away potential students. It was admitting 62 percent of its applicants, a higher percentage than any other school on *U.S. News & World Report*'s list of the top twenty-five universities. And many students who came to Hyde Park believing that they were ready for the challenge later changed their minds, dropping out or transferring. Chicago's graduation rate was the lowest among the leading private universities.

Behnke has spent his entire career recruiting students.[23] He started out at Amherst College, his alma mater, in 1971; moved on to Tufts University five years later; and in 1985, he became MIT's admissions director. Over the years he grew more managerially oriented, recruiting M.B.A.s for his staff, drawing on their marketing skills to handle the stresses of college admissions.

At universities as proudly yoked to their past as MIT and Chicago, faculty distrust the idea that their wares are being pitched to "customers." With administration backing, Behnke made it a point to search out able high school girls in order to change the school's boys' club culture. When the number of female undergraduates grew substantially, irate professors accused him of giving preferential treatment to girls, but an investigation by the faculty senate concluded that Behnke had simply done his job well. The female students were just as qualified as the males; what had changed was the effectiveness of the recruiting.

At the University of Chicago, Behnke again relied on his kit bag of marketing tools. A McKinsey & Company report concluded that the university was unknown to many potential applicants (some even confused it with the Chicago campus of the University of Illinois, the ultimate insult in Hyde Park), so Behnke tripled the amount of direct mail going to high school students. He also began to target sophomores, pitching his message to those who scored highest on the Preliminary Scholastic Aptitude Test.[24]

Pursuing sixteen-year-olds defied the conventional admissions wisdom that students are "apathetic about considering colleges until their junior or senior year."[25] But Behnke believed that with these early mailings, Chicago could become what marketers call a "first mover." The firm that gets information into the hands of the consumer first, marketing experts say, "can define a product category as a whole and thus become the 'prototype' against which all later entrants are judged." That's a big head start. "Because consumption is a learning experience, follow-on brands may be compared with the pioneer brand to their disadvantage if the latter is perceived as 'ideal.' As a result, the pioneer brand may be viewed as competitively distinct, and making competitive inroads would become difficult for later entrants."[26]

Behnke applied this first-mover principle to higher education. His hunch was that bright sophomores were already thinking hard about college, and so a school that sent them persuasive promotional material would gain a high, difficult-to-displace position on their college wish lists. He also used another tried-and-true marketing technique, the follow-up, to maintain their interest. Postcards with informal descriptions of campus life, just the kind of missives a real college student might send to a high school friend back home, were mailed out during the summer after their sophomore year. The idea, Behnke says, was to keep the Chicago "brand name" in the minds of these students as they entered their junior year, when their mailboxes would be overflowing with sales pitches from other schools.

To imprint the University of Chicago in students' minds as a desirable place, the generic viewbook, *Dreams and Choices,* the publicity material sent to prospective applicants, was replaced by *The Life of the Mind*— "What other college would put *that* on the cover of its viewbook?" Behnke asks—and *The Shocking Truths.* The content changed as well. There were fewer photos of students buried in their books, more pictures of undergrads engaged in "fun" activities like dancing, juggling, and playing football.[27] The revamped image verged on deception, and the depiction was like fingernails on the blackboard to many in Hyde Park. As one student sarcastically observed in the campus paper, "I'm proud to report there are more references to alcohol and fraternities in the viewbook of the University of Chicago then there is [sic] in the brochure of Brown University," a school known for its laid-back atmosphere.[28] Alumni complained that the new message would attract the wrong kind of applicant and undermine the school's reputation for intellectual rigor.[29]

Those fears all turned out to be groundless. When *The Life of the Mind* debuted in 1999, the number of applicants, which had dropped by 2 percent the previous year, increased 22 percent. For the first time in its history, Chicago could admit fewer than half of those who applied.[30] The pool also included more highly qualified applicants: the number with combined SAT scores of 1400 or higher increased by nearly 30 percent. This success prompted a new worry that most of these students would opt for more prestigious and less quirky places. In fact, although the entering freshman class grew by just 2 percent that year, the number of students with SAT scores of 1500 or higher rose 64 percent and the number in the top 5 percent of their high school class increased by 47 percent.[31]

The new approach to admissions had made a big difference. When the campus newspaper polled a sample of students who'd been accepted by Chicago, 88 percent said that *The Life of the Mind* was better than other schools' viewbooks.[32] Smart use of marketing tools had drawn a new kind of student to what was no longer regarded as a nasty and brutish place.

Several rungs lower on the status ladder at Beaver/Arcadia, Dennis Nostrand reported similar success. He ordered up the market research that led the school to change his name. He created radio spots touting the "London Preview" as, in essence, a $200 vacation. He sent prospective applicants more and better materials, replacing the tired viewbook with the livelier *Landmarks Magazine* that was pitched to potential students.

Nostrand's major task was to bring in more students. Mission accomplished: between 1998 and 2002, the number of undergraduates nearly doubled. He hoped to use the added tuition income to build new housing so that the college, which draws its students mainly from the region, can pitch itself to a nationwide pool. Just like any good businessman, he has a vision for the company that keeps expanding.

Colleges have also turned to new media in their quest for students. Vanderbilt pioneered in the late 1980s with personalized videos that opened with a twenty-second clip of a current student welcoming an applicant by name and mentioning his or her academic interests.[33] Now nearly all colleges are relying on the Internet, and the easily modifiable code of Web pages enables institutions to have interactive relationships with prospective students, a considerable marketing advance over one-way communication.[34]

The California State University system, for instance, offers an interactive financial aid estimator, a virtual tour of any of the system's twenty-two campuses, and a spreadsheet for making easy cross-campus comparisons. The State University of New York's Buffalo campus draws on prospective students' academic, athletic, and campus interests to help them plan an on-campus open house. And the University of Missouri at Rolla has turned instant messaging into a marketing device, sending greetings and news blurbs to anyone who has expressed interest in the university.

These interactive websites can generate lots of data from every student who creates a personal profile and uses the site. That information then gives the school a better idea of how to tailor its message. It is also valuable in the statistical analyses and predictive modeling that have become a vital part of marketing—the determination of just how big a financial aid package is needed to entice a particular applicant.[35]

▪ Pricing the Product

When higher education is being discussed, whether by parents or by politicians, cost is often the topic and grumbling defines the tone. That is understandable, since tuition keeps escalating. Between 1980 and 1995, tuition increases averaged nearly 9 percent per year, more than twice the rate of inflation.[36] The easy reaction to this bad news is to blame higher education for its own woes, an argument regularly made in articles with incendiary titles like "Our Greedy Colleges."[37] But the story is more complicated. For their part, university administrators emphasize "the usual suspects: escalating labor, material, and fuel costs; growth in faculty and staff; increased fringe benefits and student financial aid; higher administrative expenses . . . : all this with no offsetting gain in productivity."[38] But that's too simple as well. When economist Charles Clotfelter took a close look at elite universities' cost figures, most of the tuition increases remained unexplained. The best answer, he concluded, is the competitive cost of "top dog-ism."[39]

With all the concern about the big picture, less attention gets paid to what has been happening *inside* college admissions offices. During the past decade or so, there have been dramatic changes in the way schools calculate how much of a "discount" from the tuition "sticker price" to offer, and to whom—discounts that are more familiarly known as financial aid.

Financial aid has traditionally been based on a student's need. Promising scholars, the argument goes, should not be prevented from going to school because they can't afford to pay the bills. That apple pie principle is Marxism come to America—from each according to his abilities, to each according to his needs—and, like Marxism everywhere, it has given ground to market forces.

While there have always been exceptions to the rule of need—star quarterbacks, for instance—they were rarities. But then a generation ago, many colleges started increasing the number of merit-based scholarships as bait to attract students they otherwise couldn't hope to enroll.[40] These days, the admissions office is expected to recruit students with strong academic credentials in order to help their school move up in the *U.S. News* sweepstakes. As a "profit center," the admissions office is also supposed to raise as much revenue as possible from tuition. That set of demands has led to new financial aid formulas that resemble the way Priceline.com sells plane tickets.

Elite institutions aren't deeply involved in these price wars. Until the practice was halted by the U.S. Justice Department, on questionable antitrust grounds, in 1989, Ivy League schools had agreed not to use scholarship offers to compete with one another.[41] Still, when Williams College freezes tuition or Princeton converts all its student aid into scholarships, money is being used as a marketing tool in ways that only a tiny handful of schools can hope to match.[42]

The money wars are more openly and aggressively waged among striving institutions. William Elliott, vice president for enrollment management at Carnegie Mellon University, doesn't just rely on merit aid to recruit top students; he also started the first "reaction program," which sets aside over a quarter of a million dollars a year to match other schools' financial aid offers.[43] It has become common practice to invite parents to put competing bids on the table, and almost every institution that ranks below the very top is now offering proportionately more merit-based aid than it used to. Old-line admissions officers, schooled to believe that need is the only fair way to distribute aid, lament these developments. But as Michael McPherson, president of Macalester College and a distinguished higher education economist, told a *Chronicle of Higher Education* reporter, "if you go out and act altruistic, Bill [Elliott, at Carnegie Mellon] is ready to eat your lunch."[44]

The strategic uses of financial aid reach far beyond the pursuit of the ablest students. At many schools, awards are in line with an overall strategy for achieving institutional goals, as money is being leveraged with increasing precision. During the mid-1990s, when he was the dean of undergraduate enrollment at Johns Hopkins University, a school dominated by premed students, Robert Massa was eager to recruit a class with more intellectually varied tastes. He did so by offering especially sweet financial aid packages to applicants who said they planned to major in the humanities.

In making his calculations, Massa relied on econometric models of relatively recent vintage. Those models treat a student's inclination to attend a particular school as the outcome of an equation that incorporates factors such as the student's grades and SAT scores, geographic location, extracurricular activities, intended major—and, of course, what the student must pay for the education.[45] As a statistical matter, the models can only show which factors correlate with decisions made by earlier generations of students. But financial aid officers interpret the data to predict cause and effect, and then estimate how much of a discount is needed to tip an applicant's decision.

This technique can be used in ethically problematic ways. Bob Massa learned that applicants who come to Johns Hopkins for an interview— something that all colleges encourage, in the belief that students should see for themselves whether the school is a good fit—are more likely to enroll if they're admitted. That meant the university could, with relatively little risk, offer them smaller aid packages than their counterparts who had never visited the campus. Although Massa chose not to penalize campus visitors, other enrollment managers have fewer scruples. And like William Elliott of Carnegie Mellon, another early advocate of the use of statistical modeling, Massa makes smaller awards to students who apply for early admission. His reasoning is basic price discrimination: just like businessmen who don't have the flexibility to take advantage of Priceline's discounted fares, these students are captive customers.[46]

▪ Whatever It Takes: Revamping the College Experience

Until the 1970s, Brown University suffered through a long and inglorious history as the doormat of the Ivy League.[47] Unfortunately situated in the mob-plagued backwater of Providence, Rhode Island, Brown was the safety school for students rejected by Yale or Dartmouth, and the fact that almost no one wanted to be there made it an especially unhappy place. All this changed completely in the span of a decade—breathtakingly fast in higher education, where reputations once made are hard to undo. The reason was a new academic program, clevery marketed by a president whose persuasive powers put the Pied Piper to shame.[48]

Brown junked its standard-fare curriculum in 1969. What it called the "New Curriculum" was crafted mainly by campus activists, and it reads like an undergraduate's wish list.[49] The reforms abolished all distribution requirements, cut the number of courses students needed to graduate, eschewed majors in favor of individually tailored concentrations, and allowed students to take all their courses on a pass-fail basis.

"Brown's curriculum is structured in such a way," reads the college viewbook, "as to teach students the lessons of choice and responsibility." The catchphrase is "Freedom with Responsibility," and in its student-knows-best philosophy, Brown's message was perfectly attuned to the times.[50] The college also marketed its product with textbook precision. The admissions office relied on undergraduates as salespeople, flying them around the country to meet prospects. A glowing *New York Times* feature story generated invaluable publicity. Celebrities' offspring, including several members of the Kennedy clan, started to enroll, and their arrival garnered a spate of gushing stories. The new regime was promoted with tireless avidity by Vartan Gregorian, a president with a genius for generating publicity and picking donors' pockets. When Edward Fiske, the *Times* education editor, published his best-selling college guide, a precursor to the *U.S. News* rankings, in the early 1980s, Brown had become the hottest ticket in American higher education, harder to get into than Harvard. A popular T-shirt underscored the point: "Harvard University," it read, "Rejected by Brown."

Buzz can last only so long. But Brown, which still follows the philosophy of the New Curriculum, has held onto its niche as a maverick school. When Gordon Gee left for Vanderbilt, the school hired Ruth Simmons his successor—only the second woman, and the first African American, to head an Ivy League college.

Colleges are always searching for new ways to woo undergraduates. "It's not a hardship to go to college," says Kevin Kruger at the National Association of Student Personnel Administrators. That's a considerable understatement. As Mary Leonard wrote in a front-page *Boston Globe* article that surveyed the playing field, at Michigan State, lucky students can watch big-screen TV while lounging in the therapeutic bubble jets in their dorm rooms. "There's a putting green and batting cages at the new indoor tennis and track center at DePauw University. . . . At Saint Xavier University in Chicago, students can work out with a personal trainer in the fitness center and then pick up a Krispy Kreme doughnut and a Starbucks double latte, all under one roof. . . . The first college ESPN Zone at the Rochester Institute of Technology in New York [offers] sports on plasma televisions and a broadcast desk to let students practice doing play-by-play on camera. . . . The feeding of this flock has become big business. The university of Cincinnati has hired a master chef to create gourmet menus . . . Georgia Tech in Atlanta has a greengrocer in a residence hall . . . Babson College [has added a fresh juice bar at the campus center], which already had vegan and sushi stations and a full-time person preparing specialty coffees." "It's not about pampering," insists Carol Hacker, student affairs dean at Babson, all the while maintaining a straight face. "It's about community building." Kevin Kruger is more candid: "This is definitely driven by a competitive marketplace."[51]

For colleges with modest endowments, the consequences can be calamitous. "A lot of schools got into this arms race, or facilities race," an analyst at Standard and Poor's points out. "They needed a rec center because the school they compete with has a new one. Or they had to have a new dorm because the college they compete with had one. Now those buildings are done, and they have to pay for them. There's a lot of colleges out there that before they can spend a dime, they have already committed 10 or 15 percent of their budget to debt service."[52]

At many public universities, money has been poured into new "honors colleges"—small, highly selective liberal arts enclaves within the sprawl of mass education–oriented universities, which offer favored students one-on-one mentoring, special seminars, separate living quarters, and generous financial aid packages.[53] Since 1994, the number of these colleges has doubled to more than fifty, and hundreds of schools are running less intense honors programs.[54] When the Walton (Wal-Mart) family gave the University of Arkansas $300 million in 2002, the biggest single gift ever made to a public university, most of the money was designated for an honors college.

The University of Massachusetts at Amherst launched its honors college, called Commonwealth College, in 1999. Although UMass is the flagship public institution in the state, it has never received much public respect. In Massachusetts, attention goes to the private schools, which enroll two-thirds of all undergraduates, the highest proportion in the nation. The university has been derided as "ZooMass" because of its party-over-study reputation, and *U.S. News & World Report* ranked it forty-eighth among public universities in 2001, tied with Alabama and Florida State and below all the University of California's campuses.

Commonwealth College, says Aaron Spencer, board chairman of Pizzeria Uno and the trustee who proposed the idea, is designed to change all that, "to improve both public higher education and the perception of public higher education" in Massachusetts. While the state legislature was unwilling to make a major investment in such improvements, the hope was that with a few million dollars for scholarships, smaller classes, and spruced-up housing, as well as aggressive marketing, the Commonwealth Scholar degree could become an academic status symbol.

There was resistance from some undergraduates, however, including the head of the student government. In a three-hour confrontation with Spencer chronicled by the campus newspaper, they assailed the program as "racist and classist . . . not socially responsible." As the critics feared, representation of blacks and Hispanics at the honors college has been low, about half what it is on the campus as a whole. But Spencer points to Commonwealth College's clear success in attracting high-scoring undergraduates. In 2002, the median high school grade point average of the entering students was 3.9 and the median SAT score was 1329. While professing an "empathy for those from modest circumstances who try and improve themselves," Spencer misses the troubling implications of using state education money to subsidize a program for a disproportionately white and well-off selection of students. "What's wrong," he muses aloud, "with a basketball team that's predominantly black and an honors college that's predominantly white?"

What works at these flagship public universities is also being tried at regional state colleges, though training an elite was never supposed to be their mission. At little-known Indiana University in Pennsylvania, the academic profile of the 250 students in the Robert C. Cook Honors College is almost identical to that of the students at Commonwealth College, and the average SAT score of 1320 is about 260 points higher than the average among the other 11,000 undergraduates. Cook College has been a "salvation" for the university, says president Lawrence Pettit, as it pushes to be competitive with better-known state schools such as the University of Pittsburgh and Pennsylvania State University, both of which have honors colleges of their own. "Positional warfare," it appears, is occurring on all the rungs of the status ladder.[55]

▪ Rigging the Market

Colleges have also taken unsavory steps to improve their reputation—for instance, by misrepresenting the data used in determining *U.S. News* rankings. The temptation to cheat is considerable because the stakes are so high. Economists Ronald Ehrenberg and James Monks conclude that with each step upward in the rankings, proportionately more of the students a college accepts, and more of those with high SAT scores, decide to enroll.[56]

Even the most selective schools have cheated. Since the rate of giving among alumni is factored into the *U.S. News* rankings, some universities, Cornell among them, simply eliminate from their database graduates who are not likely to donate—by reclassifying them as deceased. Schools have also been known to fudge the numbers in reporting their students' SAT scores. In 1995, the *Wall Street Journal* compared the SAT scores that universities reported to bond rating agencies with those they provided to *U.S. News;* about 20 percent of the time there were notable discrepancies, with the *U.S. News* figures almost always higher. New York University failed to include the scores of about a hundred "economically disadvantaged" students, Boston University omitted the verbal scores of its international students, and Harvard could not explain a fifteen-point discrepancy in its reported SAT scores. Edward Hershey, the former director of communications at Colby College, recalled how administrators there "huddled at 'a meeting that could only be described as a strategy session on how to cheat on the system.'" When the school "mistakenly reported that 80 percent, rather than 60 percent, of Colby's freshmen were in the top 10% of their high school class . . . Colby jumped to 15th place from 20th place in the [*U.S. News*] rankings. 'The downside was that we spent the following year figuring out how to play with some other numbers to preserve our competitive advantage.'"[57]

U.S. News places great weight on a college's selectivity, that is, the percentage of applicants it admits and the percentage of those admitted who enroll. That fact, and not any academically defensible reason, is the main reason why schools have come to rely so heavily on early decision. Under this arrangement, students can apply to only one college, and promise to attend if they are accepted. Columbia and Yale, for instance, accepted nearly half their students this way in 2001, twice as many as a decade earlier. The academic records of early admits are on the whole weaker than the records of students who wait until the spring. But these applicants are irresistible to admissions officers because, since virtually all who are accepted enroll, they make the school look more selective. That's why, as a 2003 study shows, applying for early decision can improve a student's chances by as much as 50 percent—the equivalent of scoring one hundred points higher on the SAT.[58]

What is more troubling, admissions officers encourage as many students as possible to apply, knowing that the more applicants the college rejects, the more selective it appears to be. For the same reason—looking good to *U.S. News*—schools like Emory University and Franklin and Marshall do not accept their very best applicants, because the admissions office believes they won't actually come. By rejecting or wait-listing them, the school makes itself look harder to get into.

It doesn't take a Holden Caulfield to figure out that it's hypocritical to expect students to lie about themselves or dumb down their applications in order to gain admission. But not all of these students are pawns in the hands of unscrupulous officials; some collect acceptance letters like trading cards. Both sides can play this game. It's precisely the kind of thing that students with access to sophisticated advice have figured out how to do.

▪ "I Don't Guide Applications, I Guide Lives"

Chris Barrett and Luke McCabe were suburban high school kids, whiling away an afternoon in the summer of 2000 watching a golf tournament on TV, when the idea first hit them: Tiger Woods earns millions of dollars a year for wearing a black hat with a white swoosh and making a few commercials; why can't we do the same thing and get some company to pay for college? Admittedly Tiger was better known, but they were willing to do more. In return for tuition, room and board, and trips back home, the twosome were willing to become walking human billboards.

These teenagers already knew something about marketing. Chris was the youngest patent holder in U.S. history, having patented, at age five, a two-sticker system that helps youngsters tell their right shoe from their left; and Luke's band, Big Fat Huge, was a hit on the New York punk scene. Working with a publicist, they created a website, *www.chris andluke.com*, that laid out their plans to be the first corporate-sponsored college students in history. "We will drink your soda and eat your chips," they vowed, mugging for the camera. "Where we go . . . you go!"

Soon thereafter, *chrisandluke.com* was selected as Yahoo!'s website of the day. Everyone in the media wanted to tell their story—CNN and MSNBC, *Time* and *Spin,* the *New York Times* and the *Times* of London, as well. Fifteen corporations bid for their services. They settled on FirstUSA, the credit card company, which sponsored Chris at Pepperdine and Luke at the University of Southern California. For $40,000 a year apiece, the cost of a private school education, their job was to teach the coming generation how to be good consumers.

The story of Chris and Luke is more than a tale of two adolescents with an incredible idea. It takes to an extreme what has become an increasingly common activity: students marketing themselves to get into prestige schools. Even as universities retain consultants to do market research, design promotions, and devise financial aid strategies, for their part some students rely on consultants to help them put their best face forward.

There is a major difference between the two sides of this market equation. While virtually all schools are taking steps to strengthen their appeal to students, only students whose families are well off can afford a makeover. Among that select group, only those aiming for highly selective universities make the investment.[59] In a 1995 study, 79 percent of freshmen enrolled in colleges where the average SAT score was over 1300 reported that college rankings were a major influence on their choice. For those attending colleges with scores between 1001 and 1300, the figure was lower, 59 percent; and it was just 27 percent at schools where the average SAT was less than 700.

Twenty-nine thousand dollars, which is what a company called Ivywise charges for its top-of-the-line services, is a big investment. But there is no shortage of parents willing to pay handsomely for the help offered by Yale Ph.D. and former admissions officer Katherine Cohen, the firm's founder.[60] "I don't guide applications," Cohen says. "I guide lives."

Ivywise transforms students' hobbies into items that will leap off their résumés. A student interested in art would likely be advised by a high school counselor to take an advanced placement art course and include his or her best work with the college application. Katherine Cohen will showcase her client's work, but that's just the beginning. She'll also put the student in touch with a well-known artist whom she knows, persuading her friend to donate an artwork to a campus beautification project at her client's high school. And no aspiring artist's application is complete without an internship at the Metropolitan Museum of Art, courtesy of the well-connected Ms. Cohen.

What's most impressive is the effort that Cohen extracts from her charges. Students must know, inside out, every school to which they apply. This includes choosing the campus organizations they are interested in, filling out a schedule of first-year classes, and even reading a book authored by one of their prospective professors. Preparing for an interview is a similarly painstaking task. Cohen distributes a list of a hundred questions that students must answer in writing; then she conducts a mock interview which is video-taped and critiqued. That's a staggering amount of work, and Cohen's clients go through the same drill for each college to which they apply. It might be easier for these students actually to *do* something remarkable, like winning the Westinghouse science competition or getting a novel published, than to write the glittering application predictably generated by the Ivywise regimen.

As might be expected, Ivywise has been very successful—more than 80 percent of the clients get accepted into one of their two "reach" schools—and the company now offers two additional services. Ivywise Athletes caters to students whose calling card is their prowess on the sports field. Ivywise Kids is geared to the highly competitive process of admission to selective kindergartens and elementary schools. For ambitious parents, it is never too soon to start marketing one's offspring.

Parents used to depend on high school guidance counselors to guide their children though the maze of college applications. But while the admissions process has become more competitive, counselors' workloads have mushroomed. Now, with responsibility for hundreds of students, they seldom have time for pastoral duties.[61] The market abhors a vacuum. Since the mid-1980s, private counseling has become what Harvard's dean of admissions has called a "growth industry."[62]

But where does helping stop and ghostwriting begin? School counselors have complained that their counterparts in the private sector were "over-coaching" students and helping parents cheat the financial aid offices. Wealthy parents were getting huge financial aid awards for their children, the *Chronicle of Higher Education* reported in 1990, by hiring counselors to game the system.[63] "Consultants or Con Artists?" read the headline of a *New York Times* article.[64]

The private counselors went on a charm offensive. In the mid-1990s, their trade group drafted new "Principles of Good Practice," and what the signatories pledged *not* to do was eye-opening: they could no longer make guarantees about admission or accept money from schools to which they channeled students.[65] But with new revelations about counselors who all but wrote the applicants' essays—including, embarrassingly, the former president of the trade group, who himself was an ex–college admissions officer—elite schools took notice.[66] In an effort to flush out these practices, in 2002, Duke began asking applicants who had helped them write their essays.

Some counselors, Katherine Cohen among them, accept a handful of poor youngsters on a pro bono basis,[67] and companies like Princeton Review and Kaplan provide canned on-line admissions tutorials. But this system is geared to give the wealthy yet another advantage in the college admissions game. "In some ways," says Arthur Levine, president of Columbia University Teachers College, "it's an affront to the fairness of the educational process."[68] When a nonprofit organization, the Foundation for a College Education, tried providing poor school districts with high-caliber coaching, it was eaten alive by the deep-pockets competition.

In the spring of 2002, the *New York Times* ran a series chronicling how three high school seniors played the college admissions game.[69] Each story has a happy ending. Jed Resnick, a wealthy suburban adolescent, fine-tunes his image in a manner that Katherine Cohen would approve, with a summer stint at a theater company to show talent and a semester at an experimental school away from home to show spunk. Although he is turned down by Yale, his first choice, Jed is accepted by Brown. Reuben Quansah, a black teenager raised by a single mother in the Bronx, is admitted to an engineering program at Bucknell University. Gerta Xhelo, the daughter of immigrants living in the middle-class vastness of Queens, overcomes a slacker's career in high school to get into Syracuse University.

This rite of passage, once "like a secret handshake . . . is now open to all comers," the *Times* article cheerfully insists.[70] In fact, the ways in which these students approach going to college differ as much as the lives they lead. Jed would die, he says, before going to a second-tier school like Bucknell. He has been in training for this moment almost from birth, guided by hyper-ambitious parents and a counselor, Bruce Breimer, who is knowledgeable in the ways of the Ivy League schools where most of his students wind up. (Breimer even sends admissions officers a CD to showcase Jed's singing talents.) Although Reuben has done very well at a Catholic high school, no one there thinks to suggest that he should consider an Ivy League college. For his part, he just wants to enroll in a good engineering program. Gerta selects Syracuse on a whim and a virtual campus tour. And for both Gerta and Reuben, admission is only half the battle: financial aid offers determine where they can go. Jed, whose family is used to paying $21,000 a year for his prep school tuition and $7,000 more for his theater training, doesn't have to follow the money.[71]

Most stories about poor and working-class adolescents are more depressing than Gerta's and Reuben's. While they lack Jed's wealth and social capital, Gerta and Ruben both have crucial advantages that most of their peers lack. Their guidance counselors, though saddled with hundreds of students, compared with sixty for Bruce Breimer, somehow found the time to take a personal interest in these two youngsters. Their immigrant parents (from Albania and Ghana, respectively) appreciate the value of higher education and prodded their offspring to succeed. Had the *Times* decided to focus on Reuben's classmates who, the article notes, attend college fairs to check out girls, not schools, the reportorial tone would have been less chirpy, the outcome less happy, and the gulf separating winners and losers much wider.

▪ Is "Positional Arms Control" Possible?

Positional warfare, as practiced by both colleges and students, is hardly the main reason why the poor are less likely to go to college. Money is. While 80 percent of students in the highest income quintile go to college, fewer than half of those in the bottom quintile do, and this gap is considerably wider for four-year colleges.[72]

The federal government puts a thumb on the equity scale by providing scholarships, in the form of Pell grants, for which students from poor families are eligible. But these are woefully inadequate. They would nearly have to double simply to match the purchasing power of the mid-1970s; and that would be only a start, since in the intervening decades, increases in tuition have far outpaced inflation. The shift in federal policy away from grants to loan programs, tuition tax credits, and education IRAs was supposed to fix this problem. But as Michael McPherson and Morton Schapiro, two economists who are also college presidents, point out, this has actually made things worse. While Pell grants go only to poor students, all but the very wealthiest families are eligible for the new assistance programs. State scholarship programs for students with high grades have the same impact: the beneficiaries are mainly children from well-off families.[73]

The new—or at least newly sophisticated—tactics of the competitive admissions marketplace influence who gets into the top private institutions and the honors colleges in public universities; and as is true in most markets, there is nothing equitable about the system. Poorer students can't afford to remake themselves as attractive candidates for selective schools. They also fare badly when financial aid is understood "strategically." It used to be said that higher education replicated the nation's inequalities. These days it is making things worse.

What can be done? On rare occasions colleges have been able to buck the market and win. In the late 1990s, Dickinson College and Bowdoin College decided not to require applicants to submit SAT scores. They risked the wrath of *U.S. News & World Report,* which relies heavily on those test scores in ranking colleges. But the two schools were sending a signal to minority students, and the strategy worked. Nonwhites applied in considerably greater numbers—and so did a new generation of Holden Caulfields, who suddenly saw these fusty colleges as cool places. In 2002, the University of California, which is also eager to increase the number of minority students, announced it would take the same step, a declaration that unnerved admissions offices across the country. Meanwhile, Harvard threatened another kind of unilateral action, refusing to abide by other colleges' early decision admissions. If Harvard followed through with its threat, other schools would have to follow; and because only students as well-off as Jed Resnick can commit themselves to a college without knowing how much financial aid they will be receiving, this too would be a positive development.

Most of the time, though, schools are faced with a classic "prisoner's dilemma" situation: if they act alone, they lose. The competition among colleges is sometimes healthy; and so long as there is a Berkeley and a Stanford, a Harvard and a Yale, it is inevitable. But as economist Robert Frank points out, "all outcomes of open competition [among colleges aren't] good. . . . [T]he competitive dynamics . . . virtually guarantee a measure of social waste." The market for students would function better if schools were inclined, and authorized by antitrust law, to adopt what Frank calls "positional arms control agreements."[74] Rivals would commit themselves to spending less on frills and more on financial aid for those who really need it; to recruiting more heavily in working-class and inner-city schools, using the same techniques that brought more women to MIT; to democratizing access to good college advising; to converting the honors college, with its smaller classes and higher aspirations, into a model to which all of higher education should aspire; and to making need and merit, not market sophistication, the basic principles on which to allocate financial aid.[75] But with the competition getting stiffer every year and the stakes getting higher for both students and colleges, only a cockeyed optimist can imagine this scenario actually coming to pass.

2

Nietzsche's Niche
The University of Chicago

The University of Chicago is more self-absorbed—more precisely, self-obsessed—than any other institution of higher learning in America.[1] Its animating myth was manufactured by Robert Maynard Hutchins, the institution's pivotal president and promoter *non pareil*. "It's not a very good university," Hutchins declared, "it's only the best there is." Never mind Oxford or Berkeley. Harvard and Yale may fill the corridors of power, loyalists say; in the domain of ideas, Chicago rules. Nowhere else is "the Ivy League" a term of derision—the land of academic "Jay Leno-ism," it is called, a reference to its veneration of big-name professors derided at Chicago as "dying elephants." A passing remark made long ago by the philosopher Alfred North Whitehead is recycled as if it were gospel: "I think the one place where I have been that is most like ancient Athens is the University of Chicago."[2]

Three-quarters of the faculty live within a mile of the campus in the enclave of Hyde Park, a hothouse of learned chatter and salacious gossip set apart, by design, from the bombed-out inner-city landscape, peopled mainly by dirt-poor blacks, which surrounds it. The fact of isolation, it is said half-jokingly, is why the university's athletic teams are known as the Maroons. The Chicago tribe takes pleasure in furious disputations about everything from monetarism to metaphysics. While Harvard preens, Chicago navel-gazes, turning out bookshelves'-worth of histories and biographies, faculty committee reports, student newspapers, broadsheets, and websites devoted to itself. There are several hundred listings in the "introductory" bibliography of the university's history that the campus librarians have prepared.

Seemingly everyone is an amateur historian, mining the past for ammunition that can be used in the present.[3] "No episode was more important in shaping the outlook and expectations [of higher education in the decades following the Civil War] than the founding of the University of Chicago," writes Frederick Rudolph in his benchmark history of American higher education. It is "one of those events in American history that brought into focus the spirit of an age."[4] When John D. Rockefeller launched the university with a gift of $2.3 million, he expressed the hope that an institution situated far from the tradition-bound East Coast would "strike out upon lines in full sympathy with the spirit of the age."[5] Although Chicago is a great school, in this respect Rockefeller would be disappointed. The dominant trope, observes Dennis Hutchinson, professor of law and longtime dean of the undergraduate college, is that "at Chicago we've always done 'X,'" meaning whatever is being advocated at the moment.

There is another, less frequently acknowledged tradition in Hyde Park, a willingness on the part of the university's leaders, including Hutchins and William Rainey Harper, the founding president, to do whatever has been necessary to raise money for a chronically cash-starved school. Among its past ventures are a junior college and the nation's biggest correspondence school; in 1998 it attached itself to Unext.com, a for-profit business school.

These pragmatics have not been discussed in a public conversation that emphasizes the quest for knowledge. But early in the 1990s the belief that money talk was vulgar collided with the ugly bottom-line reality. The university was running huge deficits and draining the institution's modest endowment. In 1994, the trustees turned to Hugo Sonnenschein, the provost of Princeton and a distinguished economist, in the belief that he could set things right by raising money, trimming costs, and generally putting the institution on a solid financial footing. When Sonnenschein tried to do so, however, he ran straight into a buzz saw. Legions of old school loyalists disdained his managerial style and feared that his money-driven policies—especially those perceived as making undergraduate education less rigorous—spelled the "Princeton-ization" of the place they loved. Their deepest fear was that, in the quest for students, Chicago's distinctive culture would become just a marketing tool.

At both the University of Chicago and Dickinson College, a venerable and financially vulnerable liberal arts college whose response to market pressures is the focus of the next chapter, the decision to pursue students aggressively poses risks to the institution's character. At New York University, the centerpiece of Chapter 4, success has been defined as acquiring star faculty, not students, but there too the strategy potentially under-mines the academic commons. In each instance, the institution has sought a middle ground, a way to stay true to its academic mission while not ig-noring the force of the marketplace.

▪ The Ghost of Robert Hutchins

"The University of Chicago Comes to a Fork in the Road" read the head-line of a front-page article in the December 28, 1998, *New York Times.* The lead paragraph was a publicist's dream—literally so, since the publi-cist, Al Chambers, an ex–Ford Motor Company flack who had been hired as part of the university's image makeover campaign, had nursed this story into being. "Ever since its creation on the South Side of Chicago in 1892 with a pile of Rockefeller money and a group of top-flight scholars, no other academic institution has exemplified intellectual seriousness quite like the University of Chicago."[6]

But quickly the PR dream turned nightmarish. The rest of the *Times* ar-ticle dissects an institution in the throes of an "identity crisis"—a school with relatively few applicants and a high dropout rate, its endowment too modest to sustain its pretensions, and its campus a crumbling Gothic pile. Worse still, the story intimated that the very essence of the university, its fabled "cloistered approach to learning," was under assault from within. Michael Behnke, who had recently been hired as vice president in charge of enrollment, was heretical enough to doubt aloud that many students "only seek the life of the mind." President Sonnenschein spoke matter-of-factly about a new order whose mercenary character was entirely alien to the denizens of Hyde Park—a new world where the "commodification and marketing of higher education" aren't evils to be warded off but facts of life.

A month later the *Chicago Tribune* lambasted the "University of Chuckles" for a new marketing campaign that linked Chicago to "fun"—this at a campus where a popular T-shirt boasts about the university as "The Place Where Fun Comes To Die"—and the "identity crisis" story line was repeatedly retailed in the national media.[7] On campus, and among trustees and alumni as well, the *Times* article was pored over as if it were a passage from the Talmud. Quickly, the flattering lead was forgotten. The news story became a call to arms.

The fight centered on two administration initiatives: cutting back the required core curriculum and increasing the number of undergraduates.

Chicago is renowned for its take-no-prisoners approach to intellectual life. That energy was now turned full force on Sonnenschein and provost Geoffrey Stone, the former law school dean.

Seventy-four professors, among them some of the most distinguished senior faculty, sent an open letter to the trustees, warning darkly that "the intellectual tradition and academic organization of our university are being put at risk by its present leadership."[8] Ten academic ancients—icons such as Saul Bellow, David Riesman, and Mortimer Adler, the intellectual midwife to the core curriculum sixty years earlier—weighed in against this "dangerous" venture. "Making academic decisions on the basis of marketing," they intoned, "is itself a crime against the mind."[9]

A newly formed alumni group called Concerned Friends of the University of Chicago decried the administration's plans as putting in "imminent danger" the "character of the entire University," and urged fellow alumni to withhold their contributions until the old order was restored. At its peak, the website launched by the alumni group recorded ten thousand hits a month from around the globe. "What's at stake is the soul of the university," declared graduate student John Wilson in a letter to the campus paper, the *Maroon*, "which is no small thing considering that the University of Chicago, unlike most universities, actually has a soul."[10]

At a time when the technology transfer office and the heating system often seem the only things that bind institutions of higher learning together, it is remarkable that anyone should still talk about a university in such orotund terms. The tone of these missives reflects the sacredness of the partisans' cause. "The administration did not understand that if they cut the core curriculum, the natives would get restless," anthropologist Marshall Sahlins thundered in a widely circulated broadside. For faculty, students, and alumni alike, "the University itself, as mediated by their own identity with it, [has] been put at stake." Sahlins and his fellow antagonists were able to locate support for their anti-administration position in the admonition of Robert Hutchins himself. "When an institution determines to do something in order to get money," Hutchins had written sixty years earlier, "it must lose its soul."[11]

The stakes were high for the administration as well, which could mine this same Hutchins text for its own purposes. "I do not mean, of course, that universities do not need money and that they should not try to get it," Hutchins had written. "I mean only that they should have an educational policy and then try to finance it." In April 1996, Sonnenschein wrote an open letter to the faculty proposing to increase the undergraduate enrollment by 25 percent, to 4,500, within a decade: "The course I am recommending is not without risk, but the greater risk is to remain on a course that will not sustain excellence."[12]

■ The Core of the Matter

The rigors of the undergraduate experience are pivotal to Chicago's identity. The quarter system is designed to cram a semester's worth of work into ten weeks. Most classes are conducted as discussions, no more than thirty students and an instructor, and Chicago has few of the great performers who, at other top-rung campuses, lecture to multitudes. The grading system is so uninflated that students complain, with reason, that they are unfairly handicapped when they apply to graduate schools. In this spartan academic environment, where pallor is beautiful and reading Nietzsche at three in the morning or arguing the finer points of his philosophy on a first date is a badge of honor, it's not easy for a weak or lazy student to hide.

The centerpiece of this education is the required common core curriculum, which has its intellectual origins in Hutchins's *Higher Learning in America*.[13] The premise is that all students should master certain habits of mind, so that they can become independent critics of each of the major intellectual domains. This approach is the opposite of the practice at most universities, where students choose from the smorgasbord course catalogue and "general education" is demoted to "distribution" requirements.

That brand of free-form curriculum is defended as accommodating students' desires to dive straight into what most interests them. Conveniently, it also frees professors to concentrate on what most interests *them*, rather than obliging them to teach students how to think critically for themselves. The implication is that those who run the academic asylum lack the intellectual authority to mold the minds of the inmates. By contrast, the University of Chicago's philosophy of education promises bracing clarity: a stress on critical thinking in a variety of disciplines, resistance to early specialization, examination of original texts in small seminars. This approach, argued sociologist Andrew Abbott, former master of the college's social science division, "forces"—forces!—"students to achieve a breadth of knowledge and experience they would not necessarily elect for themselves."[14]

Redesigning the undergraduate curriculum has always been a donnybrook. "The absolute moral high ground," laments Geoffrey Stone, the provost during these battles, "was taken by those who said anyone who tries to change what we're doing is using false reasons and acting with evil motives." In fact, the content of the common core has changed repeatedly, expanding and contracting to fit the intellectual season. Those changes have been shaped by protracted political negotiations, carried out by professors with their own ideas—and turf—to defend. "It's the custom," says John Boyer, the administrator most responsible for the revamped core, "to have stirring fights over the curriculum."

Professors regard any administrative intervention in curricular matters as an intrusion into their exclusive terrain. In 1946, faculty members angered at changes initiated by Hutchins wrote to the trustees, beseeching them to overrule the president.[15] In 1998, it was widely rumored that Boyer was carrying out Sonnenschein's wishes. Although the central administration publicly took a hands-off stance ("This was really John Boyer's idea, what he saw as his legacy," says Stone), only the terminally naïve could miss the relationship between money and pedagogy. "The Provost [Stone]," Andrew Abbott wrote at the time, "stated to the Undergraduate Task Force [the faculty group that reviewed the core courses] that it was the administration's desire to see undergraduate education 'better and at the same time cheaper.'"[16]

"Cheaper" was understood to mean smaller, and this blunt introduction of economics into a pedagogical discourse politicized the process. In 1997, a plan that nearly halved the number of requirements was rejected, and the faculty went back to the drawing board. The revisions ultimately adopted a year later by the vote of an overwhelming majority of the faculty were quite modest. Three courses out of eighteen were cut, and the language requirement was reframed, sensibly, in terms of competency rather than seat time.

Peace seemed to have been restored. But it was a cold peace, and hostilities resumed in 1999 with the flood of media attention. Fighting had broken out again, this time publicly, and gallons of ink were spilled over a proposal whose scope had already been significantly reduced by compromise.

▪ Dante or Derrida?

"How many core courses?" was the focus of the media debate, a numbers game in which "more" was presumed to be "better." What was taught in those courses, and by whom, received no notice. The greatest threat to the common core, however, came not from the administration but from the faculty itself, which had largely given up on the project years before.

Many professors, like historian George Chauncy, author of the acclaimed *Gay New York,* favored a much smaller core because existing requirements didn't give students "enough freedom to explore their own interests, even to put together a good undergraduate major."[17] Nearly a third of all undergraduates, desperate to take courses that would engage their interest, postponed some required classes until their senior year, thus defeating the intellectual purpose of the enterprise. Faculty unhappiness with the content of the required courses was widespread. The biology courses are "in disarray," wrote the professor who oversaw the program. "Faculty are unsure what to teach, or why, and students are too often apathetic, if not hostile."[18] There were easy pathways through hard science, courses like "Physics for Poets" that belied the rigor of the requirement.

Curriculum revision also became hostage to the Kulturkampf that was sweeping academe. "There's no danger of the University of Chicago becoming less demanding," Leora Auslander told the *New York Times.* "The danger I worry about is it becoming an anachronism."[19] Auslander, who directs the Center for Gender Studies, teaches those "bizarre electives" assailed by the anti-Sonnenschein alumni group. "Shakespeare was out, gay studies was in," philosopher Daniel Garber says, recalling the heated conversations, "and the faculty traditionalists weren't pleased"—this despite the fact that the Western civilization course, which came to emblemize the tradition that was under assault, had not been required of all undergraduates since the mid-1980s. One war-weary senior, Aleem Hassain, opted for his own separate peace. He had argued strenuously for maintaining the core, he wrote in the *Maroon,* but overzealous classmates had driven him away, "people on 'my side of the issues' who argued that movies, lesbians, Cubans, and jazz had no place in a U of C education."

Only senior professors should teach the core courses, Andrew Abbott asserted, because only a widely published academic can stand as a "central authority figure who can model for the students the discipline of rethinking ideas." What a marvelous notion: Kant or Mill interpreted by Mortimer Adler or Allan Bloom, transcendent texts in the hands of master interpreters. But you would have to go elsewhere to find it. At Chicago, the ideal of a college where intellectually obsessive undergraduates are instructed in small classes by full professors, Socrates among the genius set, collides with a shabbier reality. Science courses are delivered lecture-style, as in most universities, and few sections are led by faculty members. Even in the humanities and social sciences, points out Richard Saller, the university's provost since 2001, nearly two-thirds of classes are taught by graduate students and non–tenure track faculty.

At Chicago, faculty devotion to the core isn't bred in the bone. It's a historical accident resulting from the university's peculiar division into two separate faculties. Until the 1960s, the graduate faculty, based in the disciplines, taught Ph.D. candidates, while the college faculty, hired separately, instructed undergraduates. Although the intention was to build a university that rewarded teaching as well as research, the result was a rancorous split between the discipline-based professors, who regarded themselves as the "real faculty," and the "have-not" college instructors, dismissed as glorified high school teachers. "There were people teaching economics who didn't know Milton Friedman was a professor here," Saller says, shaking his head at the oddity of it all.

This division of labor was abolished in the 1960s. Since those who have subsequently been hired, like faculty everywhere, have more specialized interests, when the college instructors retired there was no one to fill the classroom void. At the same time, in order to compete with leading universities, Chicago has cut the teaching load from six to four quarter courses, and many professors teach only one undergraduate course.

These facts on the ground made for decidedly odd bedfellows. Donald Levine, a sociology professor and the former dean of the college, for whom the common core is a passion, found himself in rare agreement with anthropologist Marshall Sahlins, whose enthusiasm for a substantial diet of required courses was premised on his fear that if undergraduates had more opportunities to take electives, people like himself would have to teach them. "I'm not a college type," Sahlins says. That's an understatement, since he refers to himself as a member of the *graduate* department of anthropology and rarely sees undergraduates.

"What we're doing has intellectual integrity!" was the rallying cry of the traditionalists. But "you can only go so far," observes one professor, "before you have to point at the faculty and ask, 'Why aren't you teaching?'"

"The contradiction we're trying to resolve," says Richard Saller, "is that we don't want to be Harvard or Yale, and use the large lecture format. We want to do as much as possible in small classes—but we can't do this with tenured faculty." The irony is palpable. At a university where devotion to general education is the watchword, until a few years ago professors were not expected to teach any undergraduates. The real challenge at Hyde Park, according to physicist Frank Richter, is "to create a culture in which teaching matters." This was not a task for which Hugo Sonnenschein was well suited.

▪ The Trouble with Hugo

When Sonnenschein arrived in 1993, campus expectations ran high. There was widespread agreement that his predecessor, historian Hannah Gray, who had governed with Thatcherite imperiousness for fifteen years, had stayed on too long. Sonnenschein looked like the perfect choice. "He had standing as an academic, and he knew how to run a complex institution," recalls one trustee, Howard Krane. "He had complete integrity. After the financial mess Stanford had gotten itself into with the federal government, that was paramount. Hugo eclipsed everyone in that search. When I met him, I never looked back."

"We were telling people we were in good financial shape," Krane adds, but that was the kind of misstatement you might expect from Arthur Andersen. Even though "I knew some of the problems and had suspicions about what the work would be," says Sonnenschein, things were much worse than he had imagined. Beyond bringing the operating budget into balance, the institution's needs were overwhelming: new laboratories and expanded libraries; more competitive salaries; new dormitories and athletic facilities; programs for study abroad. "In every place," Sonnenschein says, "the budget for staff was stripped to the bone. Services were poor, and students and faculty complained."

Sonnenschein enjoyed only the briefest of honeymoons. Within a year, his seeming high-handedness—he had imposed major changes without fully engaging the faculty—earned him vocal enemies. Quickly the attacks turned personal. Blunders were known as "Hugoisms," and an over-fondness for phrases like "fabulous thinking" and "extraordinary" was called "Hugospeak." When he told a *Wall Street Journal* reporter that he listened to public radio for its news and classical music, the natives gleefully pointed out that no public radio station in Chicago played music—another "Hugoism," more evidence that the president wasn't one of "us."

Fifteen hundred students showed up at a "Fun-In," where much of the "fun" was at the expense of the president. A photo of his face was superimposed on a cardboard cutout of Darth Vader as well as on a T-shirt depicting a can of "University of Chicago Lite . . . specially brewed by the freshest consultants and coerced into its refreshing taste." The event, its organizers proclaimed, was "a critique of an administration that thinks it needs to sacrifice some of our intellectual greatness in order to survive financially and attract more paying customers to campus. The Fun-In is a defense of the idea that intelligence and fun are not a zero-sum game."[20]

"Can we criticize these guys this hard in public without destroying any respect for them as human beings?" Adam Kissel, a graduate student who served as the student representative on the board of trustees, inquired plaintively.[21] But in an environment made poisonous by distrust, not even the most innocuous things escaped criticism. The new viewbook was assailed because of its sharp appearance; detractors feared that the color photos and the attention paid to sports and drinking would appeal to the unserious. (Only grudgingly was it acknowledged that the prominent cover text, titled "The Life of the Mind," matched the institution's self-image.) Improving the placement office was derided as a nod to vocationalism, with Silicon Valley and Wall Street recruiters brought to campus to steal the best young minds. Diehards even seized on the decision to build a new swimming pool, replacing the tiny and malodorous hundred-year-old natatorium, as representing an unseemly love of the body, a perfidious balance to the life of the mind.[22]

What lay behind Sonnenschein's specific policy initiatives, many of his critics believed, was a grand design for the wholesale makeover of the university that, by rendering it more pleasing and polished, would rob it of its cherished uniqueness. There were reasons for concern, since reforms of the scope that Sonnenschein and Stone were proposing carry their own dangers. These administrators failed "to convey a respect for the faculty's experience or their views," says Richard Saller, and the president's impromptu comments fueled the unhappiness. At one faculty gathering he tossed out the possibility of a grade-free freshman year to ease the pressure on students. That idea would be praiseworthy at many schools, but at Chicago it was treated as proof of coddling. "It's controversial at Chicago," Sonnenschein notes, "to say that students have to feel we are dedicated to their success."

"Geoff Stone and I have a great deal of analyst in us, less politician—but politician to what purpose?" asks Sonnenschein, intending the question to be rhetorical. In fact, political skill is essential in leading any community, especially one as fractious as the University of Chicago. The president was even brave, or foolhardy, enough to take on the institutional saint. "Robert Hutchins was crazy," he is said to have remarked at a College Council meeting, "and everything he stood for is crazy," an observation that made him about as popular as an atheist at a revival meeting. Even some of

Sonnenschein's allies admit that he had a tin ear for Chicago's soundtrack. "He broadcasts," says physics professor Frank Richter, summing up a widely heard sentiment, "but he doesn't receive."

▪ By the Numbers

The curriculum wars made news, but Sonnenschein's plan to increase undergraduate enrollment by 1,200 students, despite the opposition of a task force he had appointed two years earlier to consider the matter, marked the turning point in his tenure. That initiative violated another Chicago credo: Small is beautiful.

Old hands lovingly retell the tale of an astrophysicist named Subrahmanyan Chandrasekhar. While working at the university's Yerkes Observatory in the 1940s, Chandra, as he was called, drove more than a hundred miles every week to Hyde Park to teach a seminar of just two students. In 1983, he won a Nobel Prize in physics—twenty-six years after those two students had won their own Nobel Prizes.[23]

So much for economies of scale and other administrative buzzwords. The legend of Chandra distills the essence of the University of Chicago, its commitment to a handful of brilliant students and its lack of interest in educating the merely bright. No university has a lower ratio of students to faculty: there were 1,125 faculty members and 8,200 students, better than eight-to-one, in 1995, when the administration initially proposed a sizable increase in undergraduate enrollment. There are almost as many Ph.D. students at Chicago as undergraduates, and the typical Chicago professor teaches just thirty students a year.

"It is not a college but a university that is wanted," William Rainey Harper, the university's first president, announced in 1893, a remarkable ambition at the time, and that has been the rule ever since.[24] But since most Ph.D. students receive stipends, this is a costly way to run an institution. When Sonnenschein arrived in 1994, the treasurer was projecting a $55 million annual deficit by the end of the decade. Already the deficits were eating away at a $1.5 billion endowment, the smallest among top-ranked private universities. "The message is simple," provost Geoffrey Stone kept telling the faculty. "To be as good as we want to be, we need much more than we have."

Money problems are nothing new for Chicago. In the 1930s, the university came close to merging with Northwestern to form the Universities of Chicago, and twenty years later, it contemplated leaving its namesake city entirely and moving to Palo Alto or Aspen. Sonnenschein was not about to allow the latest crisis to spiral out of control. He acted quickly to trim costs and raise money. A freeze was placed on faculty hiring, and doctoral students' grants were cut back. Money-making master's programs were initiated, among them a course in financial mathematics for bankers and stockbrokers that the math department ran out of a downtown office building. In 1998, together with a number of other leading universities, Chicago entered into what promised to be a lucrative partnership with Unext.com, an on-line provider of business courses initially bankrolled by junk bond impresario Michael Milken, whose CEO happens to be a Chicago trustee. In effect, the university was renting its name to this untried venture.

Because these activities occurred at the institutional periphery, they went unnoticed, but increasing the undergraduate enrollment touched the heart of the enterprise. Still, like the curriculum reforms, it didn't represent a departure from tradition. From Robert Hutchins on, every Chicago president has had similar aspirations. In the 1960s, even as university president Edward Levi extolled the virtues of "a small college, greatly influenced by its presence in a university in which research is preeminent," he privately urged the trustees to double the number of undergraduates.[25] A decade earlier, his predecessor Lawrence Kimpton had recommended that the college expand to 5,000 students. (As one trustee observed at the time, more students would mean more tuition from "cash customers" and "potential alumni donors.") That plan had been advanced for the same reasons Sonnenschein was now offering. Under Hannah Gray, the college had quietly grown from 2,400 to 3,000 students. Even the sainted Hutchins, best remembered for his passionate commitment to the college, calculated the dollars-and-cents advantages of enrolling brigades of undergraduates. In a 1935 letter to an alumnus, he pointed out that one of the benefits of the then new core curriculum, which was being taught by an army of teaching assistants, was that it saved the university money, and that the college was "indispensable" because it paid the bills for graduate research.[26]

Previous administrations had veiled their ambitions, but Sonnenschein and Stone chose to make their budget projections public. At an open meeting, Stone handed out financial data that only the deans had previously seen. The hope was that transparency would elicit faculty understanding and support. "There should be some benefit in having people look at data clearly and be straight about it," Sonnenschein says. "This isn't just the president's responsibility." But by the time he decided to expand undergraduate enrollment, his first round of cost cutting, especially the freeze in hiring, had already left scars. When the administration developed a computer simulation of the university's parlous finances and invited professors to construct their own answers, there were few takers. The faculty didn't see themselves as "rational actors," and this wasn't a game. Only later did Stone come to appreciate that "to focus on finances was to see the university as something other than a 'pure' institution whose sole value was academic excellence."

Thus began the protracted battle of the budget. "If you put every straining dollar into maintaining an arts and sciences faculty that's larger than Harvard's, with half as many students," Sonnenschein says, "that's a tough way to run a ship." For their part, professors turned into accountants, accusing the administration of playing Chicken Little with the budget. When an administrative cost survey prepared by the accounting firm of Peat Marwick criticized inefficient management and budgeting practices, professors grumbled that the green eyeshade crowd couldn't hope to understand the arcane ways of the university. Some faculty even denied that there was a problem. "The question is not where we rank [in terms of endowment]," Marshall Sahlins argued, "but whether we have enough to meet our intellectual goals."[27] Others looked, unrealistically if longingly, to the professional schools to pick up the entire tab. The most thoughtful analysts, among them physicist Frank Richter, concluded that while the deficit wasn't chimerical, adding more undergraduates wouldn't generate enough revenue to solve the problem.

The biggest fear was that the enrollment growth would bring dumber and duller students. During the 1990s, the quality of undergraduates had declined, while the number of applicants was shrinking. To the consternation of the students, regularly reassured that they were getting the best education in the land, Chicago fell to fourteenth in U.S. News & World Report's rankings. In 1996, the university admitted 62 percent of those who applied—more than three out of five, as compared to one in eight at Harvard and Princeton. Loyalists explained away this lack of selectivity as the result of the applicants' self-selection, contending that only those who wanted Chicago's rigor actually applied, but in fact fewer than a third of those who were accepted opted to enroll.

The University of Chicago never stopped attracting some of the nation's smartest youth—the class of 2000 included three Rhodes scholars and a Marshall scholar—but it wasn't attracting enough of them. Too many students, less qualified and less motivated, wound up on campus only because Chicago was their "safe" school. Those two camps, the self-styled "brainiacs" and the Northwestern University wannabees, inhabited distinct academic worlds within the precincts of the university. This didn't happen by accident. Until the late 1990s, a quaint campus custom called "sleep-out" effectively separated the most motivated undergraduates, who camped out overnight on the frigid quad in order to be assured of getting the best professors, from the rest, who took the leftovers.

How might the university do better? The president approached the problem in his typical managerial fashion, requesting the consulting firm of McKinsey & Co. to prepare a report on the quality of student life. That study concluded that the students were unhappy. A survey the firm carried out found that for social life on campus it ranked last among 227 American universities—and that alumni, though enthusiastic about the education they'd received, were reluctant to put their children through similar rigors. Sociologist Andrew Abbott trashed the McKinsey report as shoddy research which implicitly treated Chicago's virtues as marketing problems. But the administration ignored Abbott's more rigorously designed survey, which depicted students' attitudes in a much more positive light.[28]

Soon afterwards, PR man Al Chambers made a similar gaffe. After organizing focus groups to test marketing ideas, he reported that "'intense' doesn't play well in Peoria." Predictably, the faculty responded coolly to this news. "The McKinsey report only confirmed the dour impression of collegiate life here," wrote Marshall Sahlins, "and by supposing it to be the effect of the unusual intensity of the University, made our distinctive intellectual traditions into something the matter with us. Our values were our problem: the problem being that the college's academic rigor and the consequent overwork of our students would make it difficult to increase enrollment."[29] In the end, Sonnenschein's enrollment proposal was adopted over the objections of many faculty members. Three years later, when a TV interviewer asked Sonnenschein to explain his decision, he denied that money had had anything to do with it. Understandably, no one believed him.

Both professors and students worried about the kind of student who might be tempted by the more user-friendly version of the university that McKinsey and Chambers were propounding. Prototypical Chicago undergraduates pride themselves on being a breed apart, reveling in displays of quirky intelligence. Even as Chicago was arguing over the common core, Duke University moved to stiffen its undergraduate requirements. There, the undergraduates rebelled. "You can lead me to college," their T-shirts read, "but you can't force me to think." At Chicago, by contrast, the most vocal students were those who were asking for even more requirements. At the "Fun-In" rally, they displayed a mock graph that projected a precipitous decline in the percentage of nerds once Hugo's multitudes showed up. Could Chicago become, if not the Harvard of the Midwest, then the Duke of the North?

Decades before Hugo Sonnenschein came to Chicago, the campus administration had voiced concern about the preponderance of what was delicately called a "certain kind of student." Do "beauty and brawn not deserve a place on this campus as well as brains?" the dean of admissions inquired plaintively in 1959. "The ordinary American boy, who will only make a million later in life, the ordinary American girl, who wants a husband as well as a diploma, are as welcome here as the quiz kid."[30] That wasn't really true, however, either in 1959 or forty years later. Sonnenschein wanted to turn the university into an "undergraduate playground for the golden youth of white suburbia," one professor contended at a raucous public gathering, as if black students from the adjoining ghetto abounded on the campus. "The intention is to find wealthy private school students to come here, then we make the curriculum easier for them so they'll enjoy their experience here with the new swimming pool, and thus they'll give more money when they get out."[31]

This fantastic scenario, anxiety verging on paranoia, is of a piece with the complaints about color photos in the viewbook and fear of "fun"— symbols of an unwanted normality. It is also a perfect representation of the passions of a holy war.

■ After Hugo: Quieter, Gentler, and Very Much the Same

A week before the 1999 graduation, Hugo Sonnenschein abruptly announced his resignation, effective a year later. That year's commencement exercises exemplified the schism between the president and many faculty members, including the muted majority who accepted the substance of his proposals. By tradition, commencement, like the university itself, is inwardly focused, a celebration of academic achievement at which the speaker is a faculty member. Years earlier, the faculty had voted unanimously against awarding an honorary degree to Queen Elizabeth—no scholar she—but this time President Clinton was invited to speak. It was Clinton's first speech at a commencement since his impeachment, and for him the event was a ritual of legitimation. His appearance was good publicity from the campus administration's point of view; critics saw it as pandering, just the kind of thing a place like Harvard would do.

The timing of Sonnenschein's announcement, which left the institution leaderless at the very moment when alumni, awash in campus memories, are most zealously solicited for contributions, gave credence to rumors that he had been forced out. The faculty missive to the trustees, the screed of Bellow, Adler, and the rest of the ancients, the "Fun-In," the endless tomes generated on the campus, the threats voiced by up-in-arms alumni—all of these seemed to have done their job. But trustee Howard Krane tells a different story: "Hugo submitted his resignation, and the board didn't ask him to reconsider." Sonnenschein hadn't run out of ideas about how to strengthen the university, but he had outrun his mandate. "When I told the trustees I was leaving, they felt it was probably time," he says. "For some trustees, the amount of confrontation with the press was too much. They preferred to live in a world where you're doing what's right and it's easier."

Sonnenschein's critics were exuberant at the news. Former dean Donald Levine dismissed him as "the wrong president for the university, a crude misfit." Philosopher Daniel Garber, a man of the middle, was gentler in his critique. "He did what needed to be done, but he didn't act elegantly," he says. "The analysis was right, but the practice was bungled."

In the fall of 2000, a new although quintessentially Chicago tradition was born: an ongoing faculty seminar on "the idea of the University." The seminar's title is lifted from Cardinal Newman's nineteenth-century tract on higher education, which argues that teaching, rather than research, is the real mission of the university. Levine kicked off the series with a jeremiad against "the tyranny of the bottom line," an unsubtle reminder that, even though Sonnenschein himself was gone, the war against what he stood for hadn't ended. Who needs money? Levine asked. "We relish our poverty" because "energy and brains" matter so much more than up-to-date physics labs. But it is hard to preach "leaner and meaner" to physicists like Frank Richter, whose labs, he says, were "state of the art, 1948" until the capital campaign made it possible to update them.

That December, Chicago's new president, Don Michael Randel, was installed in a tradition-steeped ceremony at Rockefeller Chapel. The Motet Choir sang a Bach cantata whose final lines were altered to declare, in German: "May Randel live long! May Randel blossom!" Randel's quotation-filled inaugural address flattered Chicago, giving pride of place to "A Poet's Alphabet," written by "the University's own Mark Strand"—shades of Robert Frost at John F. Kennedy's inauguration. It was a speech that elevated rhetoric over content, and to many in the audience the lack of fireworks came as a relief.

Randel, the longtime provost at Cornell University and a Renaissance music scholar, "is a soft, plain-spoken guy," says Howard Krane. "The search committee fell in love with him. There was a desire to find someone different [from Sonnenschein]." In that, they succeeded. Randel's style soothed egos in Hyde Park. "Sonnenschein came across as a man who was relatively insensitive," says Andrew Abbott, "someone who studies all the facts on his own, comes up with an answer, and then appoints faculty committees to come up with the same answer for him. I think Don Randel is a better listener. He has a better ear for hearing what people are upset about."[32]

Yet if Sonnenschein lost the personal battle, he won the institutional war. All of his priorities remain in place. As the ex-president, who has returned to the economics department, said in 2002, "The satisfaction is in the fact that we are really getting there and that I had a role in moving it along." Former provost Geoffrey Stone agrees: "There's no discernible change in policy . . . in terms of education or research mission or goals or priorities at all."[33]

On both sides of the budget ledger, Sonnenschein's reforms have taken hold. Aggressive fund-raising coupled with the stock market boom doubled the endowment, to $2.35 billion, between 1992 and 1998, ending talk of a budget "crisis." Graduate fellowships increased, enabling Chicago to go after the best Ph.D. candidates, and faculty salaries rose to match the competition. There are more MBA and law students to boost tuition revenue, as well as new profit-generating master's programs. The buildings that Sonnenschein's master plan called for—science labs, dormitories, and a sports complex—have altered the shape and character of the campus.

Meanwhile, without much attention, the cost of an undergraduate education has been trimmed through expedients that may undermine some of its most distinctive features. Between 1997 and 2001, the number of courses that enrolled just a single student—the "Chandra"-type courses—shrank from 283 to a (still remarkable) 174. The size of the typical undergraduate "discussion" class has grown; and in economics, the fastest-growing major, most courses are taught by graduate assistants and adjuncts, not the regular faculty.

Undergraduate enrollment is growing according to plan. In 2002, there were 4,150 students, an increase of 500 in five years. By all the standard metrics, SATs and class rank, they are better qualified academically. What's more, many of them are Chicago students in the grand tradition, passionate in their nerdiness (while pleased nonetheless by the new creature comforts). The marketing strategies developed by Michael Behnke, detailed in Chapter 1, have given the university greater visibility among high school students. The much-criticized viewbook extends an invitation to engage in "what is arguably the nation's most rigorous undergraduate experience," and when a survey of freshmen asked them what characteristics they associated with the college, 97 percent answered "intellectual," while just 1 percent said "partying." So much for the "fun" image.[34] *U.S. News & World Report* took note. In large part owing to increased selectivity in admissions and higher graduation rates, Chicago jumped in the rankings from fourteenth in 1998 to ninth in 2002.

Even as most universities have been reporting lower-than-anticipated contributions from alumni, in April 2002, President Randel, together with his provost, Richard Saller, announced an ambitious $2 billion campaign, three times the size of any previous drive. His main task was to raise pots of money in order to increase the endowment and pay for his predecessor's initiatives. As Saller points out, during the previous decade the gap between Chicago and the super-rich schools such as Harvard and Yale had widened, in good part because of the run-up of the stock market, and so "we're at a competitive disadvantage, more than ever."

Seemingly no change comes to Hyde Park without controversy. While the new buildings make students and scientists happy, Marshall Sahlins, the indefatigable pamphleteer of the curriculum wars, is deeply displeased. "There are dormitories encircling and imprisoning the library instead of expanding the library," he complains. The attempt to make the new dormitories blend in with the red-brick neighborhood evokes more enmity. "This is a Gothic campus that's differentiated, architecturally and otherwise, from what surrounds it. What matters"—in more ways than one—"is the integrity of the campus."

For a time after Sonnenschein's departure, fights over the curriculum abated. In the 2000–2001 academic year, the first time that students could choose between the old core and the new, most of them picked the new. (Being Chicago undergraduates, and so gluttons for work, many opted to do a second major rather than take more electives.) But in the spring of

2002, the curricular wars flared up once more. The University of Chicago was selling students "seriously short," the *Chicago Sun-Times* intoned; a student group calling itself Education First demanded that the status quo ante be restored; outraged alumni urged fellow Maroons to "give serious consideration to withholding contributions"; and Saul Bellow, a veteran combatant in these fracases, was among a score of academics who attacked the university for surrendering to the "mindless narrowing and specialization that has characterized other universities for decades."[35]

From the pitch of the invective, no one would know that the controversy was about the kind of tinkering that would pass unnoticed anyplace else: the "Western Civilization" core course had been replaced by two new courses, "European Civilization" and "Ancient Mediterranean World." Amid the uproar, rumors flew: the courses would be taught lecture-style; Newton, Aristotle, and even the study of Christianity were disappearing from the syllabus. The fact that none of these rumors was true didn't stop the partisans from spreading them, and stories in the national press about "the death of Western Civ." read like a disinformation campaign. Randel had intended to use his column in the June 2002 alumni magazine to push the recently launched fund-raising campaign. First things first, however. He felt obliged to rebut accusations that the administration was "lowering standards."[36] To Hugo Sonnenschein, back in the world of teaching and research, the moment was all too familiar.

And so the debate continues, in vintage Chicago fashion. Donald Levine, who numbers himself among the ex-president's harshest critics, acknowledges that the university's adoption of market values is "not an isolated phenomenon"—not just a Chicago story but "a nationwide trend"—and "that makes things scarier." The former president sees things entirely differently: "It's unimaginable that the truth [about Chicago's financial picture] won't be good in the end."

Hugo Sonnenschein may someday be hailed in Hyde Park as a hero, the leader who saved an institution by dragging it into modern times. The ultimate question, though, is whether what the traditionalists refer to as the soul of the institution, its singularity, can withstand this transformation.

3

Benjamin Rush's "Brat"
Dickinson College

For William Durden, the peripatetic president of Dickinson College, the October 5, 2001, issue of the *Wall Street Journal* contained some very good news. A feature story touted Dickinson as one of "this fall's hot schools," one of just three liberal arts colleges among the sixteen institutions singled out for such praise. It's a "college for a new era," the article gushed, "poised to be a player."[1]

Such favorable publicity—*any* publicity, for that matter—marked a major turnaround for Dickinson. Although the college, tucked away in a colonial-era town in southeastern Pennsylvania, has long offered a solid liberal arts education, few people knew of its existence. Particularly galling to Dickinsonians was the fact that potential applicants regularly confused the college with Fairleigh Dickinson University, a more proletarian New Jersey institution.

This anonymity was both a symptom and a cause of Dickinson's decline during the 1990s. Beginning early in the decade, the quality of students steadily worsened. At its nadir, the college was forced to admit more than four applicants in five—and offer outsized scholarships to bribe them into enrolling. Faculty morale bottomed out, and alumni responded with a decided lack of enthusiasm to a lengthy capital campaign. For the first time in years, Dickinson was operating in the red, and its bond rating slipped. *U.S. News & World Report* confirmed and reinforced this fall from grace in 1995, when it dropped Dickinson from its list of the nation's fifty best liberal arts colleges.[2]

Bill Durden was recruited in 1999 with a mandate to turn things around. An alumnus (class of 1971), he had spent sixteen years at Johns Hopkins University, where he was a professor of German. He was also a talented entrepreneur, having taken a tiny campus center for gifted youth and turned it into the biggest program of its kind in the country. Then he left the academic straight and narrow to become president of the Sylvan Academy of Learning and vice president for academic affairs of the Caliber Learning Network, a for-profit distance learning company. That background, unheard of in liberal arts circles, prompted some Dickinson professors to go public with their concerns that, out of desperation, the school was peddling its intellectual birthright. But the paean in the *Wall Street Journal* was just another piece of evidence that, in a very short time, the new president was making remarkable progress in putting his alma mater on the map while working to maintain its integrity.

■ An Endangered Species

A century ago, liberal arts colleges were a dominating force in American higher education. Now these schools educate fewer than 4 percent of all undergraduates, and they are at risk of becoming an endangered species.[3]

Colleges such as Swarthmore and Amherst are in no trouble. With their outsized endowments and rich histories, they compete with the likes of Stanford and Yale for the nation's best undergraduates.[4] But relatively few can make a similar boast. "Schools like Amherst and Williams have the financial power and reputation to remain in control of their own destiny," economists (and college presidents) Michael McPherson and Morton Schapiro point out, "but there are not even fifty colleges about which one could say that with confidence."[5]

The situation is grim for schools on the lowest rungs of the status ladder. Every year a number of them go out of business—at least twenty-seven between 1997 and 2002, a third more than in the previous five-year period and more than 5 percent of all American liberal arts colleges.[6] The *New York Times* reported in 2002 that "dozens more are in precarious financial situations," and in a desperate effort to attract students, some have borrowed many times more than their assets.[7] Standard & Poor's, the leading bond-rating agency in higher education, made a similar prediction: a considerable number of colleges might have to "consolidate in large numbers or close as they struggle against stagnant levels of financial resources and substantially higher levels of debt."[8]

Intimate size, a residential setting, small classes taught by full-time professors rather than adjunct instructors, faculty-student collaboration, a personal commitment to students, and institutional "communities of discourse": these are virtues worth preserving.[9] But the tides of fashion in higher education are running against these colleges. Only a quarter of all undergraduates now receive liberal arts degrees, as compared with 50 percent thirty years ago—and the label "university," rather than "college," is equated in the popular imagination with seriousness of institutional purpose.[10]

With a $20 million gift from the Lilly Endowment, Wabash College, an all-male school in rural Indiana, opened the Center of Inquiry in the Liberal Arts in 2001 with the immodest aim of "serving as a catalyst for reshaping liberal arts education in the 21st century."[11] It's a worthy goal; and perhaps the scholars who gather at what is described as an "inspirational campus setting" can figure out how to convince the public that, as Todd Gitlin writes, "the strong reason to cultivate knowledge [is] to anchor a high-velocity, reckless, and lightweight culture whose main value is marketability."[12] That was the task confronting Bill Durden when he arrived at Dickinson.

▪ "No One Dies of English"

Dickinson College is steeped—enveloped—in its past. The college, sixteenth oldest in the nation, was founded in the wake of the American Revolution. It had an eloquent champion in Benjamin Rush, a signer of the Declaration of Independence and a freethinker in matters of religion who, improbably, made this Presbyterian-sponsored school his passion. And it espoused an idea that was novel for its time: to join Christian pieties with "the learned and useful arts." From the outset, though, money was a problem. Rush had to go hat in hand to solicit the funds needed to launch the school. "Get money," he urged a close friend, sounding like a contemporary development officer, "get it honorably, if you can, but get money for the College!"[13]

Lack of funds persuaded the Presbyterian clergymen to turn over control to the Methodists, but those clerics weren't able to do much better. Out of financial desperation, Dickinson closed its doors between 1816 and 1821, and again from 1832 until 1834. It has never been able to raise a substantial endowment, and so over the years has turned to improbable financial schemes to stay afloat; at one point it tried to coax parents into signing up their children when they were in elementary school. Nor has the school fared well in its choice of leaders. Ben James, emeritus dean and professor of psychology, arrived at Dickinson as a freshman in 1930 and has been associated with the college ever since. "I went through many presidents," he says. "They were not strong overall."

Still, Dickinson has always offered a solid grounding in the liberal arts. Although Rush was something of a radical in emphasizing the practical arts rather than Greek and Latin, for most of its history the school has been rigidly orthodox in its curriculum, a defender of the old order against the new. In 1800, president Charles Nisbet railed against the "spirit of free inquiry, carried almost to madness . . . air balloons, the Rights of Man, the Sovereignty of the People . . . Atheism, Socinianism."[14] James Morgan, Dickinson's president during the first decades of the twentieth century and author of a 1933 history of the college, ends his narrative with the boast that Dickinson "has held steadily to its first and only love, the liberal arts and cultural studies." Doubtless thinking of rivals like Lehigh and Gettysburg, Morgan points out that while many colleges "have offered courses in near-engineering, in commerce and business—easier courses suited to the many who are not fit for the culture of the liberal arts . . . Dickinson has never bowed to commerce."[15] As Ben James recalls, "the idea was to prove you could be a scholar, gentleman, and an athlete."

This conception of the college's mission was championed well into the 1990s by longtime academic dean George Allan—a "liberal arts purist," as Neil Weissman, who holds Allan's old job, calls him. "Coming to Dickinson is almost like joining a cult," Allan told French professor Sylvie Davidson when she first arrived; and while signs of change emerged after Allan's departure, notably the creation of an international business and management major, the commitment persisted to what is referred to as "the Dickinsonian way."

Horn-blowing was anathema to Allan and his disciples. But in this consumerist era, parents need a very good reason to spend $25,000 a year on their child's education—especially when it is so much cheaper at Penn State, another of the *Wall Street Journal*'s "hot" schools, whose honors college goes head-to-head with Dickinson. In this environment, it helps to have as a leader someone who respects both the values of academia and the imperatives of the marketplace.

With his owlish glasses and trademark bow tie, Bill Durden is the very model of the classic college president. But appearances mislead. When a headhunter initially called, Durden insisted that he wasn't interested in returning to his alma mater. "I'm the wrong guy. I'd move that place, and I don't think they've got the guts to do that." At a meeting with trustees, he offered a scathing critique of the school's recent history. "You've blown it," he told them. "The place is adrift. It's become the 'safety school' and that's outrageous."

Board chairman John Curley, the former chief executive officer of Gannett Company and the first editor of *USA Today,* regarded Durden as easily the best choice. "We needed to go up-tempo, set a fast pace. Bill has been in business as well as the academy—and he has the personality to be Mr. Dickinson." Curley and his fellow board members eventually persuaded Durden that he'd have the leeway he needed to "drive" the college.

Durden's old boss, Johns Hopkins president Steven Muller, was skeptical that he could accomplish much at Dickinson. "No one dies of English," said the former head of a university blessed with a world-renowned medical school. "That was the challenge," Durden says. "How do I find an energetic basic charge that other places get from finding a cure for cancer? How do I create buzz?"

"Distinctively Dickinson" has become the college's motto, and ever since taking the job, Bill Durden has been emphasizing what makes Dickinson College stand out from the crowd. The first member of his family to attend college, he credits the school with "creating me," and views his job with the passion of a missionary. "Soon after I got here, I hiked part of the Appalachian trail with some students," he recalls, retelling a story that he has made a part of the new Dickinson folklore. "A senior who'd done very well told me that she really didn't know what it meant to be a Dickinsonian. In retrospect, that became a defining moment of my administration."

Durden's experience at Sylvan taught him a useful lesson. "What I learned is the importance of knowing your product. Sylvan could answer the question: 'What are we?' Colleges don't have this perspective." Dickinson College needed a compelling story, a "brand . . . out of which I could lead the institution to where it was going."

As a scholar of languages, Durden knows how much can get lost in translation. "I use words like 'consumer,' but in an academic environment, students are coming to Dickinson because they like what we offer," he says. "We're different from business. We don't have to fulfill every desire, because we're an academic institution that knows what we are. We'll listen, but don't confuse our goodwill with our agreeing with you. Sometimes we'll change our mind, but we won't break. It's important to know your product . . . to know your brand."

The college had long suffered from that well-known academic malady, sclerosis caused by governance through faculty committee. In the decade before Durden's arrival, a dozen reports had been generated, running nearly 1,500 pages and covering every aspect of institutional life. These documents were earnestly debated, only to wind up filling shelf space. Durden immediately formed a task force drawn from all the campus constituencies and gave the group an ambitious charge: shape a vision, draft a coherent plan of action, and get the school to embrace it—all within the space of a single academic year.

"The discussion was civil," recalls religion professor Mara Donaldson, one of those most anxious about creeping commercialism. "The biggest disagreements were over how to integrate student life with a liberal arts education—and about money, of course." Remarkably, Durden's timetable was met; and more remarkably still, the strategic plan isn't another pallid document. This "guide to our identity as Dickinsonians," as the president calls it, proceeds in a straight line from a declaration of principles to the enumeration of specifics. It lays out measurable aspirations for everything from minority enrollment to endowment growth and campus expansion.

The key goals are printed on a laminated wallet card, widely distributed so that everyone, from the trustees to the groundskeepers, can know at a glance where Dickinson College is heading. Hokey, perhaps, but anecdotal evidence suggests the strategy is working. An e-mail message from the president of the Gettysburg College student senate plaintively expressed the wish that students there were as involved in college affairs. Durden tells a story about a family visiting the campus: "They asked the guy watering the flowers for directions and he went into a discussion of the strategic plan."

To help the school find and construct its identity, the president hired a marketing consultant, a Johns Hopkins Ph.D. named Mark Neustadt. After conducting scores of interviews and focus groups, Neustadt concluded that the college's mission could fairly be summarized in a phrase: "Freedom + Guidance = Growth." That formulation, however, didn't separate Dickinson from the pack. A better "positioning statement" was "Reflecting America, Engaging the World." It "sets Dickinson apart from its competitors," Neustadt wrote, "resonates well with prospective students . . . and elicits enthusiasm from alumni." But because Dickinson had so few minority students, he added, that slogan "does not reflect current reality, and would therefore require substantial institutional change to implement."[16]

"World-engaging" pedagogical experiments were in fact being launched well before Durden arrived. The Clarke Center, founded in 1994, carried out interdisciplinary studies of contemporary policy issues, demonstrating the link between liberal learning and the world outside Carlisle. It also brought in political figures whose talks were aired on C-SPAN, giving the college new visibility, at least among political junkies. Biology professors were winning big research grants. The pre-law program, developed in conjunction with Dickinson Law School, formerly part of the college, shaved a year off legal education. The international business and management major was delivering practical, but not vocational, education—business as seen through the lens of the liberal arts.

Students in the "American mosaic" semester were venturing into the dying community of Steeltown and the apple orchards of rural Adam County, using oral histories and ethnographic and archival research to document how communities evolved. The course spawned an "international mosaic," as similar projects have been carried out in places as varied as Patagonia and (in conjunction with historically black Spelman College and Xavier University) in Cameroon. Those experiences make a difference, Mara Donaldson writes in the alumni magazine: "Most of our students here at Dickinson are born into worlds far removed from those they experience at our centers in India, Cameroon and Mexico. Many of them learn to feel empathy for people in these less-advantaged cultures. [They] return to Dickinson changed, wanting to help."[17]

"International mosaic" is just the latest iteration of the college's longstanding commitment to international education. Dickinson runs thirty-two programs on six continents. Eighty percent of its students spend at least one semester abroad, at campuses from Bologna to Nagoya, and a fifth of them major in a foreign language, the highest percentage in the country. In 2002, *U.S. News & World Report* ranked Dickinson's international program sixth best in the nation.

The old rule was that no department should be singled out for special recognition. But now, says Durden, "we trumpet our strengths." To Robert Massa, who carries the imposing title of vice president for enrollment, student life, and college relations, this is just good marketing. The school's "programmatic brand" is the "permanent association" between Dickinson and "a handful of our premiere programs," he writes in the alumni magazine. "When the public thinks of Dickinson, we want them to think 'international' or 'workshop (hands on) science and research' or 'pre-law.'"[18]

"Here was a school I'd never heard of," says associate dean Joanne Brown, "although I'd grown up in Philadelphia. As soon as I looked at it,

I was astonished by its academic strengths." A faculty research seminar she organized has breathed life into the intellectual environs, offering a locus for professors from across the disciplines to exchange ideas about their research. Brown has also drawn on students' interests in tobacco as a public health issue, which range from biology to law and public policy, in an effort to persuade her colleagues that "public health can be taught in the Dickinson way, as a liberal arts subject—not as at Hopkins, where the aim is early specialization, but looking at the big picture."

The college is beginning to attract attention from faculty elsewhere. "Professors from Swarthmore and Haverford are impressed," says Brown. "They say, 'Wow! Look what you are doing with few resources and a young faculty.'"[19]

"Leadership is what was missing," says provost Neil Weissman, a longtime Dickinson faculty member and administrator. "Bill came, took the pieces, and added vigor and coherent packaging."

In an article titled "Gained in Translation," Durden lays out his strategy. "The themes and key words that define the [Dickinson] leadership story . . . are unequivocal: citizen-leaders; a useful, liberal education; crossing borders; interdisciplinary; reflect America—engage the world."[20] Among these "key words" are "revolutionary" and "Founding Fathers" Benjamin Rush and John Dickinson. In its new marketing campaign, the college has reached back to emphasize its roots, in the process rewriting its own history. Dickinson used to trace its lineage to a grammar school founded in 1773, immediately before the American Revolution, and it celebrated its 250th anniversary in 1998. Now Dickinson bills itself as the first "revolutionary college," since it was chartered as a college on September 9, 1783, just six days after the Treaty of Paris was signed. What Benjamin Rush proudly described as his "petulant brat" is defining itself as a school with "attitude" and "spunk."[21]

▪ Creating "Mindshare"

When New York University set out to become a great university in the mid-1980s (a history recounted in the next chapter), its top priority was recruiting faculty luminaries. But the fortunes of a liberal arts college like Dickinson depend mainly on the caliber of its students. Everything else follows from attracting abler undergraduates—more alumni giving, more high-powered professors, greater public recognition. In "repositioning" the college, all decisions, from the design of new student apartments to re-vision of the curriculum, had to be undertaken with this goal uppermost in mind.

The greatest changes were needed in admissions and financial aid. Be-ginning in the early 1990s, the college had been forced to dip deeper and deeper into its applicant pool, eventually admitting more than 80 percent of those who applied; and even so, enrollment shrank. Lee Fritschler, Durden's predecessor, kept reassuring Dickinsonians that similar declines were being posted elsewhere. But longtime rivals like Muhlenberg College were doing better in the admissions wars, and schools that had never been regarded as competitors, such as Loyola College of Maryland, were en-croaching on Dickinson's territory.

Dickinson's problems stemmed mainly from its financial aid philosophy, which held that in making awards it was wrong to take account of a stu-dent's academic record or the likelihood of his or her enrolling; the only ethically relevant consideration was a student's actual need. This is an ad-mirable principle, and one that a handful of wealthy colleges can live by, but it cost Dickinson many of its ablest applicants. Moreover, the school didn't award sizable scholarships even to needy applicants. Its "discount rate"—the difference between what the typical student pays and the full tuition—was just 20 percent, well below that of comparable institutions. So firmly did Dickinson insist on the irrelevance of money in making col-lege choices that applicants didn't even know whether they would receive any support until after being admitted. Word spread among college coun-selors that Dickinson wasn't just principled but penurious.

As the admissions situation worsened, faculty members were obliged to dumb down their courses. When Sylvie Davidson returned to the campus in 1996, having run the college's program in Toulouse for four years, she found her classes peopled by "an entirely new—and much worse—group of students." Historian David Commins likens the new breed of students to those he had taught at Illinois State University. Understandably, that drop-off in student quality dampened faculty morale, and several senior professors contacted trustees whom they knew personally, urging them to fire Fritschler.

The professors did more than complain. With uncharacteristic selfless-ness, they passed up salary raises in favor of increasing scholarships, and rejected a plan to reduce their teaching load when they realized that would mean bigger classes. But such sacrifices couldn't solve the admis-sions problem. Belatedly the college began to award scholarships based on merit. In 1998, it hired consultant Jack Maguire, who, as Chapter 1 notes, transformed admissions and financial aid into the businesslike field of enrollment management. Handed total responsibility for making financial aid awards, Maguire was able to increase the size of the freshman class by 80 students, to 620. But to achieve his result, more than 80 percent of the freshman class received financial aid, compared with about 60 percent at similar schools, and the discount rate ballooned to 52 percent, half again as high as at competitive institutions. Although Maguire had delivered a quick fix, Dickinson couldn't afford to sustain this level of largesse.

To turn things around, Durden recruited Robert Massa, whom he had known during his years at Johns Hopkins, and gave him authority over everything from admissions to student housing, alumni affairs to athletics. Like Durden, Massa, whose experience at Hopkins is described in Chapter 1, was initially reluctant to come. "I looked at the statistics and said to myself, 'Oh my God! I don't think I can do it—it's really bad.' I couldn't sleep for worrying. But Bill had confidence, and Bill has a way about him."

If Durden looks old school, Massa is the portrait of the modern corporate manager. As the nature of college admissions has evolved from counseling and gatekeeping to recruiting, his role has changed in tandem. Initially he was more interested in students' lives than what he calls the "supply and demand aspects" of higher education, but he grew to appreciate admissions and financial aid in strategic terms. Massa expresses no qualms about the commodification of higher education. The name of the game is branding, he writes in the alumni magazine. "Dickinson, in a purposeful way, is creating 'mindshare' among prospective students."[22]

Like his counterparts elsewhere, Massa junked the generic viewbook sent to prospective students, replacing it with materials studded with pointed questions and direct answers about academics and student life—about what's "distinctively Dickinson." What is more important, he turned financial aid into a key recruiting tool. "We ought not give merit aid to kids who will already enroll," he says, criticizing his predecessors for "looking at [merit aid] as a reward" rather than a way to attract students who would otherwise go elsewhere. Now "we examine past results to estimate what giving students with 1350-plus SAT scores $17,500, versus $15,000, would do for enrollment."

This strategy has done what Massa hoped. Between 1999 and 2002, the discount rate fell from 52 to 33 percent. Just 60 percent of the students receive aid, and 10 percent of the scholarships are based on merit rather than need—in line with similar schools. And even as enrollment has remained high, average SAT scores have risen to 1240. The "'Simpsons' cohort" is receding into history.

The implications for equity, however, are troubling. More Dickinson students come from richer families—that's the meaning of having fewer students on scholarship—and the intention is to increase their numbers. Meanwhile, the number of first-generation college students, the Bill Durdens of this era, has fallen dramatically. In 1999, 22 percent of freshmen fit this category; within three years, that figure was cut almost in half, to 12 percent.[23]

At Johns Hopkins, Massa developed a regression model to favor liberal arts majors over premed students. The concern at Dickinson, as at many other colleges, is with the group known in admissions circles as "disappearing males." In recent years, considerably more women than men have been applying. Once a school gets a reputation as a "women's college," the fear is that fewer and fewer men will enroll, and the prophecy will become self-fulfilling. When two-thirds of the freshmen who enrolled in 2000 were female, Massa rewrote the admissions criteria to emphasize SATs and "leadership skills," on which men do better than women, rather than grades, where women excel. Does that amount to affirmative action for men? "If all other things were equal," Massa admitted to a *Wall Street Journal* reporter, referring to about 5 percent of the applicants, "we admitted them." Whatever it is called, the approach has made a difference. In the class admitted in 2002, the proportion of males grew to 42 percent.

Dickinson is also one of the few selective private colleges that doesn't require applicants to submit SAT scores. This policy predates Massa's arrival, and though he initially favored reinstating the requirement, as one of Dickinson's rivals, Lafayette College, has done, he has since become an advocate. "Not having the SAT requirement has improved our image among counselors and students and allowed us to take kids with lower scores and intriguing profiles." For "intriguing" read minority: just 7 percent of white applicants but a quarter of all nonwhite applicants don't submit SAT scores. This makes recruiting minorities easier, and any edge in that department is vital for a college committed to diversity ("reflecting America," as its positioning statement puts it) in a semi-rural location that that is not a natural draw for nonwhite students. In 2002, 11 percent of the freshman were minorities, compared with 6 percent just two years earlier.

Something akin to "mindshare" is also being created among Dickinson's alumni. Durden is regularly on the road, pitching alumni for money, and he is getting it. In 2001 the college received, for the first time in its history, four fully endowed chairs from individual donors, and a total of seven gifts of a million dollars or more. From 1998 to 2002, the proportion of alumni who contribute rose from 38 percent to 42 percent—that's considered a big jump at a mature institution—and the amount of alumni giving more than tripled to $8.7 million.[24] Overall, gifts to the college increased by 40 percent. "I haven't had a 'no,'" says Jennifer Barendse, who became vice president for development the year after Durden arrived. "People love the place—and we're the first people who've been asking for money in a systematic way. We made more than a thousand one-on-one meetings with alumni last year." Even in the aftermath of September 11, when contributions to higher education were generally stagnant, gifts to Dickinson increased by 10 percent.[25]

Like Bob Massa, Barendse was initially reluctant to take the job. "I was stunned when I first saw the revenue chart. Even though we were in a campaign for most of the 1990s, there were no spikes in individual giving except for testamentary gifts which we hadn't solicited." Still, she turned down an offer from Duke. "Bill convinced me the college needed me," she says, sounding a familiar note. "I feel like a sponge when I'm around him, learning about leadership. Bill never lets things slow him down. He keeps charging, moving. It's all about the pace."

▪ The Brand on the Campus Gates

This activist managerial style troubles some longtime faculty members, who dreaded the idea of bringing in a "corporate guy." Although Durden didn't fire anyone, several senior administrators quit within a year of his arrival. The bevy of recruits from Johns Hopkins—Bob Massa, admissions director Seth Allen, academic dean Joanne Brown, "positioning" consultant Mark Neustadt—led campus wags to propose that the school change its name to *Johns* Dickinson College.

When Durden brought the Washington Redskins' summer camp to the campus, he saw the decision as a no-brainer, since their presence meant revenue and publicity. Some professors grumbled that no one else had ready access to the gym, but their real complaint was that the decision was made without consulting them.[26] A Sylvan Learning Center is operating on the campus, the first such deal made by the company. To Durden, who had been president of the Sylvan Academy before coming to Dickinson, this is a "a way to serve the community while bringing in money," but again the objection was lodged that the decision was made unilaterally.

Durden makes no apologies for his style: "Sometimes, failure to act means an opportunity lost. For Dickinson to achieve its vision, it must benefit from leadership and it must desire to be led." This emphasis on presidential authority hadn't been seen at Dickinson since the 1930s, when the president sat at the head of a long table dispensing edicts to the faculty, who were seated in strict order of seniority. When Durden arrived, there was a leadership vacuum at the top. Lee Fritschler was a "nice fellow, happy to preside and look good," says Ben James, who has seen it all during his seven decades at the college. "But he wasn't getting the job done, either in the academic or financial sense."

Fritschler largely left the running of the school to George Allan, the venerable dean of the faculty. "Allan operated a Soviet-style system," assistant dean Joanne Brown dryly observes. "You keep people in bread lines, constantly busy with their committees, so that there's no revolution because they're engaged in the theater of democratic process." Now, says Brown, the bases for leadership are open and visible. Historian David Cummins agrees: "There's more candor."

Brown has thought a lot about the implications of such openness. "The irony," she says, "is that initially it was producing closure, as people started blowing issues out of proportion. "The problem is partly technological," she adds. "E-mail isn't either a letter or a conversation, though it's used interchangeably with both. People began to pass e-mails around in ways that mimicked open conversation; written passages were taken out of context, and stayed in the air as conversation doesn't. The impact was distrust. People who'd been here a long time were particularly concerned. They feared for their jobs, believed that the newcomers were more conservative politically."

Over time the climate improved. "I administer out loud," Durden says, and he tries to answer all his e-mail within two hours. "People started letting go of the illusion that things had been democratic and started to think about what would make faculty governance really work—how people could speak but not waste each other's time."

The changes are evident even in the littlest things. The signs that point visitors to campus buildings are now written in an array of foreign languages as well as English, unsubtle reminders of Dickinson's commitment to internationalism. In another break with the past, these signs all carry an identical red and white seal. The old insignia, designed by the beloved

Benjamin Rush, incorporated a Latin motto, "Pietate et doctrina tuta libertas," emblazoned over an open Bible, a telescope, and a liberty cap. But consultant Mark Neustadt pointed out that these references to religion, knowledge, and freedom were obscure to today's students, while the Latin was off-putting. Something more straightforward was needed. Now everything from the English department's stationery to the lettering on the dinner trays and dump trucks is emblazoned with what Durden calls the "identity system." At campus entrances that used to be unmarked, signs arch over newly installed gates spelling out "Dickinson College" in understated gold lettering.

Some old guard faculty scoff at these touches. The entrances demarcate a "gated community," they say, but they "don't make us Yale." They dismiss the new corporate-style logo as a vulgarity which, as they correctly observe, looks like the Seattle Mariners' insignia.[27] The logo makes an easy target, but what these faculty members are really apprehensive about, says French professor Sylvie Davidson, is their slipping power. And well they should be, since Dickinson has become dramatically, irretrievably different. The new logo is just a tangible rendering of the president's great ambition: to embody the college in a single memorable image, to give it a brand that sets it apart from its rivals.

On a sultry May morning in 2002, Bill Durden delivered the commencement address. "Benjamin Rush and John Dickinson would be proud of us today," he told the graduating seniors, drawing on his vocabulary of "key words," "because we are taking up again—passionately—their vision of the College as a revolutionary instrument."

Star Wars

New York University

Above the streets of Greenwich Village, purple and white pennants fly everywhere: This is NYU territory, they announce.[1] Five miles uptown, Morningside Heights is Columbia territory. But Columbia, long unchallenged in its claim to be the best university in New York City, wouldn't dream of putting on such a brash display of dominion. That's not how things are done at an Ivy League school founded a quarter of a millennium ago. Although NYU opened its doors in 1831, it lacks a glorious history on which it can rely. Until recently it was a commuter school with little prestige and less money; in the mid-1970s, it was teetering on the knife edge of bankruptcy. But in a turnaround that would do any corporation proud, over the course of a single generation NYU has become not only a real rival of Columbia's but a nationally renowned institution that now pitches itself as the "Global University." It has earned its display of bravado. NYU is *the* success story in contemporary American higher education.[2]

Beginning in the 1980s, NYU was able to raise money remarkably fast: $2 billion in less than two decades. Rather than using that money to build its endowment, as universities typically do, it spent most of it on building and buying new facilities and recruiting new faculty.[3] Harvard, with its $18 billion endowment, can afford to stash away its gifts and live happily on the modest income that endowment throws off, but NYU's leaders believed that at their institution, such patience would be an unaffordable luxury.[4] To reverse its record of mediocrity, the administration decided that bringing in star professors was the essential first step. Attracting better students, like other beneficial changes, would naturally follow. To create the well-funded chairs that could tempt these stars cost packets of money; and so in its drive to succeed, NYU became what former president L. Jay Oliva calls a "chair machine."[5] What George Steinbrenner did for the New

York Yankees, creating the best team that money can buy, NYU's recent presidents have tried to achieve for the university.

Since the turn of the last century, when William Rainey Harper, the first president of the University of Chicago, looted the faculty of Clark University, promising to double their salaries if they jumped ship, stealing luminaries from other universities has been seen as the fastest way to climb the ladder of academic prestige.[6] The audacity of Harper's raid startled his contemporaries, but in recent years such talent searches have become more commonplace and the offers have grown more outsized.

Until the Second World War, as Christopher Jencks and David Riesman recount in *The Academic Revolution,* the academy was a parochial world in which professors fastened their loyalties to their own institutions.[7] The "revolution" was a shift in attachment, away from the campus and to the profession. Mr. Chips was a vanishing breed, as esteem among one's fellow economists or biologists came to matter more than esteem at Siwash U. Since *The Academic Revolution* was first published in 1968, there has been another shift in loyalties among the top ranks of professors, away from the discipline and toward the individuals themselves. In this new era of free agency, faculty mobility in the senior ranks is greater, and salary differentials between the most sought-after professors and everyone else are larger, than a generation ago.[8]

No one outside the world of higher education used to notice these comings and goings, but as faculty members have become media celebrities, that is no longer true. It was front-page news in the *New York Times* business section when, in 1999, Columbia offered economist Robert Barro the sun and the moon, and also carte blanche to pick five additional faculty members, in a desperate bid to lure him away from Harvard. (Barro initially accepted Columbia's offer, only to change his mind and remain at Harvard.)[9] Three years later, the Cornel West soap opera made the front pages in newspapers from Boston to L.A.: Would the Harvard professor and erstwhile hip-hop musician, his academic prowess challenged and his pride wounded by Harvard's impolitic president, decamp to Princeton, his former home? (In the end, he made the move.)

Playing the market is risky business, whether the commodity is stocks or professors. Self-promoting academics have little attachment to any institution, and a better bid (or, as with West, an apparent slight) can tempt them away. Thanks to the consummate salesmanship of Henry Louis Gates Jr., the very model of a celebrity intellectual, in the 1990s, Harvard put together an Afro-American studies department of great individual talents, only to witness the departure of the distinguished philosopher Anthony Appiah, as well as West, to Princeton; and there was speculation that Gates himself, who had migrated from Cornell to Duke to Harvard, would be the next to leave. When he chaired Duke University's English department in the mid-1980s, Stanley Fish made a splash by recruiting the brightest, or at least the trendiest, professors to verdant Durham. But things swiftly fell apart as some of Fish's catches left for even greener pastures and others abandoned teaching entirely. Demonstrating that there really are second acts in the lives of American academics, Fish surfaced a decade later in Chicago, where, against long odds, he adopted a similar strategy at the University of Illinois.[10]

A host of schools, among them Rice, Georgia Tech, and George Mason University, have gone on star treks with at best mixed success, and that record makes NYU's achievement all the more remarkable.[11] The university has been able to raise munificent sums for its "chair machine," including $150 million in a single gift.[12] Not only have the famous scholars come, drawn by salaries that regularly top $150,000, but also they have stayed, in the process situating NYU prominently on the academic map.

What has been happening in two NYU departments illustrates the transformation. Over the course of a decade, the law school went from being a well-regarded training ground for aspiring practitioners to the most intellectually exciting school in the country. That change is mainly due to the inimitable skill of law school dean (and, since 2002, NYU president) John Sexton in the fine art of faculty seduction. The transformation of the philosophy department has been even more remarkable. That department did not even have an accredited Ph.D. program in 1995, when a new chairman, Paul Boghossian, was given authority to recruit his dream team. Within just five years, the department was tied with Princeton's as the nation's best. Compared with microbiologists or even law professors, philosophers are not an expensive investment—as the joke goes, all they need is a wastebasket and postage to send the journals what's left—but for a university with aspirations to elitism, a good philosophy department is essential, and NYU has been able to build a great, if narrowly focused, one.

The pluses of the "star search" strategy are obvious enough, but there's also a price to pay. Hiring superstars creates tensions between the professional "haves" and the "have-lesses"; and precisely because they are cosmopolitans, famous academics are often inattentive to their own backyard, neglectful of the needs of the institution.

NYU's recent history illustrates the problem. In 2001, after a long and nasty fight, it became the first private university to be ordered by the National Labor Relations Board to negotiate with its graduate student union. The adjunct faculty—part-time, ill-paid instructors with no role in university governance and no chance for tenure—have organized as well, forming the nation's biggest adjuncts-only union and the first in a private university.

These two stories, the hiring of superstars and the demand for unionization among the teaching underclass, are intertwined. The relationship isn't a simple matter of cause and effect, for adjuncts are a growing presence at most American universities, but the recruitment of famed scholars hastens the process.[13] Senior professors in great demand often insist on modest teaching loads. Their reputation, their bankable asset, depends on what they write, not how they teach. The burden of instruction, especially in the big introductory courses, mainly falls on graduate assistants and adjuncts.

NYU sloughs off a great deal of its teaching onto part-timers. Twenty-seven hundred adjuncts, almost the same in number as the tenure-ladder faculty, teach 70 percent of the undergraduate classes, a figure considerably higher than at comparable universities. In a bit of bait and switch, students drawn to NYU by luminaries like Carol Gilligan and Ronald Dworkin wind up being instructed by someone like Scott Walden, an adjunct in the philosophy department who has been teaching undergraduates since 1990. This kind of instruction can be first-rate, but many of these lesser lights resent being slighted by a system that treats them as replaceable parts.[14] That's why they have resorted to a labor-management model, rejecting as irrelevant to their lives the idea of the university as a community of scholars.

Having succeeded in the frenzied world of renown, NYU must now confront a challenge of comparable difficulty: turning its prize collection of individual talents into an academic version of the peaceable kingdom, a place where conversations about the nature and quality of academic life can cross the divides of discipline and professional status.

▪ Rescued by a Macaroni Company

Because New York University has always had a modest endowment, it has had to rely mainly on tuition to stay solvent. That's a dangerous strategy.

"[The institution's] dependence on tuition," writes Mary Poovey, professor of English and director of NYU's Institute for the History of the Production of Knowledge, "has driven the university to the brink of bankruptcy more than once."[15]

Money woes have also shaped the institutional ethos. "Normally people who are invited to come to New York University are taken aback at what they find here," Sidney Hook recalled in a 1971 conversation. Hook, who chaired NYU's philosophy department during the 1960s, was for decades among the country's leading public intellectuals. "More than once . . . I've been told by people who visited us that they sensed a factory spirit at New York University. We were always limited by money in short supply. Dependent as we were on gate receipts or tuition, the administration had to hold us in short rein. Although it urged us to plan for the future, when it came to committing itself to underwrite that future it was very reluctant to do so."[16]

Between 1964 and 1973, NYU incurred budget deficits of almost $32 million. Administrators realized that "decisive action" was necessary.[17] "In simple terms," write historians Thomas Frusciano and Marilyn Pettit, "NYU needed to seek relief through increased income, or by reducing costs. The problem with cost reduction was that if stringently applied, the university ran the risk of eroding the quality of its programs and services."[18] NYU president James Hester had harbored dreams of making the university into a "Princeton on the Hudson" but instead he had to oversee drastic cuts. NYU's faculty shrank by 10 percent in the span of just two years; and in 1973, the University Heights campus in the Bronx was sold to the City University of New York.[19] Naturally enough, recalls James Rachels, an NYU philosophy professor during that era, "there was speculation that the university might be going bankrupt."

In the end, NYU was saved by the sale of the Mueller Macaroni Company, a venerable institution that had been bequeathed to the law school. Mueller fetched $115 million; and after considerable wrangling, $40 million of the proceeds went to the university. This seed money enabled NYU to begin hiring replacements for the faculty who had fled during cutback time; and with the inauguration of John Brademas as president in the fall of 1981, the pace of recovery quickened.[20]

Brademas was an unconventional choice for the job—a politician, not an educator, an eleven-term Indiana congressman who during his years in Washington had made higher education policy his passion. He was also just the right choice. At that moment in its history, the university needed a fund-raiser at the helm, and during his eleven-year tenure, Brademas proved brilliant at persuading donors to part with their money.[21]

"Fund-raising is one of the principal responsibilities of a serious college or university president in the United States," John Brademas says, and he is a very serious man.[22] After raising more than $40 million, at that time a record for NYU, during his first year in office, the president announced "the most ambitious fund-raising effort in the university's history": NYU would raise "one million dollars a week for one hundred weeks." There was a great deal of untapped money in New York City—the "new money" that wasn't going to Columbia. "If we vigorously and successfully generate enough resources now," the president declared in his first annual report, "I am confident that we will be one of the few universities in this generation to win still wider visibility and a new position of eminence in American higher education."[23] In 1984, Brademas set the bar even higher with a goal of $1 billion in private contributions by the year 2000. The university did better than anticipated. The billion-dollar mark was passed in barely a decade, and the gifts have kept pouring in.

As New York City goes, so goes NYU. The university also benefited from the city's rebirth as the greatest show on earth. During the 1970s, when New York flirted with bankruptcy ("Ford to NYC: Drop Dead!" read the memorable *New York Daily News* headline), Washington Square had been a dicey place; but by the 1980s, the time of "I ♥ NY" T-shirts, it had become trendy. NYU invested heavily in new dorms—11,000 students live in university housing—and that made it easier to recruit students nationally. By 1995, nearly three-quarters of its students came from outside New York City, compared with just 18 percent a decade earlier, and undergraduates' SAT scores had ascended into the 1300s. Jay Oliva, who succeeded Brademas in 1991, could honestly brag that "we have changed from a commuter school whose entrance requirements were in the medium range into a national university whose students come from all over the country and the world."[24]

A considerable amount of the new funding was earmarked to endow 140 professorships.[25] "Endowed chairs," says C. Duncan Rice, the dean of arts and sciences during Brademas's tenure, "were being accumulated at a great speed."

With the backing of Brademas and then Oliva, Rice set about to transform the academic enterprise at NYU. Even as the education and public policy schools soldiered on with little help from the campus administration, the liberal arts flourished.[26] "In order to make NYU fully competitive on a national and international level," says Rice, his assignment was to "rebuild the liberal arts core." This undertaking was animated by a single idea: to bring in a critical mass of topflight faculty members so that the university would be "unstoppable." That took money. Professors were making their moves—"the market in faculty was in significant development," Rice says—and "we were encouraged to be as competitive as we had to be."

The deans, not the departments, took the lead. The idea was "to spark hiring that would not happen routinely within departments," says Craig Calhoun, who himself was hired away from the University of North Carolina in 1996 to revamp the sociology department. "It was a problem of getting action, and the solution was to find ways to do things that would create more buzz." As a result of the fiscal crises of the 1960s and 1970s, Mary Poovey writes, university administrators were "encouraged to cultivate an entrepreneurial attitude that has periodically positioned them to take advantage of emergent trends in institutional finance or education."[27] Even when NYU's financial worries began to recede, this emphasis on innovation lived on as a part of the university's culture. "Relative prosperity permitted a more aggressive and ecumenical form of opportunism."[28]

Talented academics relish the chance to run their own show. Amid the bidding wars, they have demanded their own research centers, and such enterprises have become fixtures at major universities. At NYU, says Calhoun, "most of the centers are tied to a personage." These enclaves can stir intellectual excitement, especially when their work crosses traditional disciplinary lines. But they also draw intellectual excitement away from the departments, which are left with the responsibility for teaching.[29] Even as the centers were luring well-known faculty, the departments lagged behind. In the mid-1990s, a critical external review of the sociology department described it as a donut, with stars around the periphery and mediocrity in the center. Rice took these criticisms seriously. He began to recruit department chairmen, academic worthies with the talent and taste to revitalize a second-tier department, and gave them virtual control over faculty appointments. In this model, the chairman's job is to hire other outstanding figures in the field and, in the process, to draw attention to the university as well as the department.

Unless the chair is a consummate diplomat, concentrating power is a recipe for misery among old-line faculty members. They feel—and often are—disenfranchised, told that their views don't matter. The politics department is a textbook example. Russell Hardin, a game theorist from the University of Chicago, arrived as chair in 1993 with a high salary, a light teaching load, and a mandate to transform his department. That's just what he has done, turning the NYU department into a bastion of cutting-edge rational choice theory. His most prominent hire was his Chicago colleague Adam Przeworski, a comparative politics scholar who applies that methodology to the issue of democratization.

Under the leadership of Hardin and Przeworski, says politics professor Lawrence Mead, longtime NYU faculty were "put out to pasture." The "rational choice takeover," as Mead refers to it, brought with it a "new orthodoxy" that led to "the death of the [department's] intellectual life. Most of the new crowd can't do anything *except* write journal articles. They can't teach undergraduates or discuss their basic assumptions, and they simply don't have many ideas. All they really know is an analytic method." Some of the old guard, who felt bullied by the newcomers, retreated to the university's research centers.

These intramural conflicts are emblematic of ceaseless debates about the role of scientism in the social sciences—"the elimination of politics from political science," as one dissident professor puts it.[30] But they also shed light on the difficulties that NYU has experienced in its transition from the old to the new, and the particular problems associated with hiring scholars with a narrow intellectual agenda.

Similar questions have arisen in the reinvention of NYU's philosophy department. In 1995, Paul Boghossian, a philosopher of language and mind, was asked to rescue a department that lacked even an accredited Ph.D. program. He has been remarkably successful, hiring world-class talent in his own field of analytic philosophy. Within five years, NYU was ranked first in "The Philosophical Gourmet Report," the bible for prospective students. The revamped department, however, has radically de-emphasized fields that had earlier been its great strength—law, ethics, and public philosophy—and this has been controversial on the campus. Some critics recall the 1960s, before the fiscal catastrophe, when Sidney Hook brought together a pluralistic assemblage of contending characters not dominated by any single philosophical style. Could—should—that model be emulated?

■ Many Voices, Many Rooms

If a movie director were to cast the perfect college lecturer, NYU philosopher Robert Gurland would fit the bill. Even as a graduate student in the late 1960s, a time when authority was instinctively distrusted, "students would stand and applaud" his lectures, says James Rachels, a moral philosopher who was then teaching at NYU. "Once when the enrollment for his class was closed, some students staged an overnight sit-in in the dean's office, demanding that they be allowed to take the class." University departments are reluctant to hire their own graduates, preferring that they prove themselves elsewhere, but "when Gurland finished his graduate work, the dean simply informed the department that he must be hired as a regular member of the faculty."

For a third of a century, Gurland remained philosophy's most popular attraction, someone whom one colleague admiringly calls "a barker for the department." But in 2002, increasingly disaffected with the mindset of the analytic philosophers, Gurland decamped to NYU's Gallatin School of Individualized Study. Among members of the refashioned department, there is little regret over his departure. "He's certainly very popular and charismatic," says Peter Unger, who sat in on one of Gurland's lectures. But he adds—damningly—that what Gurland teaches "doesn't seem like philosophy to me."

Gurland has responded in kind, lashing out at his department's neglect of undergraduates in a presentation at the American Philosophical Association meetings. "That this department should be so highly regarded is a scandal," he says; its transformation "offers a paradigm instance of the moral failure of those entrusted to provide a viable, life-enhancing educational process to discharge their mandated responsibilities. The willingness of administrators to sacrifice substance in order to purchase cachet is contemptible and in violation of the spirit that fueled the likes of Sidney Hook."

Everything, it seems, comes down to a comparison between "the NYU of Sidney Hook" and the department of today. For nearly half a century, beginning in 1927, Hook taught in, and for more than thirty years was chairman of, NYU's philosophy department.[31] "The primary professional task of most faculty members in our colleges and universities is teaching," Hook proclaimed near the end of his life. "The importance of teaching, especially on the undergraduate level, cannot be exaggerated."[32] Some of Hook's colleagues have similar views. Recalling the department's "golden age" of the 1960s, Steven Cahn remembers "a great emphasis on the quality of teaching," and points out that Hook himself was a dedicated undergraduate lecturer.

The department thrived as a hotbed of philosophical activity. "We were not left- or right-wingers. We were philosophers using the tools of our trade to analyze the problems of society, often by subjecting the arguments of non-philosophers to higher logical standards," says Douglas Lackey, who arrived at NYU in 1970 straight out of graduate school at Yale. When Lackey was asked at his job interview what he would be working on the following year, he replied, "The ethics of nuclear deterrence." Another applicant, asked a similar question, responded, "Pronouns." Lackey got the job. "The pronoun man," he says, "was out."

The field of philosophy is almost as capacious as thought itself, and during that era the department was a place where very different kinds of philosophers were in the habit of talking with one another. "If you went in and said you wanted to talk about Schopenhauer," says Cahn, "you'd have seven people who wanted to talk with you about Schopenhauer." This give-and-take was the result of a recruitment strategy that was the "antithesis of what's been done in recent years. The whole idea was to have as diverse a group as possible."[33]

Hook's explicit endorsement of this approach is in one respect startling, since he fervently believed that communists (including an NYU colleague, whom he publicly accused of being a member of the Communist Party) surrendered their rights to academic freedom when they gave their loyalty to the party. But Hook was also a founder of the campus chapter of the American Association of University Professors (AAUP), a national organization committed to promoting academic freedom, and he was catholic in his intellectual tastes. "From the time I headed the department," he once said, "we tried to avoid developing a monolithic department with only one point of view. No one can say that we are parochial in our outlook, and that any person has been judged by the character of his views rather than by his scholarship and his ability to teach."[34]

Then came the financial crisis of the mid-1970s. Faced with the imminent meltdown of the university, faculty members started leaving in droves, among them Hook himself, who took a post at Stanford's conservative think tank, the Hoover Institute. Before long, a department of nineteen had shrunk to six. Those departures cost the department dearly in terms of its professional respectability. New York State requires that accredited Ph.D. programs be periodically reviewed; but with the decimation of the faculty the program was in disarray. "When the state's education department came calling with their survey, NYU just threw in the towel," says Steven Cahn, and the Ph.D. program was suspended.

But as the university's financial picture brightened, there was new money to hire philosophy professors. The biggest coup came in 1980, when ethicist Thomas Nagel was recruited from Princeton with a mandate to rebuild the department. Nagel writes on broad questions—his best-known books include *The Philosophy of Altruism* and *What Does It All Mean?*—and his work has an admiring readership among philosophers and non-philosophers alike.[35] His migration to NYU had a powerful signaling effect. "If Tom Nagel would come to NYU," says Catharine Stimpson, dean of the Graduate School of Arts and Science, the feeling was that "all was not lost."

Nagel chaired the department for half a decade, but he had little to show for his recruiting efforts. NYU would have to wait until the mid-1990s for its graduate program to be reborn. By then, seemingly nudged aside by philosophers with less interest in asking "What does it all mean?", Nagel was spending much of his time at the law school with a more compatible coterie of philosophers.

▪ Analytic Philosophy Equals The Best

"To go from a program that did not have a Ph.D. program in 1995 to the best philosophy department in the world in 2000—that is a remarkable story!" says John Sexton, who succeeded Jay Oliva as president of NYU. It is in considerable measure the story of Paul Boghossian, the department's chairman. Boghossian is not a household name, even in households that subscribe to the *New York Review of Books,* but in the rarefied world of analytic philosophy he is a luminary.

Superstars like Henry Gates and Cornel West draw their stock of academic capital from their extra-disciplinary profile and aim their work at a wide audience. By contrast, specialist scholars like Boghossian gain their stature through contributions in distinctly disciplinary venues, publishing in the right journals and giving presentations at the right conferences. They are carrying forward a tradition of analytic philosophy whose style deters all but the most persistent of outsiders, and eschewing celebrity in favor of academic acclaim.

When Boghossian was hired away from the University of Michigan in 1991, the philosophy department still lacked a Ph.D. program. Without the promise of new faculty positions or even a position of leadership (he didn't become head of the department until 1994), he doesn't fit the NYU model of the powerful chair lured from outside the university.

Nonetheless, he has turned out to be one of its most adept departmental entrepreneurs. "If you give me money," he told the administration, "I'll build you one of the best departments in the world."[36] At least according the rankings, he has done just that.

"The best," to Boghossian, equals analytic philosophy. The "conscious strategy was to focus on fields such as metaphysics, the philosophy of language, and the philosophy of logic"—areas that the discipline views as central. For Peter Unger, who has sought to strengthen the department's reputation since helping to lure Thomas Nagel from Princeton in 1980, this decision also made great marketing sense, since analytic philosophy is "where the customers [the graduate students] are."

"I think it would be a shame not to have various important areas represented—including, particularly, history," Boghossian says, but until 2003 he has not recruited anyone who studies the history of the field. As one historically minded NYU graduate student notes, the faculty "take the same attitude toward the history of philosophy that a modern mathematician or logician would take to the history of math or logic: useful, perhaps, for insight into the origins of present-day puzzles . . . but not a central part of the enterprise."

Plato and Descartes, Nietzsche and Kant—that's what adjunct instructors teach to undergraduates. In Boghossian's department, unlike Sidney Hook's, the "pronoun man" would get the job.

By making what he calls "conditional agreements"—I'll come if so-and-so comes—Boghossian was able to hire in rapid succession three world-class analytic philosophers, and others soon followed. The first person he recruited was Ned Block, a philosopher of mind who decamped to NYU in 1996 after a quarter-century at MIT. "NYU was showing promise," he says; and besides, "I had a pretty good idea that if I started the ball rolling, then Field and Schiffer might come as well." Hartry Field and Stephen Schiffer, who, like Block, work in the core of analytic philosophy, both held distinguished appointments at the City University of New York Graduate Center; they are close friends, and over the years have been colleagues at three different institutions. "I knew and liked and thought very well of both of them," says Block.

"With a single strike," says NYU historian Thomas Bender, "a department that had no Ph.D. program was now a [nationally] competitive department."

One of the university's biggest draws, Block says, was the city itself, as well as NYU's ability to give its top professors that rarest of New York commodities, good housing. Block is not alone, of course, in his love of New York; in almost every conversation analyzing NYU's success, the importance of its location comes up. NYU couldn't tempt Field and Schiffer with the city's bright lights, since the two professors were already living there. But the university did find them better and cheaper apartments in the heart of Greenwich Village. In housing, as in everything else in academic life, not all professors are created equal. An attractive apartment is a valuable chip that, because of NYU's chronic housing shortage, "you give to people who you are trying to recruit or people who have offers from Yale," says Jess Benhabib, an economist and former dean of the liberal arts college.

A fat salary was another enticement. "They just made tremendous offers," Schiffer says. Block reports that his NYU salary is "vastly higher than what I was getting at MIT." NYU attracted notice in the world of elite universities, says Benhabib, by "breaking the norm, not breaking the bank." And why not? "Why should professors make less, if the market will support it?"

Nonetheless, none of NYU's newly hired philosophers came just for the money. "Hartry and I were maybe a little more reluctant than the others" to make the move, says Schiffer, because their research positions at CUNY were "slightly better than no teaching at all," and so "certain concessions were made in terms of teaching and in terms of the money." Most faculty members teach two undergraduate classes, but luminaries like Schiffer and Field rarely teach undergraduates; and when they do, the class is a specialized seminar. This same story is being played out across the liberal arts at NYU, which is one reason why the demand for adjuncts has increased. Someone must teach the undergraduates.

More money, reduced teaching, a Village apartment: what more could a star philosopher ask for? The answer turns out to be a special kind of philosophical community. "Most importantly," says Schiffer, "we had the chance to be in a first-rate department." No Schopenhauer here. In analytic philosophy, where disputation is the disciplinary pastime and sheer argumentative ability of the sort familiar to litigators is prized, having adept sparring partners is invaluable for sharpening one's arguments. Boghossian's narrow-gauge hiring strategy has produced an unusually congenial environment in which professors regularly sit in on one another's seminars, and that too has been a draw.

When Christopher Peacocke gave up his position as Waynflete Professor of Metaphysical Philosophy at Oxford to come to NYU, he became the first ever to resign a chair that has been held by some of the giants of the field. Nowadays, he says, "if you are an Anglophone philosopher, you do not have reasons for being on one continent or another. And the competition for faculty is now phenomenally intense." Philosophy is one of the "most international" disciplines; "it's a free open market, and people will follow the resources."

Alongside the market in professors is a market in graduate students, and success in recruiting the top prospects is a marker of a department's reputation. In revamping the department, Boghossian concentrated first on hiring faculty, in the belief that renowned faculty would draw attention; that this attention would translate into markers of reputation; and that good students, paying attention to these signals in the academic marketplace, would respond. Things have worked exactly according to plan. "Every year, the top ten prospective Oxford graduate students decided not to attend," observes Peacocke. "Those are the people I am seeing here at NYU." That is true across the board. "We're getting virtually all the students we make offers to," says Ned Block.

In this blood sport—"We creamed Princeton," reports Schiffer—NYU professors cite "The Philosophical Gourmet Report" as evidence of where NYU stands vis-à-vis the competition. Like *U.S. News & World Report*'s college rankings, "The Philosophical Gourmet" has drawn cries of outrage from some members of the profession. More than 250 professors signed a letter, drafted by Harvard philosopher Richard Heck, complaining about "the damage 'The Philosophical Gourmet' is doing to the profession as a whole." Meanwhile, prospective graduate students are relying on it in deciding where to enroll. NYU's number-one ranking provides objective-sounding evidence, and enables the department to counter the halo effect of more established universities.

At one level, the debate over the merits of "The Philosophical Gourmet" has to do with pragmatic questions of ranking and reputation. But the deeper substantive questions concern what a good graduate education in philosophy really entails. And those questions, which ultimately address the nature of the philosophical enterprise itself, are embedded in a larger set of debates about the current state of American philosophy. Because of its aggressive department-building strategy, NYU has been a lightning rod for those disputes as well.

▪ Analytic Philosophy's Intellectual Neighborhood

Hard-core analytic philosophers are careful thinkers and precise writers, disdainful of those they regard as less careful. Some of the best among them (Wittgenstein is a notorious historical example) have had little patience for the messiness of public debate or even interdisciplinary dialogue, preferring to address only other similarly trained and skilled philosophers.[37]

As Stanford philosopher Richard Rorty, the leading proponent of pragmatism and a voluntary exile from his discipline, points out, "many analytic philosophers do not like to think of their discipline as one of the humanities. They regard their own brand of philosophy as the disciplined pursuit of objective knowledge, and thus as resembling the natural sciences. They view the humanities as an arena for unarguable clashes of opinion. Philosophers of this sort prefer to be placed, for administrative purposes, as far as possible from professors of literature and as close as possible to professors of physics."[38]

That is certainly the case at NYU, where the philosophy department's leading lights have blasted away at those cultural and social theorists outside the department who have the audacity to think of themselves as philosophers. "There are other departments in the university that 'do philosophy,'" says philosopher Kit Fine, "and they do it very badly." In fact, he continues, "'badly' is too mild a term. This is one of the saddest things that's happened in the universities. It is a huge intellectual tragedy. Whole academic disciplines have been corroded. These faculty are very political people, and so they will try to hold on to power. But it won't last. I hope I live to see the day when people look back and see what a horrible mistake it was."

Andrew Ross, who runs NYU's American Studies program, could well be characterized as one of those "very political people." For his part, Ross has little use for Fine and his colleagues, since "in general, they are not people who contribute to interdisciplinary dialogue on campus." Ross would have preferred a revamped philosophy department more amenable to colloquy with the humanities. "There was perceived to be a separate track for the philosophers," he says of the wave of hiring. "People noticed that . . . a lot of money was being spent on them, but the hires were not seen as adding a lot to the community at large." There was considerable resentment, he adds, "that all that money was spent on people who do not circulate."

Such disputes, says Liam Murphy, a philosopher who teaches at NYU's law school, are "a local version of the broader culture wars. There is a sense that the philosophy department is narrow and bigoted, and the sense among philosophers that people in the humanities are ignorant and not well trained. And there is truth on both sides. But there is also mutual mis-understanding. So there is enormous scope for improved understanding."

When would-be peacemakers from both camps have sought rapproche-ment, though, the results have been disastrous. The university annually or-ganizes a "Derrida Month," when that French intellectual luminary holds forth across the campus. But when the philosophy department invited Derrida for a seminar, says Kit Fine, "he refused to talk with us." Derrida's reluctance is readily understood, since it's no secret that many of the phi-losophers view him with contempt. "Image-making nonsense" is how Fine dismisses Derrida Month.

At a 1997 forum organized by Ned Block, intended to promote contact with the humanities, philosopher Louise Antony, then teaching at Chapel Hill, gave a talk on feminist philosophy and Columbia literary theorist Gayatri Spivak delivered a reply. "There was not any dialogue," Block re-calls. "Spivak was pretty unintelligible." Block has come to the dispiriting realization that simply "getting philosophers and other humanities faculty in the same room is an achievement in and of itself."

Paul Boghossian has maintained intellectual contact with the social the-orists, though the terms of engagement have not been friendly. Like Fine, he is unstinting in his criticism of bad philosophy, and he was one of the few analytical philosophers to weigh in publicly on what has become known as the "Sokal affair." That contretemps was sparked by physicist Alan Sokal's article "Transgressing the Boundaries: Toward a Transforma-tive Hermeneutics of Quantum Gravity," a piece written as a parody of in-tellectual relativism that was treated as serious science in the postmodern journal *Social Text*.[39] Boghossian's criticisms were blunt and brutal. "Only the complete scientific, mathematical and philosophical incompetence of the editors of *Social Text*," he and his colleague Thomas Nagel wrote in a letter to *Lingua Franca*, "can explain how they were able to accept for publication such a tissue of transparent nonsense."[40]

This missive wasn't calculated to build any bridges, especially since An-drew Ross is one of the editors of *Social Text*. But Boghossian did open the door to disciplinary self-reflection in a field not known for its willingness to probe either its own history or its relation to broader social and cultural trends. Near the end of his broadside, Boghossian wondered aloud how the "transparently refutable" tenets of postmodernism had "ever come to gain such widespread acceptance." His response pinpointed philosophy's responsibility for allowing such questions to be so frequently mishandled. Why wasn't "analytic philosophy, the dominant tradition of philosophy in the English-speaking world, able to exert a more effective corrective influence? . . . Because philosophy concerns the most general categories of knowledge, categories that apply to any compartment of inquiry, it is inevitable that other disciplines will reflect on philosophical problems and develop philosophical positions. Analytic philosophy has a special responsibility to ensure that its insights on matters of broad intellectual interest are available widely, to more than a narrow class of insiders."[41]

In identifying philosophy's need to deliver "correction" rather than invite dialogue, Boghossian reflects the paternalism of his tribe. But the provocations he addresses to his own profession deserve consideration. His unanswered questions hint at how NYU's philosophers might yet reject a self-imposed insularity, choosing neighborliness over narrowness, mutual exploration and debate over academic high-handedness and reflexive dismissal.

▪ NYU's "Second Philosophy Department"

Kit Fine's complaints about NYU professors who "do philosophy very badly" are aimed at the *Social Text* crowd. Yet outside his department, the biggest concentration of philosophers at NYU isn't in the humanities but at the law school. There, in what might be described as a second department of philosophy, questions that analytic philosophy has relegated to the periphery—issues of law, ethics, and social justice—are addressed by scholars such as Thomas Nagel (also a member of the philosophy department and a noted analytic philosopher) and Ronald Dworkin, stars within and beyond the philosophical universe.[42]

When federal court judge and polymath Richard Posner set out to assess the work of American public philosophers in *Public Intellectuals: A Study of Decline,* he was hard-pressed to list more than a handful worthy of the name. "With philosophy increasingly professionalized, jargonized, hermetic," he wrote, philosophers who speak to a broader audience are rarities. Nagel and Dworkin were on his short list, "among the most prominent of those few living American public intellectuals who are drawn from the front ranks of academic philosophy."[43]

Dworkin and Nagel, Nagel and Dworkin. In conversations among philosophers and legal scholars, these names surface repeatedly, one right after the other. Both write regularly and accessibly for non-philosophical audiences, and both have strong connections to NYU's law school. While most of the philosophers Nagel wooed when he was chair of the philosophy department declined to join, one who did accept the invitation was Ronald Dworkin. Dworkin has been widely influential in several disciplines, and many see him as America's leading legal philosopher. "No subject ever seems quite the same after one has read Dworkin's treatment of it," gushed a reviewer in the *Journal of Philosophy*.[44] Dworkin also writes magazine articles with such titillating titles as "Philosophy and Monica Lewinsky."[45] He divides his time between NYU and Oxford; and at NYU, his main responsibility is a seminar in moral and political philosophy, which he co-teaches in the law school with Nagel. "It's one of the best courses in the university," says Dworkin's colleague Liam Murphy. Yet despite his high profile in the field, Dworkin has few ties to the department of philosophy.

Thomas Nagel began his NYU career in the philosophy department, with the assignment of strengthening it, but within a few years he had migrated to the law school. Colleagues believe that, having left Princeton partly to escape departmental acrimony, he was in no hurry to reproduce such an environment at NYU.[46] Nagel does not teach often in the philosophy department; and although he regularly attends departmental meetings and colloquiums, it is telling that, unlike a full-time faculty member, he shares an office with the adjuncts.

When Liam Murphy came to NYU Law School, just before Paul Boghossian's first wave of hiring in philosophy, he had a competing offer from a leading philosophy department. But Murphy chose the law school because it was a far more interdisciplinary and welcoming place. It was John Sexton who greeted him with open arms—literally, since seemingly everyone who walks into his office is greeted with a bear hug. By the time Murphy arrived, Sexton, who had been appointed dean in 1988, had applied his passion to the task of boosting the school's endowment and recruiting distinguished faculty.[47] His approach to institution building— what might be called "let a thousand academic flowers bloom"—is the mirror opposite of Boghossian's strategy.

"Like all truly great salesmen," James Traub says of Sexton in an admiring *New York Times Magazine* cover story, "he makes you believe his own line because he believes it, too."[48] His "drive toward meaning," says Martin Lipton, chairman of NYU's board of trustees, and formerly a trustee at the law school, "is not encompassed or summed up by the standard references of the academic marketplace: prestige, rankings, or VIPs."[49]

Stories about Sexton inevitably invoke the image of the parish priest, the counselor, the confidant. That's no accident, for Sexton has a Ph.D. in religion as well as a J.D. What he calls his "theological bent" is evident in the way he views his mission as law school dean and, since 2002, NYU's president.

At the time he became dean, he says, the dominant ethos was that professors were "independent contractors, totally autonomous beings," and the school was "the anti-community." That did not sit well with Sexton, whose "single-minded devotion," as historian Stephen Englund writes, is "to a team or institution."[50] He started an informal but institutionally powerful faculty group, which he called "the Enterprise," committed to promoting both academic excellence and intellectual commonweal. Being a member of the Enterprise, says Sexton, meant "never being content, never saying we are in our golden age"; it meant being focused on "the team getting stronger." This commitment implied a willingness to subordinate personal interests to those of "the collective mission," with a "dividend of cooperation."

Initially, the Enterprise was little more than a dreamy notion. But Sexton is a visionary who possesses the uncanny ability to turn imagined communities into real ones. Eventually the Enterprise flourished. It became a well-developed marketing tool, helping to bring about a great academic migration, as NYU Law School attracted topflight talent from the best schools in the country. "The array of faculty that has moved to NYU," says Harvard Law School's Laurence Tribe, "has created a level of scholarship and intellectual distinction and range that is extremely impressive."[51]

Money is certainly one lure, and NYU's law school has lots of money to lavish on those whom it is courting; but so do other leading law schools.[52] The "coin of the realm" is not money, says Sexton. It's a model of intellectual congregation that extends beyond the law school to the university. The hiring of Stephen Holmes in 1997 is a good example. Holmes is a prominent political theorist whose move from Princeton was part of a substantial attempt, engineered mainly by the law school, to transform NYU's politics department. Recruiting scholars of Holmes's caliber has a ripple effect. "If you want to bring the very best law faculty in the world to a place," says Sexton, "you have to have political scientists and economists and business professors and philosophers around them. It creates an exchange of ideas that just makes everybody better."[53]

At NYU, the law school is almost an entity unto itself. Its special status can be traced back to the financial crises of the 1970s, when it threatened to secede from the university and attach itself to Princeton. "Cooler heads prevailed," says Sexton, and in return for giving the university some of the proceeds from the sale of the Mueller Macaroni Company, it became a largely autonomous institution that manages its own endowment and has its own board of trustees. As dean, John Sexton welcomed that arrangement, but as university president, he has defined his task as that of building a more inclusive community. That means bringing together separate, sometimes warring units, and narrowing the immense divide between NYU's superstars and those who do the bulk of the actual teaching.

▪ A Communitarian Vision for the Global University?

The photograph that appeared in the December 7, 2001, *New York Times* is quintessential John Sexton. The new NYU president had arranged a meeting with his Columbia counterpart, Lee Bollinger, as a first step in improving relations with the university's uptown rival. The *Times* photo captures Sexton embracing Bollinger in one of his trademark embraces.

But inclusiveness has its limits. In the months before his inauguration, Sexton held a series of meetings with faculty and students, as he began to define the direction of his presidency. When Sexton met a small group of activist faculty, he told them a story about two groups of professors on the NYU campus which he called "the blue team" and "the gray team." The blue team, he said, was made up of professors who could get jobs at the drop of a hat at any of the top five universities in the country; the gray team represented the rest of the faculty. Sexton told the group that his goal was to increase the size of the blue team from 10 percent to 30 percent of the faculty. "And what team are the adjuncts on?" one of the part-timers asked.

"This whole problem of adjuncts . . . is eroding the quality of education," says one of NYU's 2,700 adjuncts.[54] Michael Schutz of the German department described "a tortuous caste system in which layers of instructors, all with different titles and pay levels, are increasingly resentful of one another and protective of their privileges." Although Schutz held a full-time position, he was not on a tenure track. "I am acutely aware on a daily basis that the work I do is considered less valuable," he told the *New York Times*.[55]

The situation in Washington Square is emblematic of national trends.[56]

During the past generation, university teaching has increasingly become the responsibility of adjunct professors, who by 2002 accounted for 43 percent of all faculty.[57] Typically they are paid a pittance. "You have an army of faculty members who do the bulk of the teaching at the university and are not paid commensurate to our contribution," says Kathleen Hull, an adjunct in NYU's general studies program. Hull, who, in 2002, taught two courses a semester for $3,600 per course, is doing comparatively well; her counterparts in the education school receive just $2,500. Adjuncts have no job security (courses are sometimes canceled at the beginning of a semester), no offices ("people are carrying their offices on their backs," says one part-timer), no benefits, no health insurance, and no voice in university affairs.[58] Many adjuncts wind up teaching at several different schools—"road scholars" or "freeway fliers," they're often called—in order to make ends meet.

In just five years, between 1993 and 1998, 40 percent of all higher education institutions reduced their full-time faculty, and 22 percent of those schools replaced them with part-timers.[59] "The full-time, tenured faculty member," says Harvard education professor Richard Chait, "is about as representative of higher education today as Ozzie and Harriet are of American society."[60] Meanwhile, professors who unhesitatingly protest the working conditions of janitors in Los Angeles and picket companies like Nike for their treatment of pieceworkers in Indonesia have generally been mute about the plight of these not-quite members of the academy.[61]

Resentment among NYU's adjuncts has prompted increased union activity. The stakes were high when, in 2002, these instructors voted on whether to join Adjuncts Come Together, a United Auto Workers local. Official recognition of the union, said union organizer Jamie Horowitz of the American Federation of Teachers (AFT), "could really be the re-emergence of labor inside private universities." John Sexton invoked his beloved concept of community in opposing the union. "Dealing with one another at arm's length," he wrote in a letter encouraging adjuncts to reject the union, "bound by stringent rules, will make it more difficult to achieve the open community we envision for ourselves."[62] But despite Sexton's plea, the adjuncts voted yes, making ACT-UAW the nation's largest adjuncts-only union.

The organizers took their cue from NYU's graduate teaching assistants, who had earlier been organized by the same union. Facing a difficult job market when they receive their Ph.D.s, with large teaching loads along the way, graduate students want the university to recognize their essential role as instructors. Across the country, the unionization of graduate student assistants and adjuncts proceeds apace. By 2002, the UAW represented more than 15,000 teaching assistants nationwide, and the AFT represented 125,000 faculty members, including 50,000 adjuncts. At NYU the campus administration vigorously opposed graduate student unionization, calling the situation there "a test case for the entire nation."[63] NYU lost that case when, in 2000, the National Labor Relations Board ruled that its teaching and research assistants had the right to organize. As a result of that decision, NYU became the first private university obliged to negotiate a contract with its graduate assistants.[64]

A glimpse at the philosophy department's undergraduate offerings for 2002, with course after course identifying the instructor simply as an unnamed "adjunct," shows how heavily the department, like many others, relies on these part-timers. Although Thomas Nagel has taught an introductory course, "Central Problems in Philosophy," he is the decided exception. The department's leading lights spend almost all their teaching time with the thirty or so Ph.D. students. "It's interesting," observes Gary Ostertag, a friend and former student of Stephen Schiffer who has been an adjunct for several years, "that on one of their central Web pages the university indicates the number of their faculty and full-time employees, but fails to even mention the existence of adjuncts. Of course, it would look a little awkward [if those figures were included]. It would be a real eye-opener." The faculty member in philosophy who, by far and away, sees more undergraduates than any other is Scott Walden, who has taught two courses a semester since 1990, and Walden is an adjunct.

NYU's rapid rise has taken place from the top down, as powerful deans and department chairmen acted on their own—"getting action," as sociology professor Craig Calhoun puts it. "They decided to spend their way into high society," says American Studies chair Andrew Ross. This was the approach in the presidential search that led to Sexton's being hired. When some professors complained about being shut out of the process, board chairman Martin Lifton was dismissive: "We fully understand the faculty point of view, and we reject it."[65]

Even instinctive democrats like Ross and Calhoun acknowledge that this approach has succeeded in vaulting NYU into the top tier in many of its programs in a generation, a feat no other American university has been able to pull off. But one consequence is the absence of any sense of the commons. "NYU suffers from not encouraging its distinguished recruits to think of themselves more as institutional citizens," Calhoun says. "Instead, it encourages them to think of themselves either as barons over some small feudal domain or as self-interested private actors who maximize their autonomy." The philosophy of John Sexton's Enterprise is noticeably absent. "Loyalty is mediated more by salary and housing and life in New York and less by ties to the university as such."

Now that NYU has its "blue team" in place, can it institutionalize charisma, inviting professors to participate in managing the affairs of the university, rather than relying entirely on individually negotiated deals with those who are threatening to go elsewhere? "Just by putting the term 'faculty governance' into circulation," says Andrew Ross, "we have begun to stir up some blood." The revival of NYU's chapter of the AAUP, established years earlier by Sidney Hook, was meant "to establish a kind of faculty voice." The odds against turning his colleagues into citizens are long, Ross acknowledges, because "faculty are eternally insecure. Despite the fact that they have tenure, they simply won't speak out." But, he adds, "I am allergic to despair."

At elite schools like Harvard, where the star system has long been in place, junior professors are rarely promoted to tenure. When making senior appointments, the university brings in scholars who have made their reputations elsewhere. But while luminaries are hired for what they have already done, it's the next generation of academics, those who are obliged to depart, who often provide the intellectual spark in the field. "One of the things that has bothered me about NYU," says a philosopher from another leading department, "is the concentration on established or over-the-hill philosophers. These are people who have essentially done their best work already, and are now involved in extensive mopping-up operations." Douglas Lackey, who taught philosophy at NYU in the 1970s before moving to CUNY, echoes this concern. "How long a profession can survive while starving its young and throwing perks at a few older celebrities remains to be seen." The same might be said of a university.

As president, can John Sexton match his achievements at the law school? He understands the dimensions of the task. "The change from being a parish priest to being a cardinal," he says, the doctor of religion offering an analogy to his move from law school dean to the president's office, "is not simply a change in magnitude. It is a category change. You realize that there are octaves of the piano that you did not know existed. And the first thing that you have to do is that you have to accept the fact that there are very few general university principles."

"We are not trying to preserve a golden age or status quo," Sexton adds. "We are not afraid to fail." Talking with alumni, a group to which little attention had been paid until he took office, Sexton sounded confident. "'A small set of universities will get it right, and N.Y.U. will be one,' he promised, moving on to the clincher, asking for their help."[66]

Despite NYU's great diversity, Sexton remains convinced that building a congregation out of a disparate collection of individuals can amount to more than rhetoric. He offers his vision as an invitation rather than an imposition, and presents himself as the dynamic champion of the faculty and the institution he leads.

"One thing that unites us all," Sexton remarks of the faculty, "is the notion that ideas are improved through dialogue. So now let's figure out how to encourage people to give us the strongest possible opposing viewpoint, to develop a structure where it becomes clear that we welcome that. And of course that involves techniques for articulating criticisms in a way that is not cruel. But scholars should be good at this." His response to criticisms of the philosophy department's faculty recruitment strategy suggests how he will proceed. "If you've got something that is the best in the world, you keep it that way. Our philosophy department is the best analytical philosophy department in the world. We are not going to mess with that. Now what else you do with it, that is the question to which I do not know the answer. But I do know this: it's not for me to answer that question. It is for me to cause that question to be answered."

At one of Sexton's many get-acquainted meetings, a group of NYU scientists wished him well. "We hope you succeed," they said. "No, no," he replied, "you've got it wrong. John cannot succeed. John can fail, but John cannot succeed. We will succeed, or John will fail. One or the other."

PART II

MANAGEMENT 101

5

The Dead Hand of Precedent

New York Law School

It was a perfect late summer morning in Manhattan, the third week of classes at New York Law School, when the catastrophe called September 11 happened.[1] September 11 stories are like JFK assassination stories—everyone remembers in the minutest detail where they were and what they were doing when they heard the news—but New York Law School (NYLS) has a specially potent storehouse of memories.[2]

The law school sits in the financial and legal heart of the city, less than half a mile from where the World Trade Center towers stood. In the days after the attacks, it became a place for firefighters and police officers to recover between shifts, as well as an outpost for CNN's round-the-clock coverage. For two weeks it was shuttered, and when it reopened, there wasn't even the illusion of normality. Train and subway service was hit-or-miss (there were regular station closings because of anthrax threats), and so were power and communications. Powdered glass and other debris from the fallen towers choked the air. Some students in the evening division did daytime duty as firefighters and cops; one of them lost thirty-four co-workers. Soldiers armed with machine guns demanded that anyone venturing into the downtown area show an ID, making it feel precisely like a war zone.

Immediately after the attacks, dean Richard Matasar went from one half-empty classroom to the next, bringing the grim news. Like an anxious parent, he stood at the doorway of 57 Worth Street, hugging beleaguered students and faculty as they straggled in for shelter; and before the communications network crashed, he worked the phones, trying to locate anyone who might have been trapped in the towers.

In the weeks that followed, the law school provided office space for homeless attorneys and community organizations, helped local retail stores handle their mounting debt problems, and pulled together a coalition of law schools to catalogue and coordinate responses from lawyers who wanted to make themselves useful. While the faculty decided to make up all the lost classes—that much would be business as usual—they ceased being sticklers about attendance and became grief counselors instead, wrapped up in their students' lives. Students were allowed to decide, after their final exams, whether to take those courses on a pass-fail basis, and many of them accepted the offer. The fateful tenure clock for junior faculty was stopped for the semester. Many people had a hard time concentrating on the humdrum of getting and giving a legal education. Why teach or study law in lawless times, people were asking themselves? And why, more pointedly, continue the sometimes Sisyphean task of reviving New York Law School?

Like Hugo Sonnenschein at the University of Chicago, John Brademas at NYU, and Bill Durden at Dickinson College, Rick Matasar had been recruited to turn around a troubled institution, a free-standing law school that badly needed an infusion of new ideas. By June 2001, the end of his first year, Matasar had the faculty dreaming about "the good life," contemplating everything from an honors program for talented students and affiliations with nearby universities to "the relentless projection of mission" and "a new, better name." September 11 made him a crisis manager, but since then this academic entrepreneur has again taken up the cause of turning NYLS into a place that stands out in New York City's fiercely competitive market for legal education.

The title of the dean's September 6, 2000, memo to the NYLS faculty and administrators was innocuous enough: "Setting the Agenda." But the tone of the message, written just two months after Matasar formally took over the job, was bracing.

"Who or what is New York Law School?" the memo begins—a fair question, since almost everyone confuses the school with its infinitely better known and more successful neighbor, NYU Law School. Though it's just a chip shot from the city's courts and an easy walk to the offices of the nation's top corporate law firms, only a handful of the judges in those courts or the partners in those law firms are NYLS alumni. There are a number of nationally known scholars on the faculty, but the students are another story. Because tuition is the school's main source of revenue, there are lots of students—about 1,400—and the bottom quarter of the class is an embarrassment. At the time Matasar arrived, more than a third of the graduates were flunking the bar exam, the worst record in the state, and so couldn't practice the trade for which they had ostensibly been trained. If things were going to improve, he wrote to the faculty, NYLS had to "find a mission, proclaim it to the world, and succeed in taking a special place in the education market."

Though still in his forties, Rick Matasar was no novice at motivating law professors. He had been law school dean at Chicago-Kent and, later, the University of Florida, and at both places he was an ardent innovator. At Chicago-Kent, he initiated "majors" in environmental law and dispute resolution, a rarity in law schools, and implemented the first "E-law" section in the nation. At the University of Florida, he opened the Legal Technology Institute, which links the law school with lawyers and judges. "We talk the talk at law schools," he said at the time. "Now, we really walk the walk. We're going to have the resources of the law school linked directly to people who are practicing law."

Less than three years into his deanship at Florida, though, he was pushed out in a brouhaha over the naming of the law school after a flamboyant litigator, Frederic Levin, who secured that honor by making the largest contribution in the university's history. But when alumni criticized the decision, some citing Levin's controversial record and others because of thinly veiled anti-Semitism, the university's president backpedaled. Matasar resigned, a principled act that won him the admiration of law school deans elsewhere—and also left him looking for work.

Chicago-Kent has a solid reputation, especially in environmental law, and Florida is ranked in the top fifty schools nationwide in the *U.S. News & World Report* rankings that law schools and prospective law students treat as holy writ. In coming to New York Law School, which was then ranked in the fourth—the bottom—tier by *U.S. News,* Matasar was taking a huge downward step.

▪ The Dead Hand of *Stare Decisis*

"There are only two things wrong with conventional legal teaching," Yale law professor Fred Rodell famously quipped. "One is style and the other is content."[3]

The training of lawyers has changed startlingly little in the century and a quarter since Christopher Langdell began to use the case method instead of the lecture at Harvard. From Professor Langdell to *The Paper Chase* to today: walk into any first-year law school classroom and you're still likely to find a would-be Socrates presiding. The subjects of study aren't very

different either, even though the courses that constitute the first-year curriculum—property, torts, contracts, and the like—mask the blurring of
these once distinct fields. Lip service, but little real attention, is paid to
legal writing, oral argument, or clinical practice. There is also scant encouragement for students to specialize in sub-fields like tax law or intellectual property. Despite repeated urgings to tailor legal training for different kinds of law jobs—"Pericles and plumbers, lawyer statesmen and
legal scriveners"—the curriculum remains one-size-fits-all.[4] Especially in
schools that see themselves as elite institutions, many professors emphasize
theory, legal and otherwise, not useful skills. So, as Stanford law professor
Deborah Rhode notes, "today's law students can graduate well versed in
postmodern literary theory but ill equipped to draft a document. They
may have learned to 'think like a lawyer' but not how to make a living at
it."[5] Over the years a library shelf's worth of reports prepared by blue-rib-
bon panels, urging reforms in legal education, has gone largely ignored.

The power that, in law, the past exerts over the present is one reason for
this ossification, says Gerald Korngold, dean of Case–Western Reserve
Law School, who has known Rick Matasar since their Pennsylvania Law
School days in the early 1970s. *Stare decisis* isn't just a technique for deciding cases; it's also how legal education is constructed, and this imposes a
heavy burden on reformers. Whenever a change is proposed, says Korngold, the instinctive faculty reaction is to ask, "How was this handled before?" Don Gifford, formerly dean at West Virginia and Maryland law
schools, offers a harsher explanation. "There's no institution in the world
more status driven and hierarchy driven than law schools. My first teaching job was at Toledo. At AALS [Association of American Law Schools]
meetings, people who read my name tag and saw 'Toledo' there would
look down at my feet. When I moved to Florida, these same people were
trying to establish eye contact." Most law professors, Gifford points out,
are graduates of top-ranked law schools. "They think it's a mistake that
they wound up at a place like Toledo and want desperately to get back to
the top," so they "put as little work as they can into teaching and focus on
writing theoretical articles that Yale and Harvard [law reviews] will publish. 'Do unto them as was done unto you' is really a way to minimize your
workload, and so doesn't slow your rise in the academic hierarchy."

The American Bar Association, which accredits law schools, and so plays
the critical role of deciding who can enter the legal guild, vigorously de-
fends the status quo. The ABA "substitutes detailed regulation of educational inputs—such as facilities, resources, and faculty-student contact—

for more direct measurement of educational outputs," writes Deborah Rhode, who adds that there's no reason to believe that "these variables relate to, say, malpractice among graduates."[6] The ABA's stand-pat attitude is reflected in its response to distance learning. Even before Concord Law School, which offers all its classes on-line, was up and running, the ABA declared that it would never accredit such a program.[7]

The rating system used by *U.S. News & World Report* reinforces this traditionalism by discounting public service and diversity; and because reputation is a major factor in calculating a school's ranking, law schools are encouraged to puff themselves while denigrating the competition.[8] The losers are schools that break the mold, like the City University of New York Law School, which concentrates on training public interest lawyers, and recruits poor and minority students, including those with weak LSAT scores.

A law school's reputation endures, seemingly forever. During the past century, the only major changes in the pecking order have been the rise to prominence of California's law schools and the more recent ascent of NYU Law School into the uppermost ranks. The NYU story, recounted in Chapter 4, shows that innovation can pay off. There, John Sexton (who in 2002 became the president of the university) recruited scholars in a wide array of fields and expanded the international reach of the school, which now bills itself as the "global law school." But often the list of deans willing to break the mold has begun and ended with John Sexton and Rick Matasar.

The practice of law has changed dramatically in a single generation with the advent of new kinds of institutions—law firms that specialize in fields like cyber-law, mega-firms with branches in a dozen cities—that deliver a wide array of services to a clientele that pays more attention now to the bottom line. Will these market forces intrude upon the fortress of legal education? The ways in which three very different law schools responded to the leadership of an innovative entrepreneur offer insights into that pivotal question.

▪ Reality Bites: Chicago-Kent

Although Rick Matasar is disarmingly mild-mannered in person, in print he loves to shock. In "A Commercialist Manifesto," published in the *Florida Law Review*, he confronts the fear of academics that the hunt for money will corrupt legal education, that commercialism will crawl into our courses, taint our teaching, distort our research, and tarnish our mission." Get over it, he writes. "Commercialism is here, now, and it is not going away." Learn to embrace it. "We are a business, deal with it. . . . Go to the market and create greatness."[9]

This wasn't the kind of dean Chicago-Kent Law School believed it was hiring. "We'd had an entrepreneur; we thought we'd found a straight academic guy," says Dan Tarlock, a nationally known environmental lawyer who chaired the search committee that recruited Matasar in 1991. Until then, Matasar's career had followed the standard trajectory: law review editor at the University of Pennsylvania; a clerkship with a federal appeals court judge; a stint at Arnold & Porter, one of Washington's foremost power firms; a professorship at the mainstream University of Iowa Law School. When Tarlock called him, Matasar had been associate dean at Iowa for three years, with responsibility, as Iowa's dean William Hines puts it, "for the care and feeding of the faculty."

"I was surprised that he took the Kent job," says Hines. "He still had a lot of maturing to do. It's like a high school basketball player jumping straight to the NBA." At age thirty-eight, Matasar was one of the youngest deans in the country, though his untamed mustache made him look a bit older. Chicago-Kent, Hines adds, was "such an alien environment after Iowa, almost a for-profit school with an endless stream of problems. For Rick, it was like going to a foreign continent." It was at Kent that Matasar—learning from, sometimes struggling with, one of legal education's most successful entrepreneurs—discovered his calling.

When it was founded at the turn of the twentieth century, Kent Law School opened the door of legal education to immigrants, minorities, and women (it was one of the first schools to graduate an African American woman). But over the years, as competitors emerged, its importance diminished. The school endured as a threadbare operation with no scholarly pretensions, and its mainly part-time faculty offered night classes to just about anyone who cared to enroll.

In the mid-1960s, Kent was acquired by the Illinois Institute of Technology (IIT), an odd coupling of cultures—engineering and law. Its prospects began to brighten in 1973, when a young attorney named Lew Collens was named dean. "I wanted to find distinctiveness," says Collens, "and so we developed legal writing as a specialty, something no place else was doing, and a strong clinical program. I also wanted to build a scholarly faculty. When Dan Tarlock arrived, we got instant credibility." The dean didn't want prima donnas but rather "people committed to building the institution." Meanwhile, he raised the money for a ten-story tower, wired with forty miles of conduit to take advantage of Chicago-Kent's pioneering efforts in high-tech legal education.

In 1988, Matasar replaced Collens, who became president of IIT. "Rick was very good at picking up on core ideas and driving them forward," says Stuart Deutsch, who taught at Chicago-Kent for twenty-seven years before becoming dean at Rutgers-Newark. "He supported professors' doing what they wanted to do." When Martin Malin proposed an Institute on Labor and Employment Law, Matasar worked hard to get it off the ground. The institute boosts the law school's reputation by providing a legal Switzerland, a place where attorneys on both sides of the labor-management divide can come together—and, not incidentally, their membership in the institute helps to pay the bills.

Matasar bolstered the school's writing program and launched "majors" in subjects ranging from environmental law to dispute resolution, ideas that, though commonplace elsewhere in higher education, remain novelties in the insular world of law schools. And he built on the school's early high-tech initiatives—in the 1980s it was the first to experiment with Lexis, now an essential on-line research tool—to create "electronic law students" who came to class with electronic casebooks, complete with outlining capability and hypertext links.

One of the innovations that Matasar inherited, a fee-generating legal clinic, is anathema in law school circles. Instead of handling indigents' cases in the clinical education program, as law schools usually do, NYLS requires its clients to pay for legal help. Their fees largely cover the clinical professors' salaries, and the more money a lawyer brings in, the higher his or her salary. Clinical professors elsewhere blanch at what they regard as the intrusion of commercialism, and they have a point. When a law school clinic has to pay its own way, interesting cases get passed over for reasons that have nothing to do with pedagogy; educating students takes time, and so potentially conflicts with making money. And because paying clients are likely to want real lawyers to represent them, not trainees, law students may find themselves doing more scut work than law work. What matters most, a fee-generating clinic cannot entirely focus on promoting justice, the hallmark of clinical legal education. In response to such criticism, Matasar could have pointed out that the Kent clinic isn't solely money driven, that it does a fair amount of pro bono work and high-profile cases, including a landmark case challenging the patenting of genes. Instead, he gave the back of his hand to the critics, reminding them of the financial facts of life—or, as he put it, "Reality bites."

The role of underdog battling the legal establishment appeals to Matasar, who took on the American Bar Association accreditors and then wrote an article nicely calculated to shock. "How will we respond to distance learning," he asked, "where a professor at the Chicago-Kent home studio teaches to Chicago-Kent's southern campus in Springfield—or, better yet, where Chicago-Kent's dean teaches at our Miami campus and beams back to home? How will accreditors react to the school that tries to reduce a student's costs by offering a two-year J.D. degree? . . . What will happen to the school that uses computer exercises to teach hundreds in a class that a faculty member meets only once a week? . . . What will happen to a school that grows a large commercial law firm to pay its bills?"[10] If legal heretics were burned at the stake, Matasar would be toast.

One of the lessons Rick Matasar learned at Chicago-Kent is that enhancing a school's reputation is a big part of a dean's job. "I was the first to step up the PR wars among law school deans," he says. Chicago-Kent had already been cited by *U.S. News & World Report* as one of the country's "up-and-coming" schools, but Matasar wasn't satisfied. Since those rankings depend heavily on the appraisals of law school deans and leading practitioners, he did just what Hollywood studios with Oscar hopefuls do when they want to influence the judges: he sent reams of material to those who would participate in the survey, on the theory that "if they know what we're doing, they'll rank us higher." The strategy worked: Kent's environmental law and international programs were named among the nation's ten best. "Rick Matasar's legacy," says Tarlock in an admiring way, "is packaging and marketing."

Because of their high student-faculty ratios, law schools are often treated as moneymaking machines by their universities, and Chicago-Kent was no exception. Collens had fought hard for the school when he was dean, but as president he was presiding over a university whose engineering program was hemorrhaging money. Inevitably, he and Matasar found themselves at loggerheads over what proportion of its revenue the law school had to turn over to the university. When the offer from Florida came, the dean didn't hesitate.

Some of the initiatives that surfaced during Matasar's tenure—a law and business center, a plan to enroll college students for a "third year in Chicago"—were stillborn. Others, like the intellectual property program, had more sizzle than substance. Still others, like an "E-learn section," have since been discarded. "It's hard enough to get students to read a paragraph together in class, too cumbersome for them to jump around," notes Tarlock. "Besides, they're using computers to screw around in class."

One longtime Kent professor complains that Matasar seized upon "one harebrained scheme after another. He didn't think through an idea to see if it was solidly based." Everywhere he has gone, critics have made this same point. Yet trying out lots of ideas with the expectation that some will inevitably fail is precisely Matasar's strategy. Despite their personal disagreements, IIT president Collens remains impressed by Matasar's talents. The specific programs he initiated "matter less than his approach," says Collens. "He comes at things from a different angle; he doesn't see the world the same way that others do. Those are the kinds of people who will solve problems."

▪ "The Energizer Bunny": University of Florida

On September 7, 1996, barely two months after taking over as dean of the University of Florida Law School, Rick Matasar sent a single-spaced, thirty-one page memo to the faculty. That memo carried the same title, "Setting the Agenda," as the one he would later prepare at New York Law School, and its message was similarly blunt: "The law school has reached a point of stagnation. . . . [I]t is not planning for the future. Florida tells the world: (1) we are big; (2) we are old; (3) we are cheap; and (4) we have an excellent tax program." There was a "collective [faculty] gasp," Matasar recalls. Longtime faculty member Jeff Harrison, a vocal critic, says that many of his colleagues read the memo as saying, "This is how bad you are; I will make you a better place." That just isn't how things are done in Gainesville.

From the start, Rick Matasar and the University of Florida Law School were badly mismatched: the dean was an innovator, but the law school wasn't really interested in innovating. The University of Florida is the prototypical big fish in a modest-sized pond, *the* place to go for anyone who plans on practicing law in the Sunshine State. Gator pride, bordering on fetishism, is everywhere; many of the senior partners in the state's leading law firms are alumni, and so are many state court judges and legislators. "We're the Goliath in Florida," Harrison puts it, "but without ambition." Florida also has a reputation for devouring its deans—four in twenty years. "If he came to the law school, God would receive nasty e-mails," say George Dawson, the associate dean during Matasar's tenure.

Amid such torpor, it is remarkable that Matasar was able to accomplish anything. "Rick's response to proposals by members of the faculty and staff is: 'That's a great idea, let's try it. Have you thought about . . . ?'" says tax professor David Richardson, one of his staunch backers. "There follow a series of suggestions about how the proposed project might be strengthened. . . . These, in turn, are followed by e-mail messages, telephone calls, and faculty lounge discussion in which he asks how the project is going, once more asks whether he can help, and shares the ideas he has had since the last encounter with him. He's the Energizer bunny."

When Richardson proposed a weekly *Evening News with Jim Lehrer*-style TV show for tax professionals, the dean leaped at the prospect. He extracted $200,000 from his old contacts at LexisNexis, the on-line research service, then met with the assistant secretary of the treasury and the head of the IRS, securing a $750,000 grant. For the deal to work, though, the university had to commit itself to matching that grant. Matasar calculated that subscription income from the tax professionals would cover most of the costs, but the risk was too great for the university and the idea died.

Lawyers at the powerhouse firm of Holland & Knight, many of them old Gators, came to Matasar with the notion of developing closer ties with the law school. Again, the dean moved quickly, launching the Holland & Knight Institute, designed to bring law professors into the firm to hone their practical skills as well as importing experienced lawyers into the classroom. Although the dean insisted that similar agreements could be struck with other law firms, some faculty members feared giving a single law firm too much sway in the law school. Like many of Matasar's initiatives, this plan combines a worthy professional goal—in this instance, closing the gap between academics and professionals—with the generation of revenue. Not only would the law firm contribute substantially to the law school's modest endowment, Matasar believed, but it could also capture for the school some of the fees that law professors earn through consulting. Few faculty members were interested, however, and with the dean's departure, the institute vanished.

Matasar had much more success with his technology projects. In partnership with a nationally recognized electronics engineer, he launched the Legal Technology Institute, which consults with law firms and courts, earning substantial revenues and generating good publicity for the law school because of its outreach. He started centers on race relations and intellectual property. He persuaded his colleagues to give some coherence to a diffuse curriculum by developing specialty areas; as a result, Florida now offers certificate programs in tax law, environmental law, and international law. Service to those least well off was also on his agenda, as long as money could be found. He obtained a grant for Gator Team Child, a training program for law students interested in children's rights issues. "There was no sense of stopping or consolidating," associate dean Dawson marvels. "There was always something new on the horizon—lots of activity, pointed in every direction at once."

All these initiatives took money, of which the law school, underfinanced by the state and unable to raise tuition to competitive levels, was in perpetually short supply. Together with development director Jeffrey Ulmer, Matasar hit the road, talking to alumni across the state. "We spent hours in the car, and most of the time we were laughing," Ulmer recalls. "We'd combine the names of donor prospects to make the most ridiculous-sounding name of a law school—the Booter Stumpy Chumpy Law Center—laughing about the absurdity of the business we were in." The dean got the job done. In the eighty-seven years before Matasar's arrival, the law school's endowment had reached just $17 million. During his three-year tenure, the endowment more than tripled to $60 million.

Ironically, the largest of those gifts led directly to his ouster. The Pensacola trial attorney Fred Levin, a Florida alumnus, had masterminded the state's litigation against the tobacco companies, and when those companies settled for $13 billion, his share of the legal fees amounted to a cool $275 million. Some years earlier, Levin had contributed $1 million to fund a chair at the law school. Now, Ulmer and Matasar came to him with a bigger proposal: Make a $6 million gift and we'll name our new building for you. With a $10 million gift, Matasar added, almost as an afterthought, it might be possible to name the school for him.

Levin jumped at the chance. "I said to myself, 'What an opportunity,'" he recalls. "I've got a couple of boats, a plane. I do what I want to do. My kids are both lawyers. I mulled the idea over for about ten minutes. That Fredric G. Levin Law School will be there long after I'm gone." The litigator also had a baser motive: to hit back at Florida's legal establishment for persecuting him because he was an outsider. Twelve years earlier, he'd gotten into trouble for his unrepentant acknowledgment that he bet on football games. "You should worry about lawyers who laugh about their clients who get convicted for murder or lawyers under indictment for the theft of their clients' money," he said defiantly. "Not about gambling." For that cheekiness, he was reprimanded for bringing the Florida bar into disrepute. Later, in his closing arguments in two separate lawsuits, he referred to the defense as "ridiculous." Although neither defense attorney objected, the Florida Bar Association did, claiming that it was unethical to express a personal opinion in court. This time, Levin, facing disbarment, brought in the heavy hitters, among them the chair of the American Bar Association's grievance committee, to testify that the Florida bar's objections were unprecedented and baseless.

Although Levin won that round, he remained embittered. "All my life, I did nothing but practice law," he says. "This was my opportunity for payback." While he was talking things over with his family and law partners, Matasar and Ulmer were on the phone with the university's development director, who discussed the proposal with Florida president John Lombardi. In a matter of hours, Lombardi gave his go-ahead. That same day, Levin wired $10 million to the university's bank account, the largest single donation in the university's history; and since the state matched private donations, the gift netted the law school $20 million.

The dean was ecstatic, but some alumni were livid. An inch-thick pile of angry letters landed on Matasar's desk. "Your stealthy and thoughtless sale of our college name for money to a lawyer . . . whose 'credentials' relate mostly to money, is a bitter irony," wrote a prominent Jacksonville lawyer. The correspondence contained more than a whiff of anti-Semitism, says Steven Uhlfelder, a student activist turned lawyer who chaired the state's Board of Regents. "'Only find WASPs with money'—is that the rule? Or do we only take money from saints? What about the racists whose names grace other campus buildings: Is anyone protesting that?"

Even as others in the Florida legal establishment, among them revered former American Bar Association president Chesterfield Smith, came to Matasar's defense, Lombardi decided to backtrack. Despite reports from a number of people with intimate knowledge of the negotiations, the president began to deny that he'd signed off on Levin's gift.

Lombardi and provost Betty Capaldi had previously clashed with Matasar over how well "The Bank," the university's scheme for rewarding productive campus units, which had been designed with the needs of liberal arts education in mind, meshed with law school reality. A few months earlier, the deans of the North Carolina and Texas law schools, invited by the Board of Regents to appraise Florida's law school, questioned Lombardi about whether the formula used by "The Bank" was appropriate for the law school. The president became choleric, cursing out the deans and accusing them of being shills for the law school.

The firestorm over Levin's gift was a convenient excuse to get rid of

Matasar. "You're not a team player," Capaldi brusquely informed him. "We want to move in another direction." Resign or be fired, he was told, and Matasar opted for the less confrontational path. What followed was a second firestorm, this time directed at the campus administration. All but four members of the law school faculty signed a protest letter to Lombardi, and when a former state supreme court justice who chaired the law school's board of trustees delivered a stinging public rebuke to the president, he won an ovation from his fellow trustees and the faculty. Lombardi was already in trouble with the state's Board of Regents—he'd derided the African-American chancellor of the state university system as an "Oreo"— and when his verbal assault on the two outside deans became public, the regents fired him. It was too late, though, to save Matasar.

"A scar on the history of the University of Florida" is how Steven Uhlfelder describes the episode. Even after his ouster, Matasar still had the interests of the law school at heart. He responded to every letter he received and met with many of the irate alumni. In the fraternity of law school deans, Iowa's Bill Hines notes, "Rick is a hero. He fell on his sword."

Matasar had been fired for being too rigorous a defender of the law school's interests in the campus wars—and fired as well for being too successful an entrepreneur.

■ "If You Can Make It There . . .": New York Law School

New York Law School's history parallels Chicago-Kent's. When it was founded by renegades from Columbia Law School in 1891, NYLS had a clear mission: to use traditional legal lecture-style pedagogy, not Christopher Langdell's "case method," and to deliver a solid legal education to first-generation Americans. The school's catalogue boasts that Woodrow Wilson and Charles Evans Hughes once taught there, but over time it lost its distinctive character and became preoccupied with paying the bills. By the early 1970s, it was in such bad shape that it risked losing its American Bar Association accreditation. But at NYLS, as at Chicago-Kent, adept deans were able to recruit talented faculty members and revive the reputation of the school.

In 1990, Harry Wellington, who had been the dean at Yale Law School, was persuaded to take over at NYLS. For a school with a deep-rooted inferiority complex, the appointment was taken as a sign that it had attained respectability. But Wellington never devoted much effort to institution building—"I'm not an entrepreneur," he says flatly—and as a result, the school's fortunes declined as it fell in short order from second, to third, then to fourth tier, the lowest in the *U.S. News & World Report* rankings.

The NYLS faculty, unlike their counterparts at the University of Florida, appreciated that their school was in real trouble. That's why they selected Matasar. "We had a collective action problem," says corporate law professor David Schoenbrod. "Rick was the solution." No one imagined that the school was competing for students with Columbia or NYU, or even Fordham, but Matasar's memo revealed how bad things really were. In head-to-head competition, NYLS was losing out, by ratios of twelve-to-one, to schools like St. John's and Cardozo, which the faculty regarded as inferior. Its job placement rate had plummeted—at 70 percent, it was the worst among accredited schools in the country—and so had the percentage of its graduates who passed the bar exam. "When Rick distributed that data," says Arthur Leonard, a leading scholar on homosexuality and the law, "he made us confront reality."

Soon after sending out his incendiary memo, Matasar brought the faculty together for a day-long retreat. There, and in several weekend sessions during the following winter and spring, he encouraged professors to engage in pie-in-the-sky thinking. The topics on the table ranged from revamping the curriculum to improving how NYLS treated its "customers," the students. Faculty developed what in management jargon is called a SWOT (strength, weaknesses, opportunities, threats) analysis. Out of these conversations, Matasar hoped there would emerge a new understanding of what the place stood for—a new "legend," he called it.

Beneath their habitually cynical professorial veneer, there are lots of altruists teaching at NYLS. "Everyone shouldn't be sitting around the campfire singing 'Kumbaya,'" Matasar says, "but you can't have a faculty where most people operate as independent contractors." The faculty's ideas largely paralleled the dean's, but it was the professors who gave them substance. "It's like a herd of cattle going, without really knowing it, into a funnel," David Schoenbrod admiringly observes. "We let ourselves be directed."

The meetings, says labor law professor Seth Harris, "enrolled people who hadn't been persuaded about the breadth of the enterprise they were going to be engaged in." And while Matasar's approach had struck some at Chicago-Kent and Florida as crass—"something for Wal-Mart managers," as Florida's Jeff Harrison acidly puts it—it didn't disturb anyone at New York Law School. Perhaps that's because, as Schoenbrod says, "it's clear that he has his academic priorities intact. The market language is a trope, a way to get insiders to analyze what they're doing and a way to communicate with donors. But the substance—the improvement—will be real."

"Rick can speak scholar and speak teacher and speak manager," says Harris, who had been through two similar mission-shaping experiences during a Clinton-era stint at the Labor Department. "He can speak 'cross-culturally,' translating management language into teacher-scholar language."[11] Although Harris's tenure prospects depend mainly on his scholarship and teaching, he became deeply involved in community building, even developing a new certificate program in labor law. "This is my home. I want it to improve," he says. "It's like buying NYLS stock at 10 in the hope that the stock will rise. Besides, I'm still an altruist: I want the school to turn out better students, and for those students to improve society."

The search for better students drives many of the school's initiatives. Competition can get ugly: Rutgers has contacted NYLS students who live in New Jersey, encouraging them to switch schools, associate dean Jethro Lieberman reports, and several rival schools have fudged their students' LSAT scores to make themselves look better in the *U.S. News* rankings. Rather than resorting to such dirty tricks, Matasar relies on attention-getting innovations. An honors program entices top-ranking applicants—students who wouldn't otherwise consider enrolling in NYLS—with merit scholarships as well as perks like summer clerkships, research opportunities, and a guaranteed place on the law review. "It's a loss leader," says public affairs dean Alata Levet, "to improve the academic culture." The Justice Action Center, headed by ACLU president Nadine Strossen, is aimed at reformist-minded students, and a Media Law Center is pitched at those interested in intellectual property law.

Breaking with law school convention, NYLS decided to admit fifty students, mainly adults embarking on new careers, who hadn't taken the LSAT. (The dean wanted to eliminate the LSAT requirement entirely, but the faculty and the American Bar Association accreditors turned him down. The ABA has insisted that these specially admitted students take the test during their first year.) Meanwhile, students in the bottom quarter of the class are channeled into bread-and-butter courses, and the weakest are required to stay on for an extra semester of bar exam–oriented classes— what Matasar calls the "glorious exit." Other new ventures, including an on-line course in mental health law, master's programs in taxation and media studies, a labor law certification program, and joint ventures with nearby universities, are designed to deliver high-quality legal education while filling a niche and promoting the school "brand." They reflect, too, the dean's unflagging enthusiasm for the new. Michael Botein, who for a quarter-century has run the school's media center, recalls that when Matasar asked him what he would like to do, he pulled out all the proposals that had languished during the deanship of Harry Wellington. "I expected him to get back to me in a week or two, saying, 'I like this one.' Instead he e-mailed me the next day: 'I like them all!'"

If things had gone according to plan, the dreaming and brainstorming would have segued into the hard work of implementation in the fall of 2001. But September 11 pushed everything back. "There's a window of opportunity," Wellington points out. "Five years from now, the faculty will look back and say, 'why am I doing this work?' What's happening now is a high-wire act. I can't think of anyone else [other than Matasar] who can do it." Art Leonard agrees that "it's not easy being a faculty member at a Rick Matasar–run law school," because he constantly pushes professors to reconsider what they, and the school, are doing. But to Randolph Jonakait, a longtime NYLS professor and the inside candidate for the dean's job before Matasar was hired, it's mostly sound and fury. "Rick throws out a thousand ideas," he says, echoing a criticism heard at both Chicago-Kent and Florida, "but he doesn't follow up on them, doesn't think things through. There's no foundation, no way for ideas to be accomplished."

While Wellington was admired by many faculty members for nurturing their scholarly aspirations, he was otherwise largely invisible. "The joke," several students say, "was that we'd see him twice—when we showed up and when we graduated." By contrast, Matasar is omnipresent. He answers his e-mail promptly and keeps his office door open. At regular "town meetings" he pitches the message that the school is improving, while letting students know that he believes in tougher admissions standards. "If you're one of those students who's not making it, you have to step up to the plate."

To the outside world as well, Matasar sells the image of a school that's on the rise. "It's like building a building while you're designing it," marvels trusts and estates professor William LaPiana. "We're putting out the propaganda while we're trying to make it work." But will anyone notice? Skeptical Randy Jonakait recalls a dinner with a senior partner at a Wall Street firm whose knowledge of the New York law schools began with Columbia and ended with NYU. "The pecking order in New York is pretty fixed," he says. Matasar has a different take. "If all we care about is our ranking," he told his colleagues, "we'd better stop our conversation now. There's only so much we can do to change the pecking order. But we can create a niche outside the hierarchy, as the place where you do cool things."

Acts of creation require money—for the research centers, the honors program, the on-line courses, and all the other ideas that have been bruited about. A new building is critical, the dean says, noting that the lack of dormitory space has discouraged applicants. "If we don't build it, they won't come." Yet what had been the law school's biggest tangible asset, its location at the heart of the legal and financial world, turned into a question mark after the attacks on the World Trade Center towers. The uncertain future of the area made investors nervous, putting a hold on a $200 million project that combines new classrooms, a bigger library, and student dorms with rental apartments.

Still, New York Law School seems to have become a livelier, and a better, place. Despite the depressed economy, alumni gave more money in 2002 than ever before. More than 93 percent of the class of 2001 got jobs, and the pass rate on the bar exam crept to within hailing distance of the statewide average. That same year, a 25 percent increase in applications permitted the school to be more selective, and an unprecedented proportion of the best applicants actually enrolled. *U.S. News* has taken note, lifting New York Law School to the third tier in its rankings.

On April 3, 2002, NYLS canceled regular classes for Faculty Presentation Day, the first such event in the school's history. Some faculty members worried that they would face empty lecture rooms, but more than a quarter of the students came to hear their professors discuss their work in progress. In a school where the students' anti-intellectualism has been a persistent concern, professors were sharing the stage with their students, and students were presenting their own work alongside their professors. "This was an 'Aha!' moment," says the dean.

New York Law School and Rick Matasar seem well matched. Unlike Florida, where anything new was viewed dubiously, NYLS appreciates that an entrepreneurship that defies the conventions of legal education isn't necessarily antithetical to academic excellence. "For whatever hucksterism portion of me that exists," Matasar says—then adds, with a grin, "and that's a lot"—"this is the bottom line: Making the world a better place through law. This capacity to look for ideas, to find contingently right answers—that's what the money goes to support. That's the best thing about all of us."

6

Kafka Was an Optimist
The University of Southern California
and the University of Michigan

Entrepreneurship is not the only idea that institutions of higher learning have imported from the business world. Ever since the flow of public money began to slow in the 1970s, universities have been searching for ways to run more efficiently. To a new generation of administrators, veterans of government streamlining and corporate downsizing, schooled in business practice, it was fatuous to imagine that universities could carry on as organized anarchies.[1] "Education is an investment," as Governor O. T. Early says in Jane Smiley's novel *Moo*. "The trouble is, [universities] don't run it like an investment over there . . . they run it like welfare."[2]

These managers looked to government and business for better models. All the budget nostrums of the 1970s and 1980s eventually found their way into higher education: PPBS (planning, programming, budgeting systems), ZBB (zero-base budgeting), MBO (management by objectives), the "balanced scorecard," strategic planning, benchmarking, TQM (total quality management), outsourcing to emphasize "core competencies." Quantitative measures carried the promise of objectivity, a clear advance over experience and intuition, seat-of-the-pants decision making. Numbers could be crunched, says Robert Birnbaum in *Management Fads in Higher Education,* a stinging critique of what he calls this "bestiary," and greater efficiency extracted.[3]

The administrators who implemented these schemes made grandiose claims—for instance, hailing "management by objectives" as "the single most successful concept ever to have been picked up and put into practice in all of management history."[4] Nearly a century earlier, in a rascally tract titled *Microcosmograph Academica, Being a Guide for the Young Academic Politician,* F. M. Cornford captured this breed of academic: "Perhaps, you may prefer to qualify as a *Good Business Man*. He is one whose mind has not been warped and narrowed by merely intellectual interests, and who,

110

at the same time, has not those odious pushing qualities which are unhappily required for making a figure in business anywhere else."[5] Because universities evolve slowly, those nostrums were often being promoted on campuses just when they were being phased out in corporations and government agencies. In higher education, the borrowed strategies mainly failed for very simple reasons: universities aren't like widget-making firms or the post office, and "organizational strategies cannot be created by the logic used to assemble automobiles."[6]

The allure—the cult—of efficiency has been a staple of higher education. In 1908, the Carnegie Foundation for the Advancement of Teaching dispatched Morris Cooke, a businessman versed in the then new principles of "scientific management," to study American universities. Cooke was aghast at what he saw. "There are very few, if any, of the broader principles of management which obtain generally in the commercial field which are not, more or less, applicable in the college field, and as far as was discovered, no one of them is now generally observed." Academic autonomy, Cooke argued, echoing present-day calls for accountability, was a license for irresponsibility.[7] The main objections to this approach also carry a familiar ring. Writing in 1917, Thorstein Veblen assailed the tendency to turn the university into "a corporation of learning" that would "set [its] affairs in order after the pattern of a well-conducted business concern. . . . The intrusion of business principles into the universities goes to weaken and retard the pursuit of learning, and therefore to defeat the ends for which a university is maintained."[8]

Both "outsourcing" and "revenue center management" exemplify the attempt to introduce management principles into higher education. When applied intelligently, as aids to analysis, both techniques have their uses. But problems arise when proponents forget that they are talking in metaphors and start to believe they are *really* running a business.[9]

▪ Outsourcing: From the Dining Hall to the School "Brand"

"It is a good principle of educational administration," declared University of Chicago president Robert Maynard Hutchins in 1936, "that a college or university should do nothing that any other agency can do as well. This is a good principle because a college or university has a vast and complicated job even if it does only what it can do."[10] Hutchins's postulate has since become familiar practice as universities increasingly rely on outside firms to run the non-academic side of the institution.[11] That is often a smart move: Why, after all, should a university operate its own print shop? But the line blurs between what is "academic" and what isn't. This is where trouble lurks. If schools aren't careful, they'll wind up sloughing off not just the print shop but the very things that define a university.

Whether the practice is called outsourcing, contracting out, or privatizing, the impact is the same. Food services, health care, the bookstore, computer services, maintenance, financial management, security, Web design, student housing, "event management," campus cleanup, vending, budgeting: a seemingly endless array of activities that universities used to manage is now being handled by others. A 1995 directory lists over two thousand companies offering more than a hundred services. A 2001 survey prepared by an organization called the Center for the Study of Outsourcing and Privatization in Higher Education (the need for such a center is itself telling) reports that one university in eight relies on an HMO to provide health care, 40 percent of college bookstores are operated by companies such as Barnes and Noble, and more than 60 percent of dining halls are run by firms such as Marriott. Nearly half the schools surveyed contracted out at least five services, and those numbers keep climbing, while fewer than 5 percent say they do everything themselves.[12]

In order to promote their "core competencies," corporations hire catering firms and security companies, and pharmaceutical houses look to universities to conduct some of their research; in order to "reinvent government," cities contract with trash disposal companies.[13] Why shouldn't universities behave similarly, relying on firms to handle the mini-businesses of the institution? Books will be cheaper, the food will be more tasty, the campus grounds will be better maintained. That's the magic of the market.

When critics object to the evils of such "creeping corporatization," they are sometimes indulging in nostalgia. Despite the hand-wringing about the demise of the dining commons and the college bookstore, and their replacement by national chains, the locally run bookstore was often creakily inefficient and the venerable campus dining hall that featured "mystery meat" menus was frequently indifferent to students' wishes. Imagine the dining hall manager of yesteryear offering a money-back guarantee of satisfaction, as one company now does.

Still, the critics have a valid point. Companies aren't necessarily attentive to the quirkiness of campus culture. Sometimes, as with the University of Pennsylvania's failed experiment in contracting out building maintenance, the firm cannot do the job. Bookstore chains and HMOs go bankrupt, leaving schools in the lurch; and private firms provide less job security for their employees.[14]

What is more important, analogies between higher education and the private sector or government shouldn't be pushed too far. A university isn't the same kind of enterprise as Dell, the world's leading manufacturer of personal computers, which relies on outside contractors to supply all the components. If the university is meant to be an academic community, not just a firm, then teaching, learning, and research have to remain the responsibility of its members.

Presaging the push for outsourcing, a Carnegie Commission report published in 1973 recommended that academic institutions divest themselves of their peripheral activities.[15] But the commission didn't regard privatization as simply a money-saving device; it was supposed to enable universities to pay more attention to their educational mission. Now the mission itself is in danger of being outsourced. Today it's the dining hall and campus maintenance, tomorrow it's student recruiting and the library, the day after that it's teaching. Down the road, the very identity of the school—its "brand"—may well be defined by outsiders.

The matching of students and colleges, increasingly the province of private firms, exemplifies the problem with contracting out. If you take a close look at universities' viewbooks, the promotional material designed to recruit students, most places appear to be the same. We know to a certainty that there are real differences in undergraduate life at the University of Oregon and Reed College, or at Ohio State and Dennison, yet in the viewbook world all of them are depicted as pastoral retreats from the bustling world. With a handful of consulting firms producing these materials, mimicking one another's product, it's no wonder that the products are so much alike. Only the bravest consultant is willing to emphasize the hard work of learning, as at the University of Chicago, for fear of scaring away prospective applicants.

Bottom-feeding private colleges desperate to fill classroom seats hire companies to run their entire recruiting and admissions operation. Sometimes these outfits resort to cold-calling likely prospects, selling the college like penny stocks. An outfit called D. H. Dagley Associates, founded in 1974, operates as the admissions office, recruiting and admitting students to forty-six schools. In many cases, campus officials just sign the letters. Universities including such well-known schools as Catholic University have turned to *e-collegebid.com*—the "Priceline" of higher education, which matches students' bids with colleges' discounts—to boost enrollment, and as Chapter 1 notes, colleges across the country depend on consulting firms to devise financial aid formulas that keep enrollment up and costs down.

When the University of Phoenix, a for-profit school, proposed to open a campus without its own library, it drew cries of outrage from professors, but that may have been much ado about not very much. While it is surely anti-intellectual to downplay students' need for books, this is one case in which outsourcing may be the right approach. Libraries are such an expensive investment that when budgets are tight, it makes sense to cut costs by contracting out that service to a nearby school, as Phoenix had agreed to do.

Meanwhile, the professoriate has been remarkably silent about the outsourcing of higher education's most basic function: teaching. The practice of hiring part-time instructors is not usually understood in these terms. But as the NYU story recounted in Chapter 5 shows, adjuncts recruited on a fee-for-service basis are the academic equivalent of temp agency fill-ins or day laborers. (So, for that matter, are associate professors at Harvard, who, despite their fine title, know that their days in Cambridge are almost surely numbered.) Barry Munitz, the former chancellor of California's state universities, estimates that in that system more than half of all classes are taught by these disposable workers. This trend is increasing. Across the country, more than three out of five new full-time academic jobs offer no prospect of tenure.

From a purely financial perspective, hiring adjuncts is an obvious move because it saves so much money. The typical English composition instructor earns about $3,000 a course, less than half the pay of an assistant professor, and receives no benefits.[16] But the true costs of this practice are high. To rely on contract labor in the classroom creates a category of faceless and fungible faculty, teachers who are given no continuing responsibility for their students, scholars who are denied the possibility of attachment to the intellectual life of the school through which they are literally passing. In the name of the bottom line, the institution sacrifices faculty loyalty, undermining its academic culture in the process.

The contracting out of leadership by relying on consulting firms to decide who makes a suitable president; the contracting out of performance on the playing field by "hiring" athletes whose scholarships can be revoked if they don't live up to their billing; the contracting out of fund-raising and alumni relations—seemingly everything is being outsourced these days.[17]

Even a school's identity can be shaped by others. Sometimes, as with Dickinson College, whose history is told in Chapter 3, the consultant's proposed slogan—in that case, "Reflecting America, Engaging the World" —is just a pithy way to capture what is taking place. But recall the saga of Beaver College, described in Chapter 1, which relied on a consulting firm's wisdom to restyle itself as Arcadia University.

Whenever a college puffs itself up into a university or drops the "technical" from its name, it is doing the same thing on a less outsized scale. But what does this contracted-out identity really mean? When everything including the name of a school is outsourced—when not just the business side of the institution but decisions about who teaches and who gets taught are privatized as well—what is left of the university?

▪ "Each Tub on Its Own Bottom"

In the search for managerial rationality, one voguish approach is "responsibility center management" or "revenue center management"—RCM for short. Permutations of RCM, which is another business import, are being used at a score of major universities, among them the University of Pennsylvania, which pioneered the scheme in the 1970s, as well as Vanderbilt University, Claremont Graduate University, Indiana University of Pennsylvania, the University of Illinois, and UCLA. A 1997 survey by the National Association of College and University Business Officers found that 16 percent of the public institutions, and 31 percent of the private schools, had fully or partly implemented RCM.[18]

RCM is the management-speak version of Harvard's hoary dictum "Each tub on its own bottom."[19] Proponents contend that a university should be run like a firm, in which every academic unit carries its weight financially. In business terms, that means each unit is expected to be a profit center. Whether it's the college of arts and sciences, the dental school, or the business school, the costs—which include salaries, space, and the like—cannot exceed the revenues, whether raised through tuition, contracts, grants, or gifts. A school that runs a surplus gets to keep it, while a school with a deficit has to pay it back.[20]

Things get tricky in practice, of course. It is hard to calculate correctly the all-important income and expenses; hard to decide how to apportion the costs of the university's "public goods," what in business parlance would be called cost centers, like the library and the registrar's office; hard as well to agree about what's a fair "tax" to subsidize, say, the theater department, which can't afford to pay its own way, or to nurture academic innovations that cross traditional academic boundaries. These details matter greatly, of course, but however they are settled, the premise of RCM remains straightforward: campus units control their own financial destiny.

Though this sounds arcane, the stakes are high. The debate over the wisdom of running a university according to the principles of the corporate profit center is in essence a contest of worldviews. It is an argument between those who believe that the citizens of a university are members of a company whose chief mission is to maximize dollar profits and those committed to the idea of the university as a community in which "gift relationships" are the norm.[21]

▪ USC: The Trojan Wars

The University of Southern California is no stranger to competition. Its football team, the Trojans, has often been a serious contender for a Pac 10 bowl bid; and the school prides itself on having brought home more Olympic gold medals than any other university in the country. But competition *within* the university for students' favor is entirely different, and until the early 1990s such rivalries were the norm at USC.[22]

Imagine the scene: At the beginning of each semester, as students signed up for courses, campus units paraded their wares with the fervor of discount merchandisers. Full-page ads in the *Daily Trojan* touted courses such as the drama class that required no reading. ("Tired of reading Shakespeare? Kill off your [general education] requirement, sit back and eat popcorn, and watch it being performed.")[23] The behind-the-scenes rivalries were even fiercer. Schools that had never previously professed an interest in the liberal arts were suddenly claiming that their offerings—introduction to real estate, for example—should satisfy the university's general education requirement.

All this academically dubious behavior, and much more of the same, can be traced to a single innovation: the introduction of revenue center management.

Since its founding by the Methodist Church in 1880, the University of Southern California has had to work hard to attain academic respectability.[24] The Methodist bishops had good intentions, but with no Rockefeller or Stanford to underwrite them, the university was ruled from the outset by a survivalist mentality. Land for the campus was the gift of real estate speculators, among them an ex-governor, who hoped that the presence of the new university would resuscitate their failed development. To stay in business, USC had to sell itself on the basis of its utility to tuition-paying students and benefactors. The real estate school was begun with the financial backing of developers, who had to be convinced that their field would become respectable only if it became a proper subject of study. This was the USC pattern: professional schools developed to fill a market niche, then joined together in a loose federation. "Figueroa Tech" became the university's sobriquet.[25]

The status of the university has improved dramatically in the past half century, mainly because of strong leadership. By 2003, enrollment had grown to nearly 30,000, and the endowment had mushroomed to more than $2 billion. The average SAT score for the class of 2004 was 1308 and the average G.P.A. was 3.9, which put USC in the ranks of the elite; the school is among the top ten in the nation in the number of National Merit scholars it enrolls. A succession of astute presidents beginning with Norman Topping, who took office in 1958, pushed the university from regional status into the first rank of higher education. "If he gets the cash," *Time* magazine observed, "Topping's master plan could revolutionize USC," a status confirmed with its election to the elite Association of American Universities in 1969.[26]

Topping's strategy was to invest heavily in a handful of units, which he called "peaks of excellence." Although his approach worked brilliantly, he was an autocrat who secretly negotiated budgets and cut private deals— "the Kremlin," fearful deans called the president's office. But the Topping administration ignored crucial matters of implementation, argues John Curry, who was named vice president for budget and planning in 1986. No one worried much about the quality of the professors who were hired to staff these programs, Curry says, or about how the offices and labs these new ventures required were to be paid for. Both Curry and Jon Strauss, recruited from the University of Pennsylvania to be senior vice president of administration, were brought in to tame this Wild West institution by installing the then-new idea of "revenue center management."

At Penn, where Strauss and his colleagues had pioneered RCM, it had been called "resource center management," but whatever its name, the intention was the same: to introduce fiscal discipline into the management of the university. Openness was one means to this end. For the first time, USC's budget was made public; all the deans could see which units were contributing extra dollars and which were being subsidized by the rest of the campus.

There was no overt opposition among the faculty to the new arrangements. The release of information was meant to spur rational planning, with departments and schools—what the scheme calls "revenue centers"—taking responsibility for their own financial affairs. To its advocates, RCM simply means sound business practice. "[It] provides information on full program costs while encouraging attention to the quality and efficient production of those services . . . joining academic and fiscal conditions together in one place," Strauss and Curry argue in a pamphlet that summarizes a quarter-century of experience with RCM.[27] But that's a too-tidy view of how universities work. "Academic institutions are complex, nonlinear systems," as Robert Birnbaum points out, "and their responses to changes in one part can have counterintuitive and surprising effects in another . . . introduc[ing] more subtle and insidious problems to replace acute ones."[28] At USC, the introduction of revenue center management unleashed the academic equivalent of a Hobbesian war of all against all. Gone was any commitment to supporting the common good.

Even as RCM was being phased in, provost Cornelius J. Pings decided that the professional schools could offer general education courses, which had been the province of the liberal arts college. This was a crucial decision because tuition is, far and away, the major source of income for most of the schools at USC. With Pings's door-opening move, fiscal concerns became dominant as each unit sought ways of seducing undergraduates.

Deans demanded "instruction rights" over their own majors, as if students were chattel. USC had long promoted an undergraduate education that combined the liberal arts with the so-called practical arts. Now the liberal arts college was being pillaged as aggressive professional school administrators pursued their "harvesting rights," treating students like so many ears of corn. The engineering school launched new courses in mathematics and composition for its majors, while the public policy school inaugurated special statistics and computing classes. Although all these initiatives had pedagogical rationales—writing for prospective engineers, it was said, is different from writing generally—the true explanation was dollars and cents. Because these courses enroll many students and are taught by adjunct instructors, they are money machines.

Meanwhile, many deans were eager to cut the budgets for campus-wide activities such as student counseling, the library, the registrar's office, and building maintenance, and they vetoed proposed initiatives such as a community outreach venture. "It's *our* money," they insisted, fighting for low campus "taxes" with the ardor of George W. Bush. The dean of the film school went so far as to seek a franchise fee from the campus administration for his school, on the ground that it enhanced the university's reputation. When it came to determining these tax rates and subsidies, the trustees got into the act, lobbying for special treatment for their favorite schools.

RCM contemplates "taxing" campus units, Strauss and Curry write, but allocating the taxes "differentially and discriminately." At USC, however, these "subventions" only made things worse.[29] In a widely circulated e-mail message, one disgruntled professor warned his colleagues at UCLA, which hired Curry to implement RCM there, that "at USC, the approach seems to be a way for central administration to retain nearly all of the control they had before while finding ways to discipline us financially when we do not make at least as much as we cost."[30]

It was entirely rational from a revenue-maximizing perspective for the gerontology school to lure undergraduates with the promise that they could satisfy their science requirement without spending a single minute in the lab. Similarly, it was fiscally smart for these professional schools to erect "trade barriers" that effectively kept engineering or business school undergraduate majors from taking English classes in the liberal arts college. For much the same reason, grades turned into recruiting tactics. While the average undergraduate grade in the liberal arts college was 3.1, in professional schools the average was an astonishing 3.5, and undergraduates could do the math. An enlightened campus policy that allowed faculty and staff to enroll in any course became a burlesque, as some deans coerced their underlings to sign up for classes in which they had no interest in order to boost enrollment. In one instance, an engineer started a scuba diving course to earn tuition revenues for his school.

By the early 1990s, USC had become an institution that, as the Oscar Wilde jibe goes, knew the price of everything and the value of nothing.[31] Some schools went so far as to alter their mission in order to generate revenues. The School of Policy, Planning, and Development started hiring professors who had little sense of the profession but could give bravura lectures that appealed to undergraduates. Academic pursuits that cost more—notably graduate teaching and research, the raisons d'être for the school—suffered as a consequence. Presumably this is what Strauss and Curry are referring to when they note that "the School of Urban and Regional Planning [as it then was called] literally built [itself] on the enrollment and research revenue incentives of RCM."[32]

Amid all the gamesmanship, there was no one at USC to speak up for the academic commons. This was Runnymede come to the campus, and the deans were effectively in charge. They decided how much to tax themselves for what were, tellingly, called "peripherals"—including the central administration itself, which had to justify its expenses.

No one gamed the system better than longtime law school dean Scott Bice, who stepped down in 2001. "It's like running your own small college," he says. "I can decide what to pay my faculty and how many students to admit without having to get anyone's approval." Bice had buckets of money to spend as he pleased. Law students' tuition, which is set at market rates, generates substantial revenue; and Susan Estrich, who managed Michael Dukakis's ill-fated 1988 presidential campaign, lectured annually to hundreds of tuition-paying undergraduates. No one did better than Bice in the campus budget battles. The matter of who pays to operate the campus library is a nice example. The library is the prototype of a campus public good; but Bice successfully argued that because the law school has its own library, it shouldn't be taxed to support another pile of books.[33]

The law school receives "most favored nation" treatment from the campus administration, says Bice, but that metaphor doesn't withstand scrutiny. The law school isn't a nation, a stand-alone institution as it was until 1900, when Los Angeles Law School affiliated with the university.[34] It's in a position to benefit from the reputation of the university as a whole; the name change says as much. And the number of volumes in the campus library affects USC's standing in the pecking order of higher education. Not only is it bad citizenship to impoverish the library, it's short-sighted as well.

The law school isn't the only unit that fared well under the Strauss-Curry regime. "An essentially permanent subvention was [also] set up for the engineering school," says provost Lloyd Armstrong. The budget managers were less sympathetic to the needs of the music school. Because it is much more expensive to teach music students than business students, a music school is logically a prime candidate for a campus subsidy, yet at USC the attitude was tough love. "Music realized that, given unit costs," say Strauss and Curry, "[its] further development could not come from enrollment but had to come from gifts and endowments."[35] But because there is no Steven Spielberg to fund a music school in Los Angeles, the budget of that school, one of the best in the country, had to be slashed.

*   *   *

In the early 1990s, a new president, Steven Sample, began keeping a file of the most obvious academic embarrassments, like "Shakespeare Lite." These were brought to an end, and so were the full-page ads, the grade giveaways, and the redundant courses. Sample, together with Lloyd Armstrong, who as a dean at Johns Hopkins University had learned firsthand the dangers of RCM, sought to rein in the budgeting system—no easy task, since the existing formula greatly benefited law and engineering, two units with powerful allies among the USC trustees.

In 1994, Armstrong led a "highly contentious" strategic planning process focused on general education. In the era of the turf struggles, fully a third of general education courses had been taught in the professional schools. No longer. "Imagine the reaction of many of the deans when I announced that the general education system was corrupted by RCM," says Armstrong, "and that to return rationality and quality to the system, in the future, general education courses would only be taught where they belonged—in the [liberal arts] college."

The substance of general education was also revamped. Instead of a smorgasbord, says Armstrong, "the six courses had to have rigor, and some logical connection to one another." All undergraduates must take the full complement of general education classes, thus preventing the professional schools from gutting the requirement by increasing the number of courses required for the major. Under the RCM formula, this gave the liberal arts college $8 million in additional funding each year, and that money has enabled the school to restore the size of its faculty, which had been cut by a sixth in the heyday of RCM.[36] General education has flourished as senior professors are teaching the courses, and the students give them high marks. The only complaints, says Armstrong, come from some of the professional school deans. "Whenever one of them has a budget problem, he says, 'This wouldn't have happened if you hadn't taken away my general education,'" but over time, "even that [complaint] has become pro forma."

"Leadership's role is to restore civilized behavior," argues John Curry, but at USC that isn't how the model was sold. True believers assume that the campus "market" can be guided by the proverbial invisible hand. That's as improbable as the traditionalist position that money is too vulgar a topic for the Arcadia of higher education.

Until 1995, the provost had less than $1 million to spend on campus-wide priorities—a pittance—and attempts to claw back some of the authority relinquished under RCM met with predictable antagonism. But this changed in the mid-1990s, when an accreditation report came out in favor of greater centralization: additional money had to be set aside for campus-wide priorities if USC was to become a great institution.[37] Using that report as leverage, the administration moved to increase the tax rate to 20 percent. This "seed money," as Armstrong calls it, pays for such interdisciplinary ventures as a program on energy and an urban initiative, and also shores up chronically impoverished units such as gerontology.

To mark this shift, new wine has been poured into an old acronym: the name "revenue center management" is out, replaced by "responsibility center management." The idea, presumably, is that when it comes to running a university, dollars aren't everything. "RCM is a wonderful accounting system," says Morton Schapiro, formerly a USC dean who left to become the president of Williams College. "But if you don't have a vision it becomes your vision."

The university has every reason to appreciate this fact. In the early 1990s, at USC as at many other second-tier private universities, the proportion of accepted undergraduate applicants who actually enrolled dropped sharply, from 43 percent to 29 percent; at the same time, financial aid was increased. Several deans proposed maintaining revenues by dipping deeper into the pool of applicants to admit weaker students. Instead, president Steven Sample raised the quality of students by reducing the size of the freshman class; he also imposed a tax to underwrite scholarships that, for top-performing California students, make it no more expensive to attend USC than the University of California.[38]

To the deans, heavily dependent on tuition, this looked like a shipwreck. In fact, it has proved a turning point for USC, which with a threefold increase in applicants in less than a decade has become a certifiably "hot" school. RCM-style markets didn't get the university there. Leadership, driven by academic values, did that.

▪ University of Michigan: The Limits of "Local Commitments"

Even as USC was changing its budgetary nomenclature and moving from "revenue center management" to "responsibility center management," the University of Michigan, which began implementing RCM in 1994, was also indulging in a rhetorical transformation. In a nod to professorial sensibilities, the "R" in RCM stood for "responsibility." But the chief campus proponent, provost and ex-business school dean Gilbert Whitaker, angered many faculty members by talking about how this approach would meet the needs of the university's "customers" while speeding "thru-put, the amount of product"—in other words, students—"moving through the system."[39]

That vocabulary was grating, and not only because of its commercial lineage. Language matters because it contributes to how we construct the world.[40] Customers want to have their preferences *satisfied,* but students come to a university to have their preferences *formed.* RCM soon became caught up in a larger argument about the institution's mission. "What about the values of higher education?" professors demanded. "Is everything a business?" Whitaker responded with a name change. In 1995, he replaced RCM with VCM—*value*-centered management. If only the real difficulties, lodged in the uneasy relationship between money matters and academic values, could be so easily resolved.

Michigan's Wolverines, like the USC Trojans, are perennial football powerhouses, but that's where the historical similarities cease. The launching of the University of Michigan in 1817 was a nervy act in a frontier state. Although the new institution was initially given an archaic name, Catholepistemiad, or University, of Michigania, the project was decidedly contemporary. In an era when eastern seaboard schools were still mimicking Oxford's classic curriculum, this new publicly subsidized university stressed economics and science. It wasn't meant to be an isolated tower of learning, a Harvard in the wilderness, but rather the capstone of the state's public education system.[41] "The beginning of the American university," historians John Brubacher and Willis Rudy argue, "came, not in Cambridge or Baltimore [with the founding of Johns Hopkins], but in Ann Arbor."[42]

Unlike USC, Michigan never had to rely mainly on tuition-paying students or status-seeking realtors. It was one of the first publicly supported institutions of higher education—literally a public good. Writing in the 1850s, president and institution-shaper Henry Tappan described the university as "a powerful counter-influence against the excessive commercial spirit, and against the chicanery and selfishness of demogogueism." A generation later, his successor, James Angell, opposed the creation of a dentistry school, something that at the time existed at no other American university, on the grounds that dentistry wasn't an "intellectual calling."[43]

But Angell lost that fight when the regents, the university's elected governing board, overruled his decision. This was a rare defeat in his thirty-eight-year presidency; apparently a school of dentistry was something the citizenry desired, and in this instance the regents were responsive to those concerns. Ever since, the tension between the pressures of political accountability and the aspirations to elitism has been continually played out. How could it be otherwise in a public institution?

Among state universities, Michigan ranks second only to Berkeley in reputation. It is a paradigmatic multiversity, with 37,000 students enrolled in nineteen schools, everything from a school of kinesiology ("movement science") to a mammoth liberal arts college with 18,000 students in fifty departments. Nearly half a billion dollars a year is generated in government research funds, and more than a billion dollars a year comes from the medical center's revenues.

The political and economic climate determines how much money the school receives from the state, and with what strings attached. Legislators fix the size of the state appropriation and jawbone the administration into filling the undergraduate class mostly with in-state (and low-tuition-paying) residents. The state's economic health also shapes public generosity. When Michigan's industrial economy crashed in the 1970s and 1980s, the campus felt the impact. "We saw our mortality in the mirror," says James Duderstadt, president from 1988 to 1996.[44]

Responsibility center management and Duderstadt: the concept and the man are well matched. As president, he saw himself as the agent of institutional transformation—the engineer, as he was by training, summoned to build a new institution. Duderstadt is given to the big think rhetoric of abstract, futuristic schemes. During his tenure, he regularly turned deans' retreats into brainstorming sessions, asking the administrators to ponder how concepts like "transformational leadership" and "change" relate to the "twenty-first-century university." After being pushed out of his job by the regents, he opted to do what ex-presidents often do: he wrote a book. The word "change" appears more than twenty times in the first dozen pages.[45]

The biggest of these changes at the University of Michigan, as at all public universities, has been the decline in state financial support. The state's contribution to the general fund, 70 percent in 1960, had fallen to 36 percent by 2000. Except during Duderstadt's visits to Lansing, the state capital, the president made it a point not to describe the University of Michigan as a state university. "We used to be state-*supported*," he has said, "then state-*assisted,* and now we are state-*located.*" Some administrators, pointing to the hostility of many legislators, would go further, describing theirs as a state-*molested* university. Like it or not, the institution was evolving into what Duderstadt called "the University of Michigan, Inc.," comparing it to a Fortune 500 company, and it had to be run more like a business. Although the university had a history of decentralized management, more was wanted, says Duderstadt: "Each tub on its own bottom with someone controlling the tide."

That "someone" was provost Gil Whitaker, who used the full force of the office to implement responsibility center management. The longtime business school dean was also a longtime supporter of decentralizing the budget process. "He believed schools should get their money from outside," says Bernard Machen, who succeeded Whitaker as acting provost. The schools had to "give a nod to the university so that they could show the logo, but otherwise ran their own shop." Whitaker was given to corporate nostrums—earlier, he had made total quality management, or TQM, his cause—and what he learned from meetings with administrators from USC and Indiana, the first public university to adopt RCM, impressed him.

Indiana was a bad analogy, contends former arts and sciences dean Edie Goldenberg, because in Bloomington, a single college, arts and sciences, dominates the campus; and USC, with its fabled scuba courses, was a textbook case of how *not* to do things. But Whitaker was "intrigued by the belief that commercial businesses do it better," says John Cross, who managed the budget of the liberal arts college during those years, "that bumbling academics should try to emulate smooth-functioning IBM and General Motors." Whitaker has a different take on his mission: "The goal was to get the incentive structure better—set the right tax on expenditure, the right reward for revenue. The challenge was to keep people from doing inappropriate things, showing movies in a class of 4,000, to get revenues. People would cheat."

Beginning in 1995, Whitaker generated budget numbers showing the anticipated dollars-and-cents implications of value-centered management for all the campus units, and a full-fledged version was in place two years later. But while RCM had no vocal opponents at USC, at Michigan there was determined opposition.

The fact that the budget scheme was imposed from the top, rather than deliberated by the faculty, angered many, including political scientist Gregory Markus, who derided the process of decision making as "hierarchical, narrow, unaccountable to the affected constituencies, and generally chilling to the spirit of initiative and quality." To Markus, it called to mind Woodrow Wilson's plaint as president of Princeton: "How can I democratize this university if the faculty won't do what I say?" In circumventing the faculty, Whitaker was taking a page from Edward Whalen's *Responsibility Center Budgeting*, the bible in the field. "When responsibility center budgeting is first announced," the Indiana economist and administrator writes, "every campus busybody feels threatened . . . and is sure that she or he must understand it to maintain 'academic quality' and protect 'academic freedom.'" Administrators, Whalen says, are well advised to keep "such nosy and usually noisy people under control."[46]

The budget "guesstimates" that the administration churned out "made the deans' eyes pop in disbelief," says Cecil Miskel, the former dean of the education school. Miskel, who knows the management literature inside out, got into a shouting match with the provost about the suitability of RCM at a deans' meeting. After that session, Miskel says, Lee Bollinger, then the dean of the law school and soon to be president of the university, profusely thanked him. "I objected to the rationale that RCM would take the hard decisions out of resource allocation—that a formula would drive everything, all the way down to the professor level," says Miskel. "Whitaker was enough of a number cruncher that he would have driven it that way." (Whitaker retorts that he was always committed to the primacy of academic values.) Budget maker John Cross weighed in with an "intellectual history" of responsibility center management, pointing out how those who first broached the idea, University of Chicago economists writing about behavior in firms, believed that its principles could be applied to only the simplest of organizations.[47]

In implementing RCM, Michigan learned from USC's mistakes. At Ann Arbor, there were few curricular outrages. No department tried to meet general education requirements by offering Shakespeare without reading plays or science without labs. Still, the temptation was there to devise what provost Paul Courant calls "spiffy new programs" of dubious merit to attract students to the university. The school of architecture "mysteriously found itself with rich students from abroad so that it could make money," says Machen. The engineering school started its own writing program, enrolling hundreds of students who would otherwise have been taking English composition at the liberal arts college. The venture had been in the works for years, the engineers pointed out, and they had decided that having a separate offering was best for their students; but to Edie Goldenberg, the liberal arts dean, the timing was suspicious, since "their push gained strength during the VCM discussion." The engineering school also gave serious thought to offering its own math and physics courses, a move that would have been disastrous for those departments. Some colleges increased course requirements for their majors so that they could keep a larger share of the tuition revenue.

What mattered more, the new fiscal realities became roadblocks in the path of cross-disciplinary work, long a hallmark at Michigan. Researchers from the departments of biology, biochemistry, and chemistry, for instance, regularly collaborate with medical school and pharmacy school professors. For more than half a century, the Institute for Social Research has been the intellectual meeting ground for social science researchers; but with the advent of RCM, the psychology department pressured its professors to run their grants through the department, not the institute, so that it could keep the overhead dollars and modernize its laboratories. "Concerns about the institute's health," says provost Paul Courant, "helped to crystallize skepticism about the new system on the part of social scientists."

There were similar fights about who should pay for campus-wide services. The law school, which is largely self-supporting, objected to underwriting the campus unit that monitors compliance with the Occupational Safety and Health Administration's regulations, since those regulations apply mainly to the medical school; for its part, the liberal arts college didn't want to subsidize the graduate school. As Janet Weiss, a former business school dean, recalls, "Units came up with a hundred reasons why they shouldn't pay for things benefiting others."

Responsibility center management is supposed to make the budgetary process transparent. But to win over reluctant deans, Whitaker was willing to wheel and deal; the education school was able to boost its annual revenues by a million dollars, nearly 15 percent of its budget, because of one such arrangement. Meanwhile, the university's hospital received special treatment under the new budget formula. The "backtracking on tough issues," says Weiss, made the new instrument less powerful in practice than in theory. "If enrollment drops because demand has dropped, generating less tuition, RCM says that the unit must pay the price. That never happened. The lag before any financial impact was felt gave the schools ample time to lobby."

In 1996, after one too many arguments with Duderstadt, Whitaker quit. "He thought he could do a better job than the president and the

CFO," says his successor, Bernard Machen. Edie Goldenberg regards Whitaker as "a good manager, with good taste in people, but an administrator, not an intellect, no scholarly credentials," and at Michigan that counted heavily against him. Although Machen was chosen to succeed Whitaker in the belief that he wouldn't upset egos, the ex-dean was soon warning his former colleagues that the free ride was over; schools would start feeling the bite of value center management. But a month after Machen was named to the post, Jim Duderstadt was ousted. His successor was Lee Bollinger, who as law school dean had praised Cecil Miskel for opposing RCM. Value center management was set for a change, and not just in name.

"The university isn't a real market," as Paul Courant points out. "All the rules about free entry and going out of business aren't there." As an economist, Courant understands how markets work. Because decisions about budgets aren't identical to judgments about institutional values, to describe budgeting as value-centered management claims far too much. Besides, "the market language led faculty to the belief that the budget was being managed by people who didn't share their priorities. They started to ask, 'Who is running our university?'"

In 1997 the budget model was renamed just that—the budget model—and much more than nomenclature changed. Although schools still bear major responsibility for raising and spending money, the campus administration reclaimed authority over decisions that affect the wider community. In Ann Arbor, as at USC, there has been a renewed assertion of leadership from the center.

Nancy Cantor, Lee Bollinger's choice as provost, and her second-in-command, Paul Courant, announced the shift in a 1997 "work in progress" paper. Value-centered management, they observed, is a good system to foster what they call "local commitments"—the commitment to a professor's own work and the life of the department. But VCM exaggerates the importance of financial self-sufficiency while downplaying the commitment to collaboration and, most broadly, to the shared life of the institution, the very things that make Michigan a special place. "We are happier at Michigan," they wrote, "when we know that a rare language is taught here, or a concert has taken place, even when our happiness comes from basking in reflected glory."[48] This isn't how Gil Whittaker talked.

The administration sought to right the balance by heavily "taxing" campus units—most of them pay 22 percent of the revenue they generate—for the intellectual collaborations that Michigan so prizes. (One lovely example is described in a 2001 paper by Cantor and Courant: "The expertise of a humanist in the Department of Asian Languages and Cultures, who by the way teaches about ten students a year, made it possible for a colleague in the School of Natural Resources to successfully design an environmental intervention in rural Indonesia without interfering with local customs.")[49] Deans who undermine joint research ventures by insisting that faculty members run their grants through their home departments rather than through multidepartment institutions have been told to be better citizens or else pack their bags. Encouraging cross-disciplinary research is, as it happens, good management practice—a recognition that, in universities as in firms, the best work often gets done not in the old structures but in what the business literature describes as "functional chimneys."[50]

The provost's office also distributes extra dollars to what it regards as the best academic programs and decides how much to spend on public goods such as the library, the computing center, and the botanical gardens. Until Nancy Cantor left Michigan to become chancellor at the University of Illinois, many on campus referred to these as "Nancy goods."

These changes infuriate Jim Duderstat. "There's too much central control," the university's former president argues, dismissing the new approach as rooted in a "naïve belief that we can turn the clock back to the 1950s, when you could send a truck up to Lansing and return with money."

"The administration," he predicts, "won't be able to resist management by markets." But Duderstadt's criticism misses the mark. "Leave it to the market" is itself a political statement, a default of institutional leadership and an abandonment of the idea of university's mission.

Mr. Jefferson's "Private" College

Darden Graduate School of Business Administration, University of Virginia

The University of Virginia is surely the most architecturally renowned campus in the country.[1] Among Virginians, it is reverentially referred to as "Mr. Jefferson's university," and indeed that polymath president had a major hand in designing what he called the "academical·village."[2] A miniature version of the Roman Pantheon, the Rotunda, sits at the heart of what's called "the Lawn," the early-nineteenth-century centerpiece of the grounds (the university has "grounds," rather than a campus), flanked by two ranks of Federalist-style buildings. These serve as classrooms, faculty residences, and dormitories for seniors, who vie for the coveted places.

Even as droves of tourists annually make the pilgrimage to Charlottesville to admire the grounds, signs of neglect are visible in the shadow of the Jeffersonian grandeur. Rouss Hall, which houses the department of economics, is the sorriest case. It needs new plumbing and a new heating system, structural repairs, an elevator for the handicapped, and much more. So far, however, the university administration, chronically strapped for funds, has been able to manage only cosmetic touches. "The building is in such bad shape that I'd be embarrassed to tell my mother I work here," says professor Edgar Olsen, who in the fall of 2001 took matters into his own hands by hiring undergraduates to tackle the cleanup job. The department has proposed to build itself a new building, but other, less well-heeled liberal arts departments have ganged up to oppose such a go-it-alone initiative. It's all of liberal arts, not just economics, they say, for which money should be raised.

A mile away, the campus of the Darden Graduate School of Business Administration, completed in 1996, pays homage through imitation to Jefferson's architectural vision. Federal-style buildings frame a wide lawn. The main building is modeled on the Rotunda. The pristine interiors, painted in soothing colonial hues (among them are three shades of Jeffersonian yellow, known to Darden students as "Post-it note" yellow) and compulsively maintained, combine the echoing foyers and sumptuous decorative touches of a palace with the hip but familiar design of a Starbucks. It's a layout fit for *Better Homes and Gardens.*

This physical separation is the embodiment in brick and mortar of a more fundamental divide within the university. The schools situated on the historic grounds, among them the liberal arts college, the education school, and the school of commerce (which trains undergraduate business students), operate according to the conventions of public universities: the state doles out operating funds and specifies how those funds can be spent.

In sharp contrast, the business school, and to a lesser extent the law school, its campus neighbor, have been moving rapidly toward what is referred to as "self-sufficiency." In exchange for eschewing most of the state funds to which it would otherwise be entitled, Darden has largely been set free to build its own campus. The result is a nine-building, 340,000-square-foot complex paid for with approximately $77 million in private contributions. In essence it can decide how many professors it wants and how much to pay them.[3] It keeps 90 percent of the money it raises. It offers expensive executive training courses for senior managers and uses the market as a benchmark in determining its tuition. Even the school's website address is a tacit declaration of independence: Web-surfers can reach the school at *www.darden.edu* rather than having to go through *www.darden.virginia.edu,* which is the format for the rest of the campus. This university steeped in tradition has responded to the contemporary pressures of market competition by creating what may well be the most autonomous—the most "private"—school in any American public university.[4]

Darden is the canary in the mine, a tale of things to come, for across the country the privatization of public higher education proceeds apace. What Mark Yudof, chancellor of the fifteen-campus University of Texas system, calls the "extraordinary compact between state governments and their flagship universities" is being consigned to the junkyard of history.[5]

"For more than a century," Yudof points out, "these two parties had a deal: In return for financial support from the taxpayers, these universities would keep tuition low and provide broad access, train graduate and professional students, promote arts and culture, help solve local problems, and perform ground-breaking research." But nationwide between 1980 and 2000, the share of universities' operating expenses paid for by state tax dollars was cut by 30 percent. The share of state revenue given to higher education has dropped by one-third, from 9.8 percent to 6.9 percent.[6]

Across the country, the financial picture for state universities is grim. Not only are state funds proportionately more scarce, but also the federal government contributes proportionately less than it did a generation ago, and those dollars go mainly to students, as grants and loans, rather than to the institutions. Public universities have responded by raising tuition by as much as 125 percent since 1990, but pressure from parents and politicians effectively sets a ceiling on this source of revenue; in Virginia, the state imposed a tuition cap in 1995.[7] Universities have also been more aggressive in courting private and corporate donors, with the inevitable consequence that the donors' preferences, not the public interest, increasingly define the institutions' priorities.

By their very nature, business schools are entirely at home with the spirit of this commercial age and are keen to take advantage of its opportunities. Money is the business schools' chief subject; making money is what mainly motivates their students; and these schools are magnets for outside support.[8] This used to make business schools a target of derision for academics, but now it's what situates these schools in the vanguard of market-driven higher education. When the state of Virginia cut Darden loose, it made it easier for the school to compete with its rivals at wealthy private schools like Stanford and Harvard—but at what price to the broader aims of the university?

■ The Long Road to Autonomy

Since its founding half a century ago as the first graduate business school in the South, Darden has aspired to be an institution of national renown. "The South still in large measure belongs to the colonial economy," proponents of the new school argued, and its brightest scions were migrating north to get a business education.[9] Concern about a brain drain was nothing new—Jefferson had fretted that Virginians educated at Harvard would turn into "fanatics & Tories"—and the hope was that by creating a generation of homegrown business leaders, a business school with the ambition of becoming the "Harvard of the South" could help level the economic playing field.[10]

Darden's faculty was dominated at the outset by Harvard Business School graduates, and the school still shares Harvard's commitment to a specific pedagogy, the case method, but no longer is Harvard the touchstone. In recent years, Darden has regularly been listed among the top ten schools in the influential *Business Week* rankings—the only public university other than Michigan to appear on that list—and it has been ranked higher than better-known schools such as the University of Chicago. Darden students report that they are pleased with their education—in that category, the school ranks second nationally—and employers, whose views weigh heavily in the *Business Week* rankings, are pleased with the graduates' performance.[11]

Darden has also done remarkably well in raising money. During his three-year tenure as dean, Edward Snyder raised $209 million, making it the best-endowed business school per student in the country. (Small wonder that, as *Business Week* reported, the staff wept when they learned in the summer of 2001 that Snyder was returning to his alma mater, the University of Chicago.) Among those gifts was the biggest single donation ever made to a business school, $60 million, which fittingly enough endows a center on entrepreneurship. The donor, Frank Batten Sr., is a Harvard M.B.A., and that led some to joke that Harvard might now be called the Charlottesville of the North.

Virginians are passionate about their leading universities, and for those who manage them this is both a blessing and a curse. In a state with neither a major city nor a major league franchise in any sport, the University of Virginia and the College of William and Mary offer something for people to boast about. Virginia politicians are passionate, too, although their feelings can run to venomousness. Legislators turn into culture warriors in battles over the content of the curriculum. Members of the State Council of Higher Education have sometimes been chosen just because of their animosity toward the university. The green eyeshade crowd in Richmond, the state capital, closely monitor university budgets, and until a few years ago the state mandated a payroll system whose complexity would startle Rube Goldberg, with rules piled atop rules.

"The problem," says former UVA provost Peter Low, "is that the state contributes [a small fraction] of the revenue but wants 100 percent control." When in the spring of 2001 the legislature failed to adopt a budget, $100 million in construction projects on the Charlottesville campus were halted for six months. "It's not like Michigan," says Ted Snyder, who taught there before becoming Darden's dean. "You feel the state on a week-to-week basis."

Despite its abiding interest, the state government has never been especially generous in funding higher education. Even during the 1970s and early 1980s, when the university was cultivating an image as one of the "public Ivies," it spent considerably less per student than neighboring North Carolina spent on its flagship Chapel Hill campus. Even as public universities across the country felt the impact of the recession of the early 1990s, higher education in Virginia fared among the worst. It suffered a 13 percent budget cut in the span of just two years.[12] Out of necessity, the state's universities dramatically increased tuition—by 79 percent for in-state students, 123 percent for out-of-state students—making them among the nation's most expensive public institutions.

Politicians began meddling in tuition rates in 1994, when legislators limited increases to the rate of inflation, and two years later, Governor George Allen imposed a tuition freeze. The universities were no longer able to offer faculty competitive salaries, and many talented professors went elsewhere. Several ex-governors, both Democrats and Republicans, issued a warning that the quality of public higher education was in real danger.

The university presidents responded with an ultimatum: If Virginia didn't do a better job of funding higher education, some parts of the universities would go private. "We all sat down and argued about this in John's [UVA president John Casteen's] living room," recalls Gordon Davies, who for twenty years headed the State Council of Higher Education. "One of the presidents said, 'Christ, you really mean this.'"

The law and business schools at UVA were already committed to privatization. Although the campus administration had always treated Darden as a favored child—it was viewed as a bright light in an institution whose units are of decidedly uneven caliber—there was never enough state money to underwrite a truly first-rate business school. In the 1980s, recalls longtime UVA chief operating officer Leonard Sandridge, an accreditation team from the Association of American Law Schools warned that "the law school is in serious danger of falling behind its peers because of a lack of money." A similarly blunt message was being delivered to Darden. To be more than a good regional institution, the Indiana of the South, the business school had to raise buckets of money.

The state legislature proved surprisingly responsive to these demands for greater autonomy. A 1996 Assembly committee report concluded that "as higher education changes the way it conducts its business, the Commonwealth should consider changing its business relationship with higher education, develop[ing] a plan to grant selected institutions special independent status in state government [to free them from] stifling bureaucratic regulation. The plan should consider the possibility of allowing institutions to grant greater autonomy to selected schools that could be largely self-supporting."[13] The reasoning was pragmatic. "The plain fact is this state is not going to put up the resources to compete with Stanford and wherever else they [the University of Virginia] compete with," says Don Finley, the state's former secretary of education.

Realistically, only the law and business schools at Charlottesville could attract enough students willing to pay the market rate tuition that self-sufficiency would require. The law school's negotiations over autonomy have been protracted because state politicians, mindful of graduates' powerful role in state affairs, have been loath to cede control. They have also pressed the law school to maintain its traditional quota of 40 percent instate students, who pay lower tuition, and this constricts the school's potential revenues.

For Darden as well, securing self-sufficiency has demanded considerable finesse.[14] Ironically, the campaign for greater autonomy was almost derailed on the occasion of the dedication of the Darden grounds in 1996, when Thomas A. Saunders III, chair of the board of trustees of the Darden School Foundation, the nominally independent fund-raising arm of the business school, said the magic word "privatization" aloud.

"I know that the word 'privatization' is politically a 'hot button,'" Saunders said. "But the fact is that the state would win. Wouldn't the state subsidy going to Darden be better spent on undergraduates in the form of scholarships or better funded programs? Tonight, I am making the case that Darden must have the freedom to respond to competition in order to join the ranks of the top five or six business schools." Saunders's attempt to yoke privatization to the university's Jeffersonian heritage sounded like a marketing ploy. "The University of Virginia would still confer the degrees. Mr. Jefferson's University would still be our very identification— our intellectual, our physical, our emotional home. What would change is not the spirit and ties, but the freedom to compete with the very best business schools in the world." "It was a horrible speech. I cringed under the table," says Board of Visitors member William Goodwin. "If you were a legislator you would say, 'Boy, that isn't going to happen to my school!'" Only with considerable soothing of egos did "self-sufficiency" proceed. Now it's a fait accompli. In 2003, Darden (as well as the law school) became formally self-sufficient. Market-rate tuition for out-of-state students, combined with income from fund-raising and the endowment, as well as revenues generated by the executive education program, will support the school. Gradually, it will expand its MBA class size by one-quarter, adding another source of revenue.[15]

*   *   *

What provost Peter Low calls "an opportunity to loosen the reins" of state control is depicted by campus administrators as a win-win arrangement. It benefits Darden by enabling it to compete nationally for students, faculty, money, and ultimately prestige; and at least on the surface, the deal also benefits UVA, since state money that used to go to Darden can now be spent elsewhere on campus. "This business," says Leonard Sandridge, "like all businesses, works best if the objectives of the various parties are aligned. If there is a way that a department or school can benefit itself by making decisions that are beneficial to the corporation, the entire institution, that's the model we want to get."

Market similes are misleading, though. Higher education is not "like all other businesses," and Darden is not like the Saturn division of General Motors. It's not self-evident that what benefits Darden will also benefit the University of Virginia. Quite the contrary, the emancipation of Darden may accelerate the fissioning of that Jeffersonian "academical village," the university.

▪ Negotiating a "Franchise Fee"

"When I was deciding among deanship offers," recalls Ted Snyder, the former dean of Darden, who combines the calm demeanor of a scholar with the shark's instinct for the jugular, "I calculated the internal tax rates," the percentage of tuition revenue that a business school pays the university. "At Michigan, the rate was 24 percent, at Emory it was 40 percent. That big variation affects competition among business schools." When Snyder came to Virginia, he spent eighteen months negotiating the tax rate with chief operating officer Leonard Sandridge. Snyder initially proposed a 5 percent tax; he walked away with a rate of just 10 percent, with side payments as a sweetener. That tax rate (substantially lower than the figure at the University of Michigan or USC, two schools whose attempts at fiscal decentralization are the focus of Chapter 6) seemed entirely fair to Snyder, since "Darden doesn't make much use of university services like the computer center." And Sandridge says he wanted a figure that wouldn't cause other deans to rebel.[16]

The final deal gave Darden a degree of independence not enjoyed by its competitors, because Darden's tax is levied only on tuition revenue, not on the proceeds from its lucrative executive education programs or other private sources. While Michigan's business school pays the campus a "tax" of 24 percent on its state operating budget, it also pays a 2 percent tax on its executive education revenue and receives a subsidy from the state of 17.7 percent, giving it considerably less autonomy than Darden.[17]

At Darden, the 10 percent contribution to the campus represents nothing more than a "franchise fee," insists Mark Reisler, Darden's associate dean for administration, and the metaphor is revealing. As Peter Low acknowledges, the business school is really "a separate entity that has a contractual relationship with the rest of the university, constrained only by custom"—a "gentleman's agreement" at a university that long regarded itself as a "gentleman's university."[18] Just as a McDonald's franchise holder pays for the drawing power of the brand, the tax, as Reisler sees it, buys the Thomas Jefferson mystique—the brand—of the University of Virginia. Otherwise, the school generally behaves as if Darden were a stand-alone institution. Snyder's predecessor pointedly skipped deans' meetings because he found them irrelevant. Undergraduates are made unwelcome: signs in the classrooms read "For the Exclusive Use of Darden M.B.A. and Executive Education Students Only." While the business school has modestly supported some campus activities—joining with Institute for Public History, for instance, to bring black leaders to campus—it has done so mainly to buff its image. There are few ties to the institutionally separate, and considerably poorer, undergraduate business school.[19]

To think about a university entirely as a market is to reject the claim that the central administration should determine priorities for the institution as a whole—as, for example, Columbia University does when it identifies the liberal arts college as its centerpiece, and taxes the business and law schools in order to pay for the physicists and poets. The market mindset dismisses the claim that public goods like a computer center or campus museum benefit everyone and so should be underwritten by the entire institution. It also disregards the direct benefit to Darden; as with the USC law school, the business school's reputation is affected by the reputation of its university.

Not surprisingly, deans who can command fewer resources see things differently. Melvin Leffler, a renowned cold war historian who until the summer of 2001 was dean of the College of Arts and Sciences, went public with an attack on how the administration parcels out money—a most un-UVA thing to do. Leffler noted that in 1997–98, tuition revenues exceeded the money made available to the college by $17 million; in other words, the college was really subsidizing the rest of the university, including Darden. While that sum does not include support for institutional public goods, Leffler regards the disparity between revenues and expenditures as revealing the misleading nature of the rhetoric of self-sufficiency: the College of Arts and Sciences could pay its own bills if, like Darden, it were allowed to keep its tuition revenue.[20]

The formula that the campus administration uses to distribute state funds is arcane even to deans who have worked with it for years. Sandridge and Low initially ignored and then dismissed Leffler's claims, but even if the liberal arts college had secured a Darden-like arrangement to keep essentially all the tuition revenue it generated, it would be a bad deal since, unlike Darden, the college can neither raise its tuition nor increase its enrollment without authority from the state. Darden professor and longtime administrator Ray Smith is unsympathetic to the plight of the college. "We don't compete with the rest of the university, we compete with Harvard," he says. "I'd love to help Mel Leffler, but I can't say, 'I'm going to take my money and give you part of it, Mel, because I feel sorry for you.'"

This internal competition for funds generates what former law school dean Robert Scott calls a "poisonous atmosphere." As one campus administrator put it with delicate understatement: "There is a little bit of the 'Babylon on the Hill' phenomenon. If you are a professor of linguistics and your department is starved to death and your pay has barely kept up with inflation, you might be annoyed by what's happening at Darden."

▪ The "Hotel" on the Darden Grounds

At the entrance of the long drive that leads to Darden's grounds sits Sponsors' Hall, home for the 4,000 senior corporate executives who annually come to Charlottesville for an intense retooling course. In the school's early years, the housing was dorm-quality and the food ran to creamed white fish with beets. But with its 180 guest suites, its billiard room, and its white tablecloth dining room, Sponsors Hall rivals a Four Seasons in the quality of its services. No creamed fish here: the chef was snatched from Keswick Hall, a nearby resort that *Condé Nast Traveler* magazine named one of the world's finest small hotels, and his five-course meals—chicken stuffed with Boursin cheese and beef Madeira are among his specialties—are as good as anything for hundreds of miles around.

Such accommodations are what these executives are accustomed to, and their Fortune 500 companies have been willing to pay handsomely for the privilege—as much as $1,000 a day for lodging and classes on topics like "developing managerial excellence." These aren't off-the-shelf courses,

but material that is specially tailored to the needs of the corporation footing the bill. *Business Week* consistently rates Darden's executive program as
among the best two or three in the nation. "It's a great way to develop the
brand," points out Ray Smith.

"Having a few thousand executives come to town has really helped the
faculty stay in touch," says Ted Snyder, but even the former dean acknowledges that the scale of the program is a concern. That's not going to
change, though, since this is Darden's cash cow, generating more than half
of the school's revenues. The tuition for a two-week course is about half
that of an entire year's M.B.A. If Darden is to prosper in the era of self-
sufficiency, it has to keep attracting these managers.

Unlike other business schools, where younger faculty are discouraged
from teaching in the executive education program so that they can focus
on research, at Darden they are expected to do so. "If they can't," says associate dean James Freeland, "we will ask them to leave." Most participate
happily, since the handsome stipends they receive for a few days in the
classroom can nearly double their salaries. "The way to get to market with
faculty," says Snyder, "is to combine a light M.B.A. teaching load"—
about two hours a week—"with executive ed." The development of a new
M.B.A. course can take a year or more, but if the price is right, professors
may be asked to create a course demanded by a particular company that
will be using the materials in a matter of weeks.

These activities, coupled with the school's emphasis on devising new
cases for M.B.A. students, keep many professors from doing the kind of
research that is expected at a top-rank school. Although Darden faculty
write many of the case studies used in business schools throughout the
country, they publish far less in the leading academic journals than their
counterparts at Stanford or Chicago.[21] That troubles those who see the
creation, not just the transmission, of knowledge as vital at a great university. The school recognizes this problem. As Joseph Harder, who came
to Darden from the Wharton School at the University of Pennsylvania,
points out, it's important "to become known for our intellectual capital."
Hiring new faculty to teach in the expanded M.B.A. program has created
an opportunity to recruit more research-minded professors.

More problematic is the fact that some of the executive courses draw on
proprietary material. In those instances, instructors cannot take the case
they developed for, say, Price Waterhouse or Citibank and use it in an
M.B.A. class. In the school's early years, notes Ray Smith, professors
feared the possibility of encroachment on their academic freedom, and so

resisted teaching company-specific courses—the first such course, developed for the postal service, was rationalized as in the public interest—but they were eventually drawn to those courses by the intellectual challenge.

Darden faculty were already teaching in corporate-run programs, Smith notes, but they were doing so on their own time, since "that's how we put our kids through school." Now this teaching has been brought into the school. There's a difference, however, between private consulting and institutional involvement. When Darden offers classes that rely on proprietary teaching material developed for a specific firm, it effaces the line between the academy, where norms of openness prevail, and the instinctively property-minded corporate environment.

Such secrecy is expected at corporate universities like Dell University and Toyota University; their courses are valuable property, and so every effort is made to prevent spies from stealing the materials. Keeping course materials out of the hands of others also makes sense at a school like the University of Phoenix, where those highly proscriptive materials are the institution's stock-in-trade. But insisting on such secrecy at the University of Virginia calls into question the very idea of a public university. It turns Darden itself into a kind of consulting firm.[22]

Administrators at Darden reluctantly acknowledge this fact. Brandt Allen, dean for executive education, says he encourages companies to allow their problems to be aired publicly, in case studies and faculty research. Allen persuaded one initially reluctant firm that incorporating its problem in a case study would be invaluable advertising—especially because the school offered to plaster the company's name throughout the casebook. In the early days of custom-tailored executive education programs, Freeland scolded faculty who spent time preparing proprietary materials for custom programs which could not be published or used in research. "Our purpose in life is not just to do 'exec ed' for making that company better, but it's to generate knowledge that can be shared," he says.

In teaching company-specific material to corporate managers, Darden is no different from Dell—with the crucial exception that as a nonprofit institution it is exempt from taxes, and that as part of the University of Virginia it carries Thomas Jefferson's "brand." That's worth a great deal. As Leonard Sandridge says: "People would pay twice as much for executive education from Darden than from [nearby] James Madison University even if it were with the same professors. Reputation doesn't happen overnight, thank goodness."

▪ Thomas Jefferson's Multiversity

When he became president of the University of Virginia in 1990, John Casteen III believed he could do it all—that he could teach and conduct research as well as manage and lead, and that he could devote just one day in five to fund-raising.[23] Casteen learned otherwise at the end of his first year, when the trustees almost fired him because he hadn't brought in enough money, and he has taken that lesson to heart. UVA's capital campaign, concluded in 2001, brought in $1.43 billion, the second-highest amount raised by any public university. Since Casteen took office, the proportion of the general budget that comes from gifts and endowment earning has mushroomed, from 4–6 percent to 16–18 percent. That is larger than the state's share, which fell by almost half between 1990 and 2003.[24]

Much of Casteen's fund-raising has been undertaken not on behalf of "the university," but rather for campus units that have been able to help themselves. Foremost among them is the McIntire School of Commerce, the undergraduate business school that, borrowing from the Darden playbook, has gone into the graduate training business. Between 1998 and 2001, enrollment in its graduate degree programs jumped from forty to three hundred, and the school has opened a branch in northern Virginia. "We have taken our graduate programs private," says dean Carl Zeithaml, echoing his Darden colleagues. "They are basically a huge net cash flow into the school. We pay a tax, a franchise fee to be part of the UVA umbrella."

The McIntire School has launched the multimillion-dollar, privately funded construction of a new building—and the economics department, long eager to escape its decrepit home in Rouss Hall, harbors similar ambitions. Although the campus administration incorporated the economics department's request for new and expanded space into plans for a new "South Lawn Project," no clear timetable was fixed. Since state funds won't be sufficient to underwrite the project, the economics department has threatened to woo donors whose gifts can be used only for its own building. If that money arrives, the economists reason, the campus will have to go along.

Edgar Olsen, the economics professor who is ashamed to show his Rouss Hall office to his mother, hopes that fund-raising becomes a responsibility of departments, not schools, a prospect that chills impoverished departments such as classics. "It's true that almost any fund-raising in any field will detract from the ability to fund-raise in other areas," Olsen acknowledges. "But if the university was allowed to raise money by going through the individual departments, the total would be greater than raising money as a whole. When people complain about Darden having these lavish buildings and we have these crappy buildings, I say, 'That's fine. We should go raise our own money.'"

The rhetoric of privatization is by no means confined to the more commercial units of the campus. Melvin Leffler, the former dean of the College of Arts and Sciences, took the idea of entrepreneurialism to heart. When he failed to extract additional funds from the campus administration, he became a money raiser, hiring one of the Darden School's development officers to show the way. In 2002, when lawmakers announced cuts approaching $100 million to the university's two-year budget, President Casteen responded by saying that the university had no choice but to look to sources other than the state for funds. He pledged to embark on the "necessary next capital campaign whose goal is to move the University yet another step closer to self-sufficiency." The goal is $3 to $5 billion; but in tough economic times, that money will be very hard to raise.[25]

Even the library—the emblem of the commons in the modern university—is pursuing self-sufficiency. Librarian Karin Wittenborg declared that her goal is to move the library toward "privatization," meaning that much of its budget would be privately endowed and its operating decisions would be made not by the university administration but internally. Wittenborg has already hired a development officer and spends much of her time fund-raising. At UVA the language of privatization, once a political hot button, is now a rallying cry.

In some ways, this market-driven activity coincides with Thomas Jefferson's original vision. The University of Virginia was never meant to be the Harvard of the South. Unlike Harvard, it wasn't devoted mainly to the education of clergy, teachers, and lawyers, and it wasn't committed to a unified classical education. Jefferson imagined a collection of specialized schools in close proximity to one another, essentially graduate schools that granted specialized degrees in both traditional subjects such as philosophy and new fields such as medicine. But Jefferson believed that Virginia needed a university that deserved public funds because it would serve the public good. As he outlined his dream: "We wish to establish . . . a University on a plan so broad and liberal and modern, as to be worth patronizing with the public support, and be a temptation to the youth of other States to come and drink of the cup of knowledge and fraternize with us."[26] The evolution of the Darden School, by contrast, represents the triumph of the private over the public good.

Then as now, it was hard to secure state backing. "My hopes are kept in check by the ordinary character of our state legislatures," Jefferson wrote a friend, "the members of which do not generally posses information enough to perceive the important truths, that knowledge is power, that knowledge is safety, and that knowledge is happiness."[27] Two centuries later, faced with a mounting budget deficit, state lawmakers reduced their contribution to UVA once again, and faculty hiring was frozen in many schools and departments. The beleaguered economics department was obliged to cut thirty courses or sections from its 2002 schedule because of faculty departures and positions that remain unfilled during the hiring freeze. In 2002, Virginia slipped to second place among public universities in the *U.S. News & World Report* rankings, twenty-third overall, and many blame the lack of state support. In the category of "financial resources," UVA fell from sixty-fourth to sixty-sixth place. Virginia provides half as much funding per student as North Carolina does at the Chapel Hill campus.[28]

The lean times have focused more attention on discrepancies between the college and the professional schools. Some professors are angry about the special treatment given to Darden. Others are simply bemused by the vulgarity of a place they see imitating the style but not the substance of Jefferson's college. Even undergraduates have begun to question the priorities of the university as a whole, as library hours are reduced while the red brick and white columns flanking Darden's new parking garage are meticulously cared for. "The million-dollar question that must be asked of the school's administration," one UVA student wrote in an op-ed piece in the *Washington Times*, "is 'why does a school with a $1.7 billion endowment starve its liberal arts college?'"[29] In 2003, the editors of the student newspaper called for a tuition increase, a "rare instance of customers complaining about low prices."[30]

Because it is more self-sufficient than other campus units, Darden has less of a stake in the machinations in Richmond. And because recessions inspire a return to the safe harbor of school, at Darden as at business schools across the country, the number of applications has risen significantly since 2000. But the economic downturn has had a major long-run impact on an institution that opted to live by—and so suffer with—the marketplace.

Darden's transition to self-sufficiency coincided with the greatest unin-terrupted era of economic growth in U.S. history, and the school bene-fited accordingly. It was easy enough in that economic climate to forget that firms can cut costs even more quickly and severely than legislatures re-duce budgets. "Ailing companies, including giants like Ford, are sending far fewer managers to $100-a-day classes," observes *Forbes Magazine,* and at Darden, executive attendance fell by 15 percent in 2001.[31] The school reacted in true entrepreneurial fashion, offering a new—free—web-based course, "Leadership in Turbulent Times," as a come-on to prospective customers.

▪ The Market and the Holy Father

It's far too early to know how a privatized Darden will fare in "turbulent times." It merits recalling that, barely a quarter of a century ago, it was private institutions that were widely regarded as endangered, even as pub-lic universities were thriving; conceivably public support could be revived over the long run. Meanwhile, the strategy of privatization has had a major impact at UVA. In its eagerness to enter the elite national ranks, Darden has made the pursuit of money its main objective. In doing so, it has deemphasized research as faculty energy that elsewhere would be devoted to scholarship and theory is sapped by corporate training needs.

Still, by the conventional indices of success, the strategy has worked brilliantly, as the school's dramatic rise in the *Business Week* rankings at-tests. Other public universities are making similar deals with their business schools, and business schools are competing vigorously for lucrative exec-utive training contracts. Darden may well embody the future. And what works for business schools can be adapted to other units of the university, especially the professional schools.

So too for the "state-located" University of Virginia. The temptation to privatize has led UVA farther from being a university that emphasizes the cultivation of knowledge and closer to being a holding company. Char-lottesville is home to UVA, Inc., a great money-making engine, an institu-tion where, as the classic welfare economic model specifies, the public in-terest is conceived as the sum of all the stakeholders' interests.

That's the nub of the problem. "If you look at the history of higher ed-ucation," says Gordon Davies, the longtime director of Virginia's Council of Higher Education, "the university was controlled by, and had to fight for intellectual purity against, the church; then it had to fight against the crown; and now it's against the corporation. There has always been a tension between the university and the funding source that could control the thought. We always have to say that the earth goes around the sun even if it doesn't comport with what the Holy Father says."

In place of the Holy Father there is the impersonal market which demands that the university conform to its preferences, but the underlying question remains the same. Can a university maintain the intellectual world that Thomas Jefferson sought to represent in his design of the Lawn—professors and students with diverse academic interests coming together in a single open space to pursue and create knowledge—if learning becomes just another consumer good?

PART III

VIRTUAL WORLDS

Rebel Alliance
Classics Departments in the Associated Colleges of the South

On a humid morning in June 2001, Kenny Morrell, a philologist and classics professor at Rhodes College in Memphis, is seated at a conference table, discussing Greek poetry with faculty colleagues from several other schools.[1] A dozen new Macintosh computers ring the room. Hal Haskell, the head of the classics program at Southwestern University in Georgetown, Texas, where the workshop is taking place, keeps swinging his chair around to check airline prices on-line. As Haskell, a specialist in Bronze Age ceramics, makes last-minute arrangements for a trip to Turkey, where he and other faculty are taking students to participate in an archaeological dig, Morrell pushes the workshop session forward, reading notes from his laptop.

These academics have traveled to a small town in Texas, thirty miles north of Austin and just down the road from the headquarters of the Dell computer company, to immerse themselves in recent classical scholarship. They've also come together to launch an innovative Web-based undergraduate course on Greek elegy and lyric poetry, one of several on-line classics courses being offered to students in a handful of southern colleges.

The topic for the morning seminar, the last of an intensive three-day workshop, is Leslie Kurke's *Traffic in Praise*. Morrell plainly relishes the opportunity to perform in this setting, parsing a difficult text and rendering the poet Pindar the subject of an intellectual passion play. He's just as much at home in the world of contemporary theory as he is in the world of classical texts, easily sliding from a summation of Judith Butler on speech acts to a close reading of Bacchylides' Ode 5.

In this sense, the comparison between Kenny Morrell and Leslie Kurke seems apt, and the two scholars are more or less peers: Kurke received her Ph.D. in classics from Princeton in 1988, and Morrell earned his at Harvard a year later. But while Kurke, a Berkeley professor and the 1999 recip-

149

ient of a MacArthur fellowship, is a cutting-edge scholar well on her way to multidisciplinary renown—just the kind of professor that a star-driven institution like NYU would covet—Morrell is the chairman of a tiny department of Greek and Roman studies at a small liberal arts college whose reach is regional, not global.

Morrell isn't without ambition, but he is not fixated on academic stardom as it is generally conceived. Improving teaching and strengthening institutions are his passions. "I want to create educational experiences," he says, "that will compete with experiences at research institutions." To high school students choosing among, say, the University of Tennessee, Vanderbilt University, and Rhodes College, he'd like to say, "You can get an education in classics here that's as good as what you'll find anyplace in the country."

Morrell has gone to great lengths to make this dream a reality. Working with enterprising colleagues at campuses scattered from Virginia to Texas, and blessed with a steady stream of financial support from the Mellon Foundation, he is trying to build his own major department. Sunoikisis, the project is called. The name refers to an ancient alliance among the cities of Lesbos during an attempted revolt against the Athenian empire, but the ambition is entirely modern: to create a nationally visible "Virtual Department of Classics."

▪ "Creating Demand for Our Product"

In the fall of 1999, when the first Sunoikisis course, literature of the early Roman Empire, went on-line, outsized predictions about how the Internet would shatter the pedagogical mold were the order of the day. "The Web is revolutionizing learning," Nobel Prize–winning economist Gary Becker opined in *Business Week*.[2] "Killer apps," on-line offerings for the big introductory undergraduate courses, would sweep the field the way Amazon.com was sweeping commerce in books, CDs, and videos.[3] "Education over the Internet is going to be so big it is going to make e-mail usage look like a rounding error," said John Chambers, the CEO of Cisco Systems.[4]

This was the apogee of the dot-com era, and venture capitalists quickly got the message. They started dumping $100 million every quarter into e-learning start-ups—and that was just the beginning. A Merrill Lynch report published in May 2000 featured a picture of Albert Einstein and promised a "$2 *Trillion* [Education] Market Catalyzed by the Internet."[5]

Even though Georgetown, Texas, is a very long way from Wall Street or Silicon Valley, Kenny Morrell and his colleagues were also reacting to new market forces; and like Gary Becker, they appreciated the potential of the Internet. But there the similarities cease. No venture capitalist was going to invest in a course on the Roman Empire, because there was no money to be made. Only an intrepid foundation—a *social* venture capitalist—would underwrite such an undertaking.[6]

That was just fine with these classicists. They were excited by the new technology not because it promised to make their schools rich but because it was a tool that each of them could use to give their students the kind of first-rate education that none of these colleges could afford to offer on its own. Forget southern courtliness. These professors knew they were under siege by both classics departments at nearby universities and academic poachers within their own colleges. They had to band together or risk extinction.

The familiar image of classicists is that they are otherworldly characters, quintessential academics disdainful of "relevance." "Many of them retreated into an elitism, an ivory tower mentality," Morrell observes. "They said, 'I do not have to justify myself to you; you in fact have to justify yourself to me, because I represent the oldest, most central, most venerable discipline, the understanding of the ancient languages. You are not worthy of my thoughts unless you can understand the ancient languages as I do.'"

"So we essentially became the elitists," he adds, "the people who inhabited the highest floors of the ivory tower and tried to make our discipline as inaccessible as possible to inflate our own self-worth. And that had catastrophic consequences. But I think we have come around. We have realized that is insane."

In a field widely thought to rank high on the academic endangered species list, where both students and faculty positions are scarce, Morrell and his colleagues are devising a strategy for permanence.[7] Rather than taking a defensive stance, Morrell's preferred approach when dealing with potential audiences for classical studies, whether colleagues or students, is one that begins by reaching out.

His promotion of Sunoikisis is in large part an extension of that entrepreneurial impulse. "I want my students to have an extraordinarily rich experience in my discipline," he says, sounding like an economist discussing Pareto-optimizing moves, "and I know that my institution is not in a position to marshal all those resources independently to do that. I've got to get other people involved. To do that, we have to establish this bartering system. I need your expertise and I'm willing to share what expertise I have. We can benefit each other and each other's students."

Southwestern's Hal Haskell sounds a similar note. "We think we have a good product," he says, relying on the rhetoric of marketing, "but as traditionally delivered, it does not have a broad appeal. Yet in our view, there is a market out there that would very much enjoy this material. We can do a much better job delivering the stuff collectively, and serving our individual campuses as a result."

When Rhodes College recruited Morrell in 1993, luring him from St. Olaf College in Minnesota, it was looking for someone to devise what he calls a "flexible, modular, forward-looking" classics program, focused less on expanding the pool of potential Ph.D.s than on creating "a base of well-educated students, an informed broader public supportive of research and teaching in classics."

"The only way that we can grow as a discipline—the only way we can survive—is to create demand for our product," Morrell says matter-of-factly. "The only way we are going to survive is to get students in our classrooms. The only way that we can create a stimulating and inviting and provocative world of study for the students is collectively." This is where Sunoikisis—a technologically assisted intellectual collaboration among colleges habituated to competing for students—becomes a critical force.

▪ Classics Come to Life

Students who are participating in the classes offered by Sunoikisis gather each week in their campus computer labs or classrooms to log on to the Sunoikisis website. Using Real Player to receive the streaming audio—streaming video awaits additional funding and technological advances—they listen to a synchronous lecture broadcast live on the Internet. This virtual classroom is a natural setting for the multitasking generation. Students tune in to a live lecture and read their professor's notes on one open desktop window, while simultaneously sending questions to the lecturer, responding to questions they're being asked, and "conversing" with one another via another open window.

If the streaming audio lecture reproduces, at a distance, a familiar academic experience, the virtual conversation mimics an actual classroom exchange. That creates an unfamiliar teaching challenge, since instead of responding directly to raised hands, the lecturer has to follow the chat room discussion along with all the students. This means keeping an eye open for queries while sitting alone in front of a computer, maintaining the flow of the conversation while reading lecture notes into a small microphone. Meanwhile, whether in a "whisper" or to the entire group, students are exchanging notes in what's called the ChatSpace with someone who might be fifteen hundred miles or fifteen feet away.

The experience demands a lot from students. "It isn't standard distance education," Morrell says, "not at all like just listening in." Indeed, the very idea of "distance education" is anathema to the Sunoikisis faculty. Hal Haskell refers to the on-line courses as "team-taught." "We have our team spread throughout the South," he says, "and just use technology to bring us together." Sunoikisis, the participants insist, isn't classics on the cheap. Instead, the intention is to combine the best of the old and the new—to embed a technologically enhanced experience, one that crosses institutional boundaries, within a pedagogy that retains the traditional emphasis on face-to-face interaction.

The on-line discussion continues after the lecture, as students are expected to post their responses to the lecturer's questions on the WebBoard. In theory, "discussion" follows, with students commenting on the work of their classmates. That kind of robust on-line dialogue has been hard to generate—students mainly talk with their "live" classmates between sessions, and professors use the postings mainly to monitor their students' progress—but Morrell thinks this will change.

"My generation places such a premium on person-to-person interaction because that was the only type we really knew," he says, riffing from Marshall McLuhan.[8] "The children of the global village have come to know something quite different. Whether the members of each unique gathering are there in person or contribute to the conversation via fiber optics from points around the globe ultimately should not matter."

A majority of adolescents report that they have made a friend on the Internet; why can't a virtual intellectual community take off? Or so the Sunoikisis professors hope. The WebBoard "allows for a particular moment of coherent thought," says Rebecca Resinski, who teaches classics at Hendrix College in Conway, Arkansas. "As a result of such moments, a community and a conversation are developed." When Morrell promotes the on-line conversation to his students, he appeals to their competitive instincts. "You have the chance," he tells them, "to see how you stack up against students at other universities."

Most of these professors don't believe that on-the-ground teaching will be replaced by its virtual simulacrum. "The information technology revolution may be here," says Elise Friedland, a professor at Rollins College in Winter Park, Florida, "but technological advances can't replace the value of real-life teaching." That's why the virtual courses build in a weekly tutorial. It's also why, at least for now, basic language learning isn't part of the on-line curriculum. Hal Haskell reels off a list of what gets lost in trying to teach Greek or Latin at a distance: "nuance, gesture, intonation, facial expression." These aspects of communication, he says, are "critical elements for most of us not completely married to our machines." Kenny Morrell, ever the futurist, thinks otherwise: "In fifty years, will it be as efficient to learn a language using primarily digital resources? Without a doubt."

▪ Vanguard Classicists

The creation of a Virtual Department of Classics has been a driving ambition since Sunoikisis was launched in 1996. But the enterprise started out with a much more modest goal: to make professors comfortable using the new technologies. Sometimes this proved a challenge, since, as Glenda Carl of Southwestern University recalls, "people were still learning how to put up web pages."

Still, when it comes to utilizing the Internet in research and teaching, classicists have a big jump on their colleagues in other fields. The discipline that's most focused on the past is also the most sophisticated in looking to the future. "If we consider the evolution of our field," says Morrell, "we've gone through some incredible technological changes. The Internet is just one more incarnation."

When asked why classics has led the way in the use of advanced technology, Morrell goes back to the early 1970s and the story of a single individual, David Packard Jr. It is, as well, Morrell's own story.

As a graduate student in classics at Harvard, Packard acquired from his father, the co-founder of the computer giant Hewlett Packard, both a passion for digital technology and the money he needed to figure out how best to use this new technology. His work in compiling the first electronic concordance in the discipline became a springboard for the field, and he helped to bring into being the *Thesaurus Linguae Graecae* (TLG), an electronic database of classical texts. Interest grew in rendering classical literature into electronic form, and by the mid-1980s, select departments were receiving fifteen-hundred-foot-long magnetic tapes with Greek on them, written in Beta code, that Packard had helped create. At Harvard, Gregory Crane took an interest in these tapes, developing a Unix-based full text retrieval system for the new database.

That's when Morrell came to Harvard as a graduate student. He began working with Crane, writing documentation that would make the texts more readily available. Soon Crane got Morrell involved in the Perseus Project, which has created an electronic library of sources for classical literature.[9] "It is now impossible," says Morrell, "for anyone doing legitimate scholarship in classics not to be fluent in the use of these resources."

When Kenny Morrell arrived at St. Olaf College in 1989 as a newly minted Ph.D., he was entirely unprepared to teach undergraduates. As a graduate student he had specialized in philology, but he wouldn't have the chance to teach his specialty. Instead he was expected to convey a panoramic view of the ancient world, not only teaching courses in Latin and Greek but also offering sweeping surveys of tragedy and myth. "I don't know anything about my discipline," he remembers thinking to himself. A "massive re-tooling" was needed.

Soon enough, Morrell realized that he wasn't alone in his predicament. What saved him professionally was the collective expertise of a network of professors at other midwestern colleges that came together under the umbrella of a regional association. "It was one of those epiphanies," he says of a weekend when his classics colleagues swapped teaching strategies, "something I had never experienced."

When he was recruited by Rhodes College a few years later, charged with the grandiose task of building "a program for the twenty-first century," his advice was solicited by Wayne Anderson, president of the Associated Colleges of the South (ACS), a consortium patterned after the midwestern network that was just getting off the ground. It's vital to "get classicists together," Morrell told Anderson, especially for someone teaching at a college like Rhodes, where the department had just doubled in size—to two.

Morrell and his colleagues at the ACS schools envisioned using Sunoikisis to enlarge the number and variety of courses they could offer. Several colleges were already working jointly on the archaeological dig where Hal Haskell spends most of his summers. "There are all sorts of Mediterranean digs where undergraduates can go for a huge fee," he points out, "but they wind up doing shoveling and wheelbarrowing. Our students are out there on the mound; they are trench supervisors. That's the kind of opportunity normally available only to grad students. By pooling our resources, the ACS becomes an institution with sufficient critical mass to participate in an excavation like this."

Sunoikisis started off with the same aspiration: to pool resources in order to offer an education far better than any of the colleges could manage on its own. Out of those initial faculty conversations came the idea of using the Internet to link faculty and students through a virtual department.

As often happens with successful innovations, the stars were aligned. There was money to underwrite Kenny Morrell's dreams.[10] The Mellon Foundation had recently decided to support "economies of scale" reforms to help liberal arts colleges thrive even in a harsh economic climate, and collaborative ventures like Sunoikisis were high on the foundation's list of priorities. At the same time, the potential of the Internet was becoming more obvious to the foundation, which has been one of the major backers of campus-based distance learning projects.[11] Morrell's experience with Perseus, as well as his special talent for academic entrepreneurship, made him a natural choice to head a new venture.

"Kenny Morrell was a real intellectual and inspirational leader," says Wayne Anderson. "Early on he saw the possibilities of technology, not only in classics but across the board." For his part, Morrell regards innovations in technology and organization as intimately connected. Responding to the changing dynamics of the academic market, he thinks, requires seismic shifts in organization as well as the pedagogy of higher education—taking full advantage of the growing value of the Internet for teaching and learning, and promoting collaboration across institutional boundaries.

Universities aren't inclined to commit their own funds to educational partnerships—they have their own identities to maintain, their own "brands" to market—but the advent of e-learning has spawned a great many partnerships. Attention has focused on companies like Fathom (Columbia's for-profit offspring whose trajectory is described in the next chapter), which has placed on the Web a wealth of material from some of the world's leading universities, museums, and libraries, and Universitas 21, a virtual degree-granting university whose membership roster lists eighteen universities on four continents.[12] Far from that jet set world, community colleges from Pennsylvania to Colorado have been early adopters of Internet-based education, and the Community College Distance Learning Network brings together schools in Texas, Ohio, Arizona, and California.[13] Many historically black colleges are also banding together to bring distance learning courses to their campuses.[14]

"Collaboration through distance learning" is fast becoming a movement in higher education. But there has to be an interested faculty and student clientele—a market—and whether the Sunoikisis experiment will run long enough to become a poster child for this new movement is uncertain. "We are still trying to find our market," says Kenny Morrell. "From the perspective of those who teach in the larger [ACS] programs, these courses may not necessarily reflect an improvement on what they have developed locally. We believe they do, but until some faculty members actually try the courses and become invested in them, they won't make the transition."

■ The Problems of the Here and Now

On a mild November evening in 2001, Leslie Kurke, the rising star from Berkeley whose text the Sunoikisis faculty had been dissecting some months earlier, arrives at Rhodes College. She has come to deliver one of the Sunoikisis project's Mellon lectures, on the poetry of Sappho and Alcaeus, a talk linked to the advanced Greek course that the Sunoikisis faculty was devising during their summer meetings.

Inviting a leading scholar in the field to spend a few days at Rhodes or Hendrix or Southwestern is meant to give Sunoikisis, and classics, a bit of cachet on the campus. Intellectual luminaries seldom visit these remoter parts of academe, and there are campus "tie-ins" to go with the lecture. Because Sunoikisis is a virtual department, the intention is also to use the talk as a way of showcasing the power of the Internet, making it possible for budding classicists from Maryland to Texas to e-mail their questions for an instant response.

Kurke does her part and more. In the morning she stops by a class on myth to talk about some of Sappho's poems that these students, few of them classics majors, have been reading. She plays the guest of honor at a sorority luncheon, and at the dinner before her talk, she chats equably with a wealthy patron of the Rhodes program in Greek and Roman studies. But the technology proves a bust.

Although Kurke herself is decidedly low-tech—she writes out her talk in longhand—that isn't the problem. Kenny Morrell, the host of these festivities, has put on-line the fragments of Sappho's poetry, that "rosy fingered moon" Kurke is talking about, so anyone on-line can read the poems along with her. Yet logging on turns out to be a mighty challenge—and once you're logged on, there's almost no one with whom to chat, just Hal Haskell at Southwestern and a few others. None of them are "talking," and so all the intellectual action is taking place among the twenty-five people in the room, just as it would with any other lecture.

It's a fittingly frustrating climax to a semester when the technological glitches have been so bad that the lecturing faculty have sometimes had to revert to the earlier practice of phoning in their lectures. This aspect of Sunoikisis—in some sense its raison d'être—still bears the marks of the project's relative infancy. Nor is the demand for a virtual course in Greek as great as the course creators assumed, perhaps because it's the first time the course is being offered.[15] Even though students who are studying Greek in any of the participating colleges can enroll, the class has only five students. Three of them—all of whom are sitting in the audience, none using a laptop—are from Rhodes, and they are decidedly underwhelmed by the virtual component of the course. As one of them says, "I'm not sure if I'm getting too much from the fact that it is on the Internet."

▪ Propelled by the Professors

"The new technology of education," the historian David Noble claims in *Digital Diploma Mills,* his widely read critique of Internet-based instruction, "like the automation of other industries, robs faculty of their knowledge and skills, their control over their working lives, the product of their labor, and, ultimately, their means of livelihood."[16] But the Sunoikisis academics are badly cast for Noble's Marxist melodrama. Rather than being the hapless and unwitting victims of a technology imposed from above, they themselves are the champions of the venture.

"It does take a hell of a lot of energy and time," says Hal Haskell. "In these first years, we are not saving time. We are creating work for ourselves. It's a heck of a lot easier to sit back and do your traditional courses the way you have always done them. No one messes with you, and you have the routine down, and you go home at night and sleep and get up the next morning and come back and do the same thing. That sounds pretty nice to me right now, actually." That's why persuading faculty to become part of Sunoikisis isn't always easy. "Inertia is the greatest force in the universe," he says. "We have to overcome that to get people excited, to see that this is really neat stuff that we are doing, and we can really do a much better job of teaching it by getting students involved with this."

These professors are not afraid that their jobs are in jeopardy. Although Haskell acknowledges the obvious—"administrators are always looking for ways to cut back on numbers of faculty"—classics is an unlikely candidate for the chop. At these schools, where instructors typically teach three, and sometimes four, courses a term, classics professors regularly teach one or two extra classes. "I have a long way to go before I go to regular time," Haskell adds, "so there is no way they can save on faculty resources. We cannot get any smaller."

Kenny Morrell takes this argument one step further. "We are not losing faculty members anywhere, we are gaining faculty members," he says, pointing to new positions at Hendrix and Rhodes. "A little bit facetiously, I would say to that legion of academics out there who are worried about losing their jobs: Become classicists. Because we are going to build the market. If you want job security, come to our discipline. Forget about French, forget about Russian—become a classicist, because we are going to build a market for your services."

"This initiative was propelled by the professors," says Rebecca Resinski. "It was something we chose to do in order to collect our strengths." That's precisely as it should be, says Hal Haskell: "It worries me when faculty colleagues want to leave it to administrators to set the pace. We should set the damn pace. To hell with the administrators. We want the administrators to listen to us, or we want them to see the great stuff we are doing. But we should be driving the agenda."

So far, most administrators have been willing to go along, especially since the Mellon Foundation is underwriting the venture. But when the foundation money dries up, the deans will have to decide whether the initiative is worth paying for out of their own funds. "I think we are all willing to experiment," says A. V. Huff Jr., vice president for academic affairs at Furman University in Greenville, South Carolina, "but devoting institutional dollars is another matter." The ultimate question, Huff says, a bit ominously, "is whether the time and money involved are worth the effort—and the answer to that question is yet to be determined."

The boldness of Sunoikisis, which is what makes it interesting, also makes watchful campus administrators uneasy, fearful that, as Hal Haskell puts it with some pride, the project is "a loose cannon." "Since we are making it up as we go along," he says, "Sunoikisis is running unchecked from their perspective. They have no control. We're dreaming up all this stuff. We get all this money. And I think they wonder, 'What in hell are these people doing?'"

The project's challenges are not simply a matter of college deans' anxieties about their own administrative authority. Rather, they extend to more basic questions of institutional identity. The ACS is a microcosm of the diverse world of liberal arts colleges. Schools like Southwestern and

Hendrix are regional institutions. Davidson College in North Carolina has a national reputation; it is ranked tenth among liberal arts colleges by *U.S. News & World Report*. Where a school is situated on that prestige ladder affects its receptivity to an entity like Sunoikisis that blurs these differences.

"We have a very strong classics department," says Clark Ross, vice president for academic affairs at Davidson, "and as a result, I am not sure our faculty have seen a great need to be involved in this initiative." Davidson's faculty and administrators have their flags firmly staked in the soil of their home institution.[17] This is far from the rarefied domain of the academic luminaries who bestow prestige on the university; in this world, the school's reputation is bound up with a faculty member's professional identity. The professor's standing benefits the school, and the school's standing also affects the professor. "I prefer a real department to a 'virtual' department," adds Ross's colleague Peter Krentz, who teaches Greek and Roman history. "While I see [Sunoikisis] as having some benefits for small departments, it strikes me on the whole as more of a threat than a help to larger departments."

The same difficulties have dogged far more ambitious collaborations such as Universitas 21. In 2001, two of its biggest players, the University of Toronto and the University of Michigan, decided to withdraw from the consortium. They were troubled by encroachments on their own institutional autonomy, as well as by the effect that a more robust collaboration would have on their individual institutional identities. "We had concerns that our faculty would not be sufficiently involved in the development or quality control of the venture's academic programs," said Gary D. Krenz, special counsel to the president at Michigan. "We're also engaged in other approaches to e-learning, and we determined that our educational interests would likely be better served through those other activities." Toronto was especially worried about using its own logos and crests for degrees issued by Universitas 21. Collaboration, it was feared, would dilute the brand.[18]

Not only do the ACS colleges differ in size and academic prestige; they also vary in more mundane but equally important ways. Even getting colleges to list a course is never a simple process. What's more, each of the ACS schools operates on a different academic calendar. Classes begin and end at different times of the day, different days of the week, different weeks of the year. In that organizational miasma, the task of finding a meeting time becomes a logistical nightmare, and the innocuous façade of logistics has been used to mask deeper animosities. "Don't you dare talk to our registrar," Morrell remembers being warned by a professor at another college who was hostile to the very idea of collaboration. Only after artful negotiation was agreement reached: the Latin class would convene Monday evenings at seven o'clock, not an hour when undergraduates are used to parsing Seneca.

Pushed forward in spite of these obstacles, Sunoikisis isn't just an unthreatening technological initiative, an institutional marriage of convenience. Morrell and Haskell have also helped their younger colleagues reshape their struggling programs to attract more students. "It's incredible," says Elise Friedland, who chairs the classical studies program at Rollins College. "They just took us under their wing."

In the process, they have helped to transform the discipline at these schools, making it much more student-friendly. The name has changed from "classics" to "classical studies," with its echo of cultural studies, and the substance is new as well.[19] The classics are increasingly being taught in translation to attract an introductory-level undergraduate audience, and in courses like "Power and Persuasion," devised by Rebecca Frost Davis of the University of the South, students read Plato's *Apology* alongside Martin Luther King Jr.'s *Letter from a Birmingham Jail*. There's also a trend toward the study of "material culture," as classicists collaborate with art historians and archaeologists. "You cannot stick with just the texts," says Friedland, "because in this day and age, that is too remote for the students."

All this activity has prompted a revival in students' interest. But enrollment is a zero-sum game, and the same undergraduates who are now exploring material culture in a classical studies program would otherwise be taking classes offered by other departments. In the present money-driven environment, where the department's claim to campus resources turns on its capacity to fill the seats, jealousies inevitably arise on each campus as well as between campuses.

▪ Today the Campus, Tomorrow Harvard

Even as Sunoikisis struggles to survive, the Associated Colleges of the South is expanding its on-line offerings, and reaching outside the region to do so. A Virtual Department of Modern Languages dubbed ALIANCO (Allied Languages in a Networked Collaboration Online), patterned after Sunoikisis, is really a "tri-consortium" that includes two similar entities in the Midwest. Yet another initiative, the Global Partners Project, links schools in all three consortiums with institutions in East Africa, central Europe, and Turkey. With additional support from the Mellon Foundation, the ACS Technology Center worked with its counterpart in the Midwest to support the use of technology at a hundred liberal arts colleges nationwide.[20]

Meanwhile, Sunoikisis wants to extend its reach beyond the Mason-Dixon line, linking up with the midwestern college consortium in which Morrell first experienced the benefits of faculty collaboration. "Sunoikisis is sort of like a business," says Morrell, "and we want to grow our business. Ultimately, the long-term viability of this project is going to depend on a critical mass of people out there. We can grow internally or we can go out and acquire. We can build a critical mass much more efficiently, much more effectively, by building relationships with other institutions."

These unlikely entrepreneurs are ultimately fired by a desire to reconfigure the discipline itself—not as faculty members from Rhodes College or Southwestern University but as professors from Sunoikisis, a virtual institution powerful enough to place its graduates in the best Ph.D. programs and also to have a say in what's being taught there.

"One of the goals," says Morrell—who likes referring to Sunoikisis as a "rebel alliance"—"is to achieve a status in our field, where we can begin to exert an influence on graduate programs and say, 'Look, we cannot hire pure philologists anymore. You may want to train and graduate people who specialize in Attic oratory or tragedy or Greek lyric poetry, but they must have a grounding in the world of material culture. They have to be able to synthesize these ideas, because our students demand that, and this is the world they are living in.' It's not just about ideas and about texts, but it's about reality. And I think it is partly a function of the world we live in."

Just as top colleges and universities have been relying on early decision as a recruiting tool, Kenny Morrell is scheming about how to use early decision to expand his project's potential. His vision is to enroll early admits to Rhodes who have substantial language experience into the Sunoikisis courses while they are still seniors in high school. A high school senior from Birmingham who plans to attend Rhodes might take a Greek course via the Internet, relying on tutorial assistance from a faculty member at Birmingham-Southern. Even more than the standard Sunoikisis course, however, this idea relies on the willingness and ability of classics faculty to see themselves as part of a larger whole, one that transcends their individual institution—a Virtual Department of Classics.

Hal Haskell allows himself to dream out loud: "By the way, Harvard, this is Sunoikisis, and we've got, collectively, a very large and important program nationally, and we choose to be listened to as a result." Like Morrell, Haskell sees Sunoikisis as a potential source of disciplinary transformation. "If we package it right," he says, "it gives us the clout of the big schools."

Much more than packaging is required, though, if that dream is going to be realized. Most of Harvard's classicists haven't heard about, let alone contemplated listening to, these entrepreneurial upstarts. The original Sunoikisis, the rebel alliance among the cities of Lesbos, ultimately failed, but that doesn't faze the contemporary alliance's irrepressible founder. "We might be just ever so slightly ahead of the curve," says Morrell, "but if we do not do this, if we do not succeed, someone else will. It's just a matter of time."

9

The Market in Ideas

Columbia University and the Massachusetts Institute of Technology

Arthur Miller sounded mournful: his beloved Harvard Law School had let him down.[1] Miller loved to put on a show, and for as long as he had been teaching, he had sought out audiences beyond his classroom. Beginning in 1979, he was the host and inquisitor on the TV show *Miller's Court*, mercilessly deploying the Socratic method to extract experts' opinions on ripped-from-the-headlines topics. The noted civil procedure professor had long sold videotaped lectures of his course, and his gravelly Brooklyn voice was heard on audiotapes prepared for the market. "There was never a whisper of unhappiness" about any of this, he says. But in the fall of 1999, Harvard bluntly informed him that he couldn't provide videotaped lectures to students at Concord Law School, the nation's first virtual law school.

Professors "should not be deflected from their primary commitment to educate Harvard students by assuming competing obligations to teach for other institutions," the law school's hastily drafted guidelines declared, and that, said dean Robert Clark, is precisely what the videotaped lectures amounted to. "That's nonsense," Miller responded with some heat. "I'm just doing what I've always done—teaching law." In a six-page letter to the dean, Miller argued that he was simply helping out a brand new school and trying out a new technology.

Miller's Court Interlocutor v. *The Paper Chase* Law School. Because of who the protagonists are, this story made the front pages. Miller talked about suing Harvard, even about resigning. But the problem quietly went away, and by the fall of 2001, Miller was no longer listed as a faculty member on Concord's website.

The particulars of this case have become the stuff of law school classroom exercises. Did it matter, legally, that Miller had prepared the lectures during the summer, setting up the video equipment in his garage? That he had no personal contact with Concord students? That Concord, unaccredited by the American Bar Association, isn't exactly "competing" with Harvard?

"We want our fundamental principles to remain intact," said a university spokesman, but for Harvard this dispute was as much a matter of money as principle. The university was insistent that it retain control over the world's most prestigious higher education brand. "What distinguishes the Internet from everything else," said Miller's peripatetic colleague Alan Dershowitz, himself a regular on TV talk shows and a syndicated columnist, "is the number of zeroes."[2]

Concord is no fly-by-night operation. It is owned by Kaplan, the SAT prep course company, which has invested in a number of higher education ventures; and Kaplan, in turn, is owned by the *Washington Post*. If Arthur Miller's name became associated with Concord, the fear was that Harvard's most precious asset, its reputation—its brand—might suffer. And Miller was hardly the biggest celebrity at Harvard, or even at the law school. If he could be paid to deliver lectures to law students enrolled elsewhere, what might Alan Dershowitz command?[3]

Soon enough, academe's heavy hitters were weighing in, voicing arguments about academic freedom, intellectual property, and the nature of a professor's obligations to the university community. "How much of Arthur Miller," Miller asked himself, "does Harvard own?" His story had become a test case whose reverberations have been felt far beyond the Charles River.

At the same time, as the Arthur Miller contretemps was unfolding, David Finney, head of NYU's just-launched e-learning company, NYU Online, reached for the grand history lesson to describe the "revolution" being ushered in by the Internet. "When Gutenberg invented the printing press five hundred years ago," Finney said, "universities made a big mistake" in allowing professors to claim ownership of books they wrote. "We won't make the same mistake again with the Internet." But at the end of the twentieth century—the era of the "new new thing," when pundits saw the Internet as poised to reshape the universe of higher education and market-driven organizations as posing a lethal threat to fusty academic institutions—it seemed that even correcting that "mistake" might not be enough to save the university.[4]

Some of the most provocative speculations about the future of higher education were advanced by David Collis.[5] Because of his stature in the management field—Collis teaches at the Harvard Business School—the higher education establishment, keen as ever for help from the business sector, has listened closely to what he has to say. The powerful and "disruptive technology" of the Internet will force universities to fundamentally rethink their mission, Collis asserts, and in his paper "Storming the Ivory Tower," he draws on analogies from private sector management to lay out some of their options.[6]

The natural temptation is to guard the fortress by erecting barriers to entry, as Harvard did in keeping Concord Law School at bay. But that strategy won't work for long, Collis counsels, because the pressures of the market are simply too strong. Conceivably, universities could borrow from industry the idea of "horizontal specialization." "Why not Columbia for modern languages, Princeton for economics, Yale for history?" Collis writes. "Why not adopt the British model and offer a three-year bachelor's degree?" But even this wild notion is a defensive tactic, "a retreat to a liberal arts core" that commands an ever-narrower sector of the market. For many schools, Collis contends, the wisest option is also the boldest. Rather than holding on to the past, universities should "enter distance education, expand continuing learning, invest in Internet-based pedagogy." That can't be done half-heartedly. The core of the institution must change. "Only aggressive pursuit of these new businesses will allow universities to maintain market leadership."[7]

More radical visionaries foresaw that the Internet would replace, not revamp, the university. "Universities won't survive . . . as a residential institution," Peter Drucker, the famous futurist, confidently announced in the pages of *Business Week*.[8] *The Virtual University*, the report of a 1996 roundtable sponsored by IBM and EDUCAUSE, the professional association of education technology professionals, reached a similar conclusion: within a decade, "a model of mass customization [with] input from business and industry" would supplant classroom courses taught by professors.[9]

The new technology, the prognosticators contended, would liberate academic superstars, because they would no longer have to be tethered to an institution. Those luminaries had no need for the lecture hall stage; now they could be sages on *virtual* stages. "The day when professors make deals like rock stars and athletes . . . even hire personal agents to arrange television appearances and other promotions to drum up business," isn't far off, predicted Arthur Levine, the dean of Columbia's Teachers College. At Harvard, Arthur Miller had been taken to the woodshed for being a mini-star, but in this scenario, he'd be "sitting across the desk from Jay Leno."[10]

Meanwhile, universities would have to surrender their authority as certifiers of intellectual achievement. With students free to enroll in courses across the virtual galaxy, Levine foresaw diplomas being replaced by "educational passports," for "why should a credential from Microsoft University be less prestigious than one from a regional state college?"[11] Bank of America analyst Howard Block urged universities to view themselves as mere "content providers," playing second fiddle to companies that know how to run a business. "If Harvard is the coffee bean grower"—not exactly that institution's self-image—then the for-profits "are the Starbucks. They take the coffee beans and turn them into something more."[12]

Eli Noam, an economist and finance professor at Columbia's business school, dipped into the recesses of ancient history to forecast the demise of the campus as the seat of learning. Higher education had remained essentially unchanged from the time of the Great Library of Alexandria, 2,500 years ago, Noam asserted in a widely discussed article, pointedly titled "Electronics and the Dim Future of Higher Education." "Scholars came to the information-storage institution and produced collaboratively still more information there, and students came to the scholars," he wrote. But this entire system was on the brink of collapse. "Today's production and distribution of information are undermining the traditional flow of information and with it the university structure. . . . The ultimate providers of an electronic curriculum will not be universities (they will merely break the ice) but rather commercial firms. . . . We may well have in the future a 'McGraw-Hill University' awarding degrees."[13]

"Embrace the future!" some academics urged. During the 1990s, as president of the University of Michigan, James Duderstadt had tried to make that institution run more like a business, promoting the idea of responsibility center management.[14] To this engineer-turned-administrator, the Internet marked the logical next stage in the transformation of higher education. In the wired academy, he declared, there would be a handful of academic celebrities, a larger number of "content providers," and a still larger number of "learning facilitators" to devise "learningware products" for "an array of for-profit service companies." "Quite a contrast," Duderstadt wrote, with evident relish, "with the current enterprise!"[15]

To be sure, there were dissenters. Those with long memories recalled the claims that had been made for earlier technologies like educational TV, and wondered whether the Internet would really perform as advertised.

The equity-minded feared that the Internet age would usher in a new class divide. While Columbia's Arthur Levine likened Internet-based education to the GI Bill in its "potential to extend the reach of American higher education," he was also concerned that the gap in the quality of instruction would widen if the well-to-do were to receive "personal highly interactive campuses, and the rest will be given virtual higher education."[16] Historian David Noble, whose on-line missives made him the scourge of web-based education, darkly warned that "the major change to befall the universities over the last two decades is identification of the campus as a significant site of capital accumulation, a change in social perception which has resulted in the systematic conversion of intellectual capital and, hence, intellectual property."[17] For their part, old school faculty worried about how collegiality could be sustained when favored professors were turning into media stars and "courseware" marketers.[18]

To prophets of the "Cyber-U" age, these doubters were relics. To affirm "the importance of quality education, academic values, the historic role in personal growth and the human need for freewheeling exchange," wrote Eli Noam, might "make one feel good"—academic values reduced to psychobabble—but all these things were "beside the point. To be culturally important is necessary (one hopes) but unfortunately not sufficient for a major claim on public and private resources."[19]

University administrators didn't simply read about these developments. They were drummed into their heads by business-minded trustees. "It is important to quickly choose a strategy—any strategy—and act upon it," declared David Collis. "Given early mover advantages, speed is of the essence for those who want to embrace new markets."[20] Writing in 1997, before the peak of the mania, Kenneth Green, one of the most clear-eyed observers of this scene, watched a growing numbers of campus officials, "like the 49ers eager to stake their claims . . . rushing forward with little real planning or a good map of the terrain: certain that there is gold in distance education, [they] believe that institutions absolutely must 'be there' or at least 'shoulder-to-shoulder' with the competition (other colleges and universities as well as commercial ventures and in-house corporate training centers)."[21]

NYU's David Finney was one who caught the gold rush fever. Explaining why his university had decided to sink $20 million into a for-profit venture, he described a moment "unlike any other in higher education. If you don't change you get left behind." NYU Online stood to earn a modest profit with corporate training, specialty law courses, and international education, he said, but the real payoff would come when the company went public. "If we sell 49 percent of our shares, we'll make fifty times our investment!"[22]

In its enthusiasm, NYU was in very good company. The roll call of universities that joined forces with e-learning companies between 1998 and 2000 reads like a "Who's Who" of higher education. "Pensare teamed up with Duke. Click2Learn teamed with NYU Online. . . . The University of Pennsylvania's Wharton School teamed with Caliber. . . . Cornell spun off eCornell. . . . Unext created Cardean University and partnered with Columbia, the London School of Economics, Stanford Carnegie Mellon and the University of Chicago. . . . North Carolina, Harvard and the University of Southern California went to University Access for help in getting online."[23] To administrators and trustees at these and many other schools, the correct course of action looked simple—as simple, presumably, as the determination by those stolid seventeenth-century Dutch burghers to risk all on tulip bulbs: either take the initiative in distance education or get beaten by competitors inside and outside the academy.[24]

Columbia University and MIT both attempted to position themselves as first movers, but the two schools chose very different paths: Columbia sought to become a leading player in the e-learning bazaar, while MIT opted to put its course materials on-line for free.[25] Those choices were based partly on conflicting estimates of how much money there was to be made in e-commerce, but control over "mindshare" mattered at least as much. Both universities appreciated the value of occupying digital space with some kind of on-line learning venture; both sensed the nascent commercial possibilities; and both have a long history of exploiting knowledge for financial gain. While Columbia decided that it could best promote its "brand" with a for-profit venture, MIT concluded that, when it came to the Internet, its reputation was best served by giving everything away.

■ Marketing a "Natural Birthright": Columbia University

"If the visitor to Columbia wishes to make a favorable impression," one such visitor wrote nearly a century ago, "he will take occasion to allude to Morningside Heights as 'the Acropolis of America.'"[26] Although there is considerably less pretension nowadays about campus architecture on this densely packed urban campus, the university does like to think of itself as vying for renown with another kind of Acropolis, Harvard and Yale. But Columbia is perpetually handicapped in its efforts to compete by an endowment less than a sixth the size of Harvard's.

This disparity can be traced in part to a critical decision made long ago by Nicholas Murray Butler (Nicholas Miraculous, as he was dubbed by Theodore Roosevelt), who ruled over Morningside Heights for the first four decades of the twentieth century. In the 1920s, Butler was urged to follow the lead of Yale and Harvard and hire a professional fund-raiser to run a capital campaign. He demurred, preferring instead to solicit money from a handful of the wealthiest New Yorkers. Butler had done so in the past with considerable success, but it wasn't until 1929 that this latest effort was mounted. The rest, as they say, is history.[27]

Raising money for a university's endowment is a sound investment in an institution's future. Yet because only a small fraction of the endowment can be spent each year, typically about 5 percent, its size has only a modest impact in the present, and impatient institutions can't wait for tomorrow. That's why, as Chapter 4 shows, NYU, in its drive to become a world-class university, spent most of the $2 billion-plus it has raised in the past generation to build housing and hire faculty rather than adding to its relatively meager endowment.[28]

Columbia never saw the need for such an unconventional step. But even as it has built up its endowment, it has hunted for other ways to generate immediate income. In the early years of the twentieth century, the university made a pile from its real estate holdings. During the 1990s, it was remarkably successful in turning its professors' inventions into fees from patent licenses.[29] While science- and engineering-oriented schools like MIT and Stanford are better known for encouraging their entrepreneurial faculty, Columbia has led all universities in its earnings from patent royalties, bringing in $141 million from these technology transfer deals in 2001 alone.[30] That represents a sizable chunk of a $3 billion annual budget, and as Michael Crow, the executive vice provost during much of this era, points out, it equals the income from a $3 billion endowment.

In his seminal 1910 book on "great American universities," Edwin Slosson was most favorably impressed by Columbia. It "has the essential qualities for success," he wrote, "initiative, adaptability, and opportunity." The university's strength, he added, "is due to the spirit of initiative in the individuals."[31] That spirit is still valued in Morningside Heights.

By the late 1990s, a mini-crisis loomed at Columbia because several of its most lucrative patents were about to expire. Revenue from licensing fees would fall precipitously, from $141 million in 2001 to $67 million just three years later, and there were no blockbuster inventions in the pipeline. The then-nascent virtual education market held out the promise of astonishing riches. Several trustees, including David Stern, commissioner of the National Basketball Association, and banking magnate Alfred Lerner, were watching this market, and they urged the administration to act aggressively. "I don't want to wake up one morning," said Stern, "and find out that Harvard and Microsoft have put $5 million on the table." It was essential that the university be out front in distance learning.

Columbia's top officials needed no persuading, because they knew first-hand that Microsoft was already setting itself up as a competitor. "Microsoft saw themselves as the content authenticators"—that is, those who create knowledge—"as well as the distributors," says Michael Crow. "At a meeting they informed us they would no longer be buying the *Columbia Encyclopedia* for on-line distribution. Since they had purchased the *Funk and Wagnall's* name and hired their own experts, they said they didn't need academics anymore."

This was a watershed moment in Columbia's approach to the Internet. "The challenge," says Columbia provost Jonathan Cole, "was to keep dot-com at bay," and that required being "fleet of foot." Decisions about how to enter this uncharted e-terrain would be made by the administration rather than by faculty, many of whom, Cole comments, reside in "the world of town hall meetings," where "an idea gets debated until there is total consensus."

Once before, Columbia had been a leader in distance learning, but that was not a happy chapter in its history.[32] The first decades of the twentieth century were the golden era of the correspondence school movement, and Columbia was a leading force, ranking second in enrollment behind only the University of Chicago. The correspondence schools' advocates claimed that their courses were better than "anything possible in the crowded classroom of the ordinary American university," and certainly better than the dubious offerings of the for-profit schools. Columbia's advertisements promised first-rate classes taught by university professors.

But reality fell far short of enticement. There were no Columbia professors, and the courses were slapdash affairs. In 1928, amid growing suspicion about the quality of education offered by the correspondence schools, the Carnegie Foundation asked Abraham Flexner, whose earlier report had led to the overhaul of medical education, to carry out an investigation. He unearthed a scandal in the universities' midst.

Flexner focused his ire on Chicago and Columbia, which had "abandoned their unique and essential social function of disinterested critical and creative inquiry [and] thoughtlessly and excessively catered to fleeting, transient, and immediate demands." The indictment was relentless. These institutions had "needlessly cheapened, vulgarized, and mechanized themselves," reducing themselves to "the level of the vendors of patent medicine. . . . Columbia, untaxed because it is an education institution, is in business: it has education to sell [and] plays the purely commercial game of the merchant whose sole concern is profit." An embarrassed President Butler ordered an end to the ads, and the correspondence school closed completely in 1937.

There was little risk that Columbia would make the same error in judgment with the Internet, because the triumvirate that shaped the university's policy was united in its insistence that academic values not be compromised. "[President] George Rupp realized that the moment was like the late nineteenth century, when leaders created new kinds of higher education," says Arthur Levine, a historian as well as president of Teachers College. "Jonathan Cole had a better grasp of the potential of technology to affect universities than any senior administrator in higher education—a real surprise from an Ivy League university. And Michael Crow was the entrepreneur, always willing to try things, looking for the academic payoff."

By the late 1990s, Internet-based education programs abounded in Morningside Heights. Columbia's business school was the first to sign up with the virtual M.B.A. program from Unext and its academic entity, Cardean University, and its imprimatur made it easier for that company to enlist other top-ranked business schools such as Stanford and Chicago. Columbia was well rewarded for going first; in return for the right to adapt the school's courses, Unext promised the university $20 million as well as a 5 percent stake in the company.[33] The liberal arts college made a similar kind of deal with Pensare; and subsequently, Teachers College decided to create its own on-line offshoot, a nonprofit called Teachers College Innovations. The intention, says Levine, is to use the school's "intellectual capital" to generate an income stream for the college's core activities and to scale up innovations: "We've been handed the biggest megaphone in the history of higher education."

It was essential that any arrangement that had Columbia's imprimatur be consistent with the institution's principles. Unlike "holding company" universities, where campus units are generally expected to pay their own way, Columbia believes that its first obligation is to its liberal arts college, which is regarded as the heart of the university. Professional schools are taxed, often over their strenuous objections, for an "academic quality fund"—a Robin Hood arrangement that Jonathan Cole describes as a "counter-market" effort to keep resources for the common.[34] "Columbia didn't want to be behind the curve," says political scientist and longtime Columbia professor Ira Katznelson, "but it was also self-consciously insistent on maintaining high intellectual standards. At every faculty briefing by Jonathan [Cole] and Mike Crow, and in private conversations as well, this was always the theme."

Even as the administration was setting rules for Internet ventures, a committee on intellectual property chaired by Katznelson was convened to discuss the Arthur Miller question. "We wanted a strong sense," he says, "based on the values of intellectuality, to find a way between two extremes—the University of Chicago's policy, that anything produced except traditional properties like books is the property of the university, and Stanford's policy that individual professors are presumed to have complete ownership rights." Katznelson's committee ultimately opted for the same formula Columbia used in dividing patent royalties: income from on-line materials is split among the university, the department, and the professor. "The result," he says, "is that the money goes to further the intellectual endeavor."

Crow's dedication to the primacy of intellectual, rather than market, values proved especially important, since his portfolio included a spate of new intellectual capital ventures. Technology transfer officers are frequently émigrés from commerce who view their job as pressuring the faculty to be responsive to industry's needs.[35] In this domain Crow, a public policy Ph.D., is a welcome rarity, an administrator who combines a talent for raising revenues with an unwavering dedication to the public purposes for which those revenues are being raised. This devotion to principle provoked a donnybrook with Meyer Weinberg, the business school dean who had negotiated the Unext agreement. "On a hundred different terms—finances, control of intellectual property, the brand—the initial deal wasn't acceptable to us," says Crow, and Jonathan Cole agrees. Although Weinberg was willing to let Unext use Columbia's name in its promotions, the campus administrators were not. In the ensuing dispute the administrators prevailed, and the Unext contract became a part of Crow's portfolio.[36]

The key element in Columbia's e-learning strategy was a company called Fathom, launched amid much fanfare in the spring of 2000. Fathom was a consortium of fourteen leading U.S. and British universities, libraries, and museums, but more than 90 percent of its financing came from Columbia, which drew on its stream of patent revenues to contribute an initial $20 million. The intention was to develop a knowledge-rich website that re-created the great bricks-and-mortar academic institutions—to establish a commanding presence for Columbia in what Cole describes as "the high-end, high-quality distance learning marketplace." Because it was structured as a for-profit entity separate from the university, Fathom could go to investors for infusions of capital, and, ultimately, it could go public.

While Fathom was only one element of Columbia's multipronged effort to harness the potential of cyberspace, because it was the most generously funded university-based e-learning venture, it garnered much attention.[37] The company's CEO, Ann Kirschner, fit the Columbia administrative profile. Cole and Crow selected her because, as a Ph.D. in English from Princeton, she understood academic folkways, and as the person who made the National Football League's sports sites the most popular ones on the Web after ESPN's, she understood the business.[38]

The idea of the world's best universities making their knowledge widely available is seemingly irresistible. But in the marketplace, timing is everything, and Fathom's timing was off. A few months after the unveiling, venture capital essentially dried up for e-learning business; and the revenues anticipated from on-line courses hadn't materialized.[39] In 2001, strapped for cash, Fathom received another $20 million infusion.[40] Meanwhile, Michael Crow was forming a variety of university-based organizations to spin off new digital media companies through an entity called Morningside Ventures, which then became Columbia Media Enterprises and later changed its name to Digital Knowledge Ventures. Some faculty object to Crow's eager embrace of so many risky ventures. "The big criticism," says political science professor Robert Jervis, "is that he goes off in five directions at once."

The faculty senate, troubled by the money drain and peevish that big decisions were being made under the benign guise of expanded institutional reach, sought an accounting from the administration. Its April 2002 report pointedly observed that "Fathom is both a privately held for-profit corporation entirely separate form the University and an integral component of the University's online strategy. While it is a for-profit enterprise, it is also described as a 'place-holder' in the space of knowledge aggregation." Those apparent contradictions are "endemic in the overall strategy, where potentially worthwhile ventures are developed with little or no reference to one another."[41]

Fathom "could have been part of the dot-com craze," Cole acknowledges. "Did we think about the commercial potential? Yes." But he cautions against reducing the origins of Fathom to purely economic motives. "Was that the most important part? No. We were never interested in getting rich quick." What the company allowed us to do was to occupy on-line space "commercially *and* educationally."

"What alternative did we have?" Ann Kirschner asks rhetorically. "Should we have left the space to the likes of Microsoft?" Columbia's big advantage is supposed to be its brand—what Kirschner calls its "natural birthright"—but it's far from certain that this great university can be captured for cyberspace and then sold for a profit. Even though, by the fall of 2002, 45,000 students had signed up for one of Fathom's on-line courses, the venture remained what Cole calls "an undone, half-baked cookie . . . a very good idea before its time." In January 2003, Columbia decided to shut down Fathom. In its thirty-month history it generated just $700,000 in revenues, including contributions from its partner organizations.[42]

In the virtual world as elsewhere, modesty can be a virtue. The one Columbia distance learning project that actually makes money has been running since 1986—the Video Network, sponsored by the School of Engineering. Its technology is decidedly old-fashioned, just a step up from the correspondence school: lectures are taped and made available on the Internet via streaming video. But it is not the technology that makes the course such a success. It's the fact that the engineering school knows its market—highly qualified students who can't relocate to New York City— and offers those students the simulacrum of a Columbia classroom education and a Columbia master's degree.[43]

The engineering school's enterprise, little known even in Morningside Heights, isn't the brave new world of the Internet. It doesn't promise the great ideas and the luminaries who propound them. But the lesson from Fathom's demise may be that few people are willing to pay very much for those great ideas, that potential customers want something the university isn't prepared to give them, namely, a course of study that leads to a Columbia degree.

What Fathom was doing—making iconic content from fabulous places electronically available—has immense value, even if it didn't turn out to be a quick moneymaker.[44] Presumably that's why the university rejected overtures from potential Fathom investors whose ambitions were, as Michael Crow says, too "commercial." In the rapidly evolving market for ideas, the vital question is this: Which parts of the intellectual forest should be sold off and which should be open to all? "Maybe Fathom is something that we contribute to the larger scholarly world for education and research," muses Columbia's librarian, James Neal. "After all, MIT has gotten foundation funding to do the same thing."[45]

▪ "The Commons of the Mind": MIT

Columbia's senior administrators bristle when asked about MIT's decision to make its course materials "open source"—that is, freely available to anyone. "Columbia had 900 of its courses on-line, far more than MIT," Jonathan Cole points out. "And by the time MIT went public with their decision, in 2001, there was no money to be had from the market."

Cole has the facts right, but he is ignoring the symbolism of MIT's decision. What MIT calls "OpenCourseWare" is more than what he labels that school's "moral hobbyhorse." It represents a radically different view of the university's role in the marketplace of ideas, one that recreates in the virtual world the idea of an intellectual commons. That MIT, of all institutions, should champion this concept comes as a surprise, for no other research university in the world has been so successfully, and so unapologetically, tied to the world of enterprise.

MIT is the country's leading engineering school, and it looks the part. It sits in the Cambridge flats, two miles down Massachusetts Avenue from Harvard, in a neighborhood where new office towers jostle for space with warehouses and factories. Its buildings are sternly functional, built as places of work and not temples of learning. The contrast with ivy-entwined Harvard Yard could not be more striking.

This difference isn't just aesthetic; here, form *does* reveal function. Harvard lays fair claim to being the best private university in the world, and although MIT's $6 billion endowment is among the top five in the nation (roughly double the size of Columbia's), its aspirations are narrowly focused. While MIT has made a point of recruiting distinguished economists, city planners, management scholars, and the like, at its core it remains a school for engineers.[46] And while Harvard, like most great research universities, publicly agonizes over the right balance between the marketplace and the academic commons, as well as over the nature of its ties to what Dwight Eisenhower famously called "the military-industrial complex," these matters have rarely troubled MIT, where links to industry and the military are what makes the place run.

That has been true since MIT opened its doors in 1861, not as a university but as an institute with a charter to promote the "advancement of the industrial arts and sciences and practical education in the Commonwealth."[47] The school traces its intellectual lineage to Thomas Jefferson's belief in the growing importance of science, which breaks down "the old unity, the old sameness" of higher education.[48] The approach that MIT took, combining "original research in applied science with the diffusion of popular knowledge," set "the pattern for the mushrooming technological schools of the later nineteenth century."[49]

Because MIT was committed from the outset to such a practical orientation, instead of being a haven from market forces it eagerly embraced them. General Electric started the first broad-based industrial research laboratory on the campus in 1900; and the school pioneered in placing student interns in factories. In 1910, Dugald Jackson, chairman of the electrical engineering department, encouraged the institute's faculty to "undertake some of the most distinctively commercial investigations under the patronage or support of the great manufacturing or other commercial companies."[50] The professors needed little encouragement. "When Institute President Karl Taylor Compton ruled in the 1930s that professors could spend 20 percent of their time on outside consulting, this was done to rein in the outside activities, not to encourage them."[51]

In the years following the Second World War, the military underwrote much of MIT's research (military police were a regular presence on the campus, guarding labs where classified work was being done), and that support enabled the institute to maintain its national preeminence in engineering and basic science.[52] In the complex web of relationships among government, business, and academia during the postwar period, MIT became the biggest player in higher education. Projects such as the Research Laboratory of Electronics and the Instrumentation Laboratory bolstered its academic reputation even as they responded to the needs of the military—and MIT is still the university whose research agenda is most closely aligned to the needs of the military.[53]

Contacts with industry have also remained intimate and lucrative. The Industrial Liaison Program, begun in 1948, enables firms that pay for the privilege to get advance insight into MIT research; Standard Oil, Goodyear, and IBM were among the founding members of this club. More industrially supported research—including what one professor calls a "'Death Star Alliance' with Microsoft"—is conducted on MIT's campus than at any other university in the world.[54]

This storied record of academic entrepreneurialism makes it all the more remarkable that MIT should take the lead in making its courses available for free.[55] This $100 million digital project, announced in April 2001, was expected, over the course of several years, to place on-line materials from MIT's more than 2,000 courses. Lecture notes, problem sets, syllabuses, pop quizzes, and exams would be available, at no charge, to anyone with access to the Internet. The only limitations would be set by the professors themselves, who would determine what materials to make available. MIT opted to avoid Arthur Miller–type fights over ownership. Those predictable disputes, says engineering professor Hal Abelson, who helped set up the project, would occur "someplace else."[56]

Top MIT officials heralded the initiative as representing a principled stand against the forces of commercialization in academe—an anti-Fathom. "OpenCourseWare looks counter-intuitive in a market-driven world," President Charles M. Vest declared. "It goes against the grain of current material values." By "making the primary materials for nearly all of our 2,000 courses available on the World Wide Web," it opens a new chapter in the quintessentially American story of democratizing higher education. "The glory of American higher education is its democratizing reach."[57] What Andrew Carnegie's libraries represented a century earlier— knowledge "free to the people"—OpenCourseWare is meant to embody for the present era.[58]

The story ran on the front page in scores of newspapers, including the *New York Times,* and without exception, the reviews were laudatory. MIT's press releases quoted liberally from the thousands of supportive e-mail messages that poured in from everywhere. "I have dreamt all my life of studying at MIT," a Nigerian student wrote. "Thanks a lot for making this dream come true, for if I can't come to MIT, MIT has now come to me." A Ugandan educator predicted that "professors . . . will be inspired and motivated to be on par with MIT standards. . . . I would like to thank you for your generosity." Another well-wisher regarded the initiative as so important that he made MIT the beneficiary of his estate: "I had no heirs—until now! If there's anything left when I'm done, it's going to be yours for being the first to attempt what my vision has been since I first went online."[59]

MIT has earned these hosannas. Yet while it chose the high road to digital education, that isn't because it rejected out of hand the commercialization of on-line learning. On the contrary: OpenCourseWare (OCW) emerged as a direct response to the temptations of the market. Late in 1999, as Columbia was readying the launch of Fathom, Ann Kirschner sought out prestigious academic partners. MIT was a top choice because of its stellar reputation in science and engineering, but when she approached the institute, she was rebuffed. MIT officials were skeptical about the market potential of digital education. While they understood the importance of securing first mover advantage in Internet ventures—MIT was a key partner in the development of high-tech companies along Route 128, the Massachusetts counterpart to Silicon Valley—they nonetheless decided to act with characteristic deliberateness.

Working with consultants from Booz Allen Hamilton, MIT conducted a "visioning exercise" that encompassed the widest possible array of options for the future. Among the possibilities considered were "Venture-tech," a Fathom-type approach; "Techtech," focusing on being an educational provider to the corporate world; and "Global Tech," aimed at MIT-quality students who couldn't come to the campus.[60] Those sessions provided the impetus to explore the commercial potential of "lifelong learning." A study group headed by Dick Yue, associate dean of engineering, assessed the various alternatives. "What would it take for MIT to seize leadership of the on-line learning space?" the group asked. "Was it institutionally feasible? Did it have the potential for commercial success?" The working group drafted a mammoth report that mapped out more than a dozen scenarios, examining technological requirements, business models, and organizational structures, and developing feasibility plans for each option.

The idea for OpenCourseWare, says Yue, emerged from this months-long deliberation. "There was no proverbial 'Eureka!' moment in the shower between squash and drinks." A "viable model" for an e-business did exist, the committee concluded, but only if the venture were conducted on a very large scale. Although MIT lacked the "existing capacity" to pursue this approach, Yue had no doubt that the school could manage the transformation if it so chose. But he and his colleagues wondered whether there might be "another game," one that acknowledged MIT's responsibility to the world beyond the "few thousand students it can take into its walls each year." At some point, the idea emerged: "Heck, let's just give it away."

Why did MIT and Columbia reach such different conclusions about how best to capture the virtual marketplace? The answer has little to do with academic values, for in this respect Jonathan Cole and Michael Crow at Columbia are no different from Dick Yue at MIT, and a great deal to do with how universities make decisions.

In the tortoise-like world of higher education, Columbia is a freewheel-

ing place. Writing in the early 1990s, Cole defended the need for nimbleness. "We must recognize that the rhythms of the external world have
changed and that these changes directly affect the internal life of universities. The faster pace and rapid growth of the institution requires more
rapid, year-round responses and initiatives, a clearer process of decision-
making so that universities can make meaningful changes and adaptations
in a timely way."[61] As vice provost, Crow had broad authority to seize the
commercial-*cum*-academic opportunities that presented themselves, pursuing an array of loosely defined and constantly evolving digital initiatives.

It's striking that Columbia was able to make a substantial financial commitment to Fathom so quickly, becoming overnight a serious player in this
new marketplace. With few institutional barriers between the entrepreneurial idea and its execution, the result was a time-to-market that would
impress a venture capitalist. The intricacies of the business plan, the delin-
eation of a market niche, the fit between these commercial and educational endeavors and Columbia's overall mission as a leading institution of
higher education—none of these considerations was as important as securing first mover advantage and locking in the revenues that seemed available for the taking. Everything else could—and did—wait.

That MIT's decision-making style is risk averse, even stodgy, has become conventional wisdom since Annalee Saxenian's much-cited study of
technological innovation and regional development around Route 128 in
Massachusetts and in Silicon Valley.[62] While Stanford was becoming an active partner with high-tech start-ups, Saxenian argues, MIT adopted a
conservative, hierarchical, and bureaucratic approach, one that mirrored
the culture of the Wall Street firms and federal agencies to which it had
long been tied. This characterization matches MIT's cautious reaction to
the moneymaking potential of e-learning. But the same style of reasoning
that led MIT to lose out to Stanford in the high-tech start-up race may
well have saved it from a Fathom-style failure.[63]

President Charles Vest immediately fell in love with the idea of giving away
courses on the Web. He was particularly struck by the fact that it defied
the conventional wisdom. "Everybody went left," Vest says, "and we went
right." But the plan carried a $100 million price tag, and, although MIT is
a wealthy school, help was wanted to pay the bills. Foundations were an
obvious place to turn. In late 2000, senior MIT officials shared their ideas
with William Bowen, president of the Mellon Foundation and former
president of Princeton. In a lecture he had delivered at Oxford a few

months earlier, Bowen voiced his concern about the commercialization of higher education. "Universities are not businesses," he said. "They are highly unusual institutions with missions and attributes unlike those of any other entity. . . . Society depends on them to do much more than produce 'products' at a fair price. . . . If these venerable institutions become too market-driven, and come to be regarded in too instrumental a way . . . they could lose the distinctive 'angle to the universe' they need to retain if they are to function at their best."[64]

Here was a chance to help one university maintain that "angle." In seeking foundation support, MIT took great pains to stress the noncommercial aspect of its venture; its message sounded a bit like the Sunoikisis Project, described in the preceding chapter, which was already being funded by Mellon. "The OCW concept will help transform the way colleges and universities define their role in disseminating knowledge, their outreach to new audiences around the world, and their institutional and faculty engagement with the Internet as a vehicle for service, not just for profit."[65]

Bowen proved an easy sell, as did the Mellon Foundation's trustees. The trustees "admire and support the philosophy of openness and non-exclusivity that motivates your initiative," Bowen wrote to Vest. "The sometimes unthinking rush to commercialize the academic content of our colleges and universities is cause for serious concern."[66] Paul Brest and Marshall Smith at the Hewlett Foundation were just as enthusiastic. "Our hope," said Brest, "is that this project . . . will reinforce the concept that ideas are best viewed as the common property of all of us, not as proprietary products intended to generate profits."[67] Within a matter of months, breakneck speed for foundations, Hewlett and Mellon agreed to underwrite an $11 million pilot program. How MIT would secure the nearly $90 million balance of the OpenCourseWare funding remained uncertain.

Even though MIT had opted not to pursue capital in the form of cash profits, Vest and his colleagues recognized that the venture would bring valuable symbolic capital. OpenCourseWare would attract favorable press; it would cast MIT as a leader in the Internet field; and it would help make MIT a truly global presence in science and engineering education. When Dick Yue and his colleagues made a slide show presentation to the Hewlett Foundation, one slide enumerated "The Values to MIT and Society." There was no venture capital talk about capturing "mindshare," but the intangible benefits were plainly laid out. "MIT takes intellectual, educational, and moral leadership"; "MIT sets an example for other leading educational institutions worldwide"; "MIT contributes to improving the quality and standard of education at all levels"; "MIT contributes to bridging the national and worldwide 'digital divide'"; "MIT redefines and becomes the clear leader in the field of distance/lifelong learning."[68]

It doesn't detract from MIT's initiative to say that OpenCourseWare is less a paradigm-breaking escape from the market than a displacement of competition from one marketplace to another, from the domain of money to the domain of reputation. As it happens, defying the ethic of the market for money capital has proved to be the best way for MIT to succeed in the market for symbolic capital. In the fall of 2002, the website was finally up and running. During its first five weeks, it registered 46.5 million hits by 361,000 unique visitors from 177 countries and all seven continents, including Antarctica.

▪ Lessons from Dot-Com U

On May 23, 2000, Merrill Lynch released a report titled "The Knowledge Web." In its bullishness on investing in e-learning companies, the report was as badly timed as an October 1929 "buy" recommendation. Nasdaq was already beginning its downward slide, and the market was turning with particular ruthlessness on the higher education sector. Merrill Lynch wasn't the only company to misread the times. The very corporations that were dubbed "dominant" by the *Financial Times* in May 2000 were gone a year later.[69] Hungry Minds was lionized in the March 2000 cover story of *University Business* magazine; that June, the company was sold for next to nothing to the firm that publishes the *Dummies* books and *Cliffs Notes*.[70]

Among universities, Columbia's plight was hardly unique. Very few of the for-profits survived the dot-com crash; and by 2002, none of them had seen a profit. Pensare, Duke's partner, was gone. Unext/Cardean—the virtual university that in its halcyon days had fretted that it might sweep the field and face Microsoft-type antitrust problems—was barely hanging on. With little to show except some corporate deals to deliver bite-sized versions of its elegant courses, it had laid off half its workforce and turned to Thomson, the international publishing conglomerate, for an infusion of cash. Hat in hand, Unext asked its partner universities, to which it had promised $20 million apiece, to "restructure" the arrangement. NYU Online shut its doors, and so did the University of Maryland's pioneering online unit, University College.[71] Cornell's e-learning operation had few students and modest earning expectations. Caliber, the Wharton School's partner, filed for bankruptcy. University Access, which worked with Harvard, the University of North Carolina, and USC, changed its name and withdrew from higher education.[72] Temple University, which established a for-profit, abandoned it without offering a single course. "I didn't see any profit potential there," said president David Adamany. "Good luck to [other universities]. When they make money, tell them to call me."[73]

It's hard for anyone residing outside this bubble to resist the temptation to crow. In higher education, as across the landscape of high-tech, the dot-com crowd was so hubristic—so sure of itself and its market models, so contemptuous of the virtues of old institutions—that its comeuppance seems only just.[74] But schadenfreude isn't an entirely apt response. Nuance rather than dismissal is needed to make sense of this e-learning moment.

Despite all the dot-com failures, the hype about Internet-based learning does contain an essential truth: the Internet is transforming education. The number of students who acquire part of their education on-line will grow rapidly; and as bandwidth increases, the ways they use the Internet will evolve, with the astonishing speed that Moore's Law ascribes to the semiconductor industry.[75] Where the promoters went badly wrong is in forgetting that technology is just a means, not an end—that the critical choices have to do with how it will be used, and for what purposes. The technology, argues Randy Bass, an English professor at Georgetown University who heads the Visible Knowledge Project, a study of distance learning, "must be used as engines of inquiry, not engines of productivity."[76]

"Designing educational experiences around technology is a foolish chase," contends Jack Wilson, whose low-tech venture at the University of Massachusetts, UMass Online, is one of the few companies that actually turns a profit. "Technology changes very rapidly and human beings change very slowly."[77]

High-tech enthusiasts believed that Internet-based education would sweep the boards, making conventional universities obsolete, because it could deliver better instruction at lower prices. Their error lay in thinking that the economies of scale of e-commerce would work in on-line learning. To produce a sophisticated Internet course costs a great deal (Unext reports that it spends a million dollars on a single course; Open University courses, discussed in Chapter 10, cost three times as much), and course development isn't the main expense. Despite the vision of a robotic educational universe, teachers are still needed—even more so, it turns out, than in conventional courses. A generation earlier, in the best-seller *Megatrends,* John Naisbitt had made the same point: "Whenever new technology is introduced into society, there must be a counterbalancing human response, or the technology is rejected. The more high tech, the more high touch."[78]

Even as students become more habituated to virtual learning, many of them are looking for more than on-line bells and whistles. They want to learn in ways that computers cannot replicate; they want to earn their degrees from real schools, not contrivances like Cardean University or Universitas 21; they want to talk with faculty and fellow students, and not just in chat rooms. They want, in other words, to participate in a community.

E-commerce companies complain, and not without cause, that universities make difficult business partners.[79] High-tech firms must be exceedingly fast off the mark and willing to take risks if they are going to survive; universities operate on an entirely different time clock. To conceive of universities as the producers of "knowledge products" or "courseware," as some in the e-learning world do, casts the institution as more like a factory (or a coffee plantation, in the ineffable imagery of the Bank of America analyst) than an academic commons, a place where the faculty more closely resemble knowledge workers like drug testers or chip designers than free minds. "Stock prices fluctuate widely if companies miss quarterly earnings estimates by pennies," the Mellon Foundation's William Bowen points out. "New ideas . . . germinate over long periods and almost always take longer to correct than they did to create."[80]

These differences in the rhythm of decision making reflect deeper value divides. "While the universities often strive for access, quality, research excellence, service, and teaching for teaching's sake," writes UMass Online's Jack Wilson, "a corporation is driven by financial consideration first and then other values to the extent that they are compatible with financial success."[81] As Columbia has learned to its sorrow, despite all the talk of "first mover advantage," higher education isn't one of those races that inevitably goes to the swift.[82]

10

The British Are Coming—and Going
Open University

Imagine the following scenario: In 1971 a new university opens its doors. Its mission is to educate anyone over age twenty-one who wants to pursue a postsecondary degree.[1] While the instructional regimen includes limited face-to-face contact between instructors and students, most of the teaching comes at a distance; there are packets of readings, courses on audiotape, on TV, and, eventually, on the Internet. Thirty years later, when the university's engineering program is evaluated by the government's quality assessment agency, it ranks higher than those at Yale and Harvard.

Were this the tale of an American university, it would be far-fetched. It sounds entirely fanciful if Oxford and Cambridge are substituted for Harvard and Yale, since in Britain, Oxbridge's preeminence has been a fact of life for centuries, and there is no tradition of mass higher education.[2]

But the story is actually true. The institution is the Open University (OU, as it is called), and almost from the day it opened its main campus, an hour's drive north of London in Milton Keynes, one of the postwar planned "garden cities," it has set the international gold standard in distance learning.[3] As the high marks awarded to its engineering program indicate, OU takes the quality of its instruction very seriously. It could also teach American e-learning companies like Unext and Fathom a thing or two about marketing, as its staggeringly large enrollment demonstrates. One and a half million Britons have taken an OU course: that's 3 percent of the population. With 180,000 students currently pursuing degrees, it is among the largest universities in the world; and in recent years it has successfully expanded into Europe, Asia, and Africa.

When Open University tried to clone itself in the United States, however, it failed miserably. In 2002, it shut down most of its American operations after having been in existence less than three years. The rationale for pulling the plug was simple economics. Having spent $20 million, the university was unwilling to continue covering the losses of its American off-spring.

During the dot-com era, distance learning was promoted with mission-ary zeal. But as the previous chapter shows, the virtual market proved elu-sive, and many ventures were scaled back or shut down. There's little rea-son to mourn most of these departures. With so much attention focused on high-tech and quick killings, little notice was paid to offering some-thing of value. But Open University is the decided exception, an institu-tion with intelligently conceived and well-packaged multimedia courses—nearly 200 year-long undergraduate courses in fields ranging from biology to business, and almost as many graduate courses.

The fact that OU is so good at what it does makes the demise of its American operation cause for regret. Its failure is also instructive. Sorting out why a university that has been such a remarkable success in Britain and Europe fared so abysmally in the United States provides insights into the workings of the new international market in distance learning and the persistent "not made here" syndrome in higher education. It is at once a story of the emerging power of globalization and the persisting power of localism.[4]

▪ "The College of the Proletariat"

Thirty years ago, it was easy to dismiss distance education as the province of the "matchbook" schools—"become a butcher, baker, or candlestick-maker while studying at home," the advertisements promised. While many of those places were, and remain, fly-by-night operations established to extract money from the gullible, distance learning also has a respectable pedigree.[5] The idea dates to 1830s England, where educators were search-ing for ways to spread higher learning throughout the empire; and over the years, Columbia and Chicago, among leading American research uni-versities, have operated large-scale correspondence schools.[6] That history continues: Herriot-Watt University, a venerable Scottish institution, en-rolls 9,000 M.B.A. students in twenty countries, including more than 2,000 in the United States, in an old-fashioned, textbook-only correspon-dence course.

The aspiration for Open University was infinitely bolder: to shatter the deeply rooted elitist traditions that ruled British higher education by pro-viding opportunities for the masses. In the *Brideshead Revisited* prewar world, the university was a preserve for the privileged. Although several new universities opened in Britain during the 1950s and 1960s, fewer than 10 percent of eighteen- to twenty-four-year-olds were enrolled in higher education, the lowest proportion among western European countries. As late as 1963, nearly half of the children of high-level professionals, but only 4 percent of skilled workers' children, attended university.[7]

The situation was anathema to the British Labour Party, ideologically committed to providing equal opportunity for all.[8] Party intellectuals like Michael Young, whose influential 1958 book *The Rise of the Meritocracy* had skewered elitism, argued that many more students deserved a post-secondary education; in particular, those who had gone directly into the workforce were entitled to a second chance.[9] Nor was there any reason for a one-size-fits-all model of higher education, the familiar English pattern of three years of full-time residential instruction. There had to be room in the system for part-time students who could both "earn and learn," doing most of their studying at home.[10]

American presidents pay attention to higher education only when delivering commencement speeches; but in 1963, Harold Wilson, the leader of the Labour Party and aspiring prime minister, made it a major campaign issue. If Labour won, he promised, his government would start a "University of the Air."[11] Wilson pledged to provide "equality of opportunity for *millions* of people," a radical concept in a country where the one-on-one tutorial remained the benchmark of higher learning. The *Times* of London doubted whether there would be any demand for it, and the chairman of the Conservative Party dismissed the idea as "blithering nonsense."[12] The proposal stirred "some not very well concealed social resentment," a former OU senior administrator recalls, but there was mostly a jokey indifference to the scheme. Oxford and Cambridge didn't fight it because they "really didn't think it would work."[13]

Open University has been as important to Britain as the opening of the land grant universities was to the United States a century earlier. Both developments "provided serious and sustained learning opportunities for large numbers of people for whom higher education had never previously been available." In one sense, the OU story is the more remarkable of the two, since the land grant schools "took at least seventy-five years to achieve a fully established place in American society, while [OU] had to be brought into full-scale operation [instantaneously]."[14] Eight years after Harold Wilson's speech, Mach speed by the academic calendar, OU admitted its first class. It numbered nearly 24,000 students, and almost as many had to be rejected because the school couldn't handle the volume. A class of that great size suggested the magnitude of unmet educational desire. From then on, says Sir John Daniel, who came to the Open University as an unpaid intern in 1972 and returned twenty years later as vice chancellor, OU was "politically unstoppable."[15] When he stepped down as prime minister in 1976, Harold Wilson declared that OU was his proudest legacy.

Open University's birth was nearly a stillbirth, however, because the Labour government was defeated before the first students began their studies, and the Conservatives weren't keen on the project.[16] As the story goes, the Tory finance minister had an order to close OU on his desk but had a heart attack before he could sign it. What saved the institution was the fact that it was cheap. The cost of an OU education is half that of a traditional university education, and such parsimony appealed greatly to an education minister named Margaret Thatcher.[17]

Luck is the residue of design, as the wise old baseball hand Branch Rickey once said. Critical decisions—the creation of a regional structure, heavy reliance on tutors—were made early and on the run, but they have proved to be robust. Months after OU opened, a lengthy postal strike made it impossible to send out course materials. "A Dunkirk spirit developed," Daniel recalls, "as tutors started driving to depots to hand materials to their students; the school had a human glue." As the university grew in size, adding continuing education and graduate programs, its reputation grew apace. "The first converts were the academics at other universities, who were massively associated as members of course teams and assessors; then came the students; and finally the business community, when the first OU graduates were hired."

The business school, which opened in 1981, was an immediate success, and now a quarter of all British M.B.A.s are OU graduates. In 2001, government inspectors ranked OU sixth among 124 institutions in the proportion of its departments rated "excellent" in teaching. That's remarkably high—it places OU ahead of the London School of Economics—and what's even more remarkable, OU ranks thirty-second in research.[18] It certainly didn't hurt the school's image when its team, average age forty-six, beat the striplings of Oxford's Oriel College on *University Challenge,* Britain's popular version of *College Bowl.*

The "college of the proletariat," Tory opponents dubbed Open University, and the institution wears that sobriquet as a badge of honor. OU applicants aren't required to take the subject area examinations, the "A levels," that university-bound secondary school students take after high school. They don't even have to take the basic "O level" tests given to fifteen-year-olds. All they have to do is sign up. Initially, students under age twenty-one weren't permitted to apply, the rationale being that they lacked the maturity needed for distance learning; but once the vast demand for higher education became evident, the age restriction was dropped.[19] In 2002, the youngest OU student was twelve years old and the oldest in her mid-nineties.

The hope of its founders was that "Open University will redeem the failure of the traditional universities, and offer education to those who were deprived by their social background."[20] In reality, OU has never been a school for the common man and woman; all but a small fraction of its students (4 percent in 2000) have taken at least one "A level" exam. That's a reflection of the sad reality that those who never gave higher education a passing thought while in high school aren't likely to do so later in life. Still, the profile of the OU student body much more closely matches the demographics of the country than that of any other British university. Fewer than a third of its students have taken the three "A level" exams that traditional universities require, and were it not for OU, those students wouldn't have access to higher education. Open University students differ from the typical British undergraduate in other ways as well. Consistent with the idea of "second chance" education, the median age of the students is thirty-four, and just 8 percent are twenty-five or younger. Half of them are the children of blue-collar workers, compared to one-fifth in the traditional universities. And unlike at any other British university, a majority of the students are women, mostly working, who have grabbed the chance to pursue an education part-time.

"I came to Open University because it promotes social justice," says Brenda Gourley, who succeeded John Daniel as vice chancellor in 2002. Gourley has initiated short courses, with lots of counseling, in order to entice "the truly socially disadvantaged—people who otherwise would never have dreamed they could make it in higher education."

Dropouts are the biggest problem at OU, as in distance education generally. Learning at a remove requires self-discipline, since without the stimulation of the classroom, it's all too easy to lose interest, and for part-time students, the demands of quotidian life make studying a challenge. Every element of an OU education—the structure of the degree programs, the way courses are organized, the quality of tutoring—is designed to keep students engaged. A bachelor's degree takes at least three years to complete, as long as at a traditional university; and because almost all students are enrolled part-time, the average student takes twice as long to graduate, which also makes dropping out more likely. Despite this, about 30 percent of those who start at OU complete a degree. That's a considerably higher dropout rate than at residential British universities, but the comparison is inapt. OU is educating a very different population—older, part-time students, many of whom are interested only in taking particular courses rather than earning a degree. The open universities in Germany, Spain, the Netherlands, and Israel make a better comparison, and there, just one student in ten receives a degree.[21]

The Open University is most famous for the quality of its courses, and rightly so. Although there have been many imitators, no other place is so rigorous in the design of its courses, so attentive to the complementary and clashing possibilities of different media, so willing to submit draft curricula to outside critique, or so concerned about the usefulness as well as the jazziness of its teaching materials. What's more, no other place spends so much, which is why its course readers are the most thumbed-through material in many universities' libraries and its course materials are regularly pirated for use by faculty elsewhere.

With its well-maintained quadrangles and its hodgepodge of buildings laid out with no architectural regard for one another, the Milton Keynes campus, OU's headquarters, looks like one of Britain's postwar universities. But there are no undergraduates in residence, only professors and administrators. When a new course is to be designed, a battalion of experts gathers at Milton Keynes; during the next year and a half, this group turns out draft syllabi, visions, revisions, evaluations, paper topics, and examinations. OU's professors take the lead: the nine hundred faculty members, many of them recruited from similar posts at other British universities, are expected to be pedagogues as well as scholars.[22] The team also includes senior tutors, who supervise instruction when the course is in the field; text editors, who sharpen the prose of books specially written for the course; TV producers; software designers; test and measurement specialists; library consultants; outside assessors, who critique what's being prepared—as many as forty people working together on a single project. A "caretaker course team" does periodic updates, and after eight years the course is entirely rebuilt.[23]

The cost of producing a single course is comparable to the price tag for a low-budget Hollywood movie. The Pacific Studies course, which includes four books and five half-hour TV shows (scenes were shot on three continents), cost $2.5 million, and other courses have cost as much as a million dollars more.[24] Production values are high. Some of the TV shows initially developed for OU students have been adapted for airing on the BBC; a million people a week tune in to these shows, even though they are aired in the small hours of the morning. Course preparation is OU's biggest expense, accounting for about 40 percent of the university's budget. But the mega-enrollments, which enable the university to publish its own books as well as manufacture its own cassettes and science lab kits, make this approach financially feasible.[25] In 2000, the year it was first taught, a course called "Understanding Social Change" drew nearly 13,000 students.[26]

When John Daniel wrote about that course for an American audience, he made a point of stressing the fact that it was "low-tech." Of course, the materials incorporate more than the printed word. It's a credo at OU that different kinds of information are best conveyed through different media. What Daniel had in mind is that this course makes little use of the Internet.

At a time when distance learning is widely regarded as synonymous with on-line instruction, and the World Wide Web is touted as the best way to reach masses of students, the Open University, which already reaches masses of students, has been a late and cautious adopter of this technology.[27] Only a handful of courses, all of them in the computer sciences and distance education, are entirely Internet-based. At OU these are viewed as special cases.[28] "If you tried to teach philosophy like that," Dominic Newbould, a longtime administrator, told a *Chronicle of Higher Education* reporter, "you'd be laughed out of court." Revamping courses to boost reliance on the Web is a costly business, especially at an institution with "rich, varied and tightly integrated courseware."[29] But Daniel argues that the reason the Web isn't more prominently featured is that most students prefer things that way. Although they use the Internet for many purposes—in Britain alone, 150,000 messages are sent daily in 16,000 OU chat rooms —students "want to read books as books, not as downloaded computer files."[30]

The fact that most current OU students are adults who didn't grow up learning on-line partly explains why the Internet isn't more popular; when the wired generation shows up, there will surely be more demand for web-based instruction. OU administrators can't risk being out of date. In order to succeed in the increasingly crowded market of distance learning, they must pay close attention to what students want. Still, the pedagogy comes first. Before revamping a course, though, the Milton Keynes faculty need solid evidence that the new medium offers more than just razzle-dazzle.

There have been endless debates about the relative merits of on-line education versus classroom education, file cabinets'-worth of studies comparing dropout rates, student satisfaction, and the like. While the "Which is better?" question is often cast in empirical terms, it's really more a matter of ideology and economics. Professors have a powerful interest in proving that they are indispensable, while the advocates of virtual learning, including cost-driven administrators and academic entrepreneurs, are equally committed to the value of technological change. In this tiresome quarrel, to favor distance learning means being regarded as a philistine and to oppose it means being dismissed as a naïf.

Because the Open University has witnessed several waves of technological change, its faculty and administrators understand the benefits of patience. They don't reflexively seize the new, but recognize that in getting ideas across to students, it makes sense to use a variety of media. "[We're] not developing technology solutions and then finding the problems to apply them to," Jerzy Grzeda, operations manager of OU's Knowledge Media Institution, told a reporter from *Crosstalk* magazine.[31] Consistent with OU's commitment to promoting good teaching, a research unit has been assigned the mission of "rethinking university teaching in a digital age," and it is investing heavily in research on new media.[32] Still, John Daniel takes pleasure in pointing out that in the winter of 2000, Hungry Minds, a dot-com company that fancied itself the Amazon.com of e-learning, threatened to take over OU if it didn't agree to a partnership. Within a matter of months, the upstart firm went out of business, and "rational discussion of the impact of online technologies on colleges and universities became possible again."[33]

Some critics still dismiss the Open University as a correspondence school in fancy dress, but that jibe misses the mark. In accounting for its enviable reputation, the network of personal relationships between students and their tutors may matter as much as the thick packet of readings and video and audio cassettes that students receive.

Those who designed the curriculum had the one-on-one student-to-tutor model of Oxford and Cambridge in the back of their minds, and though the school doesn't pretend to mimic that approach, instruction still accounts for more than 20 percent of the university's budget. Group tutorials in the foundation courses, where dropouts are most likely, as well as individual tutorials for the advanced courses, are conducted weekly, at thirteen regional offices and 300 study centers scattered across the country, which also serve as recruiting stations. Although students aren't obliged to attend these sessions, many say it is what they like best about the university. The 7,000 tutors, many of them moonlighting from jobs at other universities, represent the human link between the institution and its students. They are in regular e-mail and phone contact with the twenty students to whom they're assigned; and they grade and write comments (still mainly in longhand) on students' papers. To ensure that the tutors are doing their jobs well, faculty members at Milton Keynes regularly read a random sample of students' papers. Week-long summer sessions crammed with seminars and, for the science students, lab work have also been a staple of the program. A flourishing student life shrinks distances in this distance education world, with thousands of study groups, a noisy student newspaper, and scores of graduations and reunions.

The Open University calls this balance between self-study and hands-on teaching "supported open learning," and that's probably why it is the best in the world at providing distance education. "The secret weapon are the tutors," says Jerzy Grzeda—and his assignment is to develop new technologies for the university.

▪ At Home Abroad

It was a change of policy at home that pushed Open University into making its initial forays abroad. For eons, British universities were underwritten almost entirely by the government, but beginning in 1993, the Conservative government, which had earlier hacked away at universities' budgets, ended the practice of awarding fixed sums to institutions, instead tying support directly to enrollment. This was bad news everywhere in higher education and especially worrisome at OU. The older universities, which once sniggered at distance education, started their own programs, and the competition affected enrollment at OU. Meanwhile, the cost of preparing new courses to the university's exacting standards was steadily climbing. Money had to be found someplace.[34]

In the 1980s, OU began to offer training courses for classroom teachers; over 100,000 teachers have taken these classes. To supplement the university's revenues, the business school started delivering management seminars for executives at British Petroleum, British Telecom, and other leading companies. These generated large sums, because the companies were paying for their managers' training, and so OU could charge full market rates.

Neither of these ventures affected the core of the Open University, its degree programs. But in the wake of the government's budget cuts, the university significantly reduced its course requirements, partly in response to student calls for more intellectual flexibility and partly to improve the balance sheet. The residential summer program was made optional for some courses and eliminated entirely for others. Though beloved by many, the summer session was resented by students who were working full-time and didn't want to use up their vacation attending classes; by the time the requirement was weakened, a fifth of all students were being excused from attending. But the decision wasn't simply a response to the inevitable. It mattered greatly that the summer program is also a money-losing operation.

From the start, the required foundation courses had been regarded as the intellectual entry point in all the degree programs. But potential students who wanted a less prescriptive curriculum were going elsewhere, and to capture that market, OU reduced the requirement from two foundation courses to one, then none. "There was considerable soul-searching," says Daniel. "It was through foundation courses that people learned to study at a distance, for there was more tutorial support for those courses." While the university defended the change as a response to student demand, critics charged that OU was abandoning its principles for cash, mimicking "the general trend toward fast-track degrees in which support for the individual has been replaced by a complete open-entry system in which students purchase whatever courses at whatever level they wish."[35]

OU officials are very clever at raising money. They cut a deal with an insurance company to market home and life insurance policies to their alumni, getting a percentage of each premium as a commission, and established an Open University Visa card. But Britain is not the world, and in the early 1990s, with domestic revenue sources beginning to be exhausted, Open University looked to opportunities in other lands.

*   *   *

When Americans think about international education, they generally have in mind junior year abroad in places like Paris or Rome. For their part, college administrators focus on students who come from abroad, bringing with them several years' premium tuition payments. Still, they usually dismiss the topic as one that's best left to the subalterns in the international studies office. During the past generation, however, global education has taken off, fueled by growing worldwide demand for highly skilled workers, made easier to deliver by new technologies, and made more essential by eroding geographic and political constraints and new interdependencies among institutions and nations.[36] It's a huge and growing business: in 2000, U.S. exports of education and training amounted to more than $14 billion.[37]

That this development hasn't attracted more notice in the United States reflects the fact that the trade in higher education mainly involves American universities and e-learning companies selling their wares overseas, rather than their being confronted by overseas competitors. "Foreign involvement within America will not be the main driver of globalization in U.S. higher education," writes Simon Marginson. "Rather it will be American activities offshore, and the need to reconcile the international and domestic agendas."[38] The traffic in thinking about higher education policy runs the same way. Other countries are learning from the American example, depending less on their governments and more on the market to provide postsecondary instruction.

Governments are also relying more on other countries' public institutions. Historically, higher education has been the way the keys to the culture are passed on from one generation of the elite to the next, and this isn't a task that foreign universities can be trusted to perform. Even as higher education has everywhere become more accessible, this commitment to cultural nationalism remains intact, especially when it is perceived as under siege from American cultural products—*le Mickey Mouse,* as it were.[39] But national borders have been all but effaced in fields like computer technology, where skills count for more than national ideologies. The same holds true in business, where the tool kit of techniques—cost accounting, marketing, product development, and the like—is universal.

Students have been voting with their feet, moving from one country to the next in search of the best education in their field. Then, more timidly, the universities have followed, pushed by the forces of free trade into acknowledging the need for international standards that weren't simply market driven. In negotiations over the General Agreement on Trade and Services, or GATS, there has been little understanding that higher education should be treated differently from any other service on the international market, that in higher education—unlike, say, accounting—lifting trade barriers isn't always the right move. Responding to GATS became a case of hanging together or hanging separately. Universities around the globe have had to speak out, since otherwise, as a matter of international law, the market would become the sole arbiter of quality.[40]

By its very nature, on-line education is no respecter of geography, which is why e-learning institutions based in Australia can train multitudes of Indian and Chinese students in computer programming or corporate management. Schools that rely at least partly on face-to-face teaching have been somewhat slower to react, but that is changing. Universities from Australia, western Europe, and the United States have come together to form a consortium called Universitas 21, bankrolled by the Thomson Corporation, an international publishing company. More and more universities are opening overseas campuses—Johns Hopkins Medical School in Dubai, Wharton School of Business in Singapore, the University of Phoenix in Rotterdam, Australia's Monash University in Kuala Lumpur. Frequently there is news about the British Open University, which appears to be setting up shop around the globe.

This development should come as no surprise, because among all the universities in the world, OU is probably best situated to expand on a global scale. It has developed superior teaching materials; its books and video and audio cassettes can be readily adapted and translated. The Open University brand carries cachet throughout the Commonwealth, as well as in European countries that have used it as a model in setting up their own open universities.[41] Although OU is less high-tech and more "high-touch" than some of its rivals, this gives the school its niche in the marketplace.

Open University's first foray overseas, in 1992, was close to home, in Ireland and western Europe, where there existed a ready and lucrative market. With course materials, the biggest expense, already on the shelf, the only additional cost was providing tutors, who can be monitored from Milton Keynes. The university has such a stellar reputation that it can charge as much as twice what British OU students pay and still attract a crowd: in 2001, 8,000 students were enrolled in thirty-four study centers. When searching out new markets, OU has devised an array of business models. Partnerships with universities in central and eastern Europe, Singapore, Hong Kong, the United Arab Emirates, India, and South

Africa add another 15,000 students. The commercial arm, Open University Worldwide, licenses course materials and consults with countries and institutions interested in setting up their own distance learning programs.[42] So adept is OU in its dealings abroad that in 1997 it won the Queen's Award for Export Achievement.

For "one of the major British intellectual exports"—a "colossus now contriving to straddle the globe," as a *Times* of London reporter called it—entering the U.S. market made apparent good sense.[43] "The Open University is at a crossroads," Bob Masterson, director of OU's entrepreneurial unit, Open University Worldwide, said in 1999. "It has the opportunity to be a global player. The question is, does it have the will. My answer is, yes, it should, and we should get on with it."[44]

▪ Quality Isn't Everything

If being the best were a guarantee of success, then Open University would be well on its way to becoming preeminent in the United States. That's what OU must have believed in 1999, when it set up shop in Baltimore. Vice-Chancellor John Daniel, who was dispatched from Milton Keynes to set up the U.S. operation, expressed OU's vision in terms as immodest, for their time, as the original charter. The new institution, he said, would lay "the foundations of a 'global confederation for distance learning . . . a genuinely multi-national university.'"[45]

But even as Daniel was delivering this speech to a group called the World Education Market, warning signs were already visible. The British Open University received 40,000 applications when it opened its doors in 1970. In its first three months of operation, the U.S. branch had recruited fewer than a hundred American students. "Slow growth," said Daniel, with the British flair for understatement, "seems to be a feature of new U.S. institutions."

The situation was different in other ways as well. Higher education has become more a marketplace than a meritocracy. Aside from quality, other things matter: gaining name recognition, which costs money; and getting certified by higher education's gatekeepers, the accrediting agencies, which takes time. But Open University was impatient to enroll students and strike deals with American academic partners, and intent on doing so with a relatively modest cash outlay. It had neither the bankroll nor the patience required to succeed.

When Open University officials looked at the United States, they saw great opportunity. Distance education is potentially a multibillion-dollar market, or so the Wall Street investment firms kept saying; and although schools like the University of Phoenix were making money with business courses, none of the leading American universities was prepared to offer a full liberal arts curriculum at a distance. OU believed it could fill the void. "What we can provide," Richard Lewis, the acting chancellor of the U.S. Open University, bluntly told an American reporter, "is decent distance education, because you've not been very good at it."[46] The marketing strategy proceeded along two parallel tracks: OU entered into partnerships with American institutions and also offered its own bachelor's and master's degrees. Neither approach panned out.

Well before its official launch, OU had been negotiating with several big American universities, and profitable deals seemed to be in the offing. Florida State University was ready to create a joint distance learning program for that state's community college graduates. The twenty-two-campus California State University system was poised to sign a $5 million contract to train 14,000 California classroom teachers who lacked state credentials. Western Governors University, a virtual institution, announced "an unprecedented new distance learning initiative for students throughout the U.S." But none of these deals came to pass. "We decided that it was just as easy to start from scratch and put together our own programs," Alan Mabe, dean of graduate studies at Florida State, told a *National Crosstalk* reporter. A California State University faculty committee bought the philosophy of OU but rejected the specifics of its courses, faulting them for being "culturally limited." Even as negotiations with Western Governors University proceeded fitfully, that prospective partner was floundering.[47]

A clash of institutional cultures doomed those prospective deals. In places like Singapore and Hong Kong, says Brenda Gourley, "there were no concerns about cultural imperialism; and, John Daniel adds, eastern Europe wanted its education "hot, strong, and Western." But Florida State administrators complained that the materials were too English— "too much Queen and cricket." OU tried to rectify the problem. Year-long courses were divided into semester-long chunks, Britishisms were excised from the texts, pounds were converted to dollars, and American programming languages were introduced into the computer courses.[48] OU's commitment to blending a variety of media, rather than relying mainly on the Internet, also drew objections. The materials "weren't at all high-tech," the complaint ran, a reflection of faith that the Internet was the only way to offer distance education.

Underlying these concerns was an unhappiness that a British university—and not Oxford or Cambridge but an unknown upstart—was imposing its standards of good practice on an American university, and doing so in what seemed a patronizing manner. "The 'not invented here' syndrome is very real. Faculty are normally quite protective of their courses," says Jennifer Preece at the University of Maryland's Baltimore campus, which was negotiating a joint master's program.[49] "Charlie, the British have a very different interpretation of the Revolutionary War than we do," one Cal State professor told chancellor Charles Reed.[50] The skirmishes in Concord and Lexington were, in effect, being refought in Fullerton and Tallahassee.

Open University officials kept a stiff upper lip in the face of these failures. Their main mission, they insisted, was to create a new university, a self-sufficient entity. They had done it in Britain, after all. Why couldn't the same thing be accomplished in the United States, with its millions of nontraditional students potentially interested in a well-designed university education that they could pursue part-time—the very group that swelled enrollment at home?

But the British and American institutions weren't really the same. For one thing, the U.S. Open University initially offered only the last two years of an undergraduate education. OU hoped to attract community college graduates, and so it carried on negotiations with community college districts for "two plus two" programs in which students who had received their associate degree could continue their studies at OU. The problem was that community college graduates have ready access to better-known state universities. "You have to ask yourself if an American student will want a degree from the Open University or Florida State," an administrator in Tallahassee said, explaining his university's decision to develop its own distance learning program, and he meant the question to be rhetorical.[51]

The hallmark of the British Open University is the mix of virtual and hands-on instruction. Yet in the United States, the realities of geography made it impossible to recreate that system; instead, advising, counseling, and grading were done on-line. Although the school tried to compensate with on-line technologies such as real-time meetings with study groups and professors, which weren't available in Britain, that couldn't be a true substitute for human interaction. This was an attempt to make a virtue of necessity, but there was no way to estimate the impact of becoming "Virtual Open U" on students' satisfaction, performance, and dropout rates.

In persuading American students to enroll, OU treated its prestige as its biggest asset. "What makes us different?" its marketing materials asked. "Recognized as the world's leader in part-time education," came the answer. Yet in the insular world of American higher education, unless the school is Oxford or Cambridge, a reputation earned abroad means almost nothing. From the moment that it announced its arrival, OU has remained an unknown commodity to American audiences. No one is aware that its engineering department is rated more highly than Oxford's.

What's more, no one really cares. In choosing a university, it matters to American undergraduates that they can obtain federal loans, that their course credits will be recognized if they transfer to another school, that the institution's name will be an asset when they're looking for a job, and that *U.S. News & World Report* gives the school high marks. For any of this to happen, a university must be accredited. Otherwise, it carries the taint of the matchbook school. "Students ask if the school has been accredited," says OU's former marketing director, Josephine Feldman. "Without accreditation, the phone conversation stops right there." But this rite of institutional passage takes time, and time ran out on Open University.

Accreditation is meant to ensure quality control. "It's a gatekeeper's job. Open the gate too wide, and standards are lowered. Close the gate, and run the risk of pressure building until the gate is broken or—wore yet— another route is discovered, which makes the gate a relic of the past."[52] Yet in fact, the accreditors have had little to say about quality.[53] Instead, they focus on things that can be counted, such as books in the library and degrees held by faculty members. In Britain, a single national government agency conducts academic audits and produces "quality assurance" reports—it is these reports that put Open University above Oxford in engineering—but accreditation in the United States is a crazy quilt of fifty-five regional, national, and other specialized organizations.[54]

In late 2001, U.S. Open University won accreditation from the Distance Education and Training Council, which reviews distance learning schools, but it is the regional associations whose stamp of approval really matters.[55] Because OU had its headquarters in Baltimore, this assignment fell to the Middle States Association of Colleges and Schools, which acted with all deliberate speed. Three years after applying for accreditation, OU still hadn't moved beyond "candidacy status."

The Open University story illustrates what's wrong with how accreditation is carried out.[56] The system has long been attacked for its bias toward traditionalism; it "suppresses creativity," a 1973 Carnegie Commission on Higher Education charged. The rise to prominence of distance and e-learning ventures has spawned a host of new problems.[57]

Regional accrediting agencies, which date to the nineteenth century, are premised on the assumption that a university's campus is situated on terra firma. But a school like OU educates students around the globe. Why should the Middle States Association have taken on, as it did, the accrediting of Touro University International, an on-line branch of a New York City college with its office in Los Angeles and instruction carried out in cyberspace? The gatekeepers have not been able to devise a template to assess distance education. Should person-to-person education be the model, or does the new technology require an entirely new paradigm?[58] Even though OU was offering no on-the-ground classes, it should have been an open-and-shut case for approval because of its array of courses and a thirty-year track record of excellence.

After the Open University folded, the Middle States officials said that they had liked what they'd seen. The problem was that they couldn't act quickly enough to help OU withstand the fierce pressures of the market.

Accreditation, "Queen and cricket," professors' opposition to "not made here" distance courses, the missing personal element: all these factors help explain the failure of Open University. But money is what mattered most, and the institution's pockets simply weren't deep enough. "Open University might have triumphed eventually, if we had put enough money into it," says vice chancellor Brenda Gourley. "Clearly the U.S. is a big market, but you don't get into that market without a big up-front investment. Universities don't have 'high risk' profiles, and no one was queuing up to bankroll the venture."

Open University spent $20 million on its American operation.[59] Though that's not chump change, by current standards it isn't much. Columbia committed an estimated $40 million to Fathom, its virtual education dot-com., and that venture failed; Cardean University, the for-profit business school sponsored by several leading American universities, had burned through an estimated $125 million by the end of 2002. The

Apollo Group, which runs the on-line University of Phoenix courses, annually spends more than $20 million on marketing alone.

▪ Money and the "Meaningful Revolution"

The advent of on-line education "is the beginning of a meaningful revolution," says Columbia's provost, Jonathan Cole. "The challenge is to achieve the democratizing effect. If we can produce this knowledge for other parts of the world, then we've done something of great benefit, not only for commercial purposes."

If is the key. Crucially, the direction this "revolution" will take has yet to be fixed. Cole was talking specifically about Fathom, Columbia's failed attempt to garner money for the university by putting a storehouse of knowledge on-line, but the Open University makes an even better example. OU had created "something of great benefit," the best of what distance learning can offer, only to find out to its sorrow that, at least in the lucrative U.S. market, the best isn't enough. To talk about "the democratizing effect" of the Internet recalls the high hopes of its creators. But just as, with startling quickness, the Internet has become a shopping mall and a porn shop, higher education on the Web may be destined to be driven not by academic virtue but by the bottom line.

It misses the point to contrast "free" on-line courses with what's being offered by the market. On the Web, as in life, there is no such thing as a free lunch. The real question is who pays. The analysis of Open University, as well as the assessments in Chapter 9 of Fathom, MIT's OpenCourse-Ware, and various e-learning ventures, all point to the same conclusion: in this high stakes world, money, not quality, talks the loudest.

Without a continuing infusion of outside funding, the likeliest survivors in the virtual universe are schools like the University of Phoenix, which offer well-packaged instruction to well-defined niche markets.[60] A cash-rich company like Thomson, the publishing giant, might eventually succeed as well. In 2002, Thomson invested heavily in Cardean University, reviving its hopes of becoming not just an M.B.A. program but a world-class university, and it was trying to achieve something similar with Universitas 21. The company has deep pockets, and it has been prepared to continue dipping into them to support these ventures; but it was by no means certain that Thomson could succeed where the likes of Rupert Murdoch and Michael Milken have failed.

The grander aspiration to open access—Jonathan Cole's "democratizing effect"—remains at best a long shot. Foundations can jump-start these ventures, as the Mellon Foundation did in underwriting Sunoikisis, the confederation of classics departments described in Chapter 8, and (in tandem with the Hewlett Foundation) MIT's OpenCourseWare project. A host of schools would like to emulate MIT, but no foundation has the necessary resources. Neither do the universities themselves; they lack a credible business plan. No one at Columbia ever believed that Fathom should be treated like its own campus library, that the university had an obligation to maintain the website at a perpetual deficit because it is a public good for the world. It was, after all, Fathom.*com,* not Fathom.*edu.*

Government could step in to subsidize projects like Open University and OpenCourseWare. Perhaps that will happen in countries that opt to rely mainly on the Internet, not campus-based learning, to deliver mass higher education. In the United States, an organization called Digital Promise, founded in 2002 and boasting such heavyweight names among its founders as former NBC president Lawrence Grossman and former Federal Communications Commission chairman Newton Minow, is urging that $18 billion in revenues from FCC auctions of the radio spectrum be used to promote e-learning. "This parallels the historic use of revenues from the sale of public lands," declares the Digital Promise manifesto, "which helped finance public education in every new state and created the great system of land-grant colleges."[61] It's a fine vision, but there are no realistic prospects for a twenty-first-century counterpart to the 1862 Land Grant Act, no e-learning version of the GI Bill or the Pell grant program that would make universally available the best that distance learning has to offer.

The implication is as evident as it is troubling. If no one will underwrite an enterprise like Open University, with its promise of a world-class education for virtually everyone, will the on-line higher education world be ruled by the likes of Thomson and the Apollo Group?

PART IV

THE SMART MONEY

A Good Deal of Collaboration
The University of California, Berkeley

Gary Baldwin gets excited when he shows off the brilliantly colored tubes of light lining the corridor of Berkeley's Cory Hall, where the Gigascale Silicon Research Center is housed. Although they look like ordinary neon lights, they're actually diodes, like those in a watch or a calculator. What excites him is that they're as bright as ordinary incandescent lights—and nearly ten times more energy efficient.[1]

These power-saving colored lights represent the kind of "fundamental change" in how we live that prompted Baldwin to quit Hewlett Packard after a quarter-century, taking a sizable pay cut to join Berkeley's department of electrical engineering and computer science. At Berkeley, he says, people have a "fire in the belly" about doing this kind of visionary work.

Baldwin manages the Gigascale Silicon Research Center, a key component in an ambitious partnership among the federal government, higher education, and Silicon Valley known as MARCO, the Microelectronics Advanced Research Corporation. MARCO links the research branch of the Department of Defense, twenty-two universities, and some two dozen firms in the semiconductor industry, including such Fortune 500 names as Intel, Motorola, and Advanced Micro Devices.

The Gigascale Center aspires to revolutionize the science behind the silicon chip. The goal is to reach "gigascale"—a billion transistors on a single chip, nearly twenty-five times more than Intel's Pentium 4 processor. It's an immodest goal, and nothing less than revolutionary research is needed to achieve it—"a moon shot," in the words of MARCO's 2000 annual report.

Since its inception, immodesty has been the hallmark of the semiconductor field. Moore's Law—the axiom proposed by Intel's founder, Gordon Moore, that the number of transistors on a chip will double every eighteen months—has held up for more than a third of a century. But as transistors shrink in size below fifty nanometers, 1/20,000 the width of a pinhead, electron behavior becomes much harder to regulate. Still, gigascale proportions are essential if engineers are to build the smaller, cheaper, and more powerful semiconductors of the next generation.[2]

Can university-based electrical engineers accomplish that feat? And is their freedom of inquiry constricted when industry and government are setting the agenda?

■ Universities for Rent?

Ties between universities and industry have received a good deal of media coverage in recent years, much of it hostile. "The Kept University," the cover story in the *Atlantic Monthly*'s March 2000 issue, paints a troubling picture of multimillion-dollar deals that put higher education in thrall to the needs of big business. "Disinterested inquiry" has become hard to sustain, the authors argue, because "universities themselves are behaving more and more like for-profit companies."[3]

This topic has been an especially touchy one at Berkeley, since "The Kept University," like scores of stories (even a piece in *Le Monde Diplomatique*),[4] focuses on the $25 million, five-year contract, signed in 1998, between Berkeley's College of Natural Resources and the Swiss pharmaceutical giant Novartis, part of which supports research on genetically engineered crops. When dean Gordon Rausser announced that deal—which gives Novartis the first look at much of the research carried out by the plant and microbial biology department—he proudly proclaimed that it raised university-industry partnerships "to a new level"; but when *Nature* ran an editorial that asked, "Is the university-industry complex out of control?" the focus was on the Novartis deal.[5] In an unscientific poll of the Berkeley faculty, more than half said they feared that the deal would undermine the university's commitment to "publish," rather than sell, "good research," and three-fifths believed it would interfere with scientists' free exchange of ideas.[6] Can this be what the president of the University of California meant when he announced that "the University of California means business"?

In the years following World War II, most of the funding for large-scale scientific research projects came from Washington. A new national policy articulated by Vannevar Bush, President Truman's science adviser, took what was then a daring step, making universities rather than government agencies or think tanks the principal sites for basic inquiry.[7] Although the government determined the broad research priorities, academics were responsible for getting the job done. Public officials treated universities generously, allowing them to bill upwards of 40 percent for "indirect costs," and that money could be spent as the recipients wished.[8] It is an exaggeration, but not by much, to say that a quarter-century of such handsome public support built the modern research university.

But federal legislation passed in 1970, partly to punish universities for countenancing widespread student protests, demanded greater emphasis on "mission-oriented"—that is, more obviously useful—studies. Government's share of research costs has been declining ever since.[9] With the price tag for science escalating rapidly, universities started turning to business for support. In his 1982 book *Beyond the Ivory Tower,* Derek Bok used the bully pulpit of the Harvard presidency to praise these new patrons as a bulwark against the mounting demands of government.[10] Alliances with industry would not only provide an alternative to federal largesse but also revitalize intellectual life in universities, as corporate America injected real world problems and contributed state-of-the-art technology to the musty precincts of academe.

Since then, industry has picked up an ever larger share of the tab—corporate contributions now exceed $2 billion a year—but this has proved to be a decidedly mixed blessing.[11] Less than a decade after extolling the benefits of business ties, Bok returned to his theme. This time, however, he cautioned that the "mounting requirements of the state" might prove less onerous than the demands made by the market.[12]

At Berkeley, where firms sponsored $27.9 million in research in 2000, the Gigascale Center has sought to insulate itself by operating in an environment that approximates "open source"—give-it-away—science. By subsidizing the center's research, the sponsoring Silicon Valley semiconductor companies have in essence paid membership dues to join an intellectual club where there are no secrets—a scientific community where everyone has a chance to learn from everyone else.

The Gigascale Center, with an annual budget of $8.3 million, gets more money from industry than the Novartis project, and its corporate backers are more directly involved in setting its agenda. But outside a narrow circle of specialists, it has gone unnoticed. When examined side by side, these two enterprises situated less than a mile from each other illustrate the consequences, both good and bad, of universities' reliance on the market to pay for scientific research.

■ Putting the Pieces Together

In the summer of 1994, Peter Verhofstadt, then the chief scientist at the Semiconductor Research Corporation, or SRC, an industry research group in Silicon Valley, was launching a project on what he termed the "research gap." Verhofstadt sought the counsel of his old friend Sonny Maynard, an industry veteran who had spent thirty years administering microelectronics research for the Department of Defense and five years at McDonnell Douglas before becoming a solo consultant.

Although the SRC, like its member firms, was adept at handling short-term problem-solving assignments, Verhofstadt believed that the industry needed to invest in exploratory research. A generation earlier, that kind of work was being done at such storied places as AT&T's Bell Labs and Xerox PARC. Yet while these think tanks made great advances—the transistor, the Xerox photocopier, the laser—the companies that fronted the costs often didn't reap the financial benefits.[13] When cost-conscious managers radically shrank the labs' budgets, there was nothing to replace the labs. Concern mounted that the knowledge needed to create the next—or third or fourth—generation of semiconductors wouldn't be there when it was needed.

When it comes to marketing their products, Silicon Valley companies are fierce competitors. But the industry also has a long history of acting in firms' mutual best interest by collaborating on "pre-competitive" research that potentially benefits all of them.[14] Since the early 1980s, spurred by the threat that Japanese would monopolize the field, joint research projects have sprung up among companies as well as between the industry and government. This time, though, Verhofstadt thought it made sense to call on the universities, since that's where many of the most highly regarded long-range thinkers make their home.[15]

At about the same time, the Semiconductor Technology Council, an advisory board established by Congress, determined that industry and government should be jointly funding university research. If the semiconductor manufacturers contributed half the needed funds and their suppliers chipped in a quarter, then Washington would pay for the rest.

Verhofstadt set out to convince the members of SRC that it was in their best interests to sign up. Craig Barrett, then the chief operating officer, subsequently CEO, at Intel, one of the Silicon Valley giants, needed no convincing. A former Stanford professor, he had long been a supporter of such links. Berkeley's engineering dean Richard Newton, not usually given to encomiums, sings Barrett's praises. It was Barrett's "vision and persistence and drive," he says, and Intel's willingness to put up more than its fair share, that clinched the deal.

Meanwhile, Sonny Maynard was using his old government contacts to drum up support. The natural ally in Washington was the Defense Advanced Research Projects Agency, or DARPA, Maynard's old employer. Ever since the invention of the stirrup, Maynard quips, the military has been supporting research in technology. After World War II, the army funded Bell Labs' work on the transistor, while the air force underwrote the integrated circuit—and then, once the circuit had been invented, it made a further commitment to build an integrated circuit computer, even though no one knew whether it would work or what to do with it even if it did work.

The military is good at "finding an idea whose time has come and shoving a lot of money at it," says Maynard. "Writing a big check is therapeutic." While industry wants to solve the seemingly intractable problems, the military wants "to be there when whatever it is . . . turns up," so that it can use this latest new thing to build state-of-the-art weapons systems.

From several quarters, the idea for MARCO was taking shape. This would be a national network of scientists working in university labs, doing long-term research projects paid for by both the semiconductor companies and the federal government. Sonny Maynard, a born manager who was growing restless sitting on the sidelines, jumped at the chance to head up the new venture.

▪ Enter Berkeley

It was a foregone conclusion that MARCO would rely heavily on Berkeley for ideas and talent. Berkeley's graduate programs in engineering are ranked second by *U.S. News & World Report,* and its semiconductor research is widely regarded as without peer. When MARCO was still in its planning stage, says engineering dean Richard Newton, Berkeley's scientists were among the key figures doing the planning.[16]

Although you can still hear the native Australia in his speech, Newton has been at Berkeley since 1975. He was Berkeley's first Ph.D. student whose dissertation was entirely funded by the computer industry (Hewlett Packard underwrote his investigation of computer-assisted design (CAD) tools for minicomputers, the precursors to the personal computer), and that experience shaped his view of university-industry collaboration. "I learned as much—more—from them," he says of his corporate sponsors, "than they ever got from me."

After finishing his degree, Newton joined the Berkeley faculty. He helped raise nearly $8 million from industry to add a fifth floor atop the engineering building, Cory Hall, where the Gigascale Center is now housed, and the way he went about it illustrates the "one hand washes the other" character of Berkeley's ties to Silicon Valley. When the Digital Equipment Corporation (DEC), then one of the big computer makers, asked Newton to rewrite some source code, he did the work for free, asking only that the firm donate some of its new minicomputers to the campus. Later, when he was soliciting funds for the Cory Hall expansion, Newton went back to DEC. "The implication was, 'I sort of think you owe us,'" he says. "There was no problem. They appreciated what Berkeley had done for them and were happy to contribute."

Like many members of the scientific fraternity, Newton is as committed to academic openness—a world without intellectual borders—as he is to working with industry, but he's not a believer in the sanctity of the academy. In his view, the university justifies its privileged status mainly by its contributions to society. Nor is he averse to making money; he's a millionaire several times over because of a number of start-ups with which he has been associated. Rather, his ideas about openness, like his thoughts on collaboration, stem from his experience at Berkeley. Free source products get better, Newton says, because of the contributions of the virtual community, "all the persons who have worked—and are still working—to improve them."[17]

Newton views the purpose of university science as maximizing impact on the world, and for the electrical engineering department that has often meant giving something away. The most famous instance is Berkeley Unix, a much-improved version of AT&T's proprietary Unix platform. While users had to pay AT&T thousands of dollars, Berkeley Unix was essentially given away. What mattered most, though, was that it was open source—its code was available to all comers. In the mid-1970s, DARPA chose Berkeley Unix as a platform for networking its computers for precisely this reason: Open source products get better because of the contributions of the virtual community. As a result, Berkeley Unix became immensely important during the 1980s and 1990s, when DARPA's computer network evolved into the Internet.[18]

Newton's favorite story along these lines is the tale of a program called SPICE. During the early 1970s, Berkeley's computer scientists were developing circuit simulation programs, predecessors of the Gigascale Center's research, creating a virtual chip that obeyed all the rules of a physical chip. Testing the design for a new chip on such a program dramatically improved the likelihood that the prototype would work, at a fraction of what it would cost to build it. A group of graduate students devised a program that fit the bill. But because they wanted no part of related Defense Department research on radiation analysis—indeed, in that era they wanted no part of any classified Defense Department research—they gave it a fittingly countercultural acronym. CANCER is what they called it: Computer Analysis of Nonlinear Circuits, Excluding Radiation.

Fairchild Semiconductor obtained an exclusive license for CANCER, but soon afterward the professor who launched the project decided to develop a similar program, one that anyone would be free to use. That program bears the friendlier acronym SPICE: Simulation Program with Integrated Circuits Emphasis. While companies can add proprietary material, the basic code must remain public, and programs based on SPICE are expected to acknowledge the source of their original material. The punch line is that while CANCER died at Fairchild, even today SPICE remains the basis for many circuit simulators.

The SPICE story, Newton says, is a natural experiment that proves the value of keeping inventions in the public domain. And it's not only Berkeley academics who are committed to openness; this attitude permeates Silicon Valley. "Competitors [in Silicon Valley] consulted one another on technical matters with a frequency unheard of in other areas of the country," writes Anna Lee Saxenian. "The president of the Western Electronics Manufacturers Association (WEMA) compared the openness of Silicon Valley to the East: 'Easterners tell me that people there don't talk to their competitors. Here they will not only sit down with you, but they will share the problems and experiences they have had.'"[19]

This faith in openness is evident in MARCO's research centers. The planners, Berkeley academics like Rich Newton among them, were trying to figure out how best to organize research for that proverbial moon shot.[20] They knew this meant bringing together the best researchers from around the country. The breadth of the intellectual community at the Gigascale Center is staggering: thirty-seven faculty members, fifteen post-docs, and ninety graduate students drawn from fourteen of the nation's top research universities including Carnegie Mellon, MIT, Michigan, and Stanford. Engineers from Silicon Valley firms are also working at the center.

When Newton started phoning leading scientists, everyone wanted to get involved. The center's structure is "designed to cherry-pick all the best guys," Sonny Maynard at MARCO points out, and "give them a lot of freedom—but at the same time, to keep them talking to one another, to avoid the 'I'm the king of this little hill' problem." And it is working. "You can pretty much plug into any part of the center," says Maynard, "and you won't find some guy off in the corner doing his own thing and ignoring everyone else. [The center] has pushed forward the notion that professors can actually work with each other on teams."

As might be expected from computer scientists, many exchanges occur virtually, on a website—*www.gigascale.org*—that functions as a lively work space. But a remarkable amount happens in real time. Four times a year the researchers spend several days together, swapping notes and ideas. Such intensity of interaction, rare in academe, is considered essential in crafting a research vision grander than what any one engineer might conceive.

Like most truly good deals, the Gigascale Center is an arrangement from which all the parties—the university, the government, and the semiconductor industry—stand to benefit. Berkeley gets the money it needs to underwrite research that its scientists want to do, as well as the chance to bring in outside researchers eager to work collaboratively on a sky's-the-limit venture. The semiconductor industry gets to be tutored by some of the smartest engineers in the country. The Defense Department is betting that the research findings, though generic and not classified, will be valuable for designing the next generation's instruments of war.

One of the biggest challenges in university-industry partnerships, says David Hodges, Berkeley's emeritus dean of engineering, who helped launch the Gigascale Center, is encouraging people on both sides to speak a common language. That's why Hodges pursued Gary Baldwin, whom Hodges hired for his first job after graduate school, to run the center. "He's been on both sides of the fence," says Hodges. For his part, Baldwin was tired of the backbiting in the Hewlett labs. The lure of managing a coterie of world-class engineers was irresistible.

Baldwin's years in industry show in the way he structures that work. While he talks, he pulls out an organizational chart with three columns. The left-hand column lists the administrative contacts at the sponsoring firms, "the people who get to give MARCO a thumbs-up or thumbs-down." In the middle column are the key technical contacts, the researchers who "often provide the decision makers with a lot of input about whether this is worthwhile or not." The right-hand column identifies "key account managers." A key account manager in the business world is the liaison to a client whose task is to build customer loyalty. Baldwin sees the Gigascale Center's relationship with its industry sponsors as essentially similar, and he has assigned a scientist to be the key account manager for each semiconductor company.

In *Nice Work,* one of novelist David Lodge's send-ups of academic life, Robyn Penrose, a professor of Victorian literature at a cash-starved British university, is sent off on what the administration calls the "Shadow Scheme." Her mission is to follow Vic Wilcox, the managing director of an engineering firm, as he does his job, meanwhile convincing him of the joys of higher learning, and Lodge has great fun with the ensuing culture clash. "Does the world really need another book on nineteenth-century fiction?" Wilcox asks, to which Penrose tartly replies, "I don't know, but it's going to get one."[21] At a place like Berkeley, where faculty autonomy is a jealously guarded prerogative, most professors would take Penrose's side, chafing if asked to be the helpmate to industry. But these engineers, many with Silicon Valley experience, see things more pragmatically. An engineer's job is to solve problems, and solving problems takes money. That requires staying in close touch with the people who have the money.

▪ Keeping Things Open

Private enterprise and universities have conventionally been seen as representing opposing views about the value of openness. Companies typically make money by keeping secrets, while university-generated science has historically been available to all—undertaken to build a wider base of knowledge and published to enhance the common good. Academic scientists belong to a "gift culture . . . where reputation and sense of self-worth is tied to one's contributions: you are what you give away, not what you hoard."[22]

In a classic 1942 article, the sociologist Robert Merton described the culture of science as "communist" in character: "The substantive findings of science are a product of social collaboration and are assigned to the community."[23] For scientists, "priority of discovery is the goal," sociologists Walter Powell and Jason Owen-Smith point out. "The public nature of scientific knowledge encourages its use by others, and in so doing, increases the reputation of the researchers. In contrast, patents are the coin of the realm in the technologist's world. Rewards are pecuniary and the incentive to divulge new information quickly is not as potent."[24]

When universities cut deals with business, however, the line between public and private, profit and prestige, gets blurred. A sea change in federal policy has played a big part in redrawing those lines.[25]

Until a generation ago, universities generally weren't authorized to patent inventions stemming from research paid for by the government.[26] The theory was that since the funding was public, higher education shouldn't benefit financially from the results. Those belonged in the public domain, where anyone could use them. But as a consequence, the impressive advances made in university laboratories often went unnoticed and unused by industry.

The 1980 Bayh-Dole Act, which assigns patent rights to universities, takes a market-driven approach. That is, the opportunity to make money by patenting their inventions gives universities the necessary incentive to take their products to market.[27] Universities have taken advantage of these potential financial windfalls—the number of patent applications increased twentyfold in a generation, to about five thousand a year—but the character of their research has also changed, in disquieting ways. In biotechnology, where most of the patent money is to be found, academic research teams "acquire the character of 'quasi-firms' as scientists eagerly pursue R&D programs aimed at commercial application."[28] A handful of schools generate more than $100 million a year—the equivalent of the income generated by a $2 billion endowment—from licensing blockbuster drugs.

The difference in how value gets created in biotech and high-tech means that there can be no "one-size-fits-all" model for managing relations between universities and industry. Profits in biotech come from having a monopoly on a product; that's one reason why the Novartis deal caused such a ruckus.[29] To Berkeley's plant biologists, what made the deal so tempting was the fact that the company owns a huge database of plant genome data. Access to this material is invaluable, because information that would otherwise take years to assemble can be pulled together literally in seconds. "Without modern laboratory facilities and access to commercially developed proprietary databases," argues Gordon Rausser, dean of the College of Natural Resources, "we can neither provide first-rate graduate education nor perform the fundamental research that is part of the University's mission."[30]

Novartis was willing to share this information with the Berkeley scientists, since it anticipated making money when it patented their findings, but not with the world. That just isn't how things work in agribusiness, where openness is unknown and ownership is everything.[31] To protect its interests, Novartis required faculty who were working with its databases to sign confidentiality agreements.

From the corporate perspective this was a rational move, but in academic circles any agreement to keep a secret is an engraved invitation to controversy.[32] That's why Michael Crow, who oversaw Columbia University's technology transfer program for a decade, says he would never make a deal like the one Berkeley struck with Novartis. Crow knows what he's talking about. In 2001, his last year at Columbia (in 2002, he became president of Arizona State University), the university earned $141 million in licensing fees, the second-largest amount in the nation. Still, he says, every deal should be negotiated on a project-by-project basis: "You don't sell the store."

"One company said it could raise $400 million if we gave them a stream [of licenses] and we turned them down. No firm should have a steady stream of *anything* from the university," Crow argues. "Giving one company that kind of control can stifle research—and it is important to decide, on a case-by-case basis, whether a technology should mainly be used for private purposes or the public interest."

In the semiconductor industry, by contrast, nimbleness matters more than ownership. Although some inventions do get patented, patents rarely generate much revenue. A new chip may use hundreds of patents, and if chip makers had to license each one, they wouldn't accomplish anything else. Besides, the technology changes so quickly that no single patent matters for very long. That's why most firms have cross-licensing agreements: you let me use your patents and I let you use mine.[33]

▪ Dancing with the Devil

Arguments over whether a university is making a Faustian bargain when it signs eight-figure deals with big business grew fierce during the economic boom of the late 1990s. At the time there was little doubt that companies had bucketfuls of money at the ready. The worry was that they would use that money to control the research agenda.

The recession that began in 2000 introduced a different species of problem. Companies' balance sheets mutate faster than higher education's research priorities, and that means any university that lives by the rules of the market must risk dying by those same rules. As Columbia's provost Jonathan Cole writes, "Motivated more by the bottom line than universities, businesses that invest in university-based research can and will make rapid decisions to cut support when and if they feel it lacks profitability."[34]

Getting money from many sources is advantageous, argues Paul Gray, who negotiated such deals as Berkeley's dean of engineering before becoming executive vice chancellor and provost, since when one source of funds falters, another can step in. The harsh economic climate offered a good test of Gray's axiom.

The semiconductor industry was especially hard-hit, and MARCO, the grand alliance of the semiconductor industry, government, and universities that bankrolls the Gigascale Center, felt the impact. The original plan was to open six research centers patterned on this model, but in 2001 that number was scaled back to four. Companies that supply parts to the semiconductor manufacturers initially paid a quarter of the center's budget, but with no cash to spare on dreams of the future, many of them dropped out, and so did several big manufacturers. Consequently, while these firms can make free use of the products generated in the Berkeley labs, they no longer get to participate in the researchers' salons, and that has caused some hard feelings.

Having multiple sponsors has indeed softened the blow to Berkeley. Some of the sponsoring companies increased their contributions, and so did the Pentagon. That support permitted the center to operate at full tilt while its original backers regroup and new backers are recruited. If government hadn't reasserted its long-standing role in supporting research, Gigascale Center director Gary Baldwin might have had to look for a job.

While the setbacks in the biotech industry are no worse than in high-tech, the plant biologists will feel the pain more directly because only one company, Novartis, signed a contract with Berkeley's College of Natural Resources. In 2001, faced with persisting criticism, the university recruited an outside scholar to evaluate whether the deal undermined the ideal of open scientific inquiry. There may be less reason for concern than the critics suspect, since by all accounts the company has essentially left the researchers alone. "The deal creates a pool of money for basic, unconventional research of their own choosing," an appraisal in the *Chronicle of Higher Education* concludes, "in a way that no grant from the government, a company, or even a foundation ever would."[35]

Since this contract was signed, however, the agribusiness division of Novartis was spun off to become part of Syngenta, an international biotechnology firm. That company has absorbed the Berkeley PR hit, while not seeing the blockbuster products it had hoped for. Four years into the contract, it had not signed a single license to commercialize a patent. Moreover, because of concern, especially in Europe, about genetically modified foods, the agricultural biotechnology industry has been in decline. In 2003, when Syngenta announced that it was shutting down its main United States research operation, it was apparent that the Berkeley contract would not be renewed.[36] This may be one of those occasions when, as a biotech researcher writing in *The Lancet* observed, "the increasing pressures on universities to get into bed with industry are not always resulting in a good night's rest for either partner."[37]

▪ Gigascale II, Gigascale III

Being useful to society, Rich Newton's measure of what matters most in science, is one important purpose of universities, but it's not the only one. Were things otherwise—were it true, as many state lawmakers say, that higher education's claim to public funds rests entirely on its contribution to the economy—then fields less closely tied to the making of money (or, as with business and economics, fields in which the subject *is* money) would be threatened with elimination.[38]

This point has often been made by Lit. professors, who know in a thousand ways that in many schools they have become bit players, and who also know how to get their own back in gothic tales and novels of manners.[39] What's much less obvious but perhaps more disturbing, a contemporary version of Bell Labs, the kind of place that does the sort of curiosity-driven investigation that's pivotal to the academic enterprise, is also superfluous in an environment where measurable productivity is all that matters.

The fact that this story involves Berkeley, rather than some other similarly renowned public institution, makes it irresistible, since in the popular imagination, and the minds of editors as well, Berkeley will forever represent a passionate antagonism toward what used to be called the real world. It was in the fall of 1964 on Berkeley's Sproul Plaza that Mario Savio, the leader of the Free Speech Movement, famously railed against the university for "serv[ing] the needs of American industry" and operating "as a factory that turns out a product needed by industry; rather than serving as the conscience and critic of society."[40] On a campus where the dean of the business school is now the "Bank of America Dean," was Savio simply ahead of his time?[41]

"At a place like Berkeley," Clark Kerr, former president of the University of California and, before that, Berkeley chancellor, told a *Chronicle of Higher Education* reporter, "the situation is much more likely to go well than it would at lesser places, where faculty aren't as sure of themselves. I'm much more concerned about Novartis II and Novartis III."[42] Institutions more desperate for money and shorter on prestige have been willing to give companies much more of what they want—namely, control over the research agenda as well as ownership of the resulting inventions.[43] The unseemly intimacy of university-business ties is visible on campuses that resemble industrial parks, with the corporate sponsors' buildings interspersed among the classrooms, libraries, and laboratories.[44]

Despite all the attention paid to the financial aspects of these deals, what's most interesting about the Gigascale Center isn't who pays the bills but the high-voltage community of learning, an academic commons for the twenty-first century, that has been created. The center gets world-class researchers from many universities "out of their silos," as Paul Gray says, and working together. Those who planned the venture have made a bet that this extraordinary commitment to collaboration will encourage an intellectual liveliness that characterizes academic life at its best—that this is the best way to achieve the "moon shot" they are hoping for.

The Information Technology Gold Rush
IT Certification Courses in Silicon Valley

The twelve-student class is run more like a bar review course—or boot camp, which is how it's actually billed—than a university course. Material that normally would take months to cover is crammed into a time frame that matches the pace of change in Silicon Valley, where the course takes place. Every day for two weeks straight, classes start at 8 A.M. sharp and end at 6 P.M., then there's a hands-on session till 8 P.M. and two more hours of study time after that. "Food is brought in," says James Appodaca, who runs the program, "but they don't leave the room except for the restroom or to smoke."

This class is offered on a regular basis by Unitek, a for-profit company with branches nationwide, a consulting and training firm that's off the higher education radar screen. The two-week regimen costs $8,800, which makes it more than four times as expensive on a per week basis as MIT.[1] But it carries the imprimatur of Cisco Systems, which produced the curriculum, and comes with a guarantee not even MIT would make—that those who survive this boot camp will pass the exam to become Cisco-certified network engineers, a valuable high-tech calling card.[2]

For just $132, students can enroll in the same Cisco-certified network engineering course at a community college like Gavilan in nearby Gilroy. Of course, things aren't really the same. The pace is far slower: the community college class takes three semesters, not fourteen days. Gavilan's dropout rate is much higher; and, for those who make it to the test, the pass rate is considerably lower—60 percent, as compared with 80–90 percent for Unitek students.

Gavilan does have one potential advantage over Unitek: its CISCO courses count toward an associate degree. But Jean Meehan, the dean of Computer Technology at Gavilan, says that "not many 'Cisco students' will stick around for the degree. They're focused on getting out and getting certified."

▪ Anyone Can Play

Information technology, or IT, certification training is the Wild West of postsecondary education, a brazenly competitive world where competence counts more than degrees, and where evaluation by an outside examiner, not seat time, is all that matters. Major hardware and software manufacturers like Cisco and Microsoft offer certifications that carry the company's own label: someone who passes the test becomes, for example, a "Microsoft Certified Software Engineer." The companies prepare the course materials and devise the exams; they create a sequence of certifications, with each exam leading to a new, higher designation (the basic "Cisco Certified Network Administrator," for instance, followed by the "Cisco Certified Network Professional," and ultimately the "Cisco Certified Internet Engineer").

Passing the examination is a measure of competence. Anyone who passes the Cisco engineer exam, for example, is presumed to be capable of operating and maintaining the routers and switches that are the industry's de facto standards for the working hardware of the Internet.[3] This makes certification economically valuable, just as getting a college degree is economically valuable, and certifications are featured prominently on an IT professional's résumé or "Craig's List" job ad.[4] But unlike in college, no one has to declare a major or satisfy distribution requirements or even take a single course. There are no Carnegie units here.[5] High school students can prepare for the exam in revivified vocational education programs. It doesn't matter *how* anyone learns the material. All that counts is the fact of having passed the exam.

Company-specific information technology certification is a relatively new idea—Novell started the first program in 1989—and a very smart business move. As Gary Matkin, who heads the continuing education program at the University of California at Irvine, points out, "it's a way to get fast market penetration, have quick time to market, and reach as many people as possible," while someone else is delivering the actual training. Keeping the material up-to-date and working with those who are teaching it requires a sizable and continuing corporate investment, which is why only industry giants like Cisco and Microsoft have been able to remain in the certification field.

These companies are using IT certification as a key part of a broader strategy to establish and maintain market dominance. Its success is astonishing: in 2002, just five years after Cisco started its program, more than

260,000 students from all fifty states and 145 countries were enrolled in nearly 10,000 "Cisco Academies," mainly in high schools and community colleges. The company describes its prepackaged four-semester curriculum as a charitable venture that's meant to close the digital divide, and that's part of the story. But this is an instance of doing well by doing good. The Topsy-like growth of the academies has helped to establish Cisco as the McDonald's of its field, with a market share of 80 percent and growing.[6]

Computer science departments at leading universities are educating the next generation of inventive programmers and skilled software engineers. But professors at Cal Tech aren't interested in the intellectually less exciting task of training people with very specific networking skills. As Matkin observes, "Universities put their noses up in the air at the thought of arranging software training packages." That has enabled schools of every stripe to enter the field, and in the process to alter the landscape of higher education.

Thirty years ago, the Carnegie Commission on Higher Education could map the higher education hierarchy with near-Cartesian precision.[7] At the topmost rung of the Carnegie classification ladder were the internationally renowned research universities—institutions that were highly selective in admitting students to whom they would, as higher education scholar Martin Trow wrote, "transmit 'high culture'" and "certify [as] a social elite," and that were devoted as well to the "creation of new knowledge through 'pure' scholarship." The bottom rung was occupied by colleges with no pretensions to research or selectivity, responsible for delivering "popular education," the "provision of useful knowledge and service to nearly every group that wants it."[8] For-profit schools didn't have a place on this map, since at the time they were dismissed as houses of intellectual ill repute. These rankings were the *Upstairs, Downstairs* of higher education, and whether ranked high or low, every institution knew its place.

To be sure, the demarcation between mass and elite schools has never been entirely rigid.[9] Great public universities like Berkeley and Michigan were founded with the expectation that they would be useful resources for the citizenry as well as havens of intellect, which is why at both these universities an optometry school and a linguistics department can peacefully coexist. In addition, prestigious institutions, private and public alike, have long offered "popular" education. A walk around Harvard Yard or Sproul Plaza on any mid-July day would turn up thousands of summer school students who would never have been admitted to Harvard or Berkeley. In the early twentieth century, more than seventy universities, Berkeley, Wisconsin, Chicago, and Columbia among them, were running correspondence programs, open to any who could pay their way.[10] Today, Harvard has three times as many "fee-paying participants in 'nontraditional' programs, ranging from the extension and summer schools to a bewildering variety of short-term executive education programs," as degree candidates.[11]

Such ventures are nods in the direction of populism as well as money-making machines, cordoned off from the central mission of the institution. But the familiar boundaries separating the center from the periphery are blurring as, even at leading research universities, the market-driven sector has been expanding.[12] Whatever the issue—the composition of the student body and the faculty, the array of course offerings, the sources of money and the ways it gets spent, the "outsourcing" of basic activities like teaching—what was once the "harmonious and self-contained world" of higher education is constantly being disrupted.[13]

Meanwhile, training programs for high-tech jobs have expanded into nothing less than a "parallel postsecondary universe."[14] Whether these ventures should be described as higher education is debatable, since there is no pretense of intellectual breadth but instead a single-minded focus on preparing students to acquire a credential for specific tasks defined by a particular company. What is *not* debatable is that IT certification programs potentially threaten enrollment at second- and third-tier colleges and universities. By 2003, these courses had enrolled more than 2 million students in the United States, some of whom would otherwise have attended college, and as many students abroad.[15] To budget-minded administrators, IT certification programs are also potential cash cows—that is, if universities can figure out how to milk them.[16]

In the past, mainstream institutions would never have contemplated offering courses for, say, secretarial careers, because that would have seemed antithetical to their identity. Now, however, schools up and down the status ladder are puzzling over how to react to this disruption.[17] Except for the most prestigious private colleges and universities, postsecondary institutions of every stripe—training programs, technology-focused private schools, community colleges, and public universities through their extension programs—have entered the fray. In Cisco and Microsoft "academies," high schools are giving students the kind of instruction they would otherwise have to acquire in a corporate training program or at college.[18] And all these schools must compete with the "no school" option, since anyone can prepare for the certification test on his or her own. A company named Smart Certify, for example, provides a virtual Cisco Systems Engineering Certification tutorial that's authorized by Cisco for $535.

Although certification classes are being offered around the world, Silicon Valley is the epicenter of the high-tech industry. The firms clustered there are without peer in their level of computing power. Because those companies have an unceasing need for network administrators and other IT professionals, competition among certification programs is fiercest there. "The knowledge just flows out of here," says Unitek's Appodaca, "so if you try to oversell or sell [prospective students] something else, they will just hang up on you." Even after the dot-com bust, what's happening in Silicon Valley provides a vivid display of this unabashedly market-driven corner of higher education.

▪ Heald College and Unitek: Know Your Customer

Schools like Unitek and Heald College live by their ability to sell their product. Whether they are for-profit training companies like Unitek or not-for-profit colleges like Heald matters less than their incessant need to attract students. Unlike private universities, these schools have no endowment on which they can rely; and unlike the community colleges and public university extension programs with which they compete, they aren't directly underwritten by the state.[19] Tuition revenue keeps them afloat.

This is an unforgiving sector of the market, with many competitors vying for the favor of savvy consumers. As the Internet bubble burst, a number of schools went out of business, including Master's Institute, one of Unitek's biggest rivals; and the depressed high-tech economy means that fewer people perceive careers in information technology as the royal road to riches. To persuade prospective students that they should pay a sizable tuition premium, these schools must promote their product with an aggressiveness unknown in mainstream higher education. They also have to offer something different and, perhaps, better.

Heald College was founded in 1863 as a business school for post–Gold Rush entrepreneurs. Now it has eleven campuses in Northern California and enrolls some 11,000 students, 1,000 of them at the Silicon Valley campus, the former regional headquarters of Ford Motor Corporation in San Jose. The school's most popular program is an associate degree in computer technology, which half its students are pursuing. The Cisco and

Microsoft certification classes, which in 2002 enrolled about 100 students, can be taken either as complements to the A.A. degree program or as stand-alone courses.

Entering the IT certification market was a "natural progression," says Jean Hastie, Heald's corporate director of student success, because of student demand. "As networking became increasingly important in the workplace, students expressed the need for specific networking skills." These courses appealed especially to a different potential market from the typical Heald students—people in their mid-thirties, already employed, who saw certification as a route to promotion and greater competitiveness on the job market. The academic deans liked the idea and so did the corporate division, which has much more say over academic programs than at the typical college. Decisions about which certification courses to offer have also been shaped by the market. A Novell certification class was dropped and a Cisco course added in response to changing tastes.

IT certification is a costly investment. The biggest expense is equipment. Heald had to spend $70,000 for Cisco routers. Microsoft and Cisco charge a sliding-scale fee for their on-line tutorial modules and course readers, which varies with the type of institution. High schools and community colleges get the program at the lowest rates because they are degree-granting schools, and so do nonprofit, degree-granting private schools like Heald; commercial trainers like Unitek face the steepest tariffs. Heald also pays its instructors a higher salary than its regular teachers, since they must have the academic credentials that the school expects as well as the instructor credentials that Microsoft or Cisco requires.

These expenses make certification classes less profitable for Heald than its associate degree program, but offering them gives the school an edge on the competition. TV and radio ads promote this "Heald difference— getting the double credential [the A.A. degree and the certificate] because you need both." Preparation for the Cisco certification exam takes twenty weeks and costs $6,200, and the Microsoft class requires thirty weeks. It's a hard course—harder than getting his master's degree in English, says Kevin Carpenter, Heald's manager of technology programs. Although the school doesn't keep precise records on certification pass rates, Carpenter estimates that 70 to 80 percent of the students pass the exam.

The school sees its rivals as IT training programs like Unitek on one side and community colleges like Gavilan on the other. "We compete on price," says Carpenter, "but not just on price." To the basic certification course, Heald adds "an accreditation layer" consisting of practice tests and lab work. Like the credentials of Heald's instructors, this is required by the agency that accredits the school, the Western Association of Schools and Colleges (WASC), the same agency that accredits Berkeley and Stanford. Many corporate training programs don't include these features, says Carpenter. "Sometimes it's just a slide show. I've had students come to Heald saying, 'I took a three-month intensive program and I didn't learn anything.'" He points to another institutional selling point: to set a tone of professional seriousness, Heald has a dress code and attendance requirements, something that no public institution would dream of imposing. Image matters.

To potential students just out of high school, Heald bills itself as "the school that helps you prepare for the career of your dreams," while to those on the job it presents itself as "the school that helps you upgrade your career." These aren't just slogans. In 2001, despite the recession, Heald placed 92 percent of its graduates; and the school provides a service offered by very few mainstream schools: lifetime job placement help for its graduates. That's one reason why it has been able to maintain good relationships with the human resources divisions of nearby companies (at the height of the high-tech boom, its list of prospective Silicon Valley employers numbered over 2,000). It's also why, Hastie says, word-of-mouth is the most important marketing tool.

Like all the schools in Silicon Valley, Heald has felt the impact of the high-tech recession. "A couple of years ago," says instructor Devon Lewis, "we had a much broader market [for IT professionals]. Now you have to go through multiple interviews, and they're going to ask you to explain how you would troubleshoot a sample problem." Job placement rates are down slightly in the certification courses, as are applications. An academic degree, that "double credential," has become more valuable. "In fact," says Lewis, "it never went out of fashion." Everywhere IT certification classes are offered, from the most corporate to the most academic, this refrain is heard. Degree holders are regarded as better able to unpack and analyze problems. To the gatekeepers in Silicon Valley, that kind of intellectual capital matters.

There's no mistaking Unitek for an institution of higher learning. If Heald is quasi-corporate, Unitek is the avatar of capitalism. The company, which was started in 1992 in the home of CEO Paul Afshar, mainly serves the training needs of high-tech firms. Although it's still a family operation (Afshar's wife is the CFO), Unitek itself is a high-tech success story. With clients like AT&T and Fujitsu, it's the leading IT consulting firm, and one of the hundred fastest-growing companies, in Silicon Valley. It got there by being more responsive than its rivals; if a competitor offered potential clients five-day training, Unitek promised to cover the same ground in half the time. While its consulting business has dropped off in recent years, says James Appodaca, the director of training, it has an unbroken record of growth in the training field. IT certification classes enroll 2,500 students a year at Unitek's two Silicon Valley offices.

Marketing and personnel are critical to Unitek's success. "The hardest part is getting them in the door," says Appodaca, who has worked for three of Unitek's competitors. "Getting them through is easy." Instead of using TV or radio, as Heald does, the company relies on e-mail and the Internet to spread the word. In addition, "the sales force is better trained, uses contact management software, and knows the product better." Of the company's one hundred full-time employees, only seven are full-time instructors. Appodaca stresses their quality. "Sales bring [students] here, but instructors bring them back. The teachers are not just certified, they also have real experience, unlike other centers which ramp up their instructors from scratch." The teachers must follow the Microsoft or Cisco curriculum to the letter, but they also know how to add "real world material." The hardware is also top of the line. "Unlike at community colleges, all Unitek students have their own routers and switches to work on." This one-to-one student-to-router ratio, which Heald also maintains, is the "gold standard" in IT training, a better indicator of instructional quality than more familiar measures of prestige.

Unitek's primary market is network or help desk administrators, which has only a limited overlap with Heald's targeted market. The company doesn't see itself as competing with community colleges and university extension programs; even though they cost far less, those courses take much longer, and the teaching, in Appodaca's estimation, is inferior.[20] Its real rivals are other training programs: Learnit (its training facility is "as plush as a brand new car") and New Horizons, a global presence with 270 centers. New Horizons, Appodaca complains, "is selling just about anything," sounding for the moment like an academic purist. Unitek was accredited in 2002, not by WASC, which reviews colleges and universities, but by the Bureau of Private Postsecondary Vocational Education, which appraises training programs, and this has paid off handsomely in public money. Accreditation has enabled Unitek to obtain an average of $150,000 in training contracts, a quarter of the firm's revenues, and because of accreditation, its students are eligible for federal loans, which is a key selling point.

Appodaca is confident that Unitek can beat the competition. "Within five years," he boasts, "all the other corporate trainers will have quit in Silicon Valley." This culture of braggadocio, typical among training firms, is less typical in the public sector, where the natural inclination is to downplay the fact of competition. When asked about the IT market, Cathy Sandeen, dean of the extension program at University of California–Santa Cruz, acknowledges that there are a lot of players in the game, "but then, there's a huge need."

▪ The Savvy Consumer

Mohammad Ziaee, who has taken a number of Unitek courses, can speak from firsthand experience about many of the options available in Silicon Valley. Before enrolling at Unitek, he took courses at several of the school's competitors. He started a community college class, gave Heald a look, and relied on a self-paced tutorial program. What makes Ziaee's story worth recounting is his remarkable success. While working full-time, he acquired advanced Cisco and Microsoft engineering certification in less than three years.

Ziaee is the quintessential savvy consumer. He knows how to haggle over tuition—he got Unitek to cut its fees by a third—as well as how to appraise the quality of instruction. He selected his Microsoft certification course on the basis of the trainer's reputation. His search for a good Cisco certification class took him initially to New Horizons, Unitek's biggest competitor, but he wasn't impressed: "It's franchised, and quality control is not that good." He tried a one-day course at an outfit called Hello Computers, "but the guy was reading straight out of the book." Heald "looked good, but was very expensive." Continuing his odyssey, Ziaee enrolled in the local community college; although the instructor was "knowledgeable," the pace of the course was too slow, and "you begin to lose interest." That's when he decided to complete the Cisco certificate training with a CD-ROM tutorial from Smart Certify. Even though "with things like tutorial software, you're almost guaranteed to pass the exam," Ziaee wouldn't repeat the experience. "All you've learned is what's on the examination, not the critical skills of troubleshooting."

In information technology as in other areas of inquiry, it's important to distinguish between narrowly focused certification training and the broader conception of learning—research, analysis, problem solving—that's usually associated with higher education. Ziaee has taken several courses at Unitek, and he finds them both useful and frustrating. "They have good instructors," he says, "but they only tell you the answers if you're in the 'appropriate' course. They are very time-crunched—plus they want to sell you the next course."

Many prospective computer engineers regard certification as a quick entry into the profession, but Ziaee believes that in the long run, it's smarter to pursue a degree. "IT certification is like an attractive business card. It will get you in, but it won't get you the business if you don't have the product. And in this case, the product is your knowledge. If someone really wants to work in the IT field, certification is a good way, but I would never recommend getting a certificate over a degree. The main thing that IT depends on is research, and quick courses do not teach you how to do research."

▪ Gavilan Community College: IT Training for Everyone

California's higher education Master Plan, adopted in 1960 and still the model for many states, establishes a pyramid of academic status.[21] At the pinnacle sit the nine Ph.D.-oriented research universities, Berkeley, UCLA, Davis, and the rest, almost all of them ranked among the best in the country. At the middle of the pyramid are the "state universities" like San Jose State and Cal State–Fullerton, which cater to students in the upper third of their high school graduating class. At the base are the community colleges, open to anyone who shows up, which offer courses ranging from remedial English to linguistics, gardening to law enforcement.

California's community colleges, former chancellor Gerald Hayward once said, make up "the biggest higher education system in the free world." Yet to call this a "system" stretches the concept to its breaking point, since the differences among these schools—in money, professional talent, and instructional focus—are almost as great as the differences among their students. What does unite them is the imperative of attending to the wishes of their constituents, who pay most of the bills and, through a locally elected board of trustees, set policy. In deciding what courses to offer, training companies and job-focused colleges like Heald respond to the economic market; so do community colleges, but they also have to pay close attention to the political market. The quality—indeed, the existence—of an information technology certification course depends on how these factors play out.

The tranquil town of Gilroy, self-styled "garlic capital of the world," sits at the very edge of Silicon Valley. Fields of yellow daffodils edge up to the highway, but "for sale" signs in those fields signal that they are primed to be turned into office parks, an indication of the town's ambition to be closer to the prosperous heart of things. Even amid an economic downturn, in Silicon Valley high-tech remains the route to prosperity.

The Cisco certification program at Gavilan Community College was launched in 1999, out of this hopeful impulse to become truly a part of Silicon Valley.[22] When a college trustee broached the idea, it quickly caught on among both his fellow board members and the college faculty. Although the Cisco Networking Academy training structure made it cookie-cutter easy to start—the school paid $2,000 to a nearby community college to help set up the program, and gets its course materials from Cisco at modest cost—top administrators initially balked at the $60,000 price tag for the equipment. "They knew little about computers," says instructor Victor Robinson, "even less about networking—and maybe they didn't want to know." Money is also the main reason why the school didn't add Microsoft certification. "With only two instructors available to shoulder the burdens of setup," explains instructor Ellen Venable, "it was difficult to convince the school to make the required outlay."

The administrators weren't the only ones ignorant about the high-tech world. One reason for the initial flurry of enthusiasm was the fact that Cisco was planning on building a campus (the company has borrowed the vocabulary of higher education to describe its offices) nearby. Students straight out of high school had to be disabused of the notion that they would have a job waiting for them at Cisco as soon as they completed the program, and many are still naïve. "When Cisco stocks fell," says Jean Meehan, Gavilan's dean of computer technology, "they felt it might not make sense to get Cisco certification. They don't understand."

A community college must be many things to many people, and enrollment in the Cisco certification courses reflects that reality. The daytime classes are filled with students in the associate program, just out of high school, as well as teenagers from Gilroy High School's vocational education program, enrolled in one of the many Cisco academies in the Silicon Valley, who take some of their courses at Gavilan. "So many high school students in the area are trying to do the Cisco system," says Robinson. At night the course draws a different crowd—mainly older students like Mohammad Ziaee, many of whom have college degrees and are already employed; they are looking to improve their on-the-job skills and bolster their résumés. Some are technical writers who want to understand what IT certification entails but won't make day-to-day use of the skills.

Those classes are well taught, though the wide disparities in students' knowledge and ability can frustrate the instructors; and while the school can't match the one-to-one router-to-student ratio of Heald or Unitek—the ratio is closer to three-to-one—students have adequate access. The pass rate on the exam—60 percent for the first group of graduates, in 2002—could be better. Still, at $11 a unit, $132 for the sequence of courses, and with the possibility of acquiring a degree as well, the certification program is a bargain.[23]

There is no marketing plan in place, however, for that is not how community colleges, overrun with students and less reliant on tuition revenue than schools like Unitek or Heald, are accustomed to behaving. Creating a brand is especially hard because of the built-in contradictions in the community college's mission. "We're supposed to be preparing students for university," says Robinson, "but we don't get that many university-bound types pursuing IT certification." That's regrettable, since, as Robinson notes, with the tightening of the IT job market, "certificates are more like a minimum standard. It helps to have a traditional degree." The downturn in the high-tech industry scared off many of the younger students, and enrollment in the certification classes has dropped.

Jean Meehan thinks she knows how to win these students back: by camouflaging what should really be a selling point, the fact that this is a Cisco program. "We don't even use the word 'Cisco' in our advertising. We call it the Networking Academy."

▪ San Jose State University: Head-to-Head with the For-Profits

Like the twenty-one other universities in the middle of California's Master Plan pyramid, San Jose State sees itself as the Rodney Dangerfield of academia, the school that gets no respect. Its ambition is to rise on the status ladder by offering Ph.D.s—if it can't be Berkeley, it wants to be Berkeley-like—but the Master Plan prevents it from doing so.

A few years ago the university's extension program decided to shift in the opposite direction, away from academics and toward the job-focused world of IT certification. Like many other extension programs, San Jose State had been offering liberal arts classes along with how-to and information technology courses, but there simply weren't enough paying customers to fill the seats in art appreciation or contemporary film. With the program hemorrhaging red ink, radical surgery was called for. The extension school changed its name to San Jose Professional Development, as well as its mission. Now it concentrates on helping professionals upgrade their technical and management skills. Carolyn Shadles, who runs the school, describes it as "in theory a moneymaker." But the way it has tried to make money, through Microsoft certification classes, pits it against all the other training institutions in the area.

San Jose Professional Development does not grant degrees. It offers more than a dozen programs leading to a school certificate in specific workplace skills like Java programming, technical writing, and e-commerce management. Half of these programs incorporate coursework tied to an IT certification exam. Instructor Richard Bell sounds like his counterparts in the for-profit world when he says that "employers are looking to hire people who can hit the ground running." And although the marketing efforts are primitive by comparison to, say, Unitek's—there are no salesmen using contact management software—the school is making an effort to attract students. Its catalogue, which is mailed to tens of thousands of homes throughout Silicon Valley, would almost do Neiman Marcus proud.

The school wants to have it both ways—to be a little bit IT certification–focused and a little bit university-like—and that may turn out to be its downfall. When director Shadles contrasts her school with its mercantile competitors, she emphasizes its university roots: "It's more academic and civic-focused." In addition to preparing students for Microsoft certification, the school has developed a course that introduces them to the basic characteristics of several systems, including Cisco and Microsoft. This is precisely the kind of class that an academically based program should be offering, one that adds educational value to training material. Unfortunately, it hasn't reached its intended audience, people headed for management positions who seek a basic understanding of computer engineering. While every student must sign up for one of the certificate programs, since that's how the school gets its vendor courseware at the discounted academic rates, it's the standard Microsoft IT certification classes—the same classes that can be taken at Unitek or Heald (or at many local high schools, for that matter)—that have attracted students. These students, who constitute 40 percent of the enrollment, just want the certificate, and almost all of them drop out once they have taken the classes that prepare them for the exam.

With demand for IT certification having slackened after the high-tech downturn, does Silicon Valley need yet another Microsoft provider? Beginning in 2001, enrollment dropped significantly, and the school was forced to retrench, closing one of its campuses. It responded to new student demands in the wake of September 11 by developing a certificate program in internet security. But that venture puts the school in head-to-head competition with the better-known and more prestigious extension program at the University of California–Santa Cruz.

■ UC Santa Cruz: The Ambivalence of Elitism

Prestige, which plays such a pivotal role in the competition among the elite institutions of higher education, should be irrelevant in the IT certification training arena. When students are deciding where to enroll, what ought logically to matter are a school's pass rates on the certification exams (though that information is rarely made public), the length and cost of the course, the quality of instruction, and the like. These are the factors an exemplary IT student like Mohammad Ziaee weighs. If prestige enters this equation, it's through the back door, in an employer's conviction that all IT certifications aren't created equal, that Gilroy High really isn't UC Santa Cruz (or San Jose State, or Heald College, or any of the other "vendors")—that either because of the quality of a student's experience or the power of the school's name, where one studies still counts.

Yet in this demimonde of higher education, concern about prestige can have a perverse impact on an institution. A training program like Unitek is entirely focused on the bottom line, but a university like UC Santa Cruz needs to preserve as well as exploit its brand. This may make it reluctant—rightly so—to compete for students with the sales techniques used by a Unitek and hesitant about its involvement in IT certification, even when it is the extension school, not the campus proper, that is offering the course.

When it was founded in the 1960s, the University of California at Santa Cruz was conceived as an alternative to the Berkeley-type "multiversity." The campus was situated amid a forest of towering redwoods. It was literally the academy on the hill, a few miles by the odometer but worlds away from the flatlands that were soon to become known as Silicon Valley. With its emphasis on small, self-contained undergraduate colleges rather than big graduate programs, Santa Cruz was meant to mimic Oxford or Cambridge rather than UCLA or Michigan. Its rejection of letter grades in favor of detailed faculty evaluations of students' work exemplified its commitment to the progressive pedagogy of the day.

But idyllic UC Santa Cruz soon opened a workhorse unit, an extension school with four sites, three of them in the heart of Silicon Valley. "Extension programs have been an excellent buffer between the elitist tendencies of UC and the populist demands of the state," notes Gary Matkin, who runs UC Irvine's program. Although UCSC Extension offers its share of classes in cooking, wine appreciation, and the like, it considers itself more academically focused than similar programs elsewhere. Eighty percent of its courses carry what is termed academic credit. This doesn't mean those classes count toward a degree, just that they have been approved by the chair of the corresponding campus department.

Still, the extension school, like its counterparts throughout the University of California system, has what is best described as a tough love relationship with the main campus. It doesn't receive state support and must balance its own books—including paying $600,000 to the central administration, ostensibly for services rendered—which means that the markups on its most popular courses have to compensate for its losses on the less well patronized ones.

This fiscal pressure necessarily converts decisions about curriculum into accounting exercises, with "break-even analysis" rather than judgments about intellectual worth often determining what should be offered.[24] In the information technology field, where companies have historically been willing to pay for their employees' instruction and government funds training for unemployed workers, it's not sufficient to break even. Sandra Clark, who handles corporate training contracts, builds in markups of 40 to 70 percent over cost in calculating tuition.

When the demand for IT certification classes took off, the extension school responded by offering Cisco and Microsoft certification classes. Administrators at nearby community colleges were fearful that Santa Cruz would dominate the field—that, in the words of one dean, "Extension would eat our lunch." There was ample reason for their concern. As Cathy Sandeen points out, the school is the "big guy in town" among public institutions, with more than 50,000 enrollments each year, nearly half in information technology, and a reputation for innovation. It's a high-profile institution. "A lot of companies refer students to us because their presidents were trained here," says Helen Hill, a longtime employee in the computer and information technology department. The fact that UCSC offers classes at employers' work sites as well as at its satellite campuses gives it a significant market edge over the San Jose State program.

UC Santa Cruz Extension has a big educational edge as well. Forty percent of its students have graduate degrees, and a survey conducted in 2000 reports that respondents had high expectations of the program because it was part of the university. The school trades on that image by association. "Reputation is everything," declares the website. "Think about the name UCSC Extension. We're an extension of the world-renowned University of California. Our standards are high and our reputation is stellar. We're respected for our quality of instruction and our ability to mirror the times."[25]

"UC definitely looks better on résumés," as Gary Matkin says, yet across the University of California system, continuing education programs are hampered by restrictions that don't exist at private training schools or community colleges. The programs award mainly "certificates," not degrees; and while these may have cachet value with local employers, colleges generally don't allow students to receive course credit for their extension classes.[26]

As creatures of the mother university, extension programs must answer to faculty senates and campus administrations, which often regard them with suspicion if not disdain. Company-specific classes like Cisco and Microsoft certification courses are among the most suspicion-arousing activities that an extension school can engage in—and rightly so. The information technology certification courses are "postgraduate continuing education," says Cathy Sandeen, "just not degree-based education." But that can't be right—not unless Gavilan Community College and Gilroy High are offering postgraduate education as well.

Those classes turn the University of California into the trainer for, and booster of, a single company's product. If, as UCSC Extension says, "reputation is everything," it's especially risky for a university to be delivering a canned program straight from the manufacturer's shelves. Still, some of the IT students were asking for the training, and attentiveness to local wishes has been a hallmark of extension programs. Besides, since there was the prospect of considerable money to be made, the opportunity was hard to resist. The certification courses, which were first offered in 1997, were staffed by instructors vetted by Microsoft and Cisco. They ran nights and weekends; and, shades of Unitek, there was also a "boot camp."

Yet even at the high-water mark for IT certification—1999–2000, the year before the bubble burst—only 263 students were enrolled. That's less than 2 percent of the enrollment in all UCSC Extension's information technology courses. By contrast, at San Jose State's extension program, demand for certification classes has dominated the IT program. Sandeen suggests that the explanation for the difference lies in the demographics. Most of the people who take courses at Santa Cruz are professionals; they didn't need what is typically an entry-level credential, she says, and those who wanted the credential didn't sign up for a class because they could prepare for the exam on their own. Perhaps so—but the experience of peripatetic and highly educated Mohammad Ziaee argues otherwise.

The real problem may have been marketing; for whatever reason, the school didn't aggressively promote this product. Once the boom ended, demand abruptly dried up. While Unitek responded to the new economic realities by securing accreditation from the Bureau of Private Post-secondary and Vocational Education, and so qualifying to operate a wide range of federal retraining programs, UCSC Extension didn't pursue that market as actively. It stopped offering its Microsoft certification classes in 2001 and its Cisco-specific courses a year later, retaining only vendor-neutral courses in router configuration and management.

At the time Santa Cruz pulled the plug, Daniel Clarke, the assistant dean in charge of the computer and information technology department, was clear about the reason—declining enrollment—and apologetic to those caught short by the decision. "We greatly . . . respect and recognize your commitment to your profession and career," he told them.[27] After the fact, Clarke and others at Extension couched their decision in terms of academic standards. Vendor-specific offerings are "too problematic," says Clarke. "We're positioning ourselves as a provider of 'higher-end' offerings that surpass vendor certifications in the level of abstraction involved."

All along the school has offered its own certificates in fields like network management and Internet security, and these courses examine the theory that underpins the technology applications. Dale Stansbury, who manages Extension's relations with federal training programs, questions the value of the vendor certification classes. "They probably aren't as responsive to the economic needs of students. In the high-tech world, product-specific skills are good for about a year, whereas broad, traditional skills are life-long."

"We don't feel that certification is what we do," says Cathy Sandeen, coming at this same point from another angle. "We are educators, and we offer [vendor-specific] certifications. But we do so much more. We bring a level of theory to everything we teach."

Like her colleagues, Sandeen uses the language of "high end" and "vendor neutral" to rationalize the school's pullout from the Microsoft and Cisco certification business. That vocabulary echoes familiar university norms. "High end" connotes a level of thinking that resonates in higher education, and "vendor neutral" removes the taint of product association.

These are the right values for any university-run program, but no one at UCSC Extension was talking about them when the dot-com boom was in full swing. Back then, the discussion was all about being responsive and making money.[28]

■ Do Academic Values Sell?

In Silicon Valley, as in many other places, institutions ranging from high schools to prestigious universities are delivering the same instructional product: prep courses for Microsoft or Cisco certification exams. It over-simplifies, however, to characterize the pool of IT certification students as constituting a single set of customers for which all these places are competing. Although particularly assiduous students like Mohammad Ziaee will sample many instructional offerings, few Gavilan students (let alone high school students in Cisco Academies) could afford to enroll in Unitek's boot camp. Still, many of these institutions are competing against one another, and that competition crosses familiar demarcations. When the extension arm of UC Santa Cruz offers a boot camp, it's going head-to-head with Unitek; and when a community college upgrades its computer equipment and maintains its low tuition, it is drawing students from private providers and universities alike.

IT certification is corporate training, not higher education. To companies like Unitek or trade schools like Heald, that isn't problematic, since their bottom line *is* the bottom line. Service to the local citizenry is the mission of community colleges and high schools, which have a long record of delivering instruction directly tied to the needs of local businesses. Cisco and Microsoft Academies are just the latest examples of this kind of responsiveness.

It's a different matter, however, when universities like San Jose State and UC Santa Cruz become involved, through their extension units, in preparing students for vendor-specific certification. Although those courses are defended with the rhetoric of responsiveness, the schools' behavior shows that they can be just as market-driven as Unitek, if less well versed in the ways of this market.

Extension programs, like the phantom subsidiaries created by Enron, are a device that enables universities to slough off their less-than-Olympian chores. But like Enron's dubious offspring, this fiction doesn't survive close scrutiny. UC Santa Cruz wants to have it both ways—to recruit students by taking advantage of its good name while denying any responsibility for the content of courses that carry its name. With these courses no longer being offered, the dean of the program expresses concerns about their educational value and the propriety of offering them—concerns that, but for the promise of new revenues, would have been obvious at the outset.[29] Training schools like Unitek have an entirely different mission from UC Santa Cruz or San Jose State. To ignore those differences treats universities as simply another sector of the economy.

Ironically, the market may reach this same conclusion. Vendor certification programs were intended to capitalize on the high-tech frenzy. At a time when information technology was a sure path to career success, the courseware and examination system gave two of the nation's most powerful companies, Microsoft and Cisco, an added advantage. They also offered high schools and community colleges the chance to enter the IT universe by giving them cheap, well-designed off-the-shelf materials, and enabled schools of all stripes to bring in tuition dollars by training aspiring computer engineers.

Microsoft and Cisco, like the high-tech sector generally, have seen the value of their stock plunge in recent years, and the demand for their certification has leveled off. The next generation of training programs may be designed differently, perhaps cross-platform models and vendor-neutral certifications like those that San Jose Professional Development and UC Santa Cruz Extension have been developing. Such courses emphasize the ability to troubleshoot problems, a skill that's needed by Microsoft and Cisco engineers and by Intel and Hewlett and Compaq engineers too; a skill that won't become as quickly outmoded as an engineer's expertise with Windows 2000. In the very practical field of information technology, the values of the academy might just turn out to be the values of the market as well.

13

They're All Business
DeVry University

In October 1997, the *New Yorker* ran an article about the University of Phoenix.[1] "Drive-Thru U," the piece was titled, a jarring juxtaposition, and all the familiar markers of a university—library, bookstore, campus—appeared in quotation marks to denote that they weren't quite the real ·thing.[2] The campus, writer James Traub marveled, was an office building or industrial park: an "outlet," school officials called it. The bookstore carried only textbooks. The library was "wherever there's a computer." And the university was a subsidiary of a profit-making company called the Apollo Group. Phoenix proudly billed itself as "the second-largest private university in the United States," but to most of the magazine's readers, accustomed to thinking about higher education in pastoral and ivied terms, not as a publicly traded company, it was a dangerous interloper.

The University of Phoenix had actually been a going, and increasingly profitable, operation for a generation when the *New Yorker* happened upon it. Wall Street knew and loved the company, which trades as the Apollo Group. Between 1994, when it went public, and 1997, when the story appeared, the value of a single Apollo share had risen from two dollars to thirty-five dollars; and since then, the numbers have only gotten better. In 2002, 150,000 students were enrolled in campuses across the country and on-line; the price of the stock continued its rapid rise, defying the bear market. Between March 2000 and March 2003, the price of an Apollo share climbed 368 percent.

Other, less attention-grabbing for-profits have also been expanding rapidly. The American Schools of Professional Psychology, operated by a company called Argosy, award half of all psychology Ph.D.s. Strayer University, the oldest of these institutions—founded in 1892—targets working adults. Both *Forbes* and *Business Week* have singled it out as one of the two hundred best small companies in America.[3] Kaplan, a profitable divi-

240

sion of the *Washington Post,* is best known for its college and graduate school exam prep courses. The company buys up colleges as well, and in 1998 it opened Concord Law School, the first entirely on-line law school; despite the American Bar Association's refusal to accredit an on-line institution, Concord has the largest law school enrollment in the country.[4]

Proprietary schools have been an American fixture since the seventeenth century, when illiterate adults in New Amsterdam were taught how to read, write, and do sums.[5] But until quite recently almost all of them were mom-and-pop operations. The best among them teach a useful skill like cosmetology or auto mechanics. The worst are diploma mills—phantom operations whose degrees are literally not worth the paper on which they are Xeroxed, the topic of a *60 Minutes* exposé and a federal sting operation.[6]

The *New Yorker* story certified a transformation in higher education that had in fact been occurring for some time. A new breed of for-profit schools was emerging from the shadows, less marginal and less marginalized than its predecessors. Unlike the conventional proprietary schools, these are multi-campus operations that offer on-line as well as classroom-based instruction. While some run non-degree training courses, they mainly enroll students in degree programs for everything from the associate degree to the Ph.D. They are accredited, which gives them needed legitimacy and gives their students access to federal loan programs. They have become a force to be reckoned with.[7]

The reaction has been cacophonous. The market-minded, who often deride universities as flabby places filled with slackers and ideologues, have blessed the coming of the for-profits with "a big wet kiss," even as tradition-minded opponents churn out articles that "read like the musings of a feverish Rip Van Winkle who had awakened to find his hallowed marketplace of ideas had turned into, well, a marketplace."[8] When Bill Durden was named president of Dickinson College, the fact that he had previously worked in the for-profit sector of higher education—"the dark side," some professors called it—set off alarms at that tradition-soaked school. Richard Ruch, a dean at the University of Phoenix, begins his generally flattering account of the for-profit universe, *Higher Ed Inc.,* by "confess[ing] that until a few years ago I thought that all proprietary institutions were the scum of the academic earth."[9]

Schools such as Stanford and Williams, whose endowments allow them to subsidize their students heavily, have nothing to fear from the likes of the University of Phoenix, which must make money from tuition in order to remain in business. But this isn't the league in which for-profit schools want to compete. Like other well-run businesses, they have sought out a niche market. Most frequently that niche is degree programs for adult students—the MBA, offered evenings, weekends, and on-line, is the bread-and-butter course for Phoenix. Yet if this is not the academic war of the worlds, neither is it a tale of peaceful coexistence. The vulnerable are the less selective public and private institutions. When John Sperling, president of Phoenix, contemplates offering a B.A. in the liberal arts, these are the places he means to take on.

Those universities also represent the competition for DeVry University. Among the for-profits, DeVry ranks second in enrollment only to the University of Phoenix, with more than 50,000 students at twenty-five campuses in the United States and Canada, and it was the first of these schools to go public, in 1991. The institution, which is fully accredited, offers B.S. degrees in electrical engineering, telecommunications, and business administration. Its main rivals are regional public universities like Northern Illinois and San Jose State. Since DeVry is considerably more expensive (tuition for the bachelor of science degree runs between $35,000 and $40,000, depending on the major), in order to survive it must *be* better—or, through its advertising and recruiting, it must persuade those whom it calls its "customers" that it is better.

▪ "Reach for the Sky, DeVry"

"Reach for the Sky, DeVry": the TV commercials incessantly repeat the slogan. It's a cheesy message, the students at DeVry's Silicon Valley campus in Fremont, California, complain; and it doesn't help that the ads run late at night, at a time when car dealers ("No credit? No problem!") and bankruptcy lawyers are plying their wares. The bevy of recruiters make the same pitch, sitting in the living rooms of prospective applicants or talking with them on one of the ten thousand high school visits they make every year: "Come to DeVry for a career, not a job."

Increasing enrollment has to be the paramount concern for any for-profit university, especially one whose stock is publicly traded. DeVry spends 10 percent of its budget on recruiting; its field representatives must sound persuasive, since they are expected to meet enrollment tatgets. In their eagerness to close the deal, these salesmen sometimes oversell, skirting the border of misrepresentation when they solicit applicants who, based on their academic record, have almost no chance of success. "They make it all sound so easy," say a group of Fremont students who have been hand-picked by the campus administration to showcase the school but on this issue are off-message.

Still, there is considerable truth to the advertising. Instruction is more intense than at most community colleges and regional universities—classes run all year, and full-time students earn their degree in three years—and it is often better as well. The courses listed in the catalogue are in fact offered, not subject to cancellation on a moment's notice, as at many underfunded and understaffed public institutions. The teachers whom campus dean Kandy Simmons calls "weak links" are "fixed," one way or another, in a "total quality management" environment. The labs are generally up-to-date and open around the clock. Graduates do get hired: historically, DeVry's proudest boast has been that within six months of graduation, 95 percent of its graduates are working, and not behind the McDonald's counter but at jobs with a future. What's most remarkable, DeVry manages to accomplish something that no other undergraduate school has ever done: to maintain this level of quality and consistency across twenty-five campuses, not with cookie-cutter sameness but by modifying the instructional template to match different communities' specific workforce requirements.

The relentless pressure to enroll students; the practical and carefully thought-out curriculum, a technical core with a leavening of liberal arts classes; the impeccable job placement record: each of these elements is integral to the design of the institution. As chief operating officer and co-founder Ronald Taylor says, "The colossally simple notion that drives DeVry's business is that if you ask employers what they want and then provide what they want, the people you supply to them will be hired."

The DeVry University campus off Highway 880 in Fremont, California, opened in 1999, looks like one of the high-tech companies in the area. It's low-slung and functional, built with an eye to use, not aesthetics. With its long corridors of classrooms and labs, most of them designed for fifty or sixty students, it could be a community college, though without the gym or student center. Because the cost of nearby housing is so high, it offers rental housing to students: dorms for those straight out of high school ("they can't handle the responsibility of living on their own," says James Kho, the campus president and regional vice president) and two-bedroom apartments for working adults. The site bustles with classes twelve hours a day and on weekends as well. DeVry runs both day and evening programs:

daytime classes are mainly made up of newly minted high school gradu-ates, while evening classes are generally composed of working adults (they're much more serious, the professors say). The Keller School of Management, which is part of DeVry University, holds M.B.A. classes during the evenings.

Although most of the students at DeVry are just a few years away from their high school days, that seems like another life. It's no longer party time, and a sense of self-discipline is necessary to make the transition. Stu-dents don't cut classes—at the intense pace of instruction, they will fall fa-tally behind if they miss lab—and, remarkably for California undergradu-ates, they come to class on time. The male students are mostly enrolled in telecommunications and electrical engineering programs, while the women mainly take the business courses.

To judge from their slouchy body language and the baseball caps pulled over furrowed brows, many of the thirty-eight students in Edward Hamp-ton's "Culture and Society" class are bored. The textbook, with the un-imaginative title *Sociology*, doesn't help. It's a thick tome, slick in presenta-tion but bland in substance (the book is also widely used in California community colleges). Hampton, a young African American instructor working on his Ed.D. at the University of California at Davis, tries hard to liven things up. In a class session that focuses on the shift from agrarian to industrial societies, he points out that the basic question these societies must face is a familiar one: What should a society keep from its past, and what can it let go? Still, no one is taking notes. Although students respond to Hampton's jokes—"the 'technology' was a stick and a hoe"—his ques-tions presume they have read the assignment, and to judge from the re-sponses, many of them haven't. In an almost comic moment, Hampton tries manfully to tease out the fact that the economy in hunter-gatherer so-cieties is based on . . . hunting and gathering.

"The students are here for the technical stuff," Hampton acknowl-edges. "Many of them haven't made the connection [to social issues]." Hampton sees his vocation as forging that link—and when he succeeds, the experience is "magical." He appreciates that the textbook isn't inspir-ing, and would like to assign additional readings, but he holds back be-cause "money is tight for these students."

"I come from the underclass and grew up in a housing project. I've got to motivate these students by connecting to their culture," says Hampton. Cultures, more precisely. When the Fremont administration conducted a census of its students, it found sixty-four different language groups repre-sented. Such diversity isn't the result of school policy. In California, a state with more immigrants than any other in the Union, a Noah's Ark of students, many of them immigrants or the children of immigrants and all of them wanting good-paying jobs, walk in the door. Ed Hampton also teaches an ethics course. "I give them two main perspectives, consequentialist and deontological," he says, "and get them to look at how they make ethical decisions." That's Philosophy 1 material, just what these students would be learning at a traditional college, but Hampton knows "this is ultimately about [students'] getting a job, not learning how to learn."

The forty students in Mostafa Mortezaie's electrical engineering class are much more engaged. It's not that Mortezaie is a better teacher than Hampton, but he is talking about things that these students must learn if they're going to get hired, and they know it. When he gives them a circuitry problem, almost all of them take out their notebooks to perform the calculations.

Mortezaie, who comes from Iran, received his Ph.D. at the University of California at Santa Barbara. He was working on defense-related projects at Honeywell, but when the company lost its defense contracts and had to shut down the department, he decided to teach.

While some DeVry students lack the equipment they need for their senior research projects, Mortezaie says, the labs are much better than at community colleges. Sometimes it's possible to cadge a needed item from one of the thirty-five Silicon Valley companies whose representatives sit on the school's industrial advisory board, where their role is to keep the school on top of the latest developments in high-tech. "My students come to DeVry because it's a quick route to a good job. They know they can get an electrical engineering degree in three years." Mortezaie notes the wide variation in the students' backgrounds. "The weakest ones don't have the math needed to understand the derivation of formulas. My best student"—who did badly in high school and dropped out of DeVry's Pomona campus before getting on track at Fremont—"wants to go to Stanford for an M.S. in computer science."

The two instructors hold identical views about the quality of the DeVry students. The top 10 percent could make it anyplace, they say, but the bottom 10 percent shouldn't be in college. Still, in 2001, amidst the high-tech recession, all the electrical engineering students in Fremont's first graduating class were able to find jobs.

At DeVry, job placement is nearly as important as student recruitment, and the two functions are closely entwined. Without a good placement record, new students won't enroll.

There's rarely someone like Neil Johnson at a community college, and the community college students are the losers. Johnson used to coach high school basketball, and he brings to DeVry the energy, though not the meanness, of his coaching idol, Bobby Knight. "This job is like mental coaching," Johnson says, and he pushes students, from freshman orientation on, to prepare themselves for the job market. "Put on a suit," he coaxes them, "and come in for a mock interview." There he asks them the "killer questions . . . identify your greatest work-related disappointment; critique your manager's style." Johnson takes students on company tours, and he ferrets out jobs as well. When semiconductor manufacturing jobs became hard to find, he started making cold calls to the human resources departments of "companies no one has heard of. It's like being a basketball coach. When the big men go down, you go small. I ride up and down [Highway] 280 [where many Silicon Valley firms have their headquarters], writing down names and looking for full parking lots."

A half-dozen DeVry students, chosen by the campus administration to discuss their experiences, appreciate this kind of help. "Placement is the best—everything's focused on career." They praise the school as being "faster" and "more focused" than the community colleges and state universities that many of them considered. And they appreciate the fact that—unlike in "regular college," where instructors are remote—their professors are mentors who "want you to succeed." The school "teaches tools, not theoretical concepts," and that kind of practicality is a substitute for intellectual curiosity.

These students value the general education courses, mainly because they realize that writing matters on the job, and the communications classes "enable you to present yourself in a professional manner." Still, some of them want a bit more than nuts-and-bolts training. They note that the liberal arts classes encourage "lateral thinking" and "help you learn again what life is all about." Those courses can also be a break from the daily grind—"reading plays is a release"—and while most students at DeVry are working while going to school, some of them find time to produce literary magazines and organize poetry "slams" to break the routine.

DeVry students wield the power of consumers, especially when it comes to the quality of teaching, and they know it. "If a group of students has a complaint, something's done," they say. "If a teacher's really bad, he gets fired and we get a new teacher"—a point that dean Kandy Simmons confirms. What troubles them most, though, is the school's sketchy reputation. "People think we're just a trade school," one student says, and they are unanimous in their disdain for the "Reach for the sky" ads.

Jade Muranaka, the admissions director at Fremont, boasts that "no one else offers the same product line as we do." But she doesn't like the commercials either. "They don't really target the caliber of student we want. They put the school in the category of other proprietary schools, and don't emphasize that we're accredited and we offer a B.S. degree." The website, she adds, is better. Muranaka admits that the field representatives, who recruit students, can be overly pushy. "They are distant from the campus and don't know the environment here. They're recruiting across the system."

"The pressure is to produce the best quality, not to save money," says Kandy Simmons, but the bottom line rules. Questions about the quality of students regularly surface at "Institute Day," the DeVry counterpart of a faculty meeting, which is held once a term. "There's a desire expressed for higher admissions standards," says electrical engineering professor Mostafa Mortezaie. But those decisions, as well as determinations about which subjects should be taught, are not the faculty's to make. In this key respect, traditional safeguards of academic freedom are lacking. Similarly, admissions director Jade Muranaka lacks the authority to define the image the school projects in its ads or even to hire recruiters.

All the key policy decisions are made centrally, at DeVry's corporate headquarters in Oakbrook Terrace, Illinois, a Chicago suburb. There, the conflicts inherent in even the best for-profit universities are played out: stiffer admissions requirements versus larger enrollments; liberal arts versus specific training; and, what's most important, academic standards versus the profit margin.

The Tower is the nickname for the company's headquarters. Not only does that sobriquet fit the building, which rises twelve stories above Illinois flatlands; it's also a metaphor for the control that the corporate offices exercise over the campuses.

"The easiest way for someone to sharpen an axe on DeVry is to say it only cares about the money," says chief operating officer Ronald Taylor, "but that's not who we are."[10] In the annals of both business and higher education, Ron Taylor and chief executive officer Dennis Keller make a unique pair. They've been a team since 1972, when they left the M.B.A. mainstream, quitting fast-track jobs at Bell & Howell to start a night school in business administration in downtown Chicago—a "mini-M.B.A." for working adults, Keller calls it. He had been dreaming about such a school since his M.B.A. days at the University of Chicago, when he drafted the business plan. But the undercapitalized school (the C.B.A.

School for Postgraduate Education and Business, it was called), which opened with just seven students, almost went under. With additional funding from Keller, and a name change—the school is called the Keller Graduate School of Business—it survived, and has gone on to prosper. It enrolls nearly 10,000 students in its M.B.A. program.

In 1986, Keller and Taylor bought DeVry, which was then an eleven-campus system, from their old employer, Bell & Howell. DeVry was a rarity, a venerable and respectable entrant in the for-profit world. It had been operating since 1931, when Herman DeVry, an inventor and teacher at Bell & Howell, started a film and radio repair school. The purchase was a real stretch, and financing new campuses required a major cash infusion. Keller and Taylor took their company public in 1991. That move generated $10 million in cash—and tied the fortunes of the business to the vicissitudes of the stock market.

There's a "dynamic tension" between the business and academic sides of the house, says Patrick Meyers, vice president of academic affairs and a University of Chicago Ph.D. (Most of the senior officers have degrees from blue chip schools.) In the typical instance, the marketing group, which favors aggressive promotion, the constant rolling out of new products, and the continuous expansion of market share, clashes with the academics, who speak in terms of intellectual integrity, of what DeVry stands for.

The fighting can be fierce. When company officials decided to cut the number of hours that electrical engineering students spend in the labs, many faculty members were outraged at what they saw as fatally compromising standards in order to make the course more attractive to prospective students. "You are the death of DeVry," they told Meyers, "the death of everything we stand for"—precisely the same kind of argument that the old guard at the University of Chicago mounted against changing the core curriculum.[11] In the end, the professors lost the argument; COO Ron Taylor cut the course load. A similar fight was waged over the introduction of a science class into the business major. "Nothing can be cut," the business professors insisted, but they lost as well.

"Decisions are made by the management, by the central office, not by faculty deliberations," says Meyers. "The expectation is that [the faculty] will do it, like it or not." This arrangement isn't entirely satisfactory to the North Central States Association. When that agency accredited DeVry in 1992, it told the school to do a better job of "integrating the academic perspective into the organizational structure."

Because it has neither an endowment nor direct public subsidies, DeVry must spend considerably less to educate its students than traditional universities. The cost savings come partly from what the company regards as frills. All its sites are utilitarian; and campus administrators, like everyone above them in the corporate hierarchy, keep a watchful eye on finances.

As the account of the Fremont campus suggests, though, this doesn't mean stinting on instruction. "We want to focus our resources on issues that are critical to our success," says Ron Taylor, and high on that list is the quality of teaching. Classes at DeVry seldom exceed forty students. In the ever-changing world of high-tech, course materials are constantly being updated. Half of the faculty teach full-time, a ratio similar to that in public institutions but considerably higher than at most for-profits. They are paid somewhat better than their college counterparts, an average salary of $60,000 for three fifteen-week terms, with overtime for teaching more than the four-course load; reflecting the market, engineering faculty make more than liberal arts instructors. Adjuncts receive $55 an hour, which amounts to about $3,000 for a semester-long course. Classroom performance is regularly evaluated. Consistent with the company's philosophy of "total quality management," the aim is to help, not punish, those who aren't meeting the mark.

DeVry makes no bones about being a technical school; would-be sociologists and philosophers are advised to go elsewhere. But fully a third of the required courses are what's called "general education"—classes like Ed Hampton's sociology course at Fremont, as well as courses in economics, political science, English, and communications. During their final year, the students take a class on "social issues and technology," which is taught jointly by faculty from the two cultures. Persuading students that such classes are worthwhile is a constant struggle, says Charlie Koop, director of academic planning and technology. Many of them, who suffered through similar classes in high school, don't think the courses give them marketable skills, but this is one instance in which the consumer doesn't rule.

By and large, DeVry does good by doing well. The up-to-date content of its technical programs is necessitated by demand. "Industry representatives tell us what they want the students to know," says Pat Meyers, "and we develop the courses." The curriculum is similar from one site to the next, but DeVry isn't the McDonald's of higher education. (That description better fits the M.B.A. programs at schools like the University of Phoenix and the Keller School of Management.) Its courses vary with local employment opportunities. Because Sprint's headquarters are in Kansas City, that campus offers what Charlie Koop calls an "old-fashioned voice communication course," but in Fremont it is all high-tech. The respect that DeVry accords its faculty—the relatively high salaries, a term-long paid sabbatical after five years—is intended to cement their loyalty. Such fealty is a valuable corporate asset, because finding engineers who are willing to give up the financial rewards of the private sector is almost as big a challenge as filling the classroom seats. "The liberal arts are emphasized," says Koop, because "employers want people who think."

That's not the only reason for the general education requirement; it also satisfies the rules of the accrediting agency. Accreditation isn't valued because it brings status. Unlike traditional colleges, DeVry isn't fixated on the *U.S. News & World Report* rankings, which its prospective students rarely consult. It's important because it enables students to participate in the federal loan programs. More than 80 percent of them take out loans, and some also borrow money from the school.

These are mainly working-class students, the first in their families to go to college, and nearly half of them are nonwhite. DeVry is justifiably proud of the fact that it graduates more black and Hispanic electrical engineers than any other university in the country. "We accept students who, on paper, aren't likely to make it," Ron Taylor acknowledges, "but I wouldn't want to deny them a chance." For some students, this is an invaluable opportunity, but couple that attitude with an overly enthusiastic sales force, and the predictable consequence is a high dropout rate. Many students wash out after a term or two. Fewer than 40 percent graduate within six years, and just a quarter of the students in electrical engineering graduate in that time period.

"This is typical for the industry," Dennis Keller points out, but to him it represents a waste of human potential. "'Open the gates, washout is OK' isn't our philosophy. We should do as good a job in keeping students as we do in placing them." Keller's goal is a 50 percent graduation rate, "which would be remarkable for this population."

Community colleges don't do much better than that, despite the fact that students there can often coast to a diploma. The fact that DeVry loses too many students doesn't undermine the accomplishment of teaching marketable skills to a substantial number of people who otherwise would be working at Wal-Mart.

Between 1991, when it went public, and 2002, DeVry was a favored child of the investment community. Scores of business reporters in newspapers across the country sang the school's praises. Term after term, enrollment went up. Year after year, profits went up. And though DeVry wasn't nearly as spectacular a performer as the Apollo Group, which operates Phoenix, it did very well on the stock market.

Keller and Taylor had hoped that DeVry, which had grown during boom times, would also fare well in a recession. But in 2002, DeVry shares lost half their value. Enrollment dropped by 15 percent, something that hadn't happened in more than a decade, as prospective students became leery of high-tech careers, and the job placement rate fell to 85 percent.

"We are adapting," says Ron Taylor, "placing technical people in non-tech-based companies." In Kansas City, where Sprint laid off 30,000 workers, there was little room for adaptation, but the Fremont campus, in the heart of high-tech country, was able to place all its electrical engineers and 94 percent of its telecommunications students.

Despite the downturn, the school has continued its practice of adding two campuses a year. "If we were just motivated by the stock price in the short term, we could eliminate that growth, because there's a loss every time we open," says Taylor. "But we know there are cycles in engineering education. There will be a demand in the next few years, and we're positioning ourselves to meet that demand."

▪ But Is It Higher Education?

When the North Central States Association accredited Jones International University in 1999, awarding it the same seal of approval it bestows on the University of Wisconsin and the University of Chicago, academic watchdogs were outraged. Spokesmen for the American Association of University Professors pointed out that, despite its pretentious name, Jones—an on-line, for-profit institution—had just a handful of full-time academic employees, and far from enjoying any academic freedom, the "faculty" did the bidding of the school's owner. Moreover, Jones offered courses in only a single subject, business administration, and that mocked the conception of a university as a seat of knowledge. Jones is a trade school, the AAUP argued, not an institution of higher learning.[12]

The AAUP got it right, for whatever a university may be, it's surely not Jones International. DeVry University and the University of Phoenix are much more substantial institutions, but they too have encountered intense opposition when seeking approval from the educational establishment.

The essence of the animus is that these schools are operated as businesses. "Just how much profit do you make off the backs of your students?" the president of a nonprofit college asked his counterpart from the University of Phoenix, which was seeking permission to open a branch in Newark, New Jersey.[13] The New Jersey accrediting agency initially denied Phoenix's bid—the fact that the university had no library was one of the things that troubled them—but Phoenix revised its plan in response to the accreditors' criticisms and eventually won approval.

The absence of a library at a University of Phoenix campus is emblematic of a deeper debate over the character of higher education in our times. To most academics, libraries are sacred places; but in New Jersey, the University of Phoenix administrators argued that access to a nearby library should be good enough, since almost everything their students need is either in textbooks, on-line, or else embedded in experience, not in a pile of books.

Implicit in much of the criticism of for-profit schools is the belief that a real university should traffic in ideas rather than know-how. "Here was a university formed around the idea that practical experience is superior to abstract understanding," James Traub observed in his nuanced *New Yorker* account of Phoenix, "[and that] proposition almost seemed self-negating."[14]

Is this nuts-and-bolts school really engaged in higher education? Traub is asking. But a visit to most colleges, whether labeled public, private, or for-profit, reveals that this may be a lock-the-barn-door reaction. Since the 1970s, the "practical arts" such as recreation management and computer programming have been carrying the day; outside the elite schools, the liberal arts are everywhere in retreat.[15] Students at DeVry get at least as much exposure to the liberal arts as undergraduates at the big public universities. Whether the DeVry campus is situated in Philadelphia, San Francisco, or Detroit doesn't matter; like Burger King, Holiday Inn, or any other well-run chain, DeVry maintains a consistent level of quality throughout its operation.[16] Replication is not even on the radar screen at premier universities, which characteristically respond to increased student demand not by expanding but by setting higher admissions standards.[17]

Rather than treating these for-profits as the competition, some public universities have opted to join forces with them. Motorola University, one of the nation's pioneering corporate universities, is situated at Arizona State University's "research park." ASU offers a master's in "management of technology," and the University of Phoenix conducts several courses at the same site. Convergence along these lines, rather than the demise of the public university, seems the likeliest scenario.[18]

Despite what business analysts refer to as their "disruptive technology," the new entrants aren't going to dominate higher education anytime soon.[19] While every year some colleges flirting with insolvency are bought up by companies like Kaplan and others close their doors, public universities will soldier on for the foreseeable future. There are too many alumni in the state legislatures, too much sentiment for football teams and fraternities, for these institutions to fade away. Schools like DeVry and Phoenix are undoubtedly cheaper, simpler, and more convenient than public universities, but analogies to desktop computers in a market dominated by mainframes, or small off-road motorcycles in a world of Harley-Davidson bikes, seem inapt.[20]

Is survival really the best that the public universities can manage? Unless they are contributing to the social good, it isn't clear that they *deserve* public subsidies. If higher education is simply serving "customers," then those customers, rather than the taxpayer, should be paying the bills. If public universities really "mean business," as the president of the University of California has asserted, then why shouldn't the government rely on schools like DeVry, which *is* a business, to do the teaching? After all, as Dennis Keller says, "public universities aren't as driven to be customer-centered."[21]

During America's long love affair with the marketplace, business leaders were heroes and entrepreneurship became the highest value. It was a propitious time for the DeVry-Phoenix generation of for-profit schools, which, as one admiring observer writes, took "the traditional model of higher education . . . and subjected it to modern principles of operations management, financial management, and cost accounting."[22]

This is not, of course, the only such market-minded moment in our history. During the Gilded Age at the turn of the twentieth century, and again in the 1920s and the 1950s, markets shaped meaning.[23] In each instance, though, the embrace of commerce proved over-strong, the social costs of market dominance became obvious, and public values reasserted themselves.

Whether that history can be reenacted in higher education is a vital, and unsettled, issue. What *is* certain is that the for-profit schools won't assume this responsibility. They have no commitment to the idea of public service, no sense of their mission as tied to the good of the commonwealth. How could they and still maintain the allegiance of their profit-minded stockholders?

At the beginning of the last century, James Angell, the president of the

University of Michigan, wrote about another kind of stockholder. "I have endeavored to induce every citizen to regard himself as a stockholder in the Institution, who had a real interest in helping make it of the greatest service to his children and those of his neighbors."[24] But Angell's idea of the university as the site of "service" is out of place in this modern landscape. As John Sperling, the founder of the University of Phoenix, bluntly told James Traub, "I'm not involved in social reform."[25]

Conclusion:
The Corporation of Learning

The commercial spirit of the country and the many avenues to
wealth which are opened before enterprise, create a distaste for study
deeply inimical to education.
—Henry Philip Tappan, *University Education* (1851)

The management consultants that McDonald's hired to evaluate its training programs doubted the wisdom of flying store managers from around
the globe to the sylvan setting of Hamburger University, the company's
corporate college, for a three-week training course. If for-profit schools
like the University of Phoenix could clone themselves, then surely Mc-
Donald's, the master of corporate mitosis, could do the same.[1] Regional
sites, the consultants concluded, could teach the same material for much
less money. They recommended that the main campus be reserved for advanced management classes on leadership, group dynamics, and the like,
the corporate equivalent of graduate school.

The faculty and alumni of Hamburger U were up in arms at the proposal. The cost-cutters, said one instructor, don't realize that coming together at the flagship campus builds a sense of membership in the enterprise because they can't capture its value in a tidy cost-benefit calculation.
As one instructor said, "They are ignoring the iconic importance of the
campus experience." When Saul Bellow inveighed against the University
of Chicago's efforts to reduce the size of its core curriculum, he couldn't
have said it any better.

Only in name is "Hamburger University" a university; and despite the
fact that some community colleges award course credit for the experience,
its certificate in "hamburgerology" isn't a higher education credential.
Still, the contest over its fate is emblematic of a debate taking place seemingly everywhere. The argument sets advocates of greater reliance on the
market, with its promise of increased efficiency and productivity, against

255

defenders of the community of scholars, with its promise of discovering, sharing, and transmitting knowledge. It pits those who believe in the workings of Adam Smith's "invisible hand," the idea that the public good emerges from individuals' pursuit of their own selfish interests, against those who argue that public purposes can best be served by public and nonprofit institutions.[2]

■ Back to the Future

Like so much in higher education, these are ancient quarrels. In 1828, the fellows of Yale College appointed a committee to examine "the expediency of so altering the regular course of instruction . . . as to leave out of said course the study of the *dead languages.*"[3] The committee's report reached far beyond its mandate to encompass the entire "nature and object" of higher learning; in its time, it was the most influential American treatise on the topic. Standard histories treat it as a reactionary tract, a last-gasp defense of the old guard, but in its essence, it could have been written today.[4]

There had been considerable clamor for Yale and other colleges to take a more populist approach, to provide greater access and pay more attention to what, then and now, are called the "practical arts." The controversy was of sufficient gravity to engage the attention of the governor of Connecticut as well as local worthies and "the academical faculty." Be more businesslike, the critics were urging, or risk becoming obsolete. "From different quarters, we have heard the suggestion that our colleges must be *new-modelled;* that they are not adapted to the spirit and wants of the age; that they will soon be deserted, unless they are better accommodated to the business character of the nation." Although this was the Jacksonian age, it might as well have been the Internet age; the big difference is how Yale responded to the "suggestion." Nowadays faculty and administrators are prone to dithering. The 1828 report rejected the idea of "accommodation" out of hand.

The bedrock purpose of a college education, the report concludes, is to "form the taste and discipline the mind." That is why the study of classics should remain a requirement: far from being a "dead" undertaking, it "lays the foundations of correct taste" and "forms the most effectual discipline of the mental faculties." The old guard at the University of Chicago advanced the same kind of argument in inveighing against the perceived weakening of its hallowed core curriculum.[5]

The 1828 committee wasn't opposed to the idea of change. On the contrary: "*salutary* reform," change that solidified the "higher principle," was welcome. The curriculum had to reflect advances in knowledge; as the report notes, Yale in 1828, with its courses in chemistry, geology, and political economy, was a far better place than it had been in 1714, when it taught only "the scholastic cobwebs of a few paltry systems, that would now be laid by as proper food for worms." New York Law School would make much the same claim for its revamping of standard legal education.

Achieving a balance between teaching and research required recalibrating as well, in ways that a university like NYU would appreciate. The report urges that senior professors, the super-stars of their time, be largely freed from classroom responsibilities, enabling them to focus on research. Tutors, the nineteenth century's adjuncts (and probably better than professors in the classroom, the report surmises), should teach the basic subjects.

What a school like Dickinson College would describe as the "campus experience" was also critical to an undergraduate education. Yale needed to be appreciated as a "family . . . founded on mutual affection and confidence." One of its tasks was to develop students' "character."

Even though Yale wasn't a public university, and so wasn't "molested" by state politicians, as has been the case at schools like the University of Virginia, public opinion still mattered. Presumably the governor, whose job gave him insight into the general sentiment, was appointed to add worldly wisdom. The committee gave a nod in the direction of populism. "The public are undoubtedly right, in demanding that there should be appropriate courses of education, accessible to all classes of youth," the report observes, but Yale College wasn't equipped to deliver such instruction. While professional schools and trade schools were worthy endeavors (indeed, schools of law, medicine, and divinity were already part of the university), those narrower and more specialized subjects didn't belong in an undergraduate liberal arts education. That is the sort of argument USC's provost was making when he restored responsibility for general education to the liberal arts college.

Then and now, money was the institution's lifeblood. If the "treasury were overflowing, if we had a *surplus fund*," the report concedes, then "there might perhaps be no harm in establishing a department for a brief and rapid liberal arts course." Still, the "higher principle" ruled the day; the mission of the college, "the *discipline* and the *furniture* of the mind," must not be compromised. Such a venture needed to be "as distinct . . . as the medical or law school." In effect, the committee was proposing an extension program (though it didn't recognize what schools like the University of California at Santa Cruz, and Chicago and Columbia before them, understand very well, that extension and correspondence schools can replenish the coffers). Teaching short-term and college students together in an expanded institution was rejected because it jeopardized the value of a Yale degree. "It is a hazardous experiment, to act upon the plan of gaining numbers first, and character afterwards." Shades of USC, cutting its freshman class in the early 1990s for just that reason; or MIT, putting its course materials, but not its credential, on-line; or Columbia, refusing to award degrees to students taking courses in Fathom, its ill-fated virtual extension program.

Although a college degree mattered less in 1828 than it does today, the report points out that a liberal arts education promotes self-interest, the *private* good, by giving students the tools and the credentials they need to prosper as doctors, businessmen, and lawyers. But such an education also promotes the interest of the commonwealth, the *public* good, by molding students into citizens of the republic: "Let the value of a collegiate education be reduced and the diffusion among the people would be checked, the general standard of intellectual and moral worth lowered, and our civil and religious liberty jeopardized, by ultimately disqualifying our citizens for the exercise of the right and privilege of self-government."

In all but a handful of colleges, the classics have long since vanished from the required curriculum, but that doesn't diminish the relevance of the Yale report. The undergraduate curriculum, as the committee was at pains to point out, had been in flux since the founding of the college, and the elimination of the classics requirement a generation or so later, at Yale and elsewhere, represents just another step in that continuing process of change. What *is* pertinently different is that American colleges eventually lost control over the design of the undergraduate curriculum. Because there is less certainty about what must be part of the shared "furniture of the mind"—what belongs in the canon—in most schools (the University of Chicago being a notable exception) the common core has been abandoned in favor of innocuous "distribution requirements" that turn higher education into a shopping mall.

Much like Swiss watchmakers, today's liberal arts professors offer what is widely regarded as a luxury item to a shrinking clientele. Because these academics treat the value of their subject as self-evident, not something that needs to be explained anew, in recent years they have lost much of their audience, as career-minded undergraduates have shifted their allegiance to the "practical arts." Is it possible to reinvent the academic commons—to reinvigorate the culture of the academy, to find persuasive ways of explaining to a new generation the enduring values of a liberal education?[6]

This incoherence about what knowledge matters most goes well beyond the curriculum; it has become pervasive in higher education. Whether the topic is the nature of scholarship, the criteria for selecting and supporting students, the methods and modes of instruction, or the relationship between the university and its patrons in industry, clarifying voices of authority are rarely heard. What makes the Yale report such a wondrous anachronism is its bracing certainty about the school's mission. That committee understands what Yale College is—and what it is not.

When he delivered the Godkin lectures at Harvard in 1963, Clark Kerr, president of the University of California system and formerly chancellor at Berkeley, "knew the direction [universities] were swinging." Those lectures, published as *The Uses of the University,* describe the emergence of the bustling intellectual metropolis that Kerr labeled the "multiversity." The nineteenth-century university "was a village with its priests," and the early-twentieth-century university was "a town—a one-industry town— with its intellectual oligarchy." The new multiversity was "a city of infinite variety . . . a whole series of communities and activities held together by a common name and . . . related purposes . . . neither entirely of the world nor entirely apart from it." This was "a period of euphoria," Kerr writes, an era marked by universal access to higher education, the postwar decision to base scientific research within universities and the newfound availability of resources.[7] The tone of the lectures reflects this optimism. Clark Kerr had glimpsed the future and, by and large, he liked what he saw.

Thirty-eight years later, in 2001, the nonagenarian Kerr sat down to write a new last chapter for what had become a classic. This time he was much less confident, and far less positive, about what the future might hold. The second half of the twentieth century had been a "grand century for the cities of intellect," he writes, but that time was "now past, never to be replicated." Money was in short supply, and so were ideas. University administrators possess "no great visions to lure them on, only the need of survival for themselves and their institutions."[8]

With public universities relying less on state funds, and for-profit schools like DeVry and Phoenix coming into their own, the very idea that institutions of higher education have a mission beyond promoting their members' individual private good can no longer be taken for granted. How does the academic commons survive in a world where a renowned university like Columbia seeks to convert the promise of the Internet into a tool to position itself as a force in "the high-end, high-quality distance learning market"? How much academic freedom is available to professors at a place like the University of Virginia's business school, who cannot use course materials that they have prepared for executive training courses in their regular classes? What is the meaning of the community of scholars when a single corporation can patent the research products of an entire department, as Novartis was essentially able to do at Berkeley? What does higher education itself mean when universities compete with training companies and high schools to deliver instruction for specific company jobs, as in the IT certification market, where the courses are a "high-end" version of "hamburgerology"?

Small wonder, then, that so much attention is being paid to the proposition that higher education should be opened up to greater competition—more radically, that government should leave the field to the market. Many institutions that call themselves colleges and universities have abandoned the high ground that has given higher education a claim on the public resources of the society, forgetting that their purpose is speaking truth to power. When that happens, the university risks "losing sight of its own distinctive features and achievements," indeed, "losing control over the very means by which its own identity is formed."[9]

What is true of academic life holds true in many spheres. Why should higher education be any different from medicine—or the arts, or religion for that matter—all of which have been forced to remake themselves in response to competitive pressures? At a moment when agreement is lacking on the meaning of the public good, when even the idea itself seems vaguely old-fashioned, why should higher education receive special treatment? Since the 1970s, under considerable public pressure, universities have opened their doors to a far greater diversity of students and faculty.[10] But into what kind of place, with what values, are these newcomers gaining membership?

▪ Private Goods and the Public Good

A great deal is at stake in this contest between the values of the market and those of the commons: the commitment to test, not just replicate, the prevailing wisdoms of the day; the pride of place given to need and merit, rather than ability to pay, in determining who is to be educated; the contention that universities should be places for discovering, sharing, and passing on knowledge rather than companies for hoarding and selling it; the idea, to revive a nineteenth-century metaphor, that one can speak of the *soul* of the university.

Maintaining communities of scholars is not a concern of the market. It is axiomatic that entrepreneurs must balance the books in order to survive, which is why for-profit universities like DeVry are acting rationally when they support only research designed to strengthen their institution. But when show-me-the-money accountability becomes the mantra not just of the stock market but of the politicians who oversee public universities' budgets, who will underwrite the inquiries that academics pursue in the name of intellectual curiosity, with no hope of a quick return on investment? If the market truly reigns, will entire fields, and the intellectual capital they represent, wither away over time? Will sociology and comparative literature, and pure mathematics too, become the "dead languages" of the new millennium?

And what of access, the promise that higher education can function as an engine of mobility? While the top tier of colleges and universities can afford to admit students on a need-blind basis, subsidizing those who require such help, these schools educate only a minuscule fraction of undergraduates. Everywhere else, students from poor and working-class families are at a considerable disadvantage.

Those who enroll in for-profit schools must pay their own way, and then some, a price tag that discourages many who would benefit from such an education. Until recently, nonprofit colleges based their financial aid awards on a student's need; but many now treat the admissions office as a "profit center," and promoting equity matters less than moving up in the *U.S. News & World Report*'s pecking order. Meanwhile, a growing number of states award scholarships to students with the best high school grades, and here too the beneficiaries tend not to be the students who most need the financial help.[11]

It's easy to see who loses out because of these new rules of the game. Bill Durden at Dickinson College argues that all children, not only the well-to-do and a handful of the lucky, are entitled to the kind of education that his college offers, but that's not what's happening at his school or anyplace else.[12] The income gap in college enrollment has remained the same for a generation: in 2002 as in 1980, 30 percent more students from the wealthiest one-fifth of American households were attending college than from the poorest one-fifth; and most of the college students from the poorest families are ghettoized in two-year schools. Making federal loans more widely available was supposed to close this gap, but the policy makers miscalculated. Because the size of these loans remains inadequate and middle-class students are now eligible to receive them, the situation is actually more inequitable than before the reforms.

Free, on-line courses, along the lines of MIT's OpenCourseWare approach, potentially expand access in a different way, by giving students around the globe entree into the intellectual life of great universities. But it's naïve to think that what MIT puts on-line is truly free. As that institute's distinguished economists know well, there's no such a thing as a free lunch—or a free on-line course. Someone has to pay the bills. "If only we had 'surplus funds,'" academic leaders say, echoing the lament of the 1828 Yale committee; but it's plain that universities cannot pick up the entire tab for such projects. While foundations have made wise social investments by covering a portion of the start-up costs at MIT, as well as for Sunoikisis, the southern classics consortium, not even the richest foundation can sustain these ventures indefinitely. Only government has that kind of money. But with higher education increasingly vulnerable to budget cuts and "the digital divide" a passé slogan, there is no discernible enthusiasm for a twenty-first-century version of the GI Bill to underwrite access to the best of virtual education.[13]

The technology is only a means. Everything turns on how it gets used. In the early 1990s, when the Internet was still in its infancy, there were dreams of an infinitely richer world of ideas about to be born. Instead, the market rules, and the Web has turned into a shopping arcade. A similar fate may befall e-learning. Even as Britain's Open University, which prepares the best distance education courses in the world, failed in the United States for lack of funds, Thomson, the publishing empire, has invested heavily in such ventures as Universitas 21, an international partnership of higher education institutions, and Unext, the on-line business school with ambitions of becoming a full-fledged university. There is no altruism here. The corporation hopes to convert these enterprises into truly global institutions whose product is pitched to those who can afford the tariff.

When great public universities like Berkeley and the University of Michigan appeal for public funds, they advance a marketlike proposition for maintaining the city of intellect: that the "bundling" of teaching and research yields synergies that bring added value to the enterprise. Yet this claim, while intuitively plausible (especially to those who make their home in such places), is hard to prove in dollars-and-cents terms.

Universities could strengthen their case for favored treatment by calling a cease-fire for the worst aspects of the institutional status wars. Even as the semiconductor firms that pay for Berkeley's Gigascale Center support "pre-competitive" research that all of them can use, universities could do something similar—for instance, not using lighter teaching loads as an inducement for professors; or maintaining need as the primary basis for awarding scholarships. Such measures would make everyone better off. But with the prize to the winner and the price borne by the losers so great, only rarely is a school willing to take the lead.[14]

Meanwhile, as Willie Loman says in *Death of a Salesman,* "the woods are burning." The ultimate question is this: Can the public be persuaded that universities represent something as ineffable as the common good—more specifically, that higher education contributes to the development of knowledgeable and responsible citizens, encourages social cohesion, promotes and spreads knowledge, increases social mobility, and stimulates the economy?[15] Can the argument convincingly be made that the university offers something of such great value that it is worth subsidizing, even in the teeth of bottom-line pressures—that, as NYU's John Sexton says, in certain spheres "money is not the coin of the realm"?

With university presidents consumed by the Sisyphean burdens of fundraising and the placating of multiple constituencies, it's not clear who will take on this task.[16] Lacking such a principled defense, though, the university may degenerate into something far less palatable than the house of learning "better attuned to the business character of the nation" demanded by Yale's nineteenth-century critics—the transformation that has in fact taken place since the 1970s. It might conceivably evolve into just another business, the metaphor of the higher education "industry" brought to life in a holding company that could be called Universitas, Inc.[17] If there is a less dystopian future, one that revives the soul of this old institution, who is to advance it—and if not now, then when?

Notes

Introduction

1. This chapter draws on interviews, conducted in person and by telephone, as well as e-mail correspondence. Quotations for which no citation is provided are taken from these sources.
2. Gordon Winston and David J. Zimmerman, "Where Is Aggressive Price Competition Taking Higher Education?" *Change,* 32, no. 4 (July–August 2000), 10–18.
3. Robert Frank, "Higher Education: The Ultimate Winner-Take-All Market?" in Maureen Devlin and Joel Meyerson, eds., *Forum Futures: Exploring the Future of Higher Education, 2000 papers* (San Francisco: Jossey-Bass, 2001), 4–5. See also Gordon Winston, "Subsidies, Hierarchy, and Peers: The Awkward Economics of Higher Education," *Journal of Economic Perspectives,* 13 (Winter 1999), 13–36; Patricia Gumport, "Academic Restructuring: Organizational and Institutional Imperatives," *Higher Education: The International Journal of Higher Education and Educational Planning,* 39 (2000), 67–91 (discussing the "root metaphor" of higher education as an industry focused "on the harsh realities of market force and the urgency of doing something to stay competitive," p. 72).
4. See Richard Hofstadter, *Academic Freedom in the Age of the College* (New Brunswick, N.J.: Transaction Publishers, 1996).
5. John Henry Newman, *The Idea of a University: Defined and Illustrated in Nine Discourses* (London: Longmans, 1947); Thorstein Veblen, *The Higher Learning in America* (New York: B. W. Huebsh, 1918).
6. On canon wars and the like, see Martin Anderson, *Impostors in the Temple* (Englewood Cliffs, N.J.: Simon and Schuster, 1992); David Bromwich, *Politics by Other Means: Higher Education Group Thinking* (New Haven: Yale University Press, 1992); Dinesh d'Souza, *Illiberal Education: The Politics of Race and Sex on Campus* (New York: Free Press, 1991); Charles Sykes, *ProfScam: Professors and the Demise of Higher Education* (Washington, D.C.: Regnery, 1988); Allan Bloom, *The Closing of the American Mind: How Higher Education Has Failed Democracy and Impoverished the Souls of Today's Students* (New York: Simon and Schuster, 1987). On affirmative action, see William Bowen

and Derek Bok, *The Shape of the River: Long-Term Consequences of Considering Race in College and University Admissions* (Princeton, N.J.: Princeton University Press, 1998).

7. University of Connecticut administrator quoted in William Hathaway, "Building Uconn Inc.," *Business Week*, October 19, 1998, p. 54; Richard Atkinson, "It Takes Cash to Keep Ideas Flowing," Sepember 1998, *http://uc-industry .berkeley.edu/news/president/ittakes.htm*.

8. In *The University in Ruins* (Cambridge, Mass.: Harvard University Press, 1995), Bill Readings expresses concern about the rise of "excellence" as a benchmark. Although that book was published relatively recently, subsequent developments render his concerns almost quaint. See generally Derek Bok, *Universities in the Marketplace: The Commercialization of Higher Education* (Princeton: Princeton University Press, 2003).

9. Frank, "Higher Education," p. 5. See also Gordon Winston, "Why Can't a College Be More Like a Firm?" *Change* (September–October 1997), 33–38.

10. Arthur Levine and Jeannette Curteon, *When Hope and Fear Collide* (San Francisco: Jossey-Bass, 1998).

11. Joyce Scott and Nancy A. Bereman, "Competition versus Collegiality: Academe's Dilemma for the 1990s," *Journal of Higher Education*, 63 (1992), 684–698.

12. Hunter Breland et al., *Summary Report: Trends in College Admission 2000: A Report of a National Survey of Undergraduate Admissions Policies, Practices, and Procedures* (March 2002), *http://www.airweb.org/page.asp?page=347*. In 1999, the average acceptance rate was 68 percent for public and 60 percent for private four-year colleges. See generally Roger Geiger, "The American University in the Marketplace: Forces Shaping the University of the Twenty-first Century" (unpub. ms., 2003).

13. "During a period [1970–1995] in which the [higher education] system grew by 50 percent, almost every field which constituted the old arts and sciences core of the undergraduate college was in absolute decline." Steven Brint, "The Rise of the 'Practical Arts,'" in Steven Brint, ed., *The Future of the City of Intellect: The Changing American University* (Stanford: Stanford University Press, 2002), p. 235.

14. Richard Ruch, *Higher Ed, Inc.: The Rise of the For-Profit University* (Baltimore: Johns Hopkins University Press, 2001); Gordon Winston, "For-Profit Higher Education: Godzilla or Chicken Little?" *Change* (January–February 1999), 12–19.

15. Clifford Adelman, *A Parallel Postsecondary Universe: The Certification System in Information Technology* (Washington, D.C.: U.S. Department of Education, 2000).

16. Christopher Jencks and David Riesman, *The Academic Revolution* (New York: Doubleday, 1968); Clark Kerr, *The Uses of the University* (Cambridge, Mass.: Harvard University Press, 1964). Both books have been revised and republished, Kerr's book four times. Clark Kerr, "A Critical Age in the University

World: Accumulated Heritage versus Modern Imperatives," *European Journal of Education,* 22 (1987), 184.

17. Clark Kerr, *The Uses of the University* (Cambridge, Mass.: Harvard University Press, 2001); Simon Marginson and Mark Considine, *The Enterprise University* (Cambridge: Cambridge University Press, 2000); Burton Clark, *Creating Entrepreneurial Universities: Organizational Pathways of Transformation* (London: Pergamon, 1998); Sheila Slaughter and Larry Leslie, *Academic Capitalism: Politics, Policies, and the Entrepreneurial University* (Baltimore: Johns Hopkins University Press, 1998).

18. Neil Kotler and Philip Kotler, *Museum Strategy and Marketing: Designing Missions, Building Audience, Generating Revenue and Resources* (San Francisco, Jossey-Bass, 1998); Philip Kotler, Bryce Wrenn, and Philip Kotler, *Marketing for Congregations: Choosing to Serve People More Effectively* (Nashville: Abingdon Press, 1994).

19. Arthur Okun, *Equality and Efficiency: The Big Tradeoff* (Washington, D.C.: Brookings Institution Press, 1975), p. 19.

20. Gumport, "Academic Restructuring," describes these as "institutional" concerns and argues that they are losing out to market concerns as the legitimating idea of public higher education. See also Richard Posner, "The University as Business," *Atlantic Monthly* (June 2002), 25; Roger Benjamin, "The Environment of Higher Education: A Constellation of Changes," *Annals of the American Academy of Political and Social Science,* 585 (January 2003), 8–30; Henry Giroux, "Neoliberaism, Corporate Culture, and the Promise of Higher Education," *Harvard Educational Review,* 72 (2002), 425–463.

1. This Little Student Went to Market

1. A. R. Krachenberg, "Bringing the Concept of Marketing to Higher Education." *Journal of Higher Education,* 43 (May 1972), 370. This chapter draws on interviews, conducted in person and by telephone, and e-mail correspondence with trustees, administrators, professors, and students, as well as with others knowledgeable about the institutions. Quotations for which no citation is provided are taken from these sources.

2. Jeffrey Young, "Why Was Princeton Snooping in Yale's Admissions Website?" *Chronicle of Higher Education,* August 9, 2002, p. A37; Christine Haughney and Michael Fletcher, "Princeton Officials Punished for Breaching Yale's Web," *San Francisco Chronicle,* August 14, 2002, p. 5. Ironically, Princeton's dean of admissions, Fred Hargadon, has long been known as the best in the trade, the "dean of admissions deans." Hargadon, who wasn't implicated in the scandal, announced his retirement, effective June 2003.

3. Ben Gose, "Tuition Discounting May Rankle but Its Use Has Become Widespread." *Chronicle of Higher Education,* February 18, 2000, p. A62. See also Brian Pusser and Dudley Doane, "Public Purpose and Private Enterprise: The Contemporary Organization of Higher Education," *Change* (September–Oc-

tober 2001), 20: "Giving the people what they want has generally been an excellent business strategy, but it is not clear that it is the best national higher education strategy."

4. Robert Frank, "Higher Education: The Ultimate Winner-Take-All Market?" in Maureen Devlin and Joel Meyerson, eds., *Forum Futures: Exploring the Future of Higher Education, 2000 Papers* (San Francisco: Jossey-Bass, 2001), 4–5.

5. Howard Greene, *The Select: Students Speak Out on the Realities of Life and Learning in America's Elite Colleges* (New York: Harper Collins, 1998).

6. American Council on Education and UCLA Higher Education Research Institute, "The American College Freshman: National Norms for Fall 2001" (2002).

7. Nicholas Thompson, "Playing with Numbers," *Washington Monthly,* September 2000, pp. 16–24; National Opinion Research Center, "A Review of the Methodology for the *U.S. News & World Report*'s Rankings of Undergraduate Colleges and Universities" (1997), *www.washingtonmonthly.com/features/2000/norc.html.* Sounder approaches exist, but are often ignored. Howard Greene and Matthew Greene, "Rankings That Work," *University Business* (February 2003), 13–15.

8. Unlike in the classic market, the buyers as well as the sellers are competing. The buyers in effect *become* part of the product, since the quality of the other students is a big draw for applicants, and for that reason affects a school's prestige.

9. Robert Reich, "How Selective Colleges Heighten Inequality," *Chronicle of Higher Education,* September 15, 2000, p. B7.

10. Krachenberg, "Bringing the Concept," p. 370. See also Eugene Fram, "We Must *Market* Education—and Here Are Some Guidelines for Doing So, Effectively," *Chronicle of Higher Education,* April 17, 1972, p. 80.

11. John Maguire, "A Periodic Review of Ideas and Issues in Educational Marketing." *Lawlor Review,* 6 (Fall 1998), *www.financialaidservices.org/whatsnew/lawlorrev.htm.*

12. John Maguire, "To the Organized Go the Students," *Bridge Magazine* (Boston College alumni magazine) (Fall 1976), *www.financialaidservices.org/whatsnew/bridgmag.htm.*

13. Michael G. Dolence, "Strategic Enrollment Management," in Claire C. Swann and Stanley E. Henderson, eds., *Handbook for the College Admissions Profession* (Westport, Conn.: Greenwood Press, 1998), p. 72.

14. Ibid.

15. The program's Web site is *http://www.miami.edu/enrollment-management.*

16. Hunter Breland et al., *Summary Report: Trends in College Admission, 2000,* sponsored by ACT, Inc., the Association for Institutional Research, the College Board, the Educational Testing Service, and the National Association of College Admission Counseling, March 2002, *http://www.airweb.org/page.asp?page=347.* This figure conceals considerable variation in enrollment. Be-

tween 1979 and 1994, the annual decline was almost 700,000 students; between 1994 and 1999, there was an annual increase of almost 400,000. There has also been a substantial enrollment increase among working adults who return to college.

17. Karen Fox and Philip Kotler, *Strategic Marketing for Educational Institutions* (Englewood Cliffs, N.J.: Prentice Hall, 1985). See also Gary Armstrong and Philip Kotler, *Marketing: An Introduction* (Englewood Cliffs, N.J.: Prentice Hall, 2002); John Bowen, Philip Kotler, and James Makens, *Marketing for Hospitality and Tourism* (Englewood Cliffs, N.J.: Prentice Hall, 1996); Philip Kotler, Bruce Wrenn, and Philip Kotler, *Marketing for Congregations: Choosing to Serve People More Effectively* (Nashville: Abingdon Press, 1994).

18. Without the Ivy League brand, the jibe goes, a school like Cornell would be just another Vanderbilt.

19. Daniel Golden, "Colleges Court Jewish Students in Effort to Raise Rankings." *Wall Street Journal,* April 29, 2002, p. A1.

20. Breland et al., *Trends in College Admission, 2000,* p. 5; Donald Stewart, *College Admission Policies in the 1990s: A Look toward the Future* (New York: College Entrance Examination Board, 1992), p. 9.

21. The transformation of the University of Chicago is the topic of Chapter 2.

22. Ethan Bronner, "University of Chicago Comes to a Fork in the Road," *New York Times,* December 12, 1998, p. 1.

23. For the record, Behnke is David Kirp's Amherst College classmate.

24. See *www.collegeboard.org.*

25. Kotler, *Strategic Marketing,* p. 311.

26. Roger Kerin, P. Rajan Varadarajan, and Robert Peterson, "First-Mover Advantage: A Synthesis, Conceptual Framework, and Research Propositions," *Journal of Marketing,* 56 (October 1992), 35.

27. Joshua Lucas, "U. of C. Marketers Ditch Tradition in New Viewbook," *University of Chicago Weekly News,* September 23, 1998, *www.bayarea.net/~kins/AboutMe/Hutchins_items/UofC_marketers_ditch_trad.html.*

28. Yingtao Ho, "A Call for Action: How to Fight for the Core," *Chicago Maroon,* March 9, 1999.

29. Daniel Kingery, "Debate over College Continues at Psi U," *Chicago Maroon,* February 26, 1999.

30. Barbara Blank, "College Admissions on Course, Says Behnke," *University of Chicago Magazine,* October, 1999.

31. "Applications Up," *University of Chicago Magazine,* 91 (February 1999), *http://magazine.uchicago.edu/0102/campus-news/report-early.html.*

32. Meredith Klein, "Prospies Attracted by New College Marketing," *University of Chicago Weekly News,* March 29, 1999, *cwn.uchicago.edu/1999s/04.29/news/marketing.html.*

33. Robin Wilson, "College Recruiting Gimmicks Get More Lavish as Competition for New Freshmen Heats Up," *Chronicle of Higher Education,* March 7, 1990, p. A1.

34. Breland et al., "Trends in College Admission, 2000," p. 20.
35. Brian Williams, "To the Personalized Go the Prospects," *Journal of College Admission,* no. 166 (2000), 21–26. The Vanderbilt, SUNY-Buffalo, and University of Missouri–Rollo examples are drawn from Lisa Guernsey, "Some Colleges Try Attracting Students with Their Own On-Line Innovations," *Chronicle of Higher Education,* October 9, 1998, p. A31.
36. Thomas Kane, *The Price of Admission* (Washington, D.C.: Brookings Institution Press, 1999), p. 55.
37. William J. Bennett, "Our Greedy Colleges," *New York Times,* February 18, 1987, p. A34.
38. Morton Keller and Phyllis Keller, *Making Harvard Modern: The Rise of America's University* (New York: Oxford University Press, 2001), p. 357.
39. Charles Clotfelter, *Buying the Best: Cost Escalation in Elite Higher Education* (Princeton N.J.: Princeton University Press, 1996), pp. 26–30. See also Ronald Ehrenberg, *Tuition Rising: Why College Costs So Much* (Cambridge, Mass.: Harvard University Press, 2000).
40. Both the number of institutions that offer no-need awards and the dollar average of those awards increased between 1979 and 2000. Breland et al., "Trends in College Admission, 2000," p. 9.
41. "A Brief History of Overlap and the Antitrust Suit," *MIT Tech Talk Special Edition,* September 3, 1992, *web.mit.edu/newsoffice/tt/1992/26874/26891.html.*
42. Gordon Winston and David Zimmerman point out that graduate students receive strictly merit-based aid from every elite institution; the most sought-after students receive stipends as well as full tuition scholarships. They predict that this practice will spread to undergraduate admissions. Gordon Winston and David Zimmerman, "Where Is Aggressive Price Competition Taking Higher Education?" *Change,* 32 (July–August 2000), 10–18. Some top-tier schools practice "preferential packaging" or "merit within need." Swarthmore, for instance, which is consistently ranked first or second by *U.S. News* among liberal arts colleges, gives scholarships instead of loans to its 120 top freshmen.
43. Steve Stecklow, "Colleges Manipulate Fin. Aid Offers, Shortchanging Many," *Wall Street Journal,* April 1, 1996, p. A1.
44. Ben Gose, "Tuition Discounting May Rankle, but It Has Become Widespread," *Chronicle of Higher Education,* February 18, 2000, p. A62.
45. Any factor that correlates with a student's propensity to attend can be used this way. A school could thus factor in an applicant's race or gender.
46. Although many don't know it, those who accept early admission have struck a bargain: in exchange for the security of knowing where they're going to college, they receive smaller scholarships than students who wait anxiously until April.
47. This section draws on the research assistance of Marc Wolf.
48. Neil Miller, "How Now, Brown U?" *Boston Globe,* November 27, 1983, p. 15.
49. Their leader was Ira Magaziner, who reemerged years later as the architect of Hillary Clinton's ill-fated health care plan.

50. Hampshire College and the University of California at Santa Cruz both had essentially the same message, but in terms of selectivity, neither school has fared nearly as well.

51. Mary Leonard, "On Campus, Comforts Are Major Colleges' Hope Perks Can Boost Enrollment," *Boston Globe,* September 3, 2002, p. A1.

52. Martin Van Der Werf, "Many Colleges Could Close or Merge Because of Financial Problems, Standard & Poor's Warns," *Chronicle of Higher Education,* November 22, 2002, *http://chronicle.com/daily/2002/11/2002112701n.htm.*

53. Murray Sperber, *Beer and Circus: How Big-Time Sport Is Crippling Undergraduate Education* (New York: Henry Holt, 2000).

54. Jeffrey Selingo, "Mission Creep?" *Chronicle of Higher Education,* May 31, 2002, pp. A19–21.

55. The phrase is from Winston and Zimmerman, "Price Competition."

56. Ronald Ehrenberg and James Monks, "*U.S. News & World Report*'s College Rankings: Why Do They Matter?" *Change,* 31 (November–December 1999), 42–51.

57. Steve Stecklow, "Colleges Inflate SATs and Graduation Rates in Popular Guidebooks," *Wall Street Journal,* April 5, 1995, pp. 1, 6. The Harvard admissions director calls the SAT score disparity (between 1400 and 1385) "a mystery" and "not significant," adding that the *U.S. News* figures were accurate; Moody's reports that it printed the figures exactly as they were provided by Harvard.

58. Christopher Avery, Andrew Fairbanks, and Richard Zeckhauser, *The Early Admissions Game: Joining the Elite* (Cambridge, Mass.: Harvard University Press, 2003); Rachel Toor, *Admissions Confidential: An Insider's Account of the Elite College Selection Process* (New York: St. Martin's, 2001); Jacques Steinberg, *The Gatekeepers: Inside the Admissions Process of a Premier College* (New York: Viking, 2002); James Fallows, "The Early Decision Racket," *Atlantic Monthly* (September 2001), 37–52.

59. Patricia McDonough et al., "College Rankings: Democratized College for Whom? *Research in Higher Education,* 39 (1998), 513–537.

60. Ralph Gardner Jr., "The $28,995 Tutor," *New York,* April 16, 2001, *www.new yorkmetro.com/nymetro/urban/education/features/4579.*

61. Alvin P. Sanoff, "A Parent's Plea," *Chronicle of Higher Education,* February 12, 1999, p. B7.

62. Earl Gottschalk, "Better Odds? Parents Hire Advisers to Help Get Their Children into College," *Wall Street Journal,* November 7, 1986, p. 1.

63. These strategies included filing amendments to income tax statements to classify children as non-dependents, having a parent enroll in several community college courses (prior to 2000, when the rule was changed, the "parent contribution" per student was divided by the number of household members enrolled at least half-time in college, in accordance with federal methodology), and obtaining the "multiplier tables" that colleges use to compare home values with income and issue audit requests on suspicious applications. Thomas DeLoughry, "Colleges Say Consultants Are Suggesting Schemes That Help

Families Win Student Aid Unfairly," *Chronicle of Higher Education*, January 17, 1990, p. A25.

64. Leonard Sloane, "Consultants or Con Artists?" *New York Times*, April 7, 1991, p. A30.

65. "Principles of Good Practice" from IECA Web site, *www.iecaonline.com*.

66. Ben Gose, "Anxious Applicants to Top Colleges Seek an Edge by Hiring Consultants," *Chronicle of Higher Edcuation*, January 24, 1997, p. A31.

67. Carol Loewith, "Independent Consultants and the College Selection Process," *College Board Review*, no. 186 (Fall 1998), 24–27.

68. Liz Seymour, "The Old College Try Gets a New Sales Pitch," *Washington Post*, November 27, 1999, p A1.

69. See Jane Gross's series of three front-page articles: "Different Lives, One Goal: Finding the Key to College," "Preparing Applications, Fine-Tuning Applicants," and "At Last, Colleges Answer, and New Questions Arise," *New York Times*, May 5–7, 2002.

70. Gross, "Different Lives," p. A1.

71. Family wealth can also directly affect a student's chances of admission, as some elite universities admit applicants who otherwise would be rejected in hopes of receiving a gift from the family. Daniel Golden, "At Many Colleges, the Rich Kids Get Affirmative Action," *Wall Street Journal*, February 20, 2003, p. 1.

72. U.S. Census Bureau, Current Population Survey (CPS) Reports, ser. P20–479. Available online at *http://www.census.gov/population/www/socdemo/school.html*. By comparison, the enrollment gap between whites and underrepresented minorities is less than 10 percent. In 1999, three-quarters of all community colleges reported an increase over a five-year period in the number of students who chose a two-year, rather than a four-year, institution because of cost. Breland et al., *Trends in College Admission, 2000*, p. 15.

73. Michael S. McPherson and Morton Owen Schapiro, *The Student Aid Game* (Princeton: Princeton University Press, 1998), pp. 25–36.

74. Frank, "Higher Education," p. 3.

75. In 2001, twenty-eight private institutions agreed to tweak their financial aid formulas to grant more aid based on need and less merit-based support. But the agreed-on changes were modest; and, pointedly, neither Harvard nor Princeton signed on to the deal. Eric Hoover, "Twenty-eight Private Colleges Agree to Use Common Approaches to Student Aid," *Chronicle of Higher Education*, July 20, 2001, p. A33. As the economy worsens, the financial crunch affects more students. By 2003, increasing numbers were dropping out, and more were struggling to make ends meet. Greg Winter and Jennifer Medina, "More Students Line Up at Financial Aid Office," *New York Times*, March 10, 2003, p. A20.

2. Nietzsche's Niche

1. This chapter draws on interviews, conducted by Pablo Sandoval and David Kirp, both in person and by telephone, and e-mail correspondence with trust-

ees, administrators, professors, and students, as well as with others knowledgeable about the institution. Quotations for which no citation is provided are taken from these sources.

2. Milton Mayer, *Robert Maynard Hutchins: A Memoir* (Berkeley: University of California Press, 1993), p. 170. Alfred North Whitehead, *Dialogues of Alfred North Whitehead: As Recorded by Lucien Price* (Boston: Little, Brown, 1954), p. 137.

3. Few university websites make any reference to the history of the institution; and good university histories are notoriously hard to find. But the University of Chicago library's bibliography on the school's history, available on the university's website, includes nineteen references to general institutional history and twenty-four accounts of presidents and trustees; overall, the bibliography lists well over a hundred references—and it is identified as only "introductory." See *http://www.lib.uchicago.edu/e/spcl/introbib.html.* The best brief treatment of the university's history is John Boyer, *Three Views of Continuity and Change at the University of Chicago* (Chicago: University of Chicago Press, 1999), *http://www.uchicago.edu/docs/education/continuity-change/intro.html.* See also Thomas W. Goodspeed, *The Story of the University of Chicago, 1890–1925* (Chicago: University of Chicago Press, 1925); Richard J. Storr, *Harper's University, the Beginnings: A History of the University of Chicago* (Chicago: University of Chicago Press, 1966); Mary Ann Dzuback, *Robert M. Hutchins: Portrait of an Educator* (Chicago: University of Chicago Press, 1991); William McNeill, *Hutchins' University: A Memoir of the University of Chicago, 1929–1950* (Chicago: University of Chicago Press, 1991); and Harry Ashmore, *Unseasonable Truths: The Life of Robert Maynard Hutchins* (Boston: Little, Brown, 1989).

4. Frederick Rudolph, *The American College and University: A History* (New York: Vintage, 1962), p. 349. In 1906, John D. Rockefeller called the University of Chicago "the best investment I ever made in my life." Ibid., p. 352.

5. Annual Report of the [University of Chicago] Provost, 2000–2001, September 17, 2001, *http://www.uchicago.edu/docs/education/provost-rep00_1.html.*

6. Ethan Bronner, "The University of Chicago Comes to a Fork in the Road," *New York Times,* December 28, 1998, p. 1.

7. Ron Grossman and Patricia Jones, "At U. of C., C Stands for Chuckles," *Chicago Tribune,* January 31, 1999, p. 1.

8. "Letter from the Faculty to the Trustees of the University of Chicago," March 21, 1999, *http://www.realuofc.org/faculty/t-let.html.*

9. Scholars for the University of Chicago, April 14, 1999, *http://www.realuofc.org/public/nas.html.* This letter, though addressed to the trustees, was simultaneously made public and generated considerable publicity.

10. "Cash In, Quality Out," February 5, 1999, *http://www.realuofc.org/.* Wilson quoted in Adrienne Drell and Lon Grahnke, "U. of C. Keeps Image in Mind," *Chicago Sun-Times,* January 31, 1999, p. 1.

11. Marshall Sahlins, "The Life of the Mind and the Love of the Body; Or, the New 'Chicago Plan,' Now with Added Balance" (March 1999), 1, *http://*

www.realuofc.org/faculty/sahl-new.html. Hutchins quoted from Scholars for the University of Chicago letter.

12. Letter from the President, April 9, 1996, *http://www.realuofc.org/admin/sonnen.html*.

13. Robert M. Hutchins, *The Higher Learning in America* (New Haven: Yale University Press, 1936).

14. Andrew Abbott, "Futures of the University," *Forum: Newsletter of the Faculty Committee for a Year of Reflection* (October 1996), *http://www.realuofc.org/faculty/abbott.html*.

15. See Boyer, *Three Views*.

16. Quoted in Sahlins, "Life of the Mind."

17. Bronner, "The University of Chicago," p. A16. Among the professors who argued for this position was the noted philosopher Martha Nussbaum. See Martha Nussbaum, "Major Overhaul: Rigor and Requirements at the U. of C.," *Chicago Tribune,* March 11, 1999, *http://www.realuofc.org/faculty/nuss.html*.

18. Robert Perlman, "Biology as a Subject in the Liberal Curriculum," *College Faculty Newsletter,* 1, ser. 2 (November 1998), *http://www.cfn.uchicago.edu/no1.html#analysis*.

19. Bronner, "The University of Chicago," p. A16.

20. See "The Fun-In Mission Statement," April 1999, *http://realuofc.org/student/mission/html*. It is telling that the statement has to make the point that "the Fun-In is certainly not an attack on fun."

21. See generally Adam Kissel, "How I Became a Campus Revolutionary," *Re:generation Quarterly* (Fall 2000), *http://www.realuofc.org/student/revolutionary.html*.

22. Sahlins, "Life of the Mind."

23. Kameshwar Wali, *Chandra: A Biography of S. Chandrasekhar* (Chicago: University of Chicago Press, 1991).

24. Quoted in Marshall Sahlins, "The Metaphysical Research University" (unpublished ms., 1998), *http://www.realuofc.org/history/sahlins2.html*.

25. Levi quote from Sahlins, "Life of the Mind."

26. This historical account is drawn from Boyer, *Three Views*.

27. Sahlins, "Life of the Mind."

28. Andrew Yang and Christine Minerva, "Compromising the Core" (March 1999), *www.realuofc.org/press/yang.html*. See generally John Balz, "Success 101," *Chicago Magazine* (September 2002), *http://www.chicagomag.com/archives/0902success.htm*.

29. Sahlins, "Life of the Mind."

30. Quoted in Boyer, *Three Views*.

31. Quoted in Rudolph, *American College,* p. 495.

32. Quoted in Balz, "Success 101." In an only-at-Chicago moment Balz quotes a divinity school professor as gushing: "He [Randel] talks about me, with me. Hugo was very nice, but it was clear he hadn't read my work."

33. Ibid.

34. One remaining problem is yield: in 2002, only a third of the students who were accepted chose to enroll, just three percentage points higher than in 1997. By comparison, three-quarters of the students accepted by Harvard enroll there.

35. Scholars for the University of Chicago, press release, May 1, 2002, *http://www.goacta.org/Press%20Releases/5–1–02PR.htm*.

36. Don Randel, "Change Is in Course Offerings, Not in Our Course," *University of Chicago Magazine* (June 2002), *http://magazine.uchicago.edu/0206/departments/president.html*.

3. Benjamin Rush's "Brat"

1. "This Fall's Hot Schools," *Wall Street Journal,* October 5, 2001. This chapter draws on interviews, conducted by Jeffrey Holman and David Kirp in person and by telephone, and e-mail correspondence with trustees, administrators, professors, and students, as well as with others knowledgeable about the institution. Quotations for which no citation is provided are taken from these sources.

2. On college ranking systems and their history, see David Webster, *Academic Quality Rankings of American Colleges and Universities* (Springfield, Ill: Charles C. Thomas, 1986).

3. See generally David Collis, "Storming the Ivory Tower," Harvard Business School Working Paper, 2002.

4. Williams, Amherst, Swarthmore, Pomona, Dartmouth, and Grinnell are among the wealthiest schools, in terms of endowment per student, in the nation. "Largest Endowments per Student, 2001," *Chronicle of Higher Education,* August 30, 2002, p. 36 (citing statistics from the National Association of College and University Business Offices). In an act of noblesse oblige, in 2000, Williams College froze its tuition.

5. Michael McPherson and Morton Schapiro, "The Future Economic Challenge for the Liberal Arts Colleges," *Daedalus,* 128 (1999), 155.

6. The decline has been continuous. From 1967 to 1990, 167 private four-year colleges closed. Hugh Hawkins, "The Making of the Liberal Arts College Identity," *Daedalus,* 128 (1999), 21–47.

7. Yilu Zhao, "More Small Colleges Dropping Out," *New York Times,* May 7, 2002, p. A28.

8. Martin van der Werf, "Many Colleges Could Close or Merge Because of Financial Problems, Standard & Poor's Warns," *Chronicle of Higher Education,* November 22, 2002, *http://chronicle.com/daily/2002/11/2002112701n.htm*.

9. Steven Graubard, "Preface to the Issue: 'Distinctively American': The Residential Liberal Arts Colleges," *Daedalus,* 128 (1999), v–xii.

10. See the discussion of Beaver College/Arcadia University in Chapter 1.

11. Wabash College, Center of Inquiry in the Liberal Arts, *www.liberalarts.wabash.edu*.

12. Todd Gitlin, "The Liberal Arts in the Age of Info-Glut," *Chronicle of Higher Education,* May 1, 1998, pp. B4–5.

13. James Morgan, *The History of Dickinson College: One Hundred Fifty Years, 1783–1933* (Carlisle, Pa.: Dickinson College, 1933), p. 252, *http://chronicles .dickinson.edu/histories/morgan.* See also Charles Sellers, *Dickinson College: A History* (Middletown, Conn.: Wesleyan University Press, 1973), *http://chroni cles.dickinson.edu/histories/sellers.*

14. Morgan, *History,* pp. 68–69.

15. Ibid., p. 395. Such boasting is a familiar phenomenon, as this classic "advice" suggests: "An appeal should be made, wherever it is possible, to College Feeling. This, like other species of patriotism, consists in a sincere belief that the institution to which you belong is better than an institution to which other people belong. The corresponding belief ought to be encouraged in others by frequent confession of this article of faith in their presence. In this way a healthy spirit of rivalry will be promoted. It is this feeling that . . . differentiates more than anything else, a College from a boarding-house; for in a boarding-house hatred is concentrated, not upon rival establishments, but upon the other members of the same establishment." F. M. Cornford, *Microcosmograph Academica, being a Guide for the Young Academic Politician* (Cambridge: Metcalfe and Co., 1908), p. 55.

16. Mark Neustadt, "Focus Group Research Leading to Positioning Recommendations for Dickinson College," July 29, 1999, *http://www.dickinson.edu/ departments/polcy/neustadt.html.*

17. Mara Donaldson, "Consumed by Consumption," *Dickinson Magazine* (Spring 2002), 22.

18. Robert Massa, "The Fine Art of Admission and Enrollment," *Dickinson Magazine,* 78 (Spring 2001), 3.

19. In 2002, the college added an interdisciplinary major in archaeology. Since the keystone of the major is participation in the archaeological dig at Mycenae, instruction in modern Greek was added to the curriculum.

20. William Durden, "Gained in Translation: Leadership, Voice, and the Study of Foreign Languages," in Linda Wallinger, ed., *Teaching in Changing Times: The Courage to Lead* (Columbus, Ohio: McGraw-Hill, 2002), p. 155.

21. William Durden, "Distinctively Dickinson" (unpublished ms., 2002). On Benjamin Rush and Dickinson College, see, generally, Arthur Herman, *How the Scots Invented the Modern World* (New York: Crown Business, 2001). In a protracted on-line debate over what college deserves to call itself the first post-revolutionary college, Durden writes that "Dickinson's 1773 founding date was actually creatively introduced in the early 1940s (before that it had always been 1783). It was introduced by a trustee who was angry at the University of Pennsylvania for changing its founding date shortly before that because Penn found a grammar school existing on the same site that was begun years before its official date." February 7, 2002, *http://www.dickinson.edu/news/first/ debate.html.*

22. Massa, "Fine Art," p. 30.

23. The ethical problems associated with this strategic approach to financial aid are discussed in Chapter 1.

24. By way of contrast with some comparable colleges, the rate of alumni giving at Bowdoin is 59 percent; Colby, 51 percent; Bucknell, 40 percent; Franklin and Marshall, 40 percent; Gettysburg, 41 percent; Hamilton, 60 percent; and Hobart and William Smith, 37 percent. E-mail from Jennifer Barendse, November 18, 2002.

25. American Association of Fundraising Counsel Trust for Philanthropy, *Giving USA*," 2002, *http://www.aafrc.org*.

26. The relationship with the Redskins was terminated in November 2002. A college press release quoted Durden as saying, "Although we enjoyed having the team on campus, there were difficulties dealing with the management which were not resolved." Robert Massa explained in a subsequent e-mail message: "The college barely covered its costs with this relationship, but the community will lose, which is why we tried to put together a financial package to improve our fields for the Redskins with government help—they were obviously not impressed."

27. Some alumni agree. On a Dickinson College website, one writes: "Get rid of that ridiculous new college logo. I hope the College didn't actually pay some consultant to develop the logo. The whole idea of relegating the official college seal to the wastebasket of 'official uses only' smacks of the efforts of corporate image makers following a merger or acquisition. The new logo is really quite embarrassing to many alumni. Has Dickinson been 'taken over' by the boys from Johns Hopkins??"

4. Star Wars

1. This chapter draws on interviews, conducted in person and by telephone, and e-mail correspondence with trustees, administrators, professors, and students, as well as with others knowledgeable about the institution. Quotations for which no citation is provided are taken from these sources.

2. For-profit institutions like the University of Phoenix might dispute this conclusion.

3. As a result of rent expansion, 11,000 of NYU's 36,000 students choose to live in university housing.

4. President John Sexton describes NYU's strategy as consistent with what he calls a "New York attitude." It's "a venture capital attitude. . . . It's in the spirit of New York never to be satisfied. You're always looking for something better, and you never quite get the perfect dream that enticed you in the first place, but you can be part of this slow, constant improvement."

5. Quoted in Karen Arenson, "N.Y.U. Gets $150 Million Gift to Help Draw Top Professors," *New York Times*, February 5, 2002, p. 4.

6. John Brubacher and Willis Rudy, *Higher Education in Transition* (New

York: Harper and Row, 1976), pp. 184–185. See, generally, Dorothy Ross, *Stanley Hall: The Psychologist as Prophet* (Chicago: University of Chicago Press, 1972).

7. Christopher Jencks and David Riesman, *The Academic Revolution* (New Brunswick, N.J.: Transaction Books, 2002).
8. U.S. Department of Education, National Center for Education Statistics, Integrated Postsecondary Education Data System, "Salaries, Tenure, and Fringe Benefits of Full-Time Instructional Faculty Survey" (IPEDS-SA), selected years, *http://nces.ed.gov/programs/coe/2000/charts/chart55.asp?popup=true;* Carla Reichard, "Trends in Faculty Salary by Discipline: A Quarter-Century of Data from the OSU Faculty Salary Survey" (unpublished paper, November 2002). Bryan Chan reviewed the NCES data.
9. Sylvia Nasar, "New Breed of College All-Star: Columbia Pays Top Dollar for Economics Heavy Hitter," *New York Times,* April 8, 1998, p. D1. Columbia has since been more successful in recruiting world-renowned economists, attracting Jeffrey Sachs and Joseph Stiglitz.
10. For a skeptical appraisal, see David Kirp, "A City of Learning," *University Business* (February 2001), *www.chet.org.za/issues/DavidKirp1.doc.*
11. William Horne, "The Packaging of George Mason University," *University Business* (March–April 1998), 25–32.
12. Arenson, "N.Y.U. Gets $150 Million."
13. Leslie Berger, "The Rise of the Perma-Temp," *New York Times,* August 4, 2002, "Education Life" sec., p. 20.
14. Scott Walden himself is an exception to that proposition. A fine arts photographer, he appreciates the flexibility of the adjunct's lifestyle. "As adjunct life goes, I am probably one of the happiest on the planet," he says.
15. Mary Poovey, "Interdisciplinarity at New York University," in Joan W. Scott and Debra Keates, eds., *Schools of Thought: Twenty-Five Years of Interpretive Social Science* (Princeton: Princeton University Press, 2001), p. 290.
16. "Given our small size and our material limitations," Hook added, "and the fact that we never were at the center of the University administration in a way in which the Philosophy Department was at Columbia, we can be proud of our achievement." Milton Munitz, "History of the Department of Philosophy: A Free-Floating Recollection by Sidney Hook" (1971), "Sidney Hook—Interviews/Oral Histories," NYU archives.
17. Thomas Frusciano and Marilyn Petit, *New York University and the City* (New Brunswick, N.J.: Rutgers University Press, 1997), p. 237.
18. Ibid., pp. 238–239.
19. Ibid., p. 243.
20. William Honan, "A Decade and a Billion Dollars Put New York U. in First Rank," *New York Times,* March 25, 1995, p. 1; John Brooks, "The Marts of Trade: The Law School and the Noodle Factory," *New Yorker,* December 26, 1977, pp. 48–53.
21. Before coming to New York, Brademas had represented Indiana's Third District in Congress from 1959 to 1981.

22. John Brademas, "A Vital Philanthropy for the New Century: The Arts, The Humanities, Democracy, and Education," *HSBC Private Banking and Investments Philanthropy Forum, 1999, http://us.hsbc.com/privatebanking/wealth/pb_brademas.asp.*

23. Frusciano and Petit, *New York University and the City,* p. 254.

24. Honan, "A Decade and a Billion Dollars." See also Kenneth Weiss, "NYU Earns Respect by Buying It," *Los Angeles Times,* March 22, 2000, p. 1, *http://www.nyu.edu/financial.aid/latimesMar2000.pdf.* This change also has its critics. Andrew Ross, chair of the American Studies department, notes that "NYU is less accountable to the community on its doorstep." No longer is it "in the city and of the city."

25. Frusciano and Petit, *New York University and the City,* p. 254.

26. "At North Carolina, like many universities with national reputations, there are first-rate and second-rate departments," says Craig Calhoun, recruited to NYU from the University of North Carolina. "NYU has first-rate, second-rate, and also fourth-rate departments."

27. Poovey, "Interdisciplinarity," pp. 290–291.

28. Ibid., p. 301.

29. NYU's centers include the Neural Science Center, the Remarque Institute, the Institute for the History of the Production of Knowledge, and the Center for Media, Culture, and History.

30. Ian Blecher, "How Cult Internet Character Mr. Perestroika Divided N.Y.U.'s Political Science Department," *New York Observer,* January 7, 2002, p. 3.

31. See Sidney Hook, *Out of Step: An Unquiet Life in the Twentieth Century* (New York: Harper & Row, 1987).

32. Ibid., p. 527.

33. James Rachels recalls Hook's department as less self-consciously pluralist. "Rather than saying that Sidney strived after diversity, I'd say he assembled the faculty pretty randomly, and it was the collection of odds and ends that you might expect if there was no particular plan."

34. Hook's response to a question by Milton Munitz in "History of the Department." See also John McCumber, *Time in the Ditch: American Philosophy and the McCarthy Era* (Chicago: Northwestern Press, 2001); Ellen Schrecker, *No Ivory Tower* (New York: Oxford University Press, 1986).

35. Thomas Nagel, *The Possibility of Altruism* (New York: Oxford University Press, 1970), and *What Does It All Mean?* (New York: Oxford University Press, 1976). Nagel's other books include *Mortal Questions* (New York: Cambridge University Press, 1979), *Equality and Partiality* (New York: Oxford University Press, 1991), and *The Last Word* (New York: Oxford University Press, 1997).

36. The quotation comes from an interview with Steven Schiffer, one of Boghossian's first recruits.

37. David Edmonds and John Eidinow, *Wittgenstein's Poker: The Story of a Ten-Minute Argument between Two Great Philosophers* (San Francisco: Harper-Collins, 2001).

38. Richard Rorty, "Analytic Philosophy and Transformative Philosophy," *www.standord.edu/~rrorty*.

39. See Paul A. Boghossian, "What the Sokal Hoax Ought to Teach Us: The Pernicious Consequences and Internal Contradictions of 'Postmodernist' Relativism," *Times Literary Supplement*, December 13, 1996, pp. 14–15.

40. The letter appears in *Lingua Franca* (July–August 1996), *http://www.physics.nyu.edu/faculty/sokal/mstsokal.html*. The incompetence of the *Social Text* editors, Boghossian wrote in his *TLS* piece, could only be explained historically as part of an insidious trend within academe. "The complete historical answer is a long story, but there can be little doubt that one of its crucial components is the brush-fire spread, within vast sectors of the humanities and social sciences, of the cluster of simple-minded relativistic views about truth and evidence that are commonly identified as 'postmodernist.' These views license, and on the most popular versions insist upon, the substitution of political and ideological criteria for the historically more familiar assessment in terms of truth, evidence and argument" ("Sokal Hoax," p. 14).

41. Boghossian, "Sokal Hoax," p. 15.

42. Also at the law school are philosophers Liam Murphy, David Richards, and Lawrence Sager.

43. Richard A. Posner, *Public Intellectuals: A Study of Decline* (Cambridge, Mass.: Harvard University Press, 2001), p. 320.

44. Among Dworkin's books are *Taking Rights Seriously* (Cambridge, Mass.: Harvard University Press, 1977), *A Matter of Principle* (Cambridge, Mass.: Harvard University Press, 1985), *Law's Empire* (Cambridge, Mass.: Harvard University Press, 1986), *Life's Dominion* (New York: Knopf, 1993), and *Freedom's Law* (Cambridge, Mass.: Harvard University Press, 1996).

45. Ronald Dworkin, "Philosophy and Monica Lewinsky," *New York Review of Books*, March 9, 2000, *www.nybooks.com/articles/187*.

46. Nagel, unlike his colleagues, was not available for interviews about NYU.

47. "It is evident," longtime NYU Law School professor Norman Dorsen told a law school audience in 1990, "that John's extraordinary energy is matched by his limitless ambition for the Law School." See Norman Dorsen, "How NYU Became a Major Law School," *NYU Law Magazine* (Fall 1991), 10.

48. James Traub, "John Sexton Pleads (and Pleads and Pleads) His Case," *New York Times Magazine*, May 25, 1997, 27.

49. Steven Englund, "John Sexton: Seizing the Mile," in *Lifestyles* (Pre-spring 1999), 17.

50. Ibid., p. 10.

51. Quoted ibid., p. 6.

52. One candidate for a junior position at Harvard Law School recalls her interview with the dean. "Consider me as your rich, rich, rich uncle," he told her.

53. Sexton has promoted such synergistic exchange by crafting joint faculty appointments with other NYU schools. In addition to Holmes, he helped bring the influential psychologist Carol Gilligan, the author of *In A Different Voice*,

whose research on gender and human development has dramatically affected multiple fields, to NYU from Harvard.

54. "A spokesman for NYU, John Beckman, responded that only a small percentage of teaching was done by adjuncts within the arts and sciences, and that most adjuncts—about 1,900—are in specialized schools [like the Tisch School of the Arts, the Steinhart School of Education, and the School of Continuing and Professional Studies]." Berger, "Rise of the Perma-Temp," p. 21. Tellingly, more than one of the adjuncts with whom we spoke requested anonymity.

55. Ibid., p. 22.

56. Cary Nelson and Stephen Watt, *Academic Keywords: A Devil's Dictionary for Higher Education* (New York: Routledge, 1999).

57. American Federation of Teachers, "Marching toward Equity" (1998); Berger, "Rise of the Perma-Temp," p. 20.

58. Quoted in Mary Beth Marklein, "NYU Part-Time Faculty Vote on Forming Union," *USA Today,* July 19, 2002, p. 8D. The education department salary is for the 2000 fiscal year. See *http://www.adjunctnation.com/news/advocate/may.02/deskdrawer3.php3.*

59. Berger, "Rise of the Perma-Temp," p. 21.

60. Ibid., p. 22.

61. Faculty did hold "town hall debates" during the process of graduate student unionization at NYU.

62. Quoted in Marklein, "NYU Part-Time Faculty," p. 8D.

63. High-profile professors such as Andrew Ross and Tony Judt, director of NYU's Remarque Institute, went head-to-head in on-line discussions that were subsequently widely circulated (segments ended up in the pages of *Lingua Franca*). Ross joined a number of his NYU colleagues in asking the administration, in an open letter circulated by sociology professor Jeffrey Goodwin, to "reconsider its firm adoption of an anti-union position. Furthermore, we call upon the NYU administration to open the widest possible dialogue with faculty and refrain from making any additional, unilateral decisions"; see *http://www.nyu.edu/gsas/dept/journal/union/index.htm.* The case of Joel Westheimer, an NYU faculty member denied tenure after he supported the graduate students' right to unionize, is another interesting chapter in this story. The federal government issued formal charges against NYU, accusing the university of illegally firing Westheimer in retaliation for his testimony in support of the students before the NLRB. In May 2002, the university agreed to a financial settlement and retracted its tenure denial. For more details, see *http://www.eisner-hubbard.com/westheimer.*

64. Union elections have been held at Brown and Columbia, and union organizing is under way at other schools, including Harvard. Yale graduate students continue their struggle for union recognition. They went on strike again in the spring of 2003, together with janitors, secretaries, and dining hall workers. Graduate student unions are now active at more than sixty universities. Steven Greenhouse, "Yale's Labor Troubles Deepen as Thousands Go on Strike," *New York Times,* March 4, 2003, p. A29.

65. Hal Cohen, "Losing Their Faculties," *Village Voice,* September 12–18, 2001, *http://www.villagevoice.com/issues/0137/cohen.php.*

66. Karen Arenson, "Found: Alumni That Time Forgot," *New York Times,* November 16, 2002, p. A14. NYU's rate of alumni giving—just 16 percent, less than half that of peer institutions—reflects this neglect. Focusing on alumni gave Sexton a potential new source of revenue for the university.

5. The Dead Hand of Precedent

1. This chapter draws on interviews, conducted in person and by telephone, and e-mail correspondence with trustees, administrators, professors, and students, as well as with others knowledgeable about the institution. Quotations for which no citation is provided are taken from these sources.

2. See generally *New York Law School in Brief,* special edition (Fall–Winter 2001).

3. Quoted in Deborah Rhode, *In the Interests of Justice: Reforming the Legal Profession* (New York: Oxford University Press, 2000), p. 196.

4. William Twining, "Pericles and the Plumber," *Law Quarterly Review,* 83 (1967), 396–416. The call for diversity is an ancient one. See *Training for the Public Profession of Law* (New York: Carnegie Foundation, 1921).

5. Rhode, *In the Interests,* p. 185. On the state of American legal education, see, generally, W. Scott Van Alstyne Jr., Joseph Julin, and Larry Barnett, *The Goals and Mission of Law Schools* (New York: Peter Lang, 1990); Robert Granfield, *Making Elite Lawyers: Visions of Law at Harvard and Beyond* (New York: Routledge, 1992); David Margolick, "The Trouble with American Law Schools," *New York Times Sunday Magazine,* May 22, 1983, p. 21; David Kirp, "The Writer as Lawyer as Writer," *Journal of Legal Education,* 22 (1969), 115–123.

6. Rhode, *In the Interests,* p. 189.

7. The fact that Concord Law School is a unit of Kaplan, the for-profit education company (which in turn is owned by the Washington Post Company), is doubtless another reason for the ABA's antagonism.

8. Rhode, *In the Interests,* p. 187.

9. Richard Matasar, "A Commercialist Manifesto: Entrepreneurs, Academics, and Purity of the Heart and Soul," *Florida Law Review,* 48 (1996), 805.

10. Richard Matasar, "Perspectives on the Accreditation Process: Views from a Nontraditional School," *Journal of Legal Education,* 45 (1995), 140.

11. "Translation" is also how William Durden, at Dickinson College, describes his role. See Chapter 3.

6. Kafka Was an Optimist

1. Michael Cohen and James March, *Leadership and Ambiguity: The American College President* (New York: McGraw-Hill, 1974). This chapter draws on in-

terviews, conducted in person and by telephone, and e-mail correspondence with trustees, administrators, professors, and students, as well as with others knowledgeable about the institutions. Quotations for which no citation is provided are taken from these sources.

2. Jane Smiley, *Moo* (New York: Knopf, 1995), p. 158.

3. Robert Birnbaum, *Management Fads in Higher Education* (San Francisco: Jossey-Bass, 2000). See Robert Allen, "Why Can't Universities Be More Like Businesses?" *Chronicle of Higher Education*, July 21, 2000, p. B4. See also Patricia Gumport, "Academic Restructuring: Organizational and Institutional Imperatives," *Higher Education: The International Journal of Higher Education and Educational Planning*, 39 (2000), 67–91.

4. Birnbaum, *Management Fads*, p. 147.

5. F. M. Cornford, *Microcosmograph Academica, Being a Guide for the Young Academic Politician* (Cambridge: Metcalfe and Co., 1908), p. 33.

6. Henry Mintzberg, *The Rise and Fall of Strategic Planning* (New York: Free Press, 1994), p. 13.

7. Morris Cooke, *Academic and Industrial Efficiency* (New York: Merrymount Press, 1910), p. 6.

8. Thorstein Veblen, *The Higher Learning in America* (New York: Sagamore Press, 1957), p. 27. For a contemporary treatment of this issue, see Patricia Gumport, "Public Universities as Academic Workplaces," *Daedalus*, 126 (Fall 1997), 113–136.

9. Marvin Lazerson, Ursula Wagener, and Larry Moneta, "Like the Cities They Increasingly Resemble, Colleges Must Train and Retain Competent Managers," *Chronicle of Higher Education*, July 28, 2000, p. A72.

10. Robert M. Hutchins, *The Higher Learning in America* (New Haven: Yale University Press, 1936), *http://www.realuofc.org/libed/hutchins/hutch3.html*.

11. Michael Corbett and Associates, "The 2001 Outsourcing World Summit" (unpublished paper, 2001); Dun and Bradstreet, *Barometer of Global Outsourcing* (New York: Dun and Bradstreet, 2001).

12. See *http://nacasportal.meisoft.com/outsidelibrary/*; see also Patricia Wood, "Outsourcing in Higher Education," Eric-HE Digest Series Edo-he-2000–8, George Washington University and Department of Education, 2000; Rebecca Sausner, "Building Out of the Crunch," *University Business* (February 2002), 35–38.

13. On outsourcing by private firms, see David Collis, *The Paradox of Scope: A Challenge to the Governance of Higher Education* (Washington, D.C.: Center for Higher Education Policy Analysis, 2002), *http://www.usc.edu/dept/chepa/gov/roundtable_collis.htm*; C. K. Prahalad and Gary Hamel "The Core Competence of the Corporation," *Harvard Business Review*, 64 (1990), 74–91; Jay Barney, "Strategic Factor Markets: Expectations, Luck, and Business Strategy," *Management Science*, 31 (1986), 1231–41; Gary Pisano, "Merck's R&D Strategy," Harvard Business School Case 9–601–086, February 27, 2001. Collis, *Paradox of Scope*, cautions that outsourcing is no panacea in the private

sector: "When a company outsources an activity, it cannot abdicate responsibility for the performance of that activity. The customer still holds Dell [Computer Co.] accountable for the activities that come bundled with the product. Dell, therefore, has to structure and manage its relationship with its third party vendor of services as carefully as if it operated that activity itself. Outsourcing merely substitutes one managerial headache—managing a workforce[—]for another administrative concern—managing an arm's-length relationship with a third party. Contracts alone cannot manage the relationship, and so the firm has to learn new skills and acquire new capabilities to function adequately with these new organizational arrangements." On reinventing government, see David Osborne and Ted Gaelder, *Reinventing Government* (Reading, Mass.: Addison-Wesley, 1992).

14. Martin van der Werf, "How the U of Penn Learned That Outsourcing Is No Panacea," *Chronicle of Higher Education,* April 7, 2000, p. A38; Lynn Love, "Just What the Doctor Ordered," *University Business* (May 1999), 25–29.

15. Carnegie Commission, *Governance of Higher Education: Six Priority Problems* (New York: McGraw-Hill, 1973).

16. The data and horror tales are collected in Cary Nelson and Stephen Watt, *Academic Keywords: A Devil's Dictionary for Higher Education* (New York: Routledge, 1999), pp. 197–211.

17. Pamela Bach, "Part-Time Faculty Are Here to Stay," *Planning for Higher Education,* 27 (Spring 1999), 32–41; James Shulman and William Bowen, *The Game of Life: College Sports and Academic Values* (Princeton: Princeton University Press, 2002).

18. J. Anthony West et al., "RCM as a Catalyst," *Business Officer* (August 1997), 22.

19. In the late 1960s, Harvard's Board of Overseers voted to permit the impoverished graduate school of education to borrow from the business school's dormitory furniture replacement fund—at market interest rates.

20. The bible in the field is Edward Whalen, *Responsibility Center Budgeting* (Bloomington: Indiana University Press, 1991). Since Whalen was responsible for implementing RCM at Indiana, his is not meant as an objective account, nor does it provide any research to back its claims. Most of the critical literature is similarly devoid of empirical evidence. See, e.g., E. M. Adams, "Rationality in the Academy," *Change,* 29 (September–October 1997), 59–63; Leroy Dubeck, "Beware Higher Ed's Newest Budget Twist," *NEA Higher Education Journal* (Spring 1997), 81–91.

21. See, generally, Richard Titmuss, *The Gift Relationship* (London: Allen & Unwin, 1971).

22. The discussion in this section draws on interviews with present and former USC administrators and faculty, and with others knowledgeable about RCM.

23. These examples are drawn from both interviews and Jon Strauss and John Curry, *Responsibility Center Management: Lessons from Twenty-five Years of Decentralized Management* (Washington, D.C.: NABUCO, 2002), p. 18. This

pamphlet offers a generally nuanced description of RCM. What happened at USC and the University of Michigan, though, diverges significantly from that description.

24. Information drawn from *http://www.usc.edu/dept/CCR/theme/1.html* and interviews with USC officials.

25. Manuel Servin and Iris Wilson, *Southern California and Its University: A History of USC, 1880–1964* (Los Angeles: Ward Ritchie Press, 1969). The jibe is still in use, especially at cross-town rival UCLA.

26. USC University Park Community History Stations, *http://www.usc.edu/dept/CCR/theme/19.html*.

27. Strauss and Curry, *Responsibility*, pp. 2, 15.

28. Birnbaum, *Management Fads*, p. 194.

29. Ibid., p. 3.

30. Quoted in Wellford Wilms, Cheryl Teruya, and Mary Beth Walpole, "Fiscal Reform at UCLA," *Change*, 29 (September–October 1997), 43.

31. The phrase comes from *The Picture of Dorian Gray*, chap. 4.

32. Strauss and Curry, *Responsibility*, pp. 23–24.

33. A comment made by a dean at the University of Pennsylvania, which also lived by RCM rules, shows where such an attitude can lead. "The best way to balance his budget [the dean said] would be for him to stand on the steps of the library and prevent his students and faculty from entering and thus incurring user-based charges." Ibid., p. 27.

34. USC University Park Community History Stations, *http://www.usc.edu/dept/CCR/theme/17.html*.

35. Strauss and Curry, *Responsibility*, p. 24.

36. In October 2002, USC announced a campaign to hire 100 "world class" senior faculty for the liberal arts college, increasing its size by 25 percent. Piper Fogg, "U. of Southern California Will Add 100 to Its Faculty," *Chronicle of Higher Education*, October 4, 2002, p. A16.

37. The same criticism of RCM has been made of Harvard's venerable "each tub on its own bottom" approach. Nannerl Keohane, president of Duke, notes that "having each tub on its own bottom . . . may not be an advantage when the whole enterprise needs to head briskly in some direction." Nannerl Keohane, "Becoming Nimble, Overcoming Inertia," *Harvard Magazine* (January–February 2001), *http://www.harvard-magazine.com/archive/01jf/jf01_feat_future.html#becom*.

38. Strauss and Curry, *Responsibility*, p. 19, and USC interviews. Sample's action is the kind of exercise of authority praised by Henry Rosovsky, *The University: An Owner's Manual* (Cambridge, Mass.: Harvard University Press, 1991), pp. 277–282. See also Ronald Ehrenberg, "In Pursuit of University-wide Objectives," *Change*, 31 (January–February 1999), 29–31.

39. This section relies in considerable part on telephone and e-mail interviews and with administrators and faculty members.

40. Gumport, "Academic Restructuring," p. 74.

41. Howard Peckham, *History of the University of Michigan* (Ann Arbor: University of Michigan Press, 1997).

42. John Brubacher and Willis Rudy, *Higher Education in Transition* (New York: Harper and Row 1976), p. 109, paraphrasing Andrew White, *Autobiography* (Englewood Cliffs, N.J.: Prentice-Hall, 1905), vol. 1, pp. 291–292.

43. James Angell, *Reminiscences* (New York: McKay, 1912), p. 128.

44. On the increasing role of the state, see, generally, Patricia Gumport and Brian Pusser, "University Restructuring: The Role of Economic and Political Contexts," in John Smart and William Tierney, eds., *Higher Education: Handbook of Theory and Research* (New York: Algathon, 1999), 14:146–199.

45. James Duderstadt, *A University for the Twenty-first Century* (Ann Arbor: University of Michigan Press, 2000).

46. Whalen, *Responsibility Center Budgeting,* pp. 93–94. "Some academic administrators are even more reluctant to have faculty inside the [arena of decision making] than they have been about trustee decision-making. They worry that when provided with information, faculty will be primarily concerned with their own ends." Marvin Lazerson, "Who Owns Higher Education? The Changing Face of Governance," *Change,* 29 (March–April 1997), 14.

47. John Cross, "A Brief Review of 'Responsibility Center Management'" (unpublished ms., October 18, 1996), citing Jack Hirshleifer, "On the Economics of Transfer Pricing," *Journal of Business* (July 1956), 172–184, and "Economics of the Divisionalized Firm," *Journal of Business* (April 1957), 96–108.

48. Nancy Cantor and Paul Courant, "Budgets and Budgeting at the University of Michigan: A Work in Progress," *University Record,* November 26, 1997, *http://www.umich.edu/~urecord/9798/Nov26_97/budget.htm.*

49. "Scrounge We Must: Reflections on the Whys and Wherefores of Higher Education Finance," paper prepared for CHERI Conference on Higher Education Finance, Cornell University, May 21, 2001, *http://www.ilr.cornell.edu/cheri/conf/chericonf2001/chericonf2001_10.pdf.*

50. See, e.g., Tony Davies and Brian Paine, *Business Accounting and Finance* (London: McGraw-Hill, 2002).

7. Mr. Jefferson's "Private" College

1. This chapter draws on interviews, conducted in person and by telephone, and e-mail correspondence with trustees, administrators, professors, and students, as well as with others knowledgeable about the institution. Quotations for which no citation is provided are taken from these sources.

2. For Jefferson, form *did* follow function. The alternative to the "academical village" was "a larger and common den of noise, of filth and of fetid air." Thomas Jefferson to Hugh L. White and others, May 6, 1810, in *The Writings of Thomas Jefferson,* ed. H. A. Washington, vol. 5 (New York: Derby & Jackson, 1859), p. 521.

3. The "Memorandum of Understanding" between the Darden School and the university specifies that although Darden has more managerial flexibility than

other units of the university, its personnel policies are still subject to review by the central university. But the key difference between Darden and the other schools is that Darden can set its salaries according to "peer group market levels" rather than according to salaries in other units of the university. According to the memorandum, "the University will make every effort to provide to Darden the addition of a reasonable number of state educational and general FTEs [full-time-equivalent faculty positions], consistent with growth in Darden's budget. However, for as long as the University remains subject to a Maximum Employment Level imposed by the Commonwealth of Virginia, the University's approval of increased state FTE levels remains contingent upon the Commonwealth's approval of increases to the University's overall Maximum Employment Level. . . . The University will provide the Darden School appropriate managerial flexibility to set, subject to review by the Provost (for faculty compensation) or University Human Resources (for staff compensation) and consistent with University and Commonwealth of Virginia policies, faculty salaries and bonuses and the classification and salaries of critical administrative, professional, and technical staff positions in accordance with peer group market levels." Edward A. Snyder, Leonard W. Sandridge, and Peter W. Low, "Memorandum of Understanding," June 18, 2001.

4. See David Breneman, "The 'Privatization' of Public Universities: Mistake or Model?" *Chronicle of Higher Education,* March 7, 1997, p. B4.

5. Mark Yudof, "Is the Public Research University Dead?" *Chronicle of Higher Education,* January 11, 2002, p. B24; Jeffrey Selingo, "The Disappearing State in Higher Education," *Chronicle of Higher Education,* February 28, 2003, p. A22.

6. Yudof, "Public Research University," p. B24. See generally David Breneman and Joni Finney, "The Changing Landscape: Higher Education Finance in the 1990s," in Patrick Callan and Joni Finney, eds., *Public and Private Financing of Higher Education* (Washington, D.C.: Oryx Press and American Council on Education, 1997), pp. 30–59.

7. See Ronald Ehrenberg, *Tuition Rising: Why College Costs So Much* (Cambridge, Mass.: Harvard University Press, 2000); Thomas Kane, *The Price of Admission: Rethinking How Americans Pay for College* (Washington, D.C.: Brookings Institution Press, 1999). Federal legislation that would penalize public universities that raise tuition has been proposed. Greg Winter, "Lawmaker Proposes a Measure to Restrain Tuition Increases," *New York Times,* March 7, 2003, p. A18.

8. See James Engell and Anthony Dangerfield, "The Market-Model University: Humanities in the Age of Money," *Harvard Magazine* (May–June 1998), 49–55; James Engell and Anthony Dangerfield, "Higher Education in the Age of Money" (unpublished ms., 2002).

9. See generally C. Stewart Sheppard, ed., *The First Twenty Years: The Darden School at Virginia* (Charlottesville, Va.: Colgate Darden Graduate Business School, 1975), p. 6.

10. Thomas Jefferson to Joseph C. Cabell, January 22, 1820, in *The Works of*

Thomas Jefferson, ed. Paul Leicester Ford (New York: G. P. Putnam's Sons, 1899), vol. 10, p. 154.

11. "Over time, the *Business Week* poll has emerged as the leading arbiter of business school rankings. . . . When a school moves significantly upward or downward in the *Business Week* rankings, there ensues a large and almost immediate swing in its number of applications, and ten months later, a corresponding swing in the quality of its entering class. Since business school budgets are driven largely by student tuition payments, the *Business Week* rankings have become very important. So important, in fact, that schools have begun to alter their behavior in an effort to achieve higher scores. . . . Professors experience increased pressure not to give poor grades or take other steps that might make students unhappy, lest their angry comments cost the school points in the *Business Week* poll. After having received harsh comments from its graduating class in one *Business Week* survey, a leading school was said to have written a letter to its next *Business Week* class pointing out to them that their evaluations would have direct repercussions on the economic value of their degrees." Robert Frank, "Higher Education: The Ultimate Winner-Take-All Market?" in Maureen Devlin and Joel Meyerson, eds., *Forum Futures: Exploring the Future of Higher Education, 2000 Papers* (San Francisco: Jossey-Bass, 2001), pp. 3–4.

12. "1% Decline in State Support for Colleges Thought to Be First 2-Year Drop Ever," *Chronicle of Higher Education*, October 21, 1992, p. A21.

13. The committee proposed that select colleges and universities—those that could compete in a national market—"might become quasi-public entities that are responsible for all of their own operational processes." Commission on the Future of Higher Education in Virginia, "Making Connections: Matching Virginia Higher Education's Strengths with the Commonwealth's Needs," 1996, pp. 1, 25.

14. Board members' populist impulses can clash with the desire for autonomy. One member of the Board of Visitors has argued that the professional schools should lower their admission standards in order to attract students willing to take jobs in rural Virginia, where starting salaries are well below those to which Darden graduates aspire.

15. Amy Argetsinger, "Donors Tipping Scales at U-VA," *Washington Post*, May 28, 2003, B-1. By what's termed a "gentlemen's agreement," 30 percent of Darden's entering class are Virginia residents. Those students pay $5,000 less than out-of-state students, and the state makes up half the difference. The state will also continue to contribute over half a million dollars annually in matching grants for "eminent scholars." And, of course, the state owns the buildings and the land Darden sits on, even though these buildings were paid for with private funds. In addition, the executive education programs, retooling courses for senior corporate managers, have become increasingly valuable sources of income for business schools and the faculty who teach them. In a good year at Darden, the revenue for executive education can be greater than revenue from M.B.A. tuition.

16. Under the agreement, Darden pays for all of its maintenance and construction costs, which amounted to $828,000 in the year before self-sufficiency. Over and above covering these direct costs, the 10 percent tax is "a contribution towards the indirect cost of operating the Darden School incurred by the University." Snyder, Sandridge, and Low, "Memorandum of Understanding." Also in Leonard W. Sandridge, "University of Virginia's Responses to Selected Statements in 'Mr. Jefferson's University Breaks Up,'" September 4, 2002 (e-mail).

17. In a letter summarizing the self-sufficiency agreement, Sandridge writes, "Bottom line, UVA receives a greater net tax [from Darden] from state funds, but no tax from private funds." Sandridge, "University of Virginia's Responses."

18. See *http://www.vcdh.virginia.edu/lawn/papers/lisa/gentleman.html*.

19. Over the years, a few professors have taught jointly at both, and the two schools share a technology platform.

20. Leonard Sandridge points out that Leffler's perception that the college could be self-sufficient is not consistent with the formal structure of the university budget, which is limited by the state's cap on tuition rates. Sandridge also notes that development costs and other public goods that benefit the college are subsidized by the rest of the university and by Darden's tax. While Leffler's provocative claim may be in conflict with the text of the self-sufficiency agreement, the perceptions of these actors, not the texts, govern their behavior. In the "Memorandum of Understanding," Sandridge writes: "The College of Arts and Sciences' tuition rates are not intended to provide self-sufficiency for the College, while Darden's tuition is. Undergraduate and graduate students in the College and in the schools of engineering, nursing, architecture, commerce, and education pay essentially the same tuition; yet the costs of these programs vary widely. If the intent were to apply tuition collected from students enrolled in Arts & Sciences to the operations of that school under a responsibility-centered budgeting concept, different tuition rates would need to be calculated reflecting the cost of education in each school. In-state undergraduate tuition rates are limited by the General Assembly—a practice that effectively eliminates the possibility that tuition funds will ever make the College self-sufficient." Sandridge, "University of Virginia's Responses."

21. Stan J. Liebowitz, "The Role of Research in Business School Rankings and Reputation" (unpublished ms., October 11, 2000).

22. Darden is not the only public institution that teaches proprietary materials in courses whose enrollment is restricted to company employees. Michigan Virtual Automotive College creates custom products to suit the needs of the Big Three auto companies. MVAC became "a model for similar institutions . . . : a plastics college, an office-furniture college, a hospitality and tourism college, an aviation college." Scott Berinato, "Big 3 U," *University Business* (September–October 1998), 26.

23. Michael Winerip, "Making the Ask," *New York Times,* August 1, 1999, sec. 4A, p. 22.

24. "Inside UVA Online," March 8–21, 2002, *http://www.virginia.edu/inside*

uva/2002/09/plan.html.; William Johnson, "Lawn of Averages," *Washington Post,* March 9, 2003, p. B4.

25. In the fall of 2001, the university announced that it intends to tear down or renovate the decrepit buildings on the south side of the Lawn, opposite the Rotunda, and construct the $125 million, 285,000-square-foot South Lawn Project, to be completed by 2007.

26. Thomas Jefferson to Joseph Priestly, April 25, 1800, in *The Works of Thomas Jefferson,* ed. Paul Leicester Ford, vol. 7 (New York: G. P. Putnam's Sons, 1896), p. 407. Casteen quotation from e-mail distributed in *UVA Top News Daily, www. virginia.edu/topnews/casteen_cuts.html.*

27. Thomas Jefferson to George Ticknor, November 25, 1817, ibid., vol. 10 (1899), p. 96.

28. Johnson, "Lawn of Averages."

29. Sam Bresnahan, "College Spending Inequities," *Washington Times,* July 28, 2002.

30. Johnson, "Lawn of Averages."

31. Robyn Meredith, "Re-engineer This!" *Forbes Magazine,* December 10, 2001, p. 52.

8. Rebel Alliance

1. This chapter draws on interviews, conducted in person and by telephone, and e-mail correspondence with trustees, administrators, professors, and students, as well as with others knowledgeable about the institution. Quotations for which no citation is provided are taken from these sources.

2. Gary Becker, "How the Web Is Revolutionizing Learning," *Business Week,* December 27, 1999, p. 40.

3. Samuel Dunn quoted in James Traub, "This Campus Is Being Simulated," *New York Times Sunday Magazine,* November 19, 2001.

4. Thomas Friedman, "Next, It's E-ducation," *New York Times,* November 17, 1999, p. A25.

5. Adam Newman, "Venture Dollars Get Smarter," *Eduventures,* November 2000, *www.eduventures.com/research/industry_research_resources/venture_dollars.cfm.*

6. In 2000, an investment banker and a Williams College professor teamed up to create the Global Education Network, which puts the liberal arts—courses on everything from Boccaccio's *Decameron* to AIDS—on-line. By 2003, that much-ballyhooed project still hadn't got off the ground. Traub, "This Campus," p. 90. See also Scott Carlson and Dan Carnevale, "Debating the Demise of NYU 'Online,'" *Chronicle of Higher Education,* December 14, 2001.

7. Phyllis Culham and Lowell Edmunds, eds., *Classics: A Discipline and Profession in Crisis?* (Lanham, Md.: University Press of America, 1989); David Damrosch, "Can Classics Die?" *Lingua Franca* (September–October 1995), 61–66.

8. See Marshall McLuhan, *The Medium Is the Message* (New York: Random House, 1967).

9. See *http://www.perseus.tufts.edu*.

10. Albert Hirschman, "The Hiding Hand," in *Development Projects Observed* (Washington, D.C.: Brookings Institution, 1995), is an ingenious analysis of the surprisingly common "stars aligned" phenomenon.

11. The foundation's role in supporting MIT's OpenCourseWare is detailed in Chapter 9.

12. Geoffrey Maslen, "Rupert Murdoch's Company Joins with Eighteen Universities in Distance-Education Venture," *Chronicle of Higher Education*, May 18, 2001.

13. Frank Newman and Jamie E. Scurry, "Online Learning Pushes Teaching and Learning to the Forefront," *Chronicle of Higher Education*, July 13, 2001, pp. B7–10.

14. Jeffrey Young, "Black Colleges Band Together to Get a Jump on Technology," *Chronicle of Higher Education*, March 26, 1999, p. A31. See also Dan Carnevale, "Community Colleges in Illinois Seek to Share Their Courses Online," *Chronicle of Higher Education*, March 24, 2000, p. A52. Earlier, eleven colleges in North Dakota combined interactive technologies and television to offer joint courses. Beverly Watkins, "Uniting North Dakota," *Chronicle of Higher Education*, August 10, 1994. See also Bryon MacWilliams, "Turkey's Old-Fashioned Distance Education Draws the Largest Student Body on Earth," *Chronicle of Higher Education*, September 22, 2000, p. A41 (the institution, which relies on televised instruction, enrolls over half a million students).

15. The program has addressed the problem of low enrollments by adopting a five-year course sequence, allowing the Sunoikisis professors to look beyond the coming academic year and, it is hoped, enabling them to track greater numbers of students into the Internet-assisted courses.

16. David Noble, *Digital Diploma Mills*, pt. 1, *The Automation of Higher Education* (1997), *http://communication.ucsd.edu/dl/ddm1.html*. Ironically, Noble's critique of Internet-based education was widely read when posted on the Internet.

17. For a general discussion of localism in higher education, see David Riesman and Christopher Jencks, *The Academic Revolution* (New Brunswick, N.J.: Transaction, 2002).

18. Geoffrey Maslen, "Leery About Use of Their Names, Michigan and Toronto Opt Out of Universitas 21," *Chronicle of Higher Education*, May 25, 2001, p. A38.

19. Peter Monahan, "With Archaeology and a New Vision, Macalester Students Dig the Classsics," *Chronicle of Higher Education*, May 25, 2001, p. A41.

20. See *http://www.colleges.org/~alianco*. See also Jeffrey Young, "Moving the Seminar Table to the Computer Screen,'" *Chronicle of Higher Education*, July 7, 2000, p. A11.

9. The Market in Ideas

1. This chapter draws on interviews, conducted in person and by telephone by Anthony S. Chen and David Kirp, and e-mail correspondence with trustees, administrators, professors, and students, as well as with others knowledgeable about the institution. Quotations for which no citation is provided are taken from these sources. At Columbia, Jonathan Cole, Michael Crow, and Ann Kirschner were especially generous with their time, submitting to three interviews over an interval of three years. Anthony S. Chen, assistant professor in the sociology department and the Ford School of Public Policy at the University of Michigan, provided invaluable assistance, conducting interviews and doing archival research for the Columbia and MIT cases and helping me think through the implications of those cases.

2. In October 2000, Miller reluctantly gave up his Concord course. Six months earlier, a Harvard committee had advanced a proposal forbidding faculty to teach, conduct research, or provide consulting outside of Harvard, either in person or on-line, without permission from the appropriate dean. An Associated Press wire story quoted Miller as saying, "Now I have to justify everything I do. . . . I find it offensive I now have to go through a process I haven't had to go through in 35 years." *http://www.jurist.law.pitt.edu/colloq6.htm*. The policy, Miller said in an earlier interview, offended the principle of academic freedom: "The question is whether my contract binds me exclusively to Harvard Law School, or whether I have free choice." When an upstart company adopted the name NotHarvard.com, Harvard University sued, complaining that the name gave Harvard a "consumerish image." NotHarvard changed its name. Andrea Foster, "Hoping to Avoid a Legal Clash, NotHarvard.com Changes Its Name," *Chronicle of Higher Education*, September 20, 2000, *http://chronicle.com/daily/2000/092000092001t.htm*.

3. Dershowitz says he turned down an offer from students to set up a legal advice site, Dersh.com, which they promised would bring in $100 million. Amy Marcus, "Seeing Crimson: Why Harvard Law Wants to Rein in One of Its Star Professors," *Wall Street Journal*, November 22, 1999, p. A1.

4. Michael Lewis, *The New New Thing* (New York: Norton, 1999).

5. See, by David Collis, "New Business Models for Higher Education," in Steven Brint, ed., *The Future of the City of Intellect* (Stanford: Stanford University Press, 2002), pp. 181–202; "When Industries Change: Scenarios for Higher Education," in Joel Meyerson and Maureen Devlin, eds., *Forum Futures* (New Haven: Forum for the Future of Higher Education, 1999), pp. 4–5; "'When Industries Change' Revisited: New Scenarios for Higher Education," in Maureen Devlin and Joel Meyerson, eds., *Forum Futures: Exploring the Future of Higher Education, 2000* (San Francisco: Jossey-Bass, 2000), pp. 20–28; "Storming the Ivory Tower" (Harvard Business School working paper, 2002); and David Collis and Mark Rukstad, "UNext.com: Business Education and eLearning," Harvard Business School Case #701-014, 2001.

6. Collis relies on Clayton Christensen, *The Innovator's Dilemma* (Cambridge,

Mass.: Harvard Business School Press, 1997) for the concept of "disruptive technology."

7. Collis, "Storming the Ivory Tower."

8. *Business Week,* March 10, 1997, p. 127.

9. Educause, *The Virtual University,* report from the joint Educause/IBM roundtable, November 1996, *http://www.educause.edu/nlii/VU.html.*

10. Arthur Levine quoted in Dan Carnevale and Jeffrey Young, "Who Owns On-Line Courses: Colleges and Professors Start to Sort It Out," *Chronicle of Higher Education,* December 11, 1999, p. A45.

11. Arthur Levine, "The Future of Colleges: Nine Inevitable Changes," *Chronicle of Higher Education,* October 27, 2000, p. B10.

12. Daniel McGinn, "Big Men on Campus," *The Standard,* May 20, 2001, *http://www.thestandard.com/article/0,1902,18275-5,00.html.*

13. Eli Noam, "Electronics and the Dim Future of the University," *Bulletin of the American Society for Information Science* (June–July 1996), 6–11.

14. Discussed in Chapter 6.

15. James Duderstadt, "Can Colleges and Universities Survive in the Information Age?" in Richard Katz, ed., *Dancing with the Devil: IT and the New Competition in Higher Education* (San Francisco: Jossey-Bass, 1999), pp. 1–26.

16. Quoted in Eyal Press and Jennifer Washburn, "Digital Diplomas," *Mother Jones* (January–February 2001), 36.

17. David Noble, *Digital Diploma Mills* (New York: Monthly Review Press, 2001), pp. 16–17.

18. Teresa L. Ebert and Mas'ud Zavarzadeh, "E-Education, the Opposite of Equality Internet," *Los Angeles Times,* March 23, 2000, p. 9, *http://www.latimes.com/news/comment/20000323/t000027413.html;* Mark J. Anderson, "Professors Had Better Pay Attention," *Industry Standard,* September 12, 2000, *http://www.thestandard.com/article/0,1902,18250,00.html?body_page= 4;* Sarah Carr, "Faculty Members Are Wary of Distance-Education Venture," *Chronicle of Higher Education,* June 9, 2000, p. A41; Press and Washburn, "Digital Diplomas," p. 34.

19. Noam, "Electronics," p. 9.

20. Collis, "Storming the Ivory Tower." As the era began, one observer predicted that the University of California would "explor[e] its potential role . . . as much for institutional survival as for its reputation as the leading public research university in the country." Martin Trow, "Notes on the Development of Information Technology," *Daedalus,* 126 (Fall 1997), 310.

21. Kenneth Green, "Drawn to the Light, Burned by the Flame? Money, Technology, and Distance Education," *ED Journal,* 11 (May 1997), J8.

22. Interview, November 1999.

23. Jack Wilson, "ELearning, Is It Over?" *http://www.jackwilson.com/eLearning/IsItOver.htm.*

24. On the Dutch tulip bulb craze, see Simon Schama, *The Embarrassment of Riches* (New York: Knopf, 1987).

25. Other schools have successfully developed different niches in the e-learning

universe. Regents College (New York) and Thomas Edison State College (New Jersey), both accredited public institutions in operation since the 1970s, "bundle" on-line courses from other universities with their own on-line offerings to award degrees. North Texas University has adopted the model of patent licenses. The school markets the on-line courses of its faculty; the division of royalties depends on how much the university invested in getting the course on-line. Jeffrey Young, "At One University, Royalties Entice Professors to Design Web Courses," *Chronicle of Higher Education,* March 30, 2001, p. A41. Carnegie Mellon University develops high-end courses in the specific areas of its expertise: some of these courses are sold by a for-profit company; others, such as a logic course, which lack money-making potential have been subsidized by the Hewlett Foundation. The university invests considerable resources in developing its courses and studying their efficacy, paying specific attention to the performance of minority students.

26. Edwin Slosson, *Great American Universities* (New York: Macmillan, 1910), p. 410. Other times, other perceptions: a later commentator noted that "Columbia makes no effort to seduce the eye; outwardly its ugliness is sententious, within it is brisk and businesslike." Lloyd Morris, *A Threshold in the Sun* (New York: Harper and Bros, 1945), p. 30. See also Horace Coon, *Columbia: Colossus on the Hudson* (New York: Dutton, 1947). Barnard professor Robert McCaughey has prepared a new history of the university, timed for its 250 year anniversary in 2004.

27. The incident is recounted by Robert McCaughey (unpublished ms., 2002).

28. See *http://www.nyu.edu/transition.team/sextonpr.html.* NYU's endowment, $1.1 billion in 2002, is about a third as large as Columbia's and one-seventeenth the size of Harvard's.

29. Chapter 11 discusses technology transfer programs in the context of Berkeley's Gigascale Center and Novartis projects.

30. Goldie Blumenstyk, "Knowledge Is 'a Form of Venture Capital' for a Top Columbia Administrator," *Chronicle of Higher Education,* February 9, 2001, p. A29. Michael Crow notes that Stanford and MIT are much more inclined to encourage faculty members to start their own companies, sometimes taking an equity position.

31. Slosson, *Great American Universities,* p. 72.

32. The discussion of correspondence schools is drawn from Noble, *Digital Diploma Mills.*

33. When Ron Taylor, chief operating officer at DeVry University, a for-profit institution, asked the dean of Stanford's business school why that institution would lend its name to Cardean/Unext, the dean began by noting the faculty's interest in experimenting with on-line education. "Then," says Taylor, "he smiled: 'It's really all about money.'" See Chapter 13.

34. The professional schools made the same argument that the Darden School made at the University of Virginia: we need every cent we generate to compete with much richer schools like Harvard. See Chapter 7.

35. As is discussed in Chapter 11, Crow disagrees with the way the Berkeley-Novartis deal was structured, in part because it could stifle research.

36. Blumenstyk, "Knowledge." A similar fight was waged with the dean of the liberal arts college over the terms of a deal he struck with another firm, Cognitive Arts, and once again Crow's position prevailed.

37. The university has also established Columbia Digital Knowledge Ventures, an organization whose purpose is to promote and coordinate the development of educational resources for projection beyond campus; it also is meant to "incubate selected digital media companies" like Fathom itself. A third element of the strategy, and the one least concerned with profit-making, is the Columbia Center for New Media Teaching and Learning, which works closely with faculty members to familiarize them with the pedagogical potential of new technologies and enhance campus courses through the use of digital media. Columbia describes its array of on-line projects at *http://www.columbia.edu/cu/news/special/cdigital.*

38. Kirschner was initially recruited to run an on-line project called Morningside Ventures, a for-profit company whose aim was to sell Columbia's "sages on stages" to the world. "It was a way to test dot-com at the margin," she said just before the launch of Fathom, "a holding position until there's a real collaboration among elite institutions."

39. Fathom didn't have a clear business model, "a conception of how to sustain and scale up" the venture, says James Neal, vice president for information services and university librarian (a title that nicely brackets the old and new university). Neal adds that Fathom's "broad, unfocused" mission statement—"leadership in the sustainable application of digital media to global learning and scholarship"—exemplifies the problem.

40. The balance of patent revenues was distributed to the inventors and the units where the research was carried out.

41. Columbia University Senate, Online Learning and Digital Media Initiatives Committee, "Interim Report," April 23, 2002, *www.columbia.edu/cu/senate/annual_reports/01–02/InterimReport41502.htm.*

42. Scott Carlson, "After Losing Millions, Columbia U. Will Close Online-Learning Venture," *Chronicles of Higher Education,* January 11, 2003, p. A30.

43. Stanford's engineering school runs a similar program, with similar success. The on-line students actually do better academically than the students enrolled in the traditional classroom-based course.

44. Demand can connote a desire, even if not reflected in the economist's measure of willingness to pay full costs. See William Bowen, "At a Slight Angle to the Universe" (2000), *http://www.mellon.org/romanes%20booklet.pdf.*

45. "A for-profit board has an obligation to *get out* of a bad business while a non-profit board may have an obligation to *stay in,* if it is to be true to its mission." John Whitehead, quoted in William Bowen, *Inside the Boardroom* (New York: Wiley, 1994), p. 23. Columbia law professor Eben Moglen "posits that Wall Street's dot-com boom spurred officials to create Fathom. 'But the boom

ended before they got their shoddy little enterprise to market. . . . But they can't pull the plug on it, so they say, "It's a strategic investment. We're not trying to make money." Good. Then take the dot-com out of the name.'" Scott Carlson, "For-Profit Web Venture Shifts Gears, Hoping to Find a Way to Make a Profit," *Chronicle of Higher Education,* February 9, 2001, p. A33.

46. See interviews with Paul Samuelson and others in Sylvia Nasaw, *A Beautiful Mind* (New York: Simon and Schuster, 1998), pp. 133–138.

47. Henry Etzkowitz, "MIT, Industry, and the Military, 1860–1960," in Everett Mendelsohn, Merrit Roe Smith, and Peter Weingart, eds., *Science, Technology, and the Military* (Boston: Kluwer Academic Publishers, 1988), pp. 516–519; Susan Rosegrant and David R. Lampe, *Route 128: Lessons from Boston's High-Tech Community* (New York: Basic Books, 1992), pp. 43–47.

48. Frederick Rudolph, *The American College and University: A History* (New York: Vintage, 1962), pp. 128, 245.

49. John Bubacher and Willis Rudy, *Higher Education in Transition* (New York: Harper and Row, 1976), p. 62.

50. Quoted in Annalee Saxenian, *Regional Advantage: Culture and Competition in Silicon Valley and Route 128* (Cambridge, Mass.: Harvard University Press, 1992), p. 143.

51. Rosegrant and Lampe, *Route 128,* pp. 18–19.

52. The history of research at Stanford University is not dissimilar. See Stuart M. Leslie, *The Cold War and American Science: The Military-Industrial-Academic Complex at MIT and Stanford* (New York: Columbia University Press, 1993).

53. Ibid.; Rodger Geiger, *Research and Relevant Knowledge* (New York: Oxford University Press, 1993), pp. 62–73; John C. Hoy, "Higher Skills and the New England Economy," in David Lampe, ed., *The Massachusetts Miracle* (Cambridge, Mass.: MIT Press, 1988), pp. 343–371.

54. Hal Abelson and Vijay Kumar, "MIT, the Internet, and the Commons of the Mind," *http://ishi.lib.berkeley.edu/cshe/projects/university/ebusiness/Habelson.html;* Rosegrant and Lampe, *Route 128,* p. 64. MIT states that the alliance "was initiated in October 1999 as a five-year research alliance between MIT and Microsoft Research to enhance university education through information technology. Our goal is to demonstrate leadership in higher education by sponsoring innovative projects with significant, sustainable impact at MIT and elsewhere. In the first two years . . . we have contributed to a fundamental conceptual overhaul of MIT's program in Aeronautical and Astronautical Engineering that integrates design throughout the entire curriculum. We've supported a major transformation of MIT's introduction to Computer Science that incorporates on-line lectures and automatic homework checking. We have helped replace MIT's lecture-based introduction to Mechanical Engineering by small-group engagements, supported by desk-top experiments and on-line study modules."

55. "Open content draws both its name and, to no small degree, its paradigms, from the history of open source software," something the MIT computer sci-

entists and electronic engineers were intimately familiar with. See Reid Cushman, "Open Content for Digital Public Libraries," report to the William and Flora Hewlett Foundation, September 2002.

56. Abelson and Kumar, "MIT."

57. See *http://web.mit.edu/ocw/ocwarticles.html*; Charles M. Vest, *Report of the President*, 2000–2001, *http://web.mit.edu/president/communications/rpt00–01.html*.

58. See *http://carnegie-libraries.org*.

59. News release, April 4, 2001, *http://web.mit.edu/newsoffice/tt/2001/apr11/ocwside.html*.

60. Abelson and Kumar, "MIT."

61. Jonathan Cole, "Balancing Acts: Dilemmas of Choice Facing Research Universities," in Cole, Barber, and Graubard, eds., *Research University*, p. 7.

62. Saxenian, *Regional Advantage*. "Great people" theories abound in higher education, and it is tempting to locate an explanation for these differences in the contrasting personalities of the two key administrators. Michael Crow, who in July 2002 became the president of Arizona State, consistently showed a penchant for undertaking bold, sometimes chancy initiatives. He arrived at Columbia in 1991, having earned a doctorate in public administration from Syracuse and served in a joint academic and administrative post at his alma mater, Iowa State. He became the protégé of provost Jonathan Cole, a distinguished sociologist and a member of the Columbia academic community since his undergraduate days, and his administrative career took off. Within two years he was promoted to vice provost, the third-ranking position in the university. In that job he managed an ever-expanding portfolio of responsibilities and projects, Fathom prominent among them. By contrast, Dick Yue at MIT fits the mold of a classic academic. He received both his bachelor's and doctoral degrees from MIT, became a professor at age thirty, and earned tenure on the strength of his prolific research on marine fluid dynamics. During his career, he has published more than two hundred scientific papers, and his productivity hasn't fallen off dramatically since he was appointed to the administration. Nowhere did his background as a scholar and engineer manifest itself more clearly than in the methodical approach he took when deciding whether MIT should enter the digital higher education marketplace.

63. The outcome might well have been different had Yue and his colleagues found the yellow brick road to lavish profits through on-line education. Since they didn't, even in purely economic terms the decision to give courses away was not a difficult one. Imagine the impact on academic values if MIT had announced the creation of an internal oversight board to ensure that the research agendas of faculty members were not shaped by industrial or military priorities.

64. William Bowen, *At a Slight Angle to the Universe: The University in a Digitized, Commercialized Age* (Princeton: Princeton University Press, 2001), pp. 7–8, *http://www.mellon.org/romanes%20booklet.pdf*. The same argument is

made in Derek Bok, *Universities in the Marketplace: The Commercialization of Higher Education* (Princeton: Princeton University Press, 2003).

65. Harold Abelson, Robert A. Brown, and Steven R. Lerman, "MIT Open-CourseWare: A Proposal Submitted to the William and Flora Hewlett Foundation," April 27, 2001.

66. William Bowen to Charles Vest, December 16, 2000 (on file at Hewlett Foundation).

67. Jeffrey Young, "Grants Help MIT Put Course Materials Online," *Chronicle of Higher Education,* June 29, 2001, p. A33.

68. Slide show presentation, Hewlett Foundation (n.d.).

69. Linda Anderson, "Diversity Drives Market Development," *Financial Times,* May 23, 2000, p. 6.

70. Ann Grimes, "The Hope . . . and the Reality," *Wall Street Journal,* March 12, 2001 (e-commerce special report).

71. Gerald Heeger, who founded NYU Online before moving to University of Maryland–University College, was widely regarded as one of the ablest in the business, and so the demise of UMUC was particularly crucial to insiders. Scott Carlson and Dan Carnevale, "Debating the Demise of NYUonline," *Chronicle of Higher Education,* December 14, 2001, p. A31.

72. Wilson, "ELearning." Similarly, many of the dot-coms that supplied services to universities had to close their doors. Sarah Carr and Goldie Blumenstyk, "The Bubble Bursts for Education Dot-Coms," *Chronicle of Higher Education,* June 30, 2002, p. A39.

73. Goldie Blumenstyk, "Temple U. Shuts Down For-Profit Distance-Education Company," *Chronicle of Higher Education,* July 20, 2001, p. A29.

74. Just a few years back, considerable attention was paid to analysts who predicted that the Dow Jones would soar to 36,000. James Glassman and Kevin Hassett, *Dow Thirty-six Thousand* (New York: Times Business, 1999).

75. Bowen, *At a Slight Angle,* p. 22. Gordon Moore, founder of Intel, proposed that the number of transistors on a microchip will double every eighteen months, a postulate referred to as Moore's Law.

76. Quoted in Stephen Brier and Roy Rosenzweig, "The Keyboard Campus," *Nation,* April 22, 2002, p. 30. See also Randy Bass, "Engines of Inquiry: Teaching, Technology, and Learner-Centered Approaches to Culture and History," *www.georgetown.edu/crossroads/guide/engines/html.*

77. Wilson, "ELearning."

78. John Naisbitt, *Megatrends: Ten New Directions Transforming Our Lives* (New York: Warner, 1982), p. 156. The highly successful for-profit Phoenix University prides itself on being two generations behind in technology, so that students are likely to have access to it. See Chapter 13.

79. Universities had hoped to make a fortune by floating an initial public offering (IPO) but wanted to keep a controlling stake in the venture. It's unclear why any investor (other than a charity-minded alum) would want to participate in such a scheme.

80. Bowen, *At a Slight Angle,* p. 38.

81. Wilson, "ELearning."
82. Arthur Levine at Teachers College notes that "Fathom got there faster than we could get going. We couldn't find a person to head the organization—and that saved us $2 million!"

10. The British Are Coming—and Going

1. This chapter draws on interviews, conducted in person and by telephone by Nirav Kamdar and David Kirp, and e-mail correspondence with trustees, administrators, professors, and students, as well as with others knowledgeable about the institution. Quotations for which no citation is provided are taken from these sources. Adele Grundies canvassed the literature on the history of accreditation in the United States.
2. "Viewed from a United States perspective all British universities are in effect campuses of a single national university—and such variations in quality as undoubtedly exist are comparable to, say, variations in quality between campuses of the University of California." Jeremy Tunstall, "Introduction," in Jeremy Tunstall, ed., *The Open University Opens* (Amherst: University of Massachusetts Press, 1974), p. 13.
3. United Kingdom Open University, *Profile 2001*. The rankings of engineering programs are drawn from Quality Assurance Agency, "Subject Overview Report: Engineering," 1998, *http://www.qaa.ac.uk/revreps/subjrev/All/qo6–98.pdf*.
4. See, generally, Amartya Sen, "Global Justice: Beyond International Equity," in Inge Kaul, Isabelle Grunber, and Marc Stern, eds., *Global Public Goods: International Cooperation in the Twenty-first Century* (New York: Oxford University Press, 1999), pp. 116–125.
5. John Bear, *Bear's Guide to Earning Degrees by Distance Learning* (Berkeley: Ten Speed Press, 2001), is a fascinating compendium of the best and worst of these schools.
6. David Noble, *Digital Diploma Mills* (New York: Monthly Review Press, 2001).
7. Walter Perry, *The Open University* (San Francisco: Jossey-Bass, 1977), p. 8 (citing data from the 1961 Robbins Committee report).
8. Ralph Smith, "Developing Distance Learning Systems—The UKOU Experiment: Some Lessons," in Ram Reddy, ed., *Open Universities: The Ivory Towers Thrown Open* (New Delhi: Sterling Publishers, 1988), p. 244. Changes in secondary education were also driven by equity concerns. There, the government introduced comprehensive schools in place of a three-tier hierarchy and abolished an examination system that determined a child's educational future at the tender age of twelve. Even the teaching in primary schools changed, because of government policy, to make it less highly structured, more "open."
9. Michael Young, *The Rise of the Meritocracy* (London: Thames and Hudson, 1958).
10. This history draws on Perry, *Open University*.

11. The idea of a "wireless university" had actually been bruited about since the mid-1920s, the early days of the BBC; and with the advent of TV came proposals for a "television university." Michael Young, "Is Your Child in the Unlucky Generation?" *Where?* 10, no. 4 (1962), 3–5.

12. Sarah Lyall, "Distance Education: The British Are Coming," *New York Times,* April 4, 1999, *http://www.cs.brown.edu/people/jes/distance/nyt.04.04.99.british.html.*

13. Goldie Blumenstyk, "Distance Learning at the Open University," *Chronicle of Higher Education,* July 23, 1999, p. A35.

14. Perry, *Open University,* p. x.

15. "An Interview: Sir John Daniel," *National Crosstalk,* 7, no. 3 (Summer 1999), 2.

16. See, generally, the excellent comparative account of open universities in Sarah Guri-Rosenblit, *Distance and Campus Universities: Tensions and Interactions* (London: Pergamon, 1999).

17. Walter Perry, "The Open University," in I. Muggridge, ed., *Founding the Open Universities* (New Delhi: Sterling Publishers, 1997), pp. 5–20.

18. See *http://education.guardian.co.uk/researchratings/table/0,11229,-4319756,00.html.*

19. The age restriction also meant that OU wouldn't compete for students with traditional universities.

20. Brian MacArthur, "An Interim History of the Open University," in Jeremy Tunstall, ed., *The Open University Opens* (Amherst: University of Massachusetts Press, 1974), p. 4.

21. Guri-Rosenblit, *Distance and Campus Universities.* Many students, though obliged to be enrolled for a degree, want to take only a course or two; it is misleading to refer to them as "dropouts."

22. "When Oxford and Cambridge started raiding faculty, and I won half those battles, that's when I thought, 'Gotcha—this could really be a model of higher education for the future,'" says John Daniel.

23. Open University, "University Profile," 2001.

24. Blumenstyk, "Distance Learning."

25. Perry, *Open University,* p. 101.

26. John Daniel, "Lessons from the Open University: Low-Tech Learning Often Works Best," *Chronicle of Higher Education,* September 7, 2001, p. B24. See also John Daniel, *Mega-Universities and Knowledge Media* (London: Kogan Page, 1997), p. 129.

27. OU has been moving progressively, though slowly, toward increasing its online courses. See Robin Mason, "From Distance Education to Online Education," *Internet and Higher Education,* 3, nos. 1–2 (2000), 63–74.

28. As of 2001, three on-line courses were being offered, two in computer science and one for a master's course on distance learning. See *http://www3.open.ac.uk/media/factsheets/NewTech.pdf.*

29. Chris Curran, "Universities and the Challenge of E-Learning: What Lessons

from the European Open Universities?" 2001, *http://ishi.lib.berkeley.edu/cshe/projects/university/ebusiness/Ccurran.html*.

30. Daniel's argument is bolstered by research findings that what is retained from on-line material is about 30 percent less than what is retained from books. John Dalton et al., *Online Training Needs a New Course* (Cambridge, Mass.: Forrester Research, 2000), cited in Austan Goolsbee, "Higher Education: Promises for Future Delivery," in Robert Litan and Alice Rivlin, eds., *The Economic Payoff from the Internet Revolution* (Washington, D.C.: Brookings Institution Press, 2001), p. 275.

31. Jon Marcus, "Distance Education: British Open University Sets the Standard Worldwide," *National Crosstalk,* 7 (Summer 1999), 1.

32. Diana Laurilard, *Rethinking University Teaching: A Conversational Framework for the Effective Use of Learning Technologies* (London: Routledge, 2001).

33. Curran, "Universities and the Challenge."

34. UK e-Universities Worldwide is a collaborative public-private partnership to promote distance learning. See *www.ukeuniversitiesworldwide.com*.

35. Marcus, "Distance Education," p. 1.

36. This discussion draws heavily on Simon Marginson, "Going Global and Governing It: Cross-Border Traffic in Higher Education and Some of the Implications for Governance" (unpublished ms., 2002).

37. Stephen Adam, *Transnational Education Project: Report and Recommendations* (Confederation of European Union Rectors' Conferences, March 2001), *www.crue.org/espaeuro/transnational_education_project.pdf*. See generally Manuel Castells, *The Rise of the Network Society,* vol. 1 of *The Information Age: Economy, Society, and Culture* (Oxford: Blackwell, 2000).

38. Marginson, "Going Global."

39. "In 1999 the former Education Minister for France, Claude Allegre, warned that higher education in Europe was at risk of being dominated by 'American values.'" Ibid.

40. Judith Eaton, "American Accrediting and the International Environment," *International Higher Education,* 23 (2001), 13–15; Philip Altbach, "Higher Education and the WTO: Globalization Runs Amok," *International Higher Education,* 23 (2001), 2–4; Frank Hayward, "Finding a Common Voice for Accreditation Internationally," Council for Higher Education Accreditation, Washington, D.C., 2001, *www.chea.org/international/common-voice-html*. "On 28 September 2001 four organisations—CHEA, the American Council on Education, the Association of Universities and Colleges of Canada, and the European University Association—signed a declaration opposing the inclusion of higher education services in the GATS negotiations." Marginson, "Going Global."

41. Guri-Rosenblit, *Distance and Campus Universities;* Gerhard Ortner and Friedhelm Nickolmann, eds., *Socio-Economics of Virtual Universities: Experiences from Open and Distance Higher Education in Europe* (Weinheim, Germany: Beltz Deutscher Studien Verlag, 1999).

42. The data come from Marcus, "Distance Education."

43. R. Bell and M. Tight, *Open Universities: A British Tradition?* (Buckingham, U.K.: Society of Research into Higher Education and Open University Press, 1993), p. 128; Marcus, "Distance Education," p. 1. (Although Marcus's piece was published in an American publication, *Crosstalk,* his day job was with the *Times* of London.)

44. Marcus, "Distance Education," p. 1.

45. "The Open University—Open to the World," press release, May 22, 2000.

46. Blumenstyk, "Distance Learning," p. A35.

47. William Trombley, "A New British Invasion? Open University Struggles in the United States," *National Crosstalk,* 7 (Summer 1999), 1. Not until February 2003 did Western Governors University win accreditation from a group of four accrediting agencies; at that time, it enrolled just 750 degree-seeking students. Dan Carnevale, "Western Governors U. Wins Key Accreditation," *Chronicles of Higher Education,* March 14, 2003, p. A32.

48. This kind of tailoring wasn't limited to the American market. In developing an open university in the Arab nations, says Brenda Gourley, "we can't have someone settling down to a gin and tonic." The ambition is "a to-and-fro of curriculum."

49. Trombley, "New British Invasion," p. 6.

50. William Trombley, "Teaching Teachers to Teach," *National Crosstalk,* 7 (Summer 1999), 6. Reed also ran into trouble when he tried hiring part-time tutors, circumventing the regular faculty. After failing as a stand-alone institution, OU created a commercial arm, the Open University Worldwide USA, to market its courses in partnership with American institutions. In January 2003, OU and New School University announced a joint program in management. Dan Carnevale, "New School and Open U. to Collaborate," *Chronicle of Higher Education,* February 7, 2003, p. A28.

51. Goldie Blumenstyk, "Banking on Its Reputation, the Open University Starts an Operation in the U.S.," *Chronicle of Higher Education,* July 23, 1999, p. A36.

52. Terrence Reading (CEO, OnLine Training, Inc.), letter, *Chronicle of Higher Education,* November 19, 1999, p. B5.

53. See generally William Selden, *Accreditation* (New York: Harper & Bros., 1960). The accrediting agencies aren't unaware of this criticism. The North Central Association of Colleges and Schools offers an alternative accreditation approach that stresses strategic planning rather than rule-mindedness. Ben Gose, "A Radical Approach to Accreditation," *Chronicle of Higher Education,* November 1, 2002, p. A25.

54. Quality Assurance Agency for Higher Education (QAAHE), Guidelines for the Quality Assurance of Distance Learning, *www.qaa.ac.uk.*

55. Harland Bloland, *Creating the Council for Higher Education Accreditation (CHEA),* American Council on Education (Phoenix: Oryx Press, 2001); Mil-

ton Greenberg, "What Administrators Should Know about Accreditation," *Chronicle of Higher Education,* October 26, 2001 (on-line edition only). The creation of CHEA, in 1996, was a response to criticism directed at the process of accreditation.

56. The fact that OU is an import may have prompted initial skepticism. That parochialism is not just regrettable but ironic. American schools have been the biggest abusers of accreditation internationally, with diploma mills turning "to foreign countries—almost always small ones—for 'accreditation.'" Marginson, "Going Global."

57. Alexander Mood, "The Future of Higher Education: Some Speculations and Suggestions," in Carnegie Commission on Higher Education, *A Classification of Institutions of Higher Education* (New York: McGraw Hill, 1973).

58. Simon Marginson and Marcela Mollis, "'The Door Opens and the Tiger Leaps': Theories and Reflexivities of Comparative Education for a Global Millenium," *Comparative Education Review,* 45 (2001), 581–615. The accreditation process established for Western Governors University, with four regional accrediting bodies forming a group called the Inter-Regional Accrediting Committee, could be a model. That process took several years. Carnevale, "Western Governors."

59. Michael Arnone, "United States Open University to Close after Spending $20 Million," *Chronicle of Higher Education,* February 25, 2002, p. A44.

60. In the three-year period ending March 10, 2003, Apollo Group stock increased 368 percent. Pennsylvania State University's World Campus has been successful in offering a wide array of courses, some leading to a degree and others to a certificate, in such niche fields as noise control engineering and turf grass management (a program that prepares groundskeepers for golf courses).

61. See *http://www.digitalpromise.org.* In a 1962 speech to the National Association of Broadcasters, Minow ensured his immortality in the ranks of FCC commissioners by lambasting TV as a "vast wasteland." See *http://www.janda .org/b20/News%20articles/vastwastland.htm.*

11. A Good Deal of Collaboration

1. This chapter draws on interviews, conducted in person and by telephone, and e-mail correspondence with trustees, administrators, professors, and students, as well as with others in industry and government knowledgeable about these ventures. Quotations for which no citation is provided are taken from these sources.

2. Although the breakthrough moment has yet to arrive, numerous publications—five books, nineteen papers, and fifty-eight talks in 2001 alone—attest that important work is being done. By all accounts, the Silicon Valley firms believe that the Berkeley project is a worthwhile investment, since even in economically hard times they continue to support it.

3. Eyal Press and Jennifer Washburn, "The Kept University," *Atlantic Monthly* (March 2000), 39. See also Kristi Coale, "The Contract and the Code," *University Business* (October 1999), 28–35.

4. Ibrahim Warde, "For Sale: U.S. Academic Integrity," *Le Monde Diplomatique* (March 2001), *http://mondediplo.com/2001/03/11academic*.

5. See the editorial in *Nature*, 409, no. 6816 (January 4, 2001), 11. The fact that Berkeley was developing genetically modified crops was also a target of criticism. As the *Nature* editorial notes: "The Novartis deal can all too easily be portrayed as an institution undermining both its motivation and trustworthiness to provide an independent and impartial view of one of the most contentions technologies of our time."

6. Press and Washburn, "Kept University."

7. Vannevar Bush, *Science—The Endless Frontier: A Report to the President on a Program for Postwar Scientific Research* (Washington, D.C.: National Science Foundation, 1990); Andre Schiffren, ed., *The Cold War and the University: Toward an Intellectual History of the Post-War Years* (New York: New Press, 1997).

8. Rebecca Lowen, *Creating the Cold War University: The Transformation of Stanford* (Berkeley: University of California Press, 1997).

9. Roger Noll, ed., *Challenges to Research Universities* (Washington, D.C.: Brookings Institution Press, 1998); Jonathan Cole, Elinor Barber, and Stephen Graubard, eds., *The Research University in a Time of Discontent* (Baltimore: Johns Hopkins University Press, 1994).

10. Derek Bok, *Beyond the Ivory Tower* (Cambridge, Mass.: Harvard University Press, 1982). See also Roger Meiners and Ryan Ambacher, *Federal Support of Higher Education: The Growing Challenge to Intellectual Freedom* (New York: Paragon House, 1989).

11. Sheila Slaughter and Larry Leslie, *Academic Capitalism* (Baltimore: Johns Hopkins University Press, 1997); John Servos, "Engineers, Businessmen, and the Academy: The Beginnings of Sponsored Research at the University of Michigan," *Technology and Culture*, 37, no. 4 (1996), 721–762. Between 1991 and 2000, federal funding for academic research and development increased 43 percent in real terms, state and local funding increased 25 percent, and industry funding increased 51 percent. National Science Foundation, Division of Science Resources Statistics, 2003, *http://caspar.nsf.gov*.

12. Derek Bok, *The University and the Future of America* (Durham: Duke University Press, 1990). Bok has subsequently become more concerned by the encroachment of business values into higher education. Derek Bok, *Universities in the Marketplace: The Commercialization of Higher Education* (Princeton: Princeton University Press, 2003). The concerns are real enough. Corporate dollars can become too tempting, with firms paying only for research with a dollars-and-cents, not a life-or-death, payoff: a cure for cancer but not tuberculosis. For an example-filled, though tendentious, exposition of this view, see

Lawrence Soley, *Leasing the Ivory Tower: The Corporate Takeover of Academia* (Boston: South End Press, 1995). Companies have also been known to tweak research findings in order to generate misleadingly optimistic reports about their products. See Mildred Cho and Lisa Bero, "The Quality of Drug Studies Published in Symposium Proceedings," *Annals of Internal Medicine,* March 1, 1996, pp. 485–489.

13. Xerox PARC invented the computer mouse, for example, but the idea went nowhere until Apple borrowed it a few years later. See, generally, Richard Rosenbloom and William Spencer, "The Transformation of Industrial Research," *Issues in Science and Technology,* 12, no. 3 (1996), 68–74.

14. The 1984 National Cooperative Research Act authorizes consortiums like the SRC to conduct such research. During the 1980s, in response to the threat from Japanese competition, producers, suppliers, and the Defense Department joined to establish SEMATECH, Semiconductor Manufacturing Technology.

15. Walter Powell and Jason Owen-Smith, "Universities and the Market for Intellectual Property in the Life Sciences," *Journal of Policy Analysis and Management,* 17, (1998), 253–277: "Much of industry eschewed basic research because the payoffs were either too long-run or too difficult to appropriate" (p. 254). See also Joseph Badaracco, *The Knowledge Link* (Boston: Harvard Business School Press, 1991).

16. Although the actual request for proposals was put together in a "clean room," free from formal Berkeley involvement, in effect Berkeley drafted and then responded to the specifications for the Gigascale Center. That's not an unusual arrangement, though there's reason to be concerned that it undermines the process of peer review.

17. Jeffrey Benner, "Public Money, Private Code," Salon.com, January 4, 2002, *http://www.salon.com/tech/feature/2002/01/04/university_open_source/?x.*

18. Reid Cushman, "Open Content for Digital Public Libraries," report to the William and Flora Hewlett Foundation, September 2002 (on file at the Hewlett Foundation).

19. Anna Lee Saxenian, *Regional Advantage: Culture and Competition in Silicon Valley and Route 128* (Cambridge, Mass.: Harvard University Press, 1994), p. 33. See also Susan Rosegrant and David Lampe, *Route 128: Lessons from Boston's High-Tech Community* (New York: Basic Books, 1992).

20. See generally Eric Von Hippel, *Sources of Innovation* (New York: Oxford University Press, 1988).

21. David Lodge, *Nice Work* (New York: Penguin, 1990), p. 85.

22. Cushman, "Open Content."

23. Robert Merton, "Science and Technology in a Democratic Order," *Journal of Legal and Political Sociology,* 1 (1942), 120. See also Robert Merton, "The Matthew Effect in Science, II: Cumulative Advantage and the Symbolism of Intellectual Property," *Isis,* 79 (1988), 606–623.

24. Powell and Owen-Smith, "Universities and the Market," p. 254.

25. Nathan Rosenberg and Richard Nelson, "American Universities and Technical Advance in Industry," *Research Policy,* 23 (1994), 325–348.

26. Privately funded research could, of course, be patented; and even before the law was changed, some federal agencies were able to give limited patent licensing rights to universities.

27. This shift to a market philosophy began with the Department of Health, Education, and Welfare in the late 1960s, which authorized universities to patent government-sponsored research. The 1980 Bayh-Dole legislation extended this open patent principle to all federal agencies. NASA and the Department of Energy had previously assigned all patents to the government, which made them freely available, while the Defense Department reserved the right to control patents.

28. Powell and Owen-Smith, "Universities and the Market," p. 272.

29. Ibid., p. 273. In the Novartis case, objections to secrecy were conflated, by some critics, with objections to any research on genetically engineered crops.

30. Gordon Rausser, "Novartis Revisited: Pro," *California Monthly* (February 2002), 18.

31. Vittorio Santaniello et al., eds., *Agriculture and Intellectual Property Rights* (New York: CABI, 2000).

32. The Novartis controversy was made worse by the university administration's cloak-and-dagger behavior. During the protracted negotiations, the Berkeley administration kept the deal under wraps, bypassing the traditional channels of faculty governance; and even after the deal was announced, it was hard to find out the terms of the arrangement. That fixation with secrecy naturally invites suspicion in an environment committed to transparency.

33. The University of California's system-wide Office of Technology Transfer understands this, at least in principle. As OTT memo 2000-02 (August 1, 2000) explains: "Competitive success rarely is based upon the statutory protection of intellectual property, as requirements for conformance with industry-wide standards reduce the value of proprietary technology. Rapid product development and early market entry with innovative products are the keys to market leadership and successful products."

34. Jonathan Cole, "Balancing Acts: Dilemmas of Choice Facing Public Universities," in Cole, Barber, and Graubard, *The Research University,* p. 29.

35. Goldie Blumenstyk, "A Vilified Corporate Partnership Produces Little Change (Except Better Facilities): Critics of the Berkeley-Novartis Pact Can't Point to Business Intrusions, but Fears Persist," *Chronicle of Higher Education,* June 22, 2001, p. A24. An internal campus review reached a similar conclusion. Robert Saunders, "Closing the Book on the Novartis Deal?" *Berkeleyan,* January 30, 2003, p. 1.

36. Goldie Blumenstyk, "Berkeley's Collaboration with Swiss Company Is on the Verge of Ending," *Chronicle of Higher Education,* January 10, 2003, p. A25.

37. David Weatherall, "Academia and Industry: Increasingly Uneasy Bedfellows,"

Lancet, May 6, 2000, p. 1574. The 2002 Berkeley report notes, however, that participating faculty "used their Syngenta-supported work to attract additional outside support." Blumenstyk, "Berkeley's Collaboration," p. A25.

38. James Engell and Anthony Dangerfield, "Higher Education in the Age of Money" (unpublished ms., 2002).

39. See, e.g., Richard Russo, *Straight Man* (New York: Random House, 1997); James Hynes, *The Lecturer's Tale* (New York: Picador, 2001). See, generally, David Kirp, "Poison Ivy," *American Prospect* (September 2000), 68.

40. Quoted in Press and Washburn, "The Kept University," p. 47.

41. Lest anyone at Berkeley not get the message that money matters, the vice chancellor for budget and finance distributed campuswide a booklet titled "Navigating UC Berkeley's Business Environment" (May 2002).

42. Blumenstyk, "Vilified Corporate Partnerships," p. A24.

43. Seth Shulman, *Owning the Future* (Boston: Houghton Mifflin, 1999).

44. Diane Rahm, John Kirkland, and Barry Bozeman, *University-Industry Collaboration in the United States, United Kingdom, and Japan* (Boston: Kluwer, 2000).

12. The Information Technology Gold Rush

1. In 2002–3, tuition at MIT was $28,030, or a bit less than $1,000 a week. This chapter draws on interviews, conducted in person and by telephone, and e-mail correspondence with trustees, administrators, professors, and students, as well as with others knowledgeable about the institution. Quotations for which no citation is provided are taken from these sources. Brian Pusser introduced us to the Silicon Valley IT market, and Jeffrey Green (Berkeley, B.A., 2000) wrote an initial memo on the topic.

2. Cisco routers and switches are de facto standards for Internet working hardware. Local Area Networks (LAN), Wide Area Networks (WAN), and other networking models require this technology to operate. Thus, all corporations that demand such services must have someone who can operate and maintain them, and this provides a steady—if variable, depending on the economic climate—demand for Cisco-certified engineers.

3. Although students do not take the certification courses of two companies simultaneously, the companies' offerings aren't necessarily competitive. Indeed, Cisco encourages students to come with Microsoft certification so that they'll have broader skills. Mohammad Ziaee, an IT engineer with multiple certifications, points out that "when you're working with real network components, there are three broad areas: computers, network infrastructure such as routers, and media such as filters. So my knowledge [with advanced Microsoft certification] wasn't complete." Ziaee also needed Cisco training. Interview, April 2002.

4. See, e.g., Thomas Kane, *Price of Admission: Rethinking How Americans Pay*

for College (Washington, D.C.: Brookings Institution Press, 1999). Because the certification is so valuable, a sub-industry has grown up to administer the exams and report the results.

5. "The unit was developed in 1906 as a measure of the amount of time a student has studied a subject. For example, a total of 120 hours in one subject—meeting 4 or 5 times a week for 40 to 60 minutes, for 36 to 40 weeks each year—earns the student one 'unit' of high school credit. Fourteen units were deemed to constitute the minimum amount of preparation that may be interpreted as 'four years of academic or high school preparation.'" "The Carnegie Unit: What Is It?" *http://www.carnegiefoundation.org/aboutus/carnegie-unit.htm*.

6. On Cisco demographics, see *http://cisco.netacad.net/public/academy/About.html*. Microsoft changed the name of its certification programs from Authorized Academic Trainer Providers to Microsoft Academies; in the business world, as elsewhere, imitation is the sincerest form of flattery.

7. Lewis Mayhew et al., *The Carnegie Commission on Higher Education* (San Francisco: Jossey-Bass, 1973).

8. Martin Trow, "Elite and Popular Functions in Higher Education," in W. R. Niblett, ed., *Higher Education: Demand and Response* (London: Tavistock, 1969), pp. 182, 184. Trow subsequently added "universal higher education" to his taxonomy. Martin Trow, "Reflections on the Transition from Mass to Universal Higher Education," *Daedalus*, 90, no. 1 (1970), 1–42. See, generally, Akira Arimoto, ed., *Academic Reforms in the World: Situation and Perspective in the Massification Stage of Higher Education* (Hiroshima: RIHE, 1997).

9. Martin Trow's writing on elite and mass institutions makes this point.

10. David Noble, *Digital Diploma Mills* (New York: Monthly Review Press, 2001).

11. Morton Keller and Phyllis Keller, *Making Harvard Modern* (New York: Oxford University Press, 2001), p. 492.

12. Roger Geiger, "Research Universities in a New Era: From the 1980s to the 1990s," in Arthur Levine, ed., *Higher Learning in America, 1980–2000* (Baltimore: Johns Hopkins University Press, 1993), pp. 67–85; Robert Zemsky and William Massy, "Towards an Understanding of Our Current Predicament," *Change*, 97 (1995), 40–49. In the business sector, a similar shift has been remarked. See C. K. Prahalad and Gary Hamel, "The Core Competence of the Corporation," *Harvard Business Review*, 68 (May–June 1990), 79–91.

13. David Collis, "The Paradox of Scope: A Challenge to the Governance of Higher Education" (Harvard Business School working paper, 2002). Demography is one reason for this shift. Since 1970 there has been a major shift in who is enrolling in higher education. Now, only a quarter of full-time college students have come straight out of high school and are wholly or partly supported by their parents. The change in student interest away from the liberal arts to what are called the practical arts has been similarly dramatic. Since 1970, there has been a doubling, to 35 percent, in the proportion of degrees

awarded in business, communications, health professions, leisure and fitness studies, and protective service, even as enrollment in the arts and sciences has declined in almost precisely the same proportion.

14. Clifford Adelman, *A Parallel Postsecondary Universe: The Certification System in Information Technology* (Washington, D.C.: U.S. Department of Education, Office of Educational Research and Improvement, 2000). Expenditures in a related "parallel universe," corporate training programs, are estimated as at least a quarter the size of the formal higher education market. Merrill Lynch, *The Knowledge Web* (2000).

15. Adelman, *Parallel Postsecondary Universe*.

16. Burton Clark, "The Problem of Complexity in Modern Higher Education," in Sheldon Rothblatt and Bjorn Wittrock, eds., *The European and American University since 1800* (Cambridge: Cambridge University Press, 1993), pp. 263–279.

17. Clayton Christensen, *The Innovator's Dilemma* (Boston: Harvard Business School Press, 1997).

18. The Cisco Academies situated at high schools do not directly compete with other institutions preparing students for the certification exams because they serve a different age group. What's remarkable and noteworthy, though, is that, through these academies, Cisco has played an important part in reviving vocational education programs. The firm makes it easy for high schools to set up the program: it charges a modest licensing fee, provides all the teaching materials, and makes used equipment available at a deep discount. Although the classes were initially aimed at students from regional occupational programs (ROPs), those regarded as least likely to attend college, they have attracted students from across the academic spectrum, thus removing the vocational "taint" from these courses. Because many of these students take some of their courses at local community colleges, the program also introduces them to the world of higher education. The elaborate evaluation instruments built into the program have attracted the attention of teachers from other disciplines, who have considered how that structure might be adapted for other courses. In short, one important, if inadvertent, impact of Cisco Academies is on the reform of high school education; in this instance, market-driven changes are improving practice.

19. Accredited training schools like Unitek have been able to capitalize on the availability of public funding for laid-off workers and so receive an indirect public subsidy.

20. State training funds—$150,000 a month—lessen the price disparity between training institutions and state-run programs. Those funds accounted for a quarter of the company's total revenues in 2002. Accreditation also means that Unitek students are eligible for federal financial aid.

21. On the California Master Plan, see Clark Kerr, *The Gold and the Blue: A Personal Memoir of the University of California, 1949–1967*, vol. 1, *Academic Triumphs* (Berkeley: University of California Press, 2001).

22. Gavilan, like most community colleges in the state, opted against offering Microsoft certification as well. For one thing, there weren't enough instructors to offer both Cisco and Microsoft classes; and for another, Microsoft was unresponsive to the college's requests for help.

23. The pass rate at Harbor High School is considerably higher, around 80 percent, according to Fidel Mejia, who runs the Cisco Academy.

24. Gary Matkin, director of UC Irvine's extension program, notes that extension programs sometimes deploy the Robin Hood principle, subsidizing money-losing but academically important courses in the humanities or courses in teacher training, which serve a public need, with income generated by courses in fields like IT, for which private employers are willing to pay a premium.

25. See *http://www.ucsc-extension.edu/main/info/welcome.html.*

26. Since 1997, UCSC Extension has been authorized to offer a master's degree in "Computer Engineering, Specializing in Network Engineering."

27. See *http://www.ucsc-extension.edu/to/cit/micro.html.*

28. Matkin offers a spirited defense of USCC Extension's decision to offer IT certification classes that Sandeen herself doesn't make. Because extension operations have to be more market-driven than the rest of the institution, says Matkin, "they must continually monitor, track, and provide whatever the target community wants. Not to do so, in fact, diminishes the reputation of the Extension unit as well as the parent institution. So, it is quite natural for Extension to jump on an opportunity both to serve its community and 'make money' such as IT certification. . . . UCSC Extension's response is entirely consistent with this market orientation and influenced very little by any embarrassment, recognized expediently only later, when the prospect of financial returns diminished." E-mail, July 29, 2002.

29. Dean Sandeen assumed her position after the decision to offer IT certification courses was made.

13. They're All Business

1. This chapter draws on interviews, conducted in person and by telephone, by Robert Ness, Pablo Sandoval, and David Kirp, and e-mail correspondence with trustees, administrators, professors, and students, as well as with others knowledgeable about the institution. Quotations for which no citation is provided are taken from these sources.

2. James Traub, "Drive-Thru U: Higher Education for People Who Mean Business," *New Yorker,* October 20, 1997, pp. 114–123.

3. These schools are described in Richard Ruch, *Higher Ed Inc.* (Baltimore: Johns Hopkins University Press, 2001).

4. Chapter 5 discusses the bar association's role in the accreditation of another unconventional school, New York Law School.

5. Ruch, *Higher Ed Inc.,* p. 52.

6. John Bear and Mariah Bear, *Bears' Guide to Earning Degrees Nontraditionally* (Berkeley: Ten Speed Press, 1999), provides some horrific examples.

7. For balanced appraisals, see Gordon Winston, "For-Profit Higher Education: Godzilla or Chicken Little?" *Change* (January–February 1999), 13–19; Brian Pusser, "Higher Education, the Emerging Market, and the Public Good," in Patricia Graham and Nevzer Stacey, eds., *The Knowledge Economy and Postsecondary Education* (Washington, D.C.: National Academy Press, 2002), pp. 105–126; Brian Pusser and William N. Harlow, "For-Profit Higher Education," in James J. Forest and Kevin Kinser, eds., *Higher Education in the United States: An Encyclopedia* (Santa Barbara, Calif.: ABC-CLIO, 2002), pp. 266–268; Brian Pusser and Dudley J. Doane, "Public Purposes and Private Enterprise: The Contemporary Organization of Postsecondary Education," *Change* (September–October 2001), 18–24; Brian Pusser, "The Role of the State in the Provision of Higher Education in the United States," *Australian Universities Review*, 12, no. 2 (2000), 24–37. Economists have long noted that higher education is unlike a conventional market. See, e.g., Larry Leslie and Gary Johnson, "The Market Model in Higher Education," *Higher Education*, 45 (1977), 1–20. A related development is the expansion of corporate universities, like Hamburger University (described in the introduction), Toyota University, and Motorola University. See Stan Davis and Jim Botkin, *The Monster under the Bed* (New York: Simon and Schuster, 1994), which asserts that the increase in classroom contact hours for employees in a single year, 1992, exceeded the enrollment growth of all colleges built between 1960 and 1990.

8. John Palatella, "Ivory Towers in the Marketplace," *Dissent*, 48 (Summer 2001), 70.

9. Ruch, *Higher Ed Inc.*, p. 1.

10. In 2000, DeVry ranked eleventh on *Business Ethics*' "100 best corporate citizens list," which is based on how well companies serve their employees, customers, stockholders, and the community. Michael Markovitz, the CEO of Argosy, says much the same thing: "We are educators in the business of education, not business people selling education."

11. The University of Chicago conflict is recounted in Chapter 2.

12. Accreditation is discussed in the context of the U.S. Open University in Chapter 10.

13. Ruch, *Higher Ed Inc.* Susan Friedberg, dean of academic affairs at DeVry's Du Page campus, describes part of the strategy to gain accreditation in New York, where "the state department of education treats everyone badly": "We were the first institution required to go through a public hearing. CUNY attacked us, and so did the community colleges. We pointed out that a thousand New York State residents had enrolled in DeVry's New Jersey campus—including the daughter of a CUNY professor who didn't want to go to CUNY."

14. Traub, "Drive-Thru U," p. 121.

15. Steven Brint, ed., *The Future of the City of Intellect* (Stanford: Stanford University Press, 2002).
16. This is one example of the quality control mechanisms that DeVry uses: student papers from across the system are collected and blind-graded by instructors at other campuses and at company headquarters.
17. It's hard to imagine Harvard University setting up Harvard University West in the Bay Area, although it certainly has the resources, both financial and human, to do so.
18. On the Arizona State University–Motorola linkage, see *http://www.center pointinstitute.org/bridges/SWHCategory/Project.asp?ProjectId=1002*. On the subject of Motorola and other corporate universities, see Jean Meister, "The Brave New World of Corporate Education," *Chronicle of Higher Education,* February 9, 2001, p. B10; Mark Yudof, "Is the Public Research University Dead?" *Chronicle of Higher Education,* January 11, 2002, p. B24.
19. See Chapter 7 for a discussion of the states' role in higher education.
20. See Clayton Christensen, *The Innovator's Dilemma* (Boston: Harvard Business School Press, 1997). Christensen applies his insights about manufacturing to higher education in "Improving Higher Education through Disruption," Futures Forum 2002, "Exploring the Future of Higher Education," Cambridge, Mass., 2002, pp. 5–6.
21. Keller's dream is to "give every student a scholarship for as much education as he or she can take, from nursery school to graduate school."
22. Ruch, *Higher Ed Inc.,* p. 148.
23. See, e.g., Eric Homberger, *Mrs. Astor's New York: Money and Power in a Gilded Age* (New Haven: Yale University Press, 2002); Mark Wahlgren Summers, *The Gilded Age* (Englewood Cliffs, N.J.: Prentice Hall, 1996).
24. James Angell, *Reminiscences* (New York: McKay, 1912), p. 141. Robert Knoll, *Prairie University: A History of the University of Nebraska* (Lincoln: University of Nebraska Press, 1995), describes one land-grant university's endless struggle to balance civic obligations and bottom-line realities.
25. Traub, "Drive-Thru U," p. 123.

Conclusion

1. On the workings of the McDonald's corporation, see Eric Schlosser, *Fast Food Nation: The Dark Side of the All-American Meal* (Boston: Houghton Mifflin, 2001).
2. Brian Pusser, "Higher Education, the Emerging Market, and the Public Good," in Patricia Graham and Nevzer Stacey, eds., *The Knowledge Economy and Postsecondary Education* (Washington, D.C.: National Academy Press, 2002). Typically the debate is between partisans, but individuals may at different times find themselves on opposite sides of this divide. Everything depends on the specific issue, because many professors are both members of the corporation of scholars and ardent academic entrepreneurs.

3. Quotations are from *Reports on the Course of Instruction in Yale College; by a Committee of the Corporation, and the Academical Faculty* (New Haven: Hezekiah Howe, 1828), *www.higher-ed.org/resources/Yale/1828_curriculum.pdf*.

4. See, e.g., Frederick Rudolph, *The American College and University: A History* (New York: Vintage, 1962), pp. 131–135.

5. The historian Frederick Rudolph describes Chicago's Robert Maynard Hutchins as "a kind of strange and wonderful throwback to . . . the Yale Report of 1828." Ibid., p. 479.

6. Steven Brint, "The Rise of the 'Practical Arts,'" in Steven Brint, ed., *The Future of the City of Intellect: The Changing American University* (Stanford: Stanford University Press, 2002), pp. 231–259. On the value of a liberal education, see Martha Nussbaum, *Cultivating Humanity: A Classical Defense of Reform in Liberal Education* (Cambridge, Mass.: Harvard University Press, 1998).

7. Clark Kerr, *The Uses of the University* (Cambridge, Mass.: Harvard University Press, 2002), pp. vii, ix, 31, 1.

8. Ibid, p. 209.

9. Simon Marginson and Mark Considine, *The Enterprise University* (Cambridge: Cambridge University Press, 2000), p. 6.

10. John Skrentny, *The Minority Rights Revolution* (Cambridge, Mass.: Harvard University Press, 2002), pp. 65–79; Peter Schuck, *Diversity in America* (Cambridge, Mass.: Harvard University Press, 2003), pp. 154–202.

11. Donald Heller and Patricia Marin, eds., *Who Should We Help? The Negative Social Consequences of Merit Aid Scholarships* (Cambridge, Mass.: Civil Rights Project, Harvard University, 2002), *http://www.civilrightsproject.harvard.edu/research/meritaid/fullreport.php*.

12. William Durden, "Liberal Arts for All, Not Just the Rich," *Chronicle of Higher Education*, October 19, 2001, p. B20.

13. It is unclear that this would be a wise course: the failure of the best nonprofit institutions, such as Open University, and the sorry experience of public universities like California's Virtual University, give reason for pause.

14. In allowing students who are accepted under early decision rules to apply to other schools, Yale and Stanford have taken such a step. Jeffrey Young, "Yale and Stanford End Early-Decision Options and Defy National Group," *Chronicle of Higher Education*, November 22, 2002, p. A58.

15. See, e.g., Simon Marginson, *Markets in Education* (Melbourne: Allen and Unwin, 1997); Larry Cuban and Dorothy Shipps, eds., *Reconstructing the Common Good in Education* (Stanford: Stanford University Press, 2000); B. L. Wolfe, "External Benefits of Education," in Martin Carnoy, ed., *International Encyclopedia of Economics of Education* (New York: Elsevier, 1995), pp. 159–164; Pusser, "Higher Education"; Howard Bowen, *The State of the Nation and the Agenda for Higher Education* (San Francisco: Jossey-Bass, 1982). On the ineffability of the common good, see Jane Mansbridge, "On the Contested Nature of the Public Good," and Craig Calhoun, "The Public Good as

a Social and Cultural Project," in Walter Powell and Elisabeth Clemens, eds., *Private Action and the Public Good* (New Haven: Yale University Press, 1998), pp. 3–19 and 20–35.

16. Sexton himself may well become a great institutional leader at NYU, and there are a few such leaders at public institutions as well. Some administrators are even willing to put provocative ideas down on paper. See, for instance, Durden, "Liberal Arts," and Mark Yudof, "Is the Public Research University Dead?" *Chronicle of Higher Education,* January 11, 2002, p. B24. Yudof was well known in Minnesota when, as president of the university, he tangled with Governor Jesse Ventura. But he is a rarity; none of these leaders has a national reputation outside the circle of academic professionals. Clark Kerr provides an instructive contrast. While he was presiding over the creation of a great state university, he crafted what remains the most penetrating analysis of American higher education. These days, it is ex-presidents who write the most interesting books. See, e.g., William Bowen and Derek Bok, *The Shape of the River* (Princeton: Princeton University Press, 1999); James Freedman, *Liberal Education and the Public Interest* (Ames: University of Iowa Press, 2003); Frank Rhodes, *The Creation of the Future: The Role of the American University* (Ithaca, N.Y.: Cornell University Press, 2001).

17. Such an institution might consider a suggestion made only half in jest by Harvard education professor Richard Chait: that it become a publicly held firm whose shares are traded on the New York Stock Exchange, its market value rising and falling with the "knowledge products" it develops and the caliber of the "knowledge workers" it recruits. The tax law bars a company from "owning" a nonprofit college, of course, but the suggestion is meant in the Swiftian, not the literal, sense.

Acknowledgments

To adapt a famous line, I've always depended on the kindness of *both* friends and strangers. Since you have read this far, you may be curious to know how this book came to be and whom I've turned to for help along the way.

Like many professors, I have spent most of my career teaching and writing, happily leaving it to administrators to manage the affairs of the university, but a stint as acting dean of the Goldman School of Public Policy at Berkeley was an eye-opener. At one meeting of the campus Council of Deans, a full forty-five minutes was expended on the proper and improper uses of the university seal—a presentation that initially puzzled me, since I was sure that Berkeley's mascot was a bear, not a seal. I learned enough in that job to conclude that I wanted to learn more, and this book is the result.

As with many things I've done during my life, I started out in entire innocence about the magnitude of the task I'd set for myself; were it otherwise, I would never have had the nerve to propose it. Jorge Balan at the Ford Foundation appreciated, far better than I, just how little I actually knew, but he was nonetheless willing to take a gamble. Since 1999, when the foundation initially funded the project, he has been the model of a modern foundation officer: an intellectual guide as well as a financial angel, testing and encouraging in turn, and always engaged in the enterprise.

With research funding in hand, I had no intention of securing a publisher until I finished writing. Then I encountered Elizabeth Knoll, who is as persuasive as she is smart and personable. Over the years I have been fortunate to work with a number of talented editors, and she ranks with the best. Like Jorge, she has been both a friendly critic and a critical friend, and our long talks have helped to mold the manuscript.

As I have done in the past, I looked for research assistance mainly to the ranks of Berkeley students, undergraduates and graduate students alike, trained in the social and policy sciences. "David's Raiders," the group was dubbed, and they were called on to do everything from scour primary source materials and conduct interviews to draft chunks of prose. None of them had studied how universities work, and most had to go through a crash course in methodology. As a teacher, I hope they learned from the experience. As a writer, I know that they contributed immensely.

315

Jay Tate, Ph.D. in political science and interim director of the UC Berkeley Washington Center, participated in the earliest stages of the project, sharing responsibility for drafting the grant proposal. Pablo Sandoval drafted insightful background papers on the phenomenon of faculty superstars, and in the summer of 2000 he assisted me in conducting interviews at the University of Chicago, DeVry University, and Hamburger University. Marc Wolf's research on Brown University's redesign of its undergraduate curriculum, Adele Grundies's research on the impact of *U.S. News & World Report* rankings and the history of higher education accreditation, Bryan Chan's research on market forces in higher education in South and East Asian nations, and Nirav Kamdar's research on the British and U.S. Open Universities all inform the book. Bryan was also assiduous in tracking down stray references. The fact that these students were undergraduates when they worked with me makes the caliber of their assistance all the more noteworthy. Anthony Chen, Ph.D. in sociology from Berkeley and assistant professor of sociology and public policy at the University of Michigan, collected source material, conducted interviews, and wrote initial drafts for the chapter on the market in ideas even as he was finishing his dissertation, teaching a new course, and looking for a job.

I am especially indebted to my co-authors, all but one of them Berkeley students. Elizabeth Popp Berman, a sociology Ph.D. candidate, quickly acquired a keen appreciation of the folkways of universities during the course of our examination of two Berkeley industry-university collaborations. Jeffrey Holman, a statistician by initial inclination and a Ph.D. candidate in economics, started collaborating with me while still an undergraduate. Over time, we came to understand how students and universities have constructed an elaborate market to sell themselves to each other. I worked with Patrick Roberts, a Ph.D. candidate in political science at Virginia, across a continent, through endless E-mail and telephone conversations. His passion for Jeffersonian history and his talents as archivist and interviewer were essential in explaining the University of Virginia business school's decision to become an essentially private institution. Debra Solomon, a master's in public policy candidate at the Goldman School, and Robert Ness, a Berkeley B.A. (with a triple major in economics, mathematics, and interdisciplinary field studies), looked closely at half a dozen different institutions in order to understand the new academic market preparing students to be certified by corporations such as Microsoft and Cisco. That assignment required them to analyze institutional cultures as different as a public high school and the extension program of an elite university.

I am exceptionally grateful to Jonathan VanAntwerpen, a Ph.D. candidate in sociology. He is a rarity among graduate students, a genuine intellectual with a passion for ideas. He and I worked together on two chapters—on the valiant effort of classics departments at southern liberal arts colleges to form a virtual consortium, and the strategies deployed by NYU in its rise to elite institutional status. Because of his conceptual contributions and his assiduous fieldwork, he is the first author of those two chapters.

Portions of the book appeared in earlier versions in *The Nation, American Prospect, Public Interest, Change, Chronicle of Higher Education, Lingua Franca, L, California Monthly,* and *University Business;* in many instances, talented editors at those publications measurably strengthened my work.

The Goldman School of Public Policy, which I have called my academic home for more than three decades, is a remarkable place: a genuine community of scholars and teachers drawn from many disciplines, a place for collaboration, collegial respect, and useful critique. Over countless lunches and cups of coffee, I've discussed the project with my colleagues, as well as with graduate students who participated in a seminar on higher education policy.

In recent years I've given talks at the Forum on the Future of Higher Education, the College Board, the American Association of University Professors, EduCause, the American Association of Colleges and Universities, the Center for Higher Education Policy at the University of Twente (Netherlands), and the Center for Studies in Higher Education at Berkeley. Those occasions have allowed me to test out ideas among those who know this terrain well. With the support of the Ford Foundation, I organized a two-day seminar in January 2002 on the role of market forces in higher education, which brought together some of the keenest minds in the field.

At various stages of the project, my ideas have been sharpened by conversations with Richard Chait, Steven Brint, Richard Hersh, Brian Pusser, David Brenneman, Susanne Lohmann, Joel Meyerson, William Tierney, Simon Marginson, Patrick Clinton, Derek Bok, Frank Newman, Arthur Levine, Walter Powell, Craig Calhoun, David Collis, Jürgen Enders, Guy Neave, Ray Bacchetti, and Patricia Gumport. The literally hundreds of people I interviewed during the course of research offered valuable information and invaluable perspective. In myriad ways, friends and colleagues have contributed to my thinking, among them Ira Heyman, Patricia Cross, Michael Nacht, Eugene Bardach, Robert Frank, Aron Rodrigue, Eugene Smolensky, Rachel Moran, Mark Yudof, Jeffrey Kittay, Marvin Lazerson, Ray Bacchetti, Diane Harley, Marshall Smith, Kristin Luker, Alexander Kelso, Reid Cushman, Mary Ann Mason, Norton Grubb, and Stanley Katz.

I have known Rhea Wilson as a good friend and a dream of an editor for twenty years. Her close and insightful reading of the entire draft manuscript meant much more work for me and, I hope, a stronger book.

Brian Veazey, to whom the book is dedicated, saw me through endless visions and revisions as a mountain of materials slowly took shape as a book. He is my partner in all the ways that matter—among so many other things, he is my loving, and best, friend.

Index

Abbott, Andrew, 39, 46
Abelson, Hal, 178
Academic Revolution, The (Jencks and Riesman), 67
accreditation, 200–201, 250, 303n56; University of Phoenix and, 251–252
Adamany, David, 183
adjuncts, 69, 85–87
admissions, 269n33, 271n58; positional warfare and, 11–12, 25, 31–32; image consultants and, 12–14; Maguire approach and, 14–16; attracting students and, 16–20; *Life of the Mind* and, 18; media and, 19–20; tuition and, 20–22; price wars and, 21; reaction programs and, 21; scholarships and, 21; personal visits and, 21–22; Brown's New Curriculum and, 22–23; publicity and, 22–23; presentation and, 22–25; selectivity and, 26–27; counseling and, 27–31; Ivywise and, 28–29; online services and, 29, 113–114; Pell grants and, 31; early decision, 32, 270n46; Dickinson College and, 59–63; disappearing males and, 62; Hook and, 74–75; philosophers and, 75; New York Law School and, 107–108; family wealth and, 272n71
Afshar, Paul, 227–228
ALIANCO (Allied Languages in a Networked Collaboration Online), 161–162
Allan, George, 55, 64
Allen, George, 134
alumni, 25–26
American Association of University Professors, 251
American Bar Association, 96–97, 100, 104; Concord Law School and, 164–165, 241
American Philosophical Association, 74
American Schools of Professional Psychology, 240–241
Anderson, Wayne, 156
Angell, James, 123–124, 253–254
Antony, Louise, 81
Apollo Group. *See* University of Phoenix

Appiah, Anthony, 68
Appodaca, James, 221, 228–229
Arcadia University, 14, 19, 115
architecture, 130–131, 286n2
Arizona State University, 252
Armstrong, Lloyd, 120–121
Associated Colleges of the South (ACS), 155, 157, 159–162
Association of American Law Schools (AALS), 96
Association of American Universities, 117
AT&T, 210, 212, 219, 228
Auslander, Leora, 39

Babson College, 23–24
Baldwin, Gary, 207, 214–215, 218
Barendse, Jennifer, 63
Barnes and Noble, 112
Barrett, Chris, 27–28
Barrett, Craig, 210–211
Barro, Robert, 67
Batten, Frank, Sr., 133
Bayh-Dole Act, 216
Beaver College, 12–15, 19, 115
Becker, Gary, 150
Behnke, Michael, 17–18
Bell & Howell, 248
Bell Labs, 210, 219
Bender, Thomas, 77
Benhabib, Jess, 78
Beyond the Ivory Tower (Bok), 209
Bice, Scott, 120
Birnbaum, Robert, 110, 118
Block, Ned, 77–78, 81
Boghossian, Paul, 68, 73, 76–77, 81–82, 280n40
Bok, Derek, 209, 304n12
Bollinger, Lee, 85, 126, 128
books, 112–113, 191
Booz Allen Hamilton, 179
Boston University, 15, 26
Botein, Michael, 107–108
Bowdoin, College, 31
Bowen, William, 180–181

318